W9-BGI-304

HOCKINSON
HIGH SCHOOL

KK ℓ

Going to the Source
The Bedford Reader in American History

About the Editors

Victoria Bissell Brown is an associate professor at Grinnell College, where she teaches modern U.S. history, U.S. women's history, and U.S. immigration history. She is the author of *The Education of Jane Addams* (2003) and the editor of the Bedford/St. Martin's edition of *Jane Addams's Twenty Years at Hull-House* (1999). Her articles have appeared in *Feminist Studies*, the *Journal of Women's History*, and the *Journal of the Illinois State Historical Society*. She has served as the book review editor of the *Journal of the Gilded Age and Progressive Era* and as the Ray Allen Billington Distinguished Visiting Professor at the Huntington Library and Occidental College.

Timothy J. Shannon is an associate professor at Gettysburg College, where he teaches early American and Native American history. He is the author of *Indians and Colonists at the Crossroads of Empire: The Albany Congress of 1754* (2000), which received the Dixon Ryan Fox Prize from the New York State Historical Association and the Distinguished Book Award from the Society of Colonial Wars. His articles have appeared in the *William and Mary Quarterly* and *New England Quarterly*, and he has been a research fellow at the Huntington Library and John Carter Brown Library.

Going to the Source

The Bedford Reader in American History

VOLUME 1: TO 1877

Victoria Bissell Brown

Grinnell College

Timothy J. Shannon

Gettysburg College

014013691

Bedford / St. Martin's   Boston ◆ New York

To our students, who have taught us so much

For Bedford/St. Martin's
Publisher for History: Patricia A. Rossi
Director of Development for History: Jane Knetzger
Executive Editor for History: Elizabeth M. Welch
Developmental Editor: Laura W. Arcari
Production Editor: Arthur Johnson
Senior Production Supervisor: Nancy Myers
Marketing Manager: Jenna Bookin Barry
Editorial Assistants: Elizabeth Wallace, Rachel L. Safer
Production Assistants: Kristen Merrill, Amy Derjue
Copyeditor: Richard Steins
Text Design: Claire Seng-Niemoeller
Indexer: Steve Csipke
Cover Design: Billy Boardman
Cover Art: Photograph of Stanford historian Carl Degler, © Ressmeyer/CORBIS. Photograph
   of Susquehannock pottery, c. 1575–1600, courtesy of the State Museum of Pennsylvania,
   Pennsylvania Historical and Museum Commission. *Buffalo Hunt, Chasing Back,* 1844, by George
   Catlin © CORBIS. "Matthew Brady's Traveling Photo Set-up," c. 1860, © Bettmann/CORBIS.
   "Portrait of Mary Jane Soggs and Her Little Brother, Henry," 1830, by Ammi Phillips, © Peter
   Harholdt/CORBIS.
Composition: Pine Tree Composition, Inc.
Cartography: Mapping Specialists
Printing and Binding: R.R. Donnelley & Sons Company

President: Joan E. Feinberg
Editorial Director: Denise B. Wydra
Director of Marketing: Karen Melton Soeltz
Director of Editing, Design, and Production: Marcia Cohen
Managing Editor: Elizabeth M. Schaaf

Library of Congress Control Number: 2003112719

Copyright © 2004 by Bedford/St. Martin's

All rights reserved. No part of this book may be reproduced, stored in a retrieval system, or
transmitted in any form or by any means, electronic, mechanical, photocopying, recording, or
otherwise, except as may be expressly permitted by the applicable copyright statutes or in writing
by the Publisher.

Manufactured in the United States of America.

9   8   7   6   5   4
f   e   d   c   b

For information, write: Bedford/St. Martin's, 75 Arlington Street, Boston, MA 02116
(617-399-4000)

ISBN: 0–312–40204–X

Acknowledgments

CHAPTER 1
Page 10 (Source 1): Courtesy of the State Museum of Pennsylvania, Pennsylvania Historical and Museum Commission.
Page 11 (Source 2): Courtesy of the State Museum of Pennsylvania, Pennsylvania Historical and Museum Commission.
Page 12 (Source 3): Courtesy of the State Museum of Pennsylvania, Pennsylvania Historical and Museum Commission.

*Acknowledgments and copyrights are continued at the back of the book on pages 336–37, which constitute
an extension of the copyright page. It is a violation of the law to reproduce these selections by any means
whatsoever without the written permission of the copyright holder.*

Preface for Instructors

The scene is familiar: you have only one class period in which to discuss a topic—say, anti-Irish nativism in the 1840s. The reader you are using includes a half-dozen or more documents—two newspaper editorials, a petition, a sermon excerpt, a cartoon, a letter, several job advertisements. What to do with such a wealth of material? All of it points to anti-Irish prejudice, so you focus the class meeting around that historical development, hoping the students will walk away from all those documents with a general impression of how nativism operated in the 1840s. But there are some bumps along the way. The students have a hard time distinguishing the utility of one document from another, but you lack the time to introduce and discuss the differences between these types of sources. Ultimately, the level of discussion suffers because the students focus on recalling the content of the varied materials they read rather than analyzing them as historical evidence. You end the class wishing you had the time and teaching instrument necessary to talk directly to students about how historians would actually turn such sources over in their hands and heads, assessing the advantages and disadvantages of each, before using them to write a history of anti-Irish nativism.

Our purpose in *Going to the Source* is to provide you with both the time and the instrument for coupling a discussion of historical content with a discussion of a specific type of historical source. As teachers, we have often felt uncomfortably stuffed by the smorgasbord servings of different primary and secondary documents typically offered in U.S. history readers. Our goal in writing this reader is to provide a streamlined focus on a particular topic while blending in a healthy portion of historical thinking about the nature of different types of sources, be they newspapers, letters, paintings, statistical data, or scholars' secondary writing. To achieve this, we've designed each chapter around one historical topic and one type of source in order to allow for more focused student reading and assignments, as well as an enriched classroom discussion, on the various processes that go into researching and reconstructing the past.

In the course of writing *Going to the Source*, we have read numerous discussions of how to employ primary and secondary documents in the teaching of history. Most of those discussions focus on the worthy goal of enlivening historical content; they tend to emphasize the way in which a letter from a Lowell mill worker, for example, can illuminate that particular historical experience. We were looking, however, for a method that would allow us to combine more explicitly a lively study of the past with equally lively classroom discussion of the challenges and rewards historians face in reconstructing the past with primary and secondary sources.

We have been encouraged in this endeavor by the work of Sam Wineburg, a cognitive psychologist at Stanford University, whose research reveals the difference between the way that trained historians approach a historical document and the way nonhistorians, especially undergraduate students, approach the same document.[1] Wineburg has found that historians have so absorbed their discipline's way of handling a document—looking first at its provenance and making instantaneous calculations about the date, the author, the proximity to the event discussed, the authenticity of the document, and the reliability of the document's creator—that they have difficulty describing a reading process that is as natural to them as breathing.

Wineburg has also found that students most successfully travel out of the present and into the past if their teachers can explain and demonstrate that the pathway to the past is often a rutted road comprised of more and less reliable documents that every historian must pick up, examine, and evaluate. Wineburg calls on historians to "bring this messier form of expertise into the classroom" so that students can become conscious of both the distance between now and then and the logical processes historians use to traverse that distance via their sources.

The organization of each chapter in *Going to the Source* is designed to expose historians' processes and reveal to students how historians utilize sources. The seven-part organization of each chapter includes an introduction that sets the stage for the case study that will unfold in the documents, a "Using the Source" section that examines the advantages and disadvantages inherent in the particular type of source utilized in that chapter, and a section called "Working with the Source" that provides students with tools to aid them in their analysis of the documents. The longest portion of each chapter is "The Source," a section consisting of documents that draw from a single source or single type of source. It is followed by "Analyzing the Source," which offers questions suitable for written assignments or class discussion. An epilogue entitled "Beyond the Source" provides closure on the case study, and "Finding and Supplementing the Source" suggests additional sources for further study. In addition, this book features an "Introduction for Students" that discusses the principles and practices of working with sources and a "Documenting the Source" appendix that shows students how to document the sources included in these volumes according to *The Chicago Manual of Style*.

Taken as a whole, the fourteen chapters in each volume offer documents that are personal and documents that are public; the sources included here run the gamut from popular to official, from obvious to obscure. In satisfying our own interest in Americans' struggle to realize democratic ideals out of undemocratic realities, we have provided sources from the margins of society as well as the centers of power. By including documents that balance a bottom-up with a top-down approach to U.S. history, we seek to remind students that the nation's conflicts over democratic ideals have not been confined to marginal communities or anonymous voices. Historians seeking to trace these conflicts

---

[1] Sam Wineburg, *Historical Thinking and Other Unnatural Acts: Charting the Future of Teaching the Past* (Philadelphia: Temple University Press, 2001), and "Teaching the Mind Good Habits," *The Chronicle of Higher Education* 49 (April 11, 2003), B20.

look high and low, examining congressional speeches along with the oral reports of obscure witnesses to the American scene. By exposing students to elite or official documents as well as private or anonymous ones, we seek to remind them that influence can arise from humble communities in America, that centers of power cannot be ignored when writing the history of American democracy, and that marginal people have had to learn about elite institutions in order to influence the powerful. We also seek to remind students of the span of sources a historian can draw upon to capture U.S. history and to convince them of their ability to understand—and their right to access—a vast array of documentary material.

ACKNOWLEDGMENTS

We would like to thank the following reviewers who guided us in our revisions with their suggestions and comments: James Beeby, West Virginia Wesleyan College; Jamie Bronstein, New Mexico State University; William Cario, Concordia University; John R. Chávez, Southern Methodist University; Edward J. Davies, University of Utah; Douglas W. Dodd, California State University Bakersfield; Bruce Dorsey, Swarthmore College; Chris Erickson, Indiana State University; Jim Farmer, University of South Carolina at Aiken; Gayle Fischer, Salem State College; Andrew Frank, Florida Atlantic University; Susan E. Gray, Arizona State University; Emily Greenwald, University of Nebraska–Lincoln; Bradley J. Gundlach, Trinity College; Steven Hahn, Northwestern University; Barbara Handy-Marchello, University of North Dakota; Päivi Hoikkala, Cal State Polytechnic University; Kathleen Kennedy, Western Washington University; Todd Kerstetter, Texas Christian University; David Krugler, University of Wisconsin–Platteville; Molly Ladd Taylor, York University; Charlene Mires, Villanova University; Susan Rugh, Brigham Young University; John Sacher, Emporia State University; Rebecca S. Shoemaker, Indiana State University; Michael Topp, University of Texas at El Paso; Robert Wolff, Central Connecticut State University; and David E. Woodard, Concordia University.

We extend our thanks to the editorial staff at Bedford/St. Martin's: Joan E. Feinberg, president, and her predecessor, Charles H. Christensen; Patricia A. Rossi, publisher for history; Heidi H. Hood, our first developmental editor, and her successor, Laura W. Arcari, who, in addition to working with us to bring this book to publication, was responsible for writing the "Documenting the Source" appendix; Jane Knetzger, director of development for history; our editorial assistants, Rachel Safer and Elizabeth Wallace; our production editor, Arthur Johnson, and production assistants Kristen Merrill and Amy Derjue. Thanks also to our copyeditor, Richard Steins, and to the book's designer, Claire Seng-Niemoeller. We give special thanks to Katherine Kurzman, our original sponsoring editor, who started us on our journey. This book never would have happened without her impetus.

We were greatly aided in our endeavors by the librarians at Gettysburg College, including Chris Amadure, Karen Drickamer, Linda Isenberger, and Susan Roach, as well as the Government Documents librarians at the University of

Iowa, Marianne Mason and John Elson; the collections manager at the Pennsylvania State Museum, Janet Johnson; and the staff in the archives section of the Minnesota Historical Society. Staff assistance from Carla Pavlick and Linda Price is gratefully acknowledged, as is the advice we received from colleagues who answered questions and read drafts of chapters. We are particularly grateful to Gabor Boritt, Joe Coohill, Brendan Cushing-Daniels, William Farr, Keith Fitzgerald, Matt Gallman, Tom Hietala, Jim Jacobs, Shawna Leigh, Ann Lesch, Karl Lorenz, Gerald Markowitz, Barbara Sommer, Mark Weitz, and Robert Wright. The assistance of students and former students was invaluable in this project, and we owe much to Maggie Campbell, Katie Mears, Posey Gruener, Amy Scott, Jason Stohler, Matthew Raw, and Lauren Rocco. Finally, of course, we owe thanks to our families, who encouraged us throughout this process and regularly offered much-needed relaxation from our labors. Thanks to Jim, Colleen, Caroline, Daniel, and both of our Elizabeths.

Introduction for Students

In the debate over going to war with Iraq in 2003, the American people were asked to examine and interpret different kinds of evidence from multiple sources: the United Nations' evidence on Iraqi weapons programs, Amnesty International's evidence on the Iraqi government's torture of its own citizens, the Pentagon's evidence of Iraqi ties to international terrorist organizations, British prime minister Tony Blair's evidence of Iraqi interest in obtaining nuclear weapons. Some of this evidence was unverified when the United States launched its preemptive war against Iraq in March 2003, but none of it was easily dismissed. American citizens had the responsibility of reading and listening to the evidence as it was presented by both disinterested experts and partisan analysts and reaching their own conclusions about the case for war. That process did not end when U.S. troops occupied Baghdad. The debate over the Iraq evidence continues to influence American citizens' support for their government's policies, and the debate over the evidence will be aired among historians for decades to come. The Iraq war is only the most obvious recent example of the importance of evidence, data, sources, intelligence, information, and, yes, values, beliefs, and opinion in making decisions that shape our lives. It is also the most prominent example of a contemporary story that will be told and retold in history books, drawing on evidence we have available today as well as evidence that is bound to emerge in the coming years.

Going to the Source intends to sharpen your skills at reading, evaluating, and interpreting evidence. To achieve that goal, we ask you to put yourself in the position of a historian who is interrogating different kinds of sources from the past, trying to determine what is reliable in the testimony that each type of source provides. In the end, it is our hope that your work with *Going to the Source* will leave you with a set of practices and principles that you can just as easily apply to reading your local newspaper as to examining a grandmother's letter found in the attic, an eighteenth-century oil painting, or a Vietnam war intelligence report. These principles and practices have guided our writing of every story and exercise included here, and though we do not ask that you memorize our guidelines, we offer them here as a preview of concepts that will become quite familiar to you while working with this volume.

PRINCIPLES AND PRACTICES OF WORKING WITH SOURCES

- Every tangible object that human beings produce, whether it be a piece of clothing or a laundry list, is a kind of "document" and as such has the potential to serve as a historical "source."

- Every document is created in a particular context — a particular place, a particular time, a particular culture, a particular political situation — and must be examined with that context in mind. No document can be understood on its own, in a vacuum.

- Once placed in context, the first questions we must ask of a document are: Who created it? When? Why? What was the document creator's purpose? What end was this document intended to serve? What was this document doing?

- Because all documents are human creations, all documents have a bias. That is to say, all documents are produced by someone with a particular point of view. This is not an unfortunate flaw of historical sources, it is what makes them rich with meaning.

- As human creations with a point of view, historical sources are complex witnesses to the past. Moreover, different documents from different creators are likely to present diverging angles of vision if not outright contradictions.

- The historian's job is neither to dismiss nor to adopt the bias of the source but rather to figure out what the bias is and use it as evidence of one viewpoint operating in that place, at that time. This is what we mean by "interpreting" a document: figuring out the viewpoint of a particular source and positioning that viewpoint among all the others in that historical moment.

LIMITATIONS, LOGIC, AND ETHICS IN HISTORICAL ANALYSIS

In the work you will be undertaking in *Going to the Source,* you will have multiple opportunities to see these principles and practices in operation and to apply them to your own examination and interpretation of historical documents. As you engage in these activities, which replicate the daily work of every historian, you will confront the limitations, logic, and ethics of historical source analysis. The limitations are the root of all frustration and creativity in historical work and derive from the simple fact that we do not have access to everything humans created in any time or place. We are left with what has survived, and no single piece of the surviving evidence can tell a whole story. Historians must piece together different kinds of surviving sources the way you would piece together a broken vase, hoping that the shards you have to work with are sufficient to hold water.

Logic is vital to this process because historians must consider what arguments a source can be used to support. For example, the written opinion of a majority of Supreme Court justices cannot be used as evidence of the attitudes of the majority of Americans, but it can be used as evidence of the law that ruled those Americans. The anti–woman suffrage speeches of a sexist legislator in 1910 cannot be used as evidence of the views of every male in the United States, but they can be used as evidence of the attitudes the woman suffrage movement was combating. As you work with the sources in this volume, you often will have to consider how a particular source can legitimately and logically be used in piecing together the past and what parts of the puzzle that source simply cannot address.

Ethics come into play in this process because the effectiveness of historians rests on their readers' trust that no sources were unearthed and then hidden because those sources complicated or contradicted a preconceived interpretation. For example, historians who set out to tell the story of male opposition to woman suffrage are likely to come across speeches, editorials, letters, and meeting minutes that indicate some men's active support of woman suffrage. The historians then have a choice: either they expand the parameters of their story to compare the views of those men who opposed woman suffrage with the views of men who supported it, or they tell their readers up front that their particular story focuses only on male opponents of woman suffrage and not on the other story to be told about male supporters of suffrage. Ethics do not dictate that every historian tell every story; rather, they dictate that none of us cover up evidence of the stories we are not telling and of the viewpoints we are not representing. Historians use logic and ethics to carefully and explicitly define the scope of their stories because the limitations of the surviving evidence make that a practical necessity.

THE ORGANIZATION OF *GOING TO THE SOURCE*

You will immediately notice, in your work in the first chapter of *Going to the Source*, that we are not asking you to juggle multiple types of sources on each topic. Instead, you will focus on just one type of source in the context of each chapter's story. The source types will range from archaeological findings of seventeenth-century Indian-European encounters to freed slaves' testimony before a post–Civil War congressional committee to U.S. Census Bureau data on modern immigration. We make no claim that our one-source-at-a-time approach will expose you to everything there is to know about each story told in this volume; no history text could make such a claim. Instead, we propose that this approach puts the spotlight on the nature of the sources themselves, illuminating the challenges and the opportunities a historian faces when analyzing any newspaper report, memoir, photograph, or set of song lyrics.

In order to give you a chance to apply the practices and principles that guided the creation of *Going to the Source*, we have organized every chapter into seven sections, each with a specific purpose. These sections give you a predictable framework in which to explore the historical issues, problems, and advantages unique to each type of source.

- An **introduction** at the start of each chapter provides you with historical context and tells you the broader story you need to know in order to interpret the sources in the chapter.
- **"Using the Source"**   Here we introduce the type of source you will be working with and alert you to the particular advantages and disadvantages that historians confront when using that type of source, be it magazine advertisements or child-rearing literature. An annotated example models how historians approach the source featured in the chapter, showing you how to unpack the evidence in a document. We also raise issues

here about the logical application of the particular source type, noting the questions that this type of source can address and the questions that must be answered by other types of sources.

- **"Working with the Source"**   This section offers you some strategies for pulling the chapter's documents apart and reorganizing the evidence into meaningful patterns. These strategies reflect the kinds of simple categorizing tools that historians invent in the course of sorting through mountains of documentary material.

- **"The Source"**   Each chapter will offer for your examination a single, coherent set of documents from a single source or from a single type of source. For example, all of the documents will come from one court case, or all of the documents will be individuals' autobiographical accounts. In a number of cases, these sources will be excerpts from much longer documents; you will recognize the use of ellipses—three dots that look like periods—to signal when words have been omitted. In every excerpt, we have endeavored to retain the author's purpose while remembering that you have limited time for reading and analyzing long historical documents.

- **"Analyzing the Source"**   In this section, you will encounter specific questions that build on your notes and reflections while "Working with the Source." These questions are meant to help you and your classmates explore further the nature of the source, interpret the source in the historical context of the chapter's story, and suggest ways in which this source might be combined with other sources to expand the story even further.

- **"Beyond the Source"**   There is no final word on any historical story, but this section offers information on later developments in the chapter's story and draws connections between this one story and larger themes in U.S. history.

- **"Finding and Supplementing the Source"**   Even if you do no further research on the chapter's topic, reading through this section will serve as a reminder that any topic in history attracts the attention of multiple historians, who devise new and interesting approaches and interpretations because they draw on varying sources or discover wholly new documents that shed an entirely different light on the topic. We invite you to peruse this section to enhance your awareness of the different books, articles, and Web sites that one historical topic can generate.

Going to the Source was created by human beings; therefore, it is a document with its own biases or point of view. We have already listed the principles and practices that guided our design and discussion in this book, but in the course of writing the book we became aware of another set of assumptions operating in these pages. As American historians who specialize in Native American history, women's history, and immigration history, we are acutely conscious of the contradictions in America's historical promises of equality and liberty. We are equally conscious of some Americans' historical struggle to preserve those contradictions and other Americans' equally determined struggle to eliminate them. We knew when we began this project that the stories we would choose to tell would illuminate this central theme in American life, the conflict over how to be true to American principles. We also knew that we wanted to represent that conflict with sources that came from the most humble corners of American life as well as the most elite centers. The mix of very popular, prominent, and private documents in *Going to the Source* is meant to convey two messages: historians must seek out and carefully assess a wide variety of sources when telling any story about the past; and the American struggle over equality and liberty has not been confined to only one tier of society—it must be examined in many sites and in multiple sources.

Contents

4 **Germ Warfare on the Colonial Frontier: An Article from the *Journal of American History*   65**

10   The West in Jacksonian Arts: George Catlin's Paintings of American Indians   197

12 On and Off the Record: Diplomatic Correspondence on the Eve of the Mexican-American War   244

13   The Illustrated Civil War: Photographers on the Battlefield   271

Going to the Source

The Bedford Reader in American History

CHAPTER 1

The Susquehannocks
Discover Europeans

Archaeological Data from the
European-Indian Encounter

While exploring the northern reaches of the Chesapeake Bay in 1608, Captain John Smith heard about a strange group of Indians from the coastal Algonquians who were his guides and interpreters. The Algonquians called this new group *Sasquesahanocks*, after a river that flowed through the strangers' territory, and told Smith they spoke a language unfamiliar to other Indians of the Chesapeake Bay. When Smith met some Indians who possessed "hatchets, knives, peeces of iron, and brasse" which they claimed to have acquired from the Sasquesahanocks, he became even more intrigued, and he sent some intermediaries to arrange a meeting with these mysterious people to the north.

Sixty Sasquesahanocks came to meet Smith and his party, and the Englishmen were impressed by what they saw. The Indians carried with them gifts of venison, animal pelts, bows, arrows, beads, and "Tobacco-pipes three foot in length." Smith described them as a "gyant-like people" who towered over the English and other Indians present. When these giants spoke, the sound echoed "as it were a great voice in a vault or cave." Unlike any Indians Smith had previously seen, the Sasquesahanocks dressed in the skins of wolves and bears. They carried weapons, he noted ominously, "sufficient to beat out the braines of a man."

Smith was the first Englishman to meet the Susquehannocks, an Indian nation that inhabited the lower Susquehanna River Valley in present-day Pennsylvania. Historians know much less about this group than they do about the coastal peoples who met the first wave of European colonists, but references to the Susquehannocks are scattered throughout early French, Dutch, Swedish, and English sources. Like the English, who derived their name for the Susquehannocks from Smith's Algonquian interpreters, other Europeans usually learned of this group from someone else. The French called them *Andaste*, a name used by the Hurons in Canada. The Dutch and Swedish called them *Minqua*, a name they learned from Indians along the Delaware River. No record has survived of what the Susquehannocks called themselves.

The Susquehannocks owed their fame to their location. The Susquehanna River flows out of central New York, from north to south, bisecting Pennsylvania before emptying into Chesapeake Bay. It was a highway for trade and warfare in northeastern America long before Europeans showed up, and it remained so throughout the colonial era. Unfortunately for the Susquehannocks, this geographic centrality made their homeland in the lower Susquehanna Valley the focus of intense competition for the fur trade among native peoples and colonists. By the 1670s, warfare with other Indians and European newcomers had dramatically reduced the Susquehannock population, the remnants of which lost their territorial and political autonomy as they resettled among other Indian groups. For nearly a generation, the lower Susquehanna was a no-man's-land until Indians displaced by war and colonization elsewhere, including some refugee Susquehannocks, resettled there in the 1690s. Colonists called this hybrid community Conestoga Town, because of its location near Conestoga Creek, a tributary of the Susquehanna. The Conestoga population gradually dwindled after 1740 as European settlers surrounded them and as the Pennsylvania fur trade moved into the Ohio Valley. In December 1763, a mob of colonists known as the Paxton Boys viciously murdered the twenty Indians who remained in Conestoga, wiping out the last vestige of the Indians who had so impressed Captain John Smith 150 years earlier.

While the specifics of the Susquehannocks' encounter with Europeans remain unclear, the general contours of the story seem all too familiar: a powerful Indian group meets European colonizers and is drawn into the fur trade, which disrupts their local communities and leads to warfare, dispersal, and decline. Indians who had occupied their homelands for thousands of years disappeared from the map within a few generations of meeting these invaders and their superior technology. This version of the story comes to us chiefly from the sources left by the colonists themselves. It is of course much harder to get the Indians' perspective because they did not leave the same kind of written records. This lack of native textual evidence has often resulted in depictions of Indians as the inhabitants of a Garden of Eden, frozen in time before European contact. Put another way, European sources have denied Indians a history of their own, classifying them as part of a "natural history" of the Americas before Columbus and placing them literally alongside woolly mammoths in museum exhibits.

One way in which historians can recover the Indians' perspective on the European-Indian encounter is by using material artifacts as evidence. Archaeologists and anthropologists have been using this type of source for a long time. For example, excavations of Indian sites from the pre-Columbian era (that is, before European contact) have enabled scholars to reconstruct the shape of

Indian communities, estimate the size of their populations, and describe their technology, economy, and beliefs. This archaeological fieldwork, which can be used to trace changes in Indian cultures over thousands of years prior to European contact, quickly deflates the notion of Indians living in a timeless paradise, awaiting Europeans to jump-start history for them. Likewise, the excavation of Indian sites from the colonial era can tell us much about the impact that colonization had on Indian communities in their material culture, social relations, and even spiritual beliefs.

The Susquehannocks provide an excellent case study for using archaeology to reconstruct the European-Indian encounter from a native perspective. While historians have long relied on the reports of colonists such as Captain John Smith to tell the Susquehannocks' story, archaeologists associated with the State Museum of Pennsylvania undertook major excavations of Susquehannock sites in the upper and lower Susquehanna Valley in the 1960s and 1970s (see Map 1.1 below). From their work, we know that the Susquehannocks emerged as a culturally distinct group about A.D. 1500. They were related to the Iroquoian-speaking Indians of the eastern Great Lakes (which accounts for the unfamiliarity of their language to Smith's interpreters), and they initially inhabited the north branch of the Susquehanna River, near the present-day Pennsylvania–New York border. About a generation before they encountered

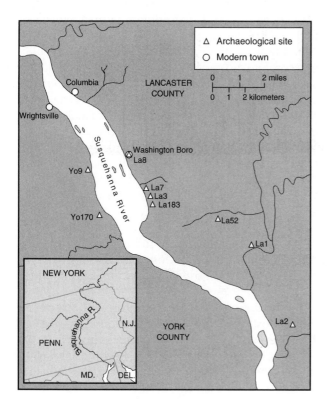

Map 1.1 Susquehannock Archaeological Sites in Lancaster and York Counties, Pennsylvania
This map shows Susquehannock sites in the lower Susquehanna River Valley of Pennsylvania. Each site has been assigned a number. The sites discussed in this chapter are: the Schultz site (La7), the Strickler site (La3), and the Conestoga Town site (La52).
Source: Barry C. Kent, *Susquehanna's Indians* (Harrisburg: Pennsylvania Historical and Museum Commission, 1989), 20.

Europeans, they concentrated their settlement in the lower Susquehanna, in what is now Lancaster County, Pennsylvania. There they displaced or assimilated another native group, known to anthropologists as the Shenk's Ferry People. The archaeological record also reveals a remarkable change in the Susquehannocks' material culture after 1600, as they incorporated European trade goods into their everyday lives.

By analyzing material artifacts recovered from Susquehannock sites, we can gain a better understanding of their participation in early colonial encounters in North America. What European trade goods did they value most? What sorts of purposes and meanings did they associate with those goods? How did the incorporation of these goods into their daily lives affect their work habits, gender relations, or notions of status? The challenge to the historian is to make this archaeological data speak in the same way as the more familiar textual sources left behind by the likes of Captain John Smith and his contemporaries, so that a more complete version of this tale might be told.

Using Archaeological Data as a Source

Academic archaeologists, unlike amateur treasure seekers and artifact collectors, pursue their work according to scientific and ethical standards agreed upon by their profession. The excavation of any site that may contain human remains or sacred objects requires balancing scholarly inquiry with sensitivity to other cultures, past and present. Native American sites can be especially controversial in this regard because of a long record of desecrations and lootings by non-Indians that has continued into the present day. Deciding to work with archaeological data, therefore, does not give historians license to take up this field on their own terms. Rather, they should familiarize themselves with how archaeologists go about their work and the professional standards they use to regulate it.

Archaeologists begin their fieldwork by finding a site that suggests previous human habitation. Once they have located such a site, they divide it into a grid pattern and systematically look for spots or "features" that suggest human activity. Trash or storage pits, for example, can yield information about the diet of the people who inhabited the site. The remains of hearths used for heating and cooking offer clues about family organization, and in the case of very old sites, can also yield the physical evidence necessary for radiocarbon dating. Post molds, or the holes left behind by the construction of homes or stockades, can reveal the physical dimensions of a home or village, information that may be useful for estimating population.

Cemeteries and burial sites can also yield a wealth of information about an individual or community. Burial position is often an indication of cultural affiliation. The Shenk's Ferry People, who predated the Susquehannocks in the lower Susquehanna Valley, buried their dead in an extended position: lying on the back, stretched out from head to feet. The Susquehannocks, on the other hand, practiced flexed burials, placing the deceased on their side in a fetal position. Forensic data recovered from human remains may tell us the sex, height, and approximate age of the deceased. The examination of bones also yields clues about the state of health of a community: what were the diseases or dietary deficiencies from which its members were likely to suffer?

In addition to human remains, burial sites may yield material artifacts. Indians of northeastern America typically interred their dead with grave goods, objects that they expected the deceased to find useful in making the journey to the next world. In the hands of archaeologists, such objects tell the story of an individual, a community, or an entire cultural group. Changes in the manufacture and decoration of pottery, for example, help archaeologists trace patterns of migration and technological change over time. Likewise, human or animal effigies carved into sacred objects such as pipes provide evidence of spiritual beliefs. Grave goods made of materials not indigenous to a particular region, such as marine shell beads recovered from an inland region, provide evidence of long-distance trade. Archaeologists also use grave goods to draw comparisons about the relative status of individuals from a set of burials. Generally speaking, the greater the quantity of grave goods, the higher the status of the individual interred with them.

In the next section, you will find two types of evidence related to archaeological excavations. The first is field notes taken by archaeologists as they worked on three Susquehannock sites: Schultz, inhabited c. 1575–1600; Strickler, inhabited c. 1645–1665; and Conestoga Town, inhabited c. 1690–1750. The Schultz and Strickler sites were named after the property owners of the sites at the time of their excavation; Conestoga Town was the historic name of the last Susquehannock-related community. As you examine this information, it is important to bear in mind that field notes are recorded on site. They are a daily log and therefore contain only information readily apparent to an archaeologist working in the field, such as descriptions of the body's burial position, an inventory of objects associated with the grave, or rough guesses about the age and sex of the deceased. The field notes do not contain conclusions drawn from the more precise forensic analysis of these materials that would be conducted in a laboratory outfitted with the necessary equipment.

The second kind of archaeological evidence that you will work with was created after the archaeologists cleaned, catalogued, and studied the objects they recovered in the field. Photographs of the objects will help you visualize items named in the field notes and compare objects of native and European manufacture. The information contained in the table comparing native and European objects found in Susquehannock burial sites (Source 14 on p. 22) is an example of the kind of data archaeologists compile about these objects after their fieldwork is complete. Taken together, the field notes, photographs, and data table will give you an idea of the process of archaeological research from start to finish, as researchers turn observations recorded in their field notes into data that can be used to draw conclusions about the site or people they are studying.

Advantages and Disadvantages of Working with Archaeological Data

The use of archaeological sources offers many advantages to the historian. First and foremost, archaeological remains provide a "text" for studying people who did not leave behind written documents, and this type of evidence helps overcome the bias toward the European perspective evident in written sources. For example, if we were to study the fur trade only by examining the inventory lists and price schedules kept by colonial traders, we could easily conclude that Indians valued brass and copper kettles because they were lighter and more durable cooking vessels than their native-made pottery. In other words, an imported metal technology rapidly supplanted a Stone Age native one. Studying the archaeological record puts an interesting wrinkle in that version of the story. Copper and brass are soft metals, and when Indians acquired kettles made from these materials, they often cut them up and reworked them into other items, such as arrow points and jewelry. They incorporated this new item into their material culture by altering its form and function in ways that had nothing to do with the kettle's original purpose. Likewise, trader inventories and accounts emphasize the monetary value of a trade good, putting a price on each item that was often set by the quantity of fur necessary to purchase it. The archaeological record provides an Indian perspective on this exchange that looks much less like a financial balance sheet. An analysis of grave good inventories shows that Indians ascribed social and spiritual value to goods acquired in the fur trade that Europeans were slow to comprehend. The glass beads and clay pipes that European traders dismissed as trinkets were valued by Indians because they resembled native-made shell beads and stone pipes that carried great spiritual and ritualistic meaning in native cultures.

One other noteworthy advantage of archaeological evidence is that it can provide a means of dating a particular group's participation in European trade or diplomacy, even if the textual record is foggy or silent on the subject. While scientific methods of dating organic materials such as bone or carbon are usually accurate only within hundreds or even thousands of years, the dating of material objects such as native pottery or European trade goods can be much more precise, often within decades. Native pottery designs provide a common means of sequencing village sites relative to each other. European trade beads and clay pipes can be used to date the site from which they were recovered with a fair degree of precision. In the case of clay pipes, maker's marks commonly left on the heel or bowl of a pipe can be traced to individuals or companies known to have been active in the pipe-making trade during a particular period. The diameter of European-made pipe stems also changed over the course of the colonial era, so by using a method known as pipe-stem dating, archaeologists can place the occupation of a site within decades. In a similar manner, particular styles of European beads fell in and out of fashion during the long history of the fur trade, enabling archaeologists to date a Native American site based upon the types of beads most commonly found there.

In the case of the Susquehannocks, an analysis of burial sites shows an enthusiastic, but selective, use of European goods acquired in the fur trade in the early seventeenth century. Consider, for example, this burial site from the Strickler (c. 1645–1665) field notes:

Location	Body Position	Sex	Age	Notes/Associations
N57-W21 (2 bodies)	extended	?	adult	cache near head: steatite pipe flints archaic projectile point pewter object steel strike-a-lite knife
				cache near hips: gun parts: flintlock pan, main spring, hammer?
	bundled	?	adolescent	Strickler pot small iron knife under pot

Labels at left, connected by lines to the table:

- Directional markings indicating position of this burial on a grid
- Question mark indicates something that cannot be readily identified or confirmed in the field
- Native stone pipe
- European fire-making tool
- Native pottery design named after site where it is most commonly found
- Collection of loose bones buried together, usually evidence of a reinterment

Source: State Museum of Pennsylvania, Strickler Site, 1645–1665 (36La3), Burial Records, 1974.

This burial featured a combination of native and European grave goods. The steatite pipe, archaic projectile point, and Strickler pot were native goods made of stone or clay. The steel strike-a-lite, small iron knife, and gun parts were metal wares commonly acquired in the fur trade. The flints and knife found with the adult's remains could have been of either European or native manufacture. What this site tells us, then, is that by the mid-seventeenth century, the Susquehannocks engaged in trade with Europeans, but their material culture still included some important native crafts, such as pottery making and pipe making.

While there is much that archaeological data can reveal, there are some limitations to working with this source. Just as libraries and archives select what documents they will preserve, so too does nature control what survives and what does not in the archaeological record. Objects that are interred, be it in a burial site or trash pit, do not all deteriorate at the same rate. Metal wares corrode but are long-lived compared to such organic materials as wood, woven cloth, and food. A typical inventory of a colonial-era burial site may include a laundry list of iron and brass items—kettles, knives, hatchets, hoes, scissors, arrow points, gun parts, jewelry—but very little in the way of cloth. Yet, we know from colonial records that cloth accounted for the greatest variety and monetary value of items that Indians acquired through the fur trade. Other significant items purchased by Indians in the fur trade are also commonly absent from burial site inventories because they were consumed quickly or lacked the durability of metal wares. For example, alcohol and tobacco figured prominently in trade and diplomacy between Europeans and Indians. However, neither item shows up very often in burial sites, even though textual records indicate that Indians incorporated both into their mourning customs. A balanced picture of the material exchange involved in the fur trade, therefore, requires supplementing archaeological data with trade lists and accounts that illuminate the role of goods not likely to find their way into the archaeological record.

Another disadvantage of this type of evidence has to do with the context in which such artifacts are recovered. An archaeologist recovers an object at its final resting place. In other words, archaeology presents goods at their last stop, not in the context of exchange or use that may have given them meaning to their original possessors. Archaeologists will look at a kettle recovered from a burial site and ascribe to it spiritual significance as a grave good. It is also important to ask how that kettle was acquired and used before it ended up in a burial. What functional purpose did it serve as a cooking utensil? Did it replace or supplement native pottery? What social meaning did it have in terms of food preparation and consumption?

Another factor to bear in mind as you examine this evidence is that historians and archaeologists do not always ask the same questions. Archaeologists tend to identify and classify objects first according to the materials from which they are made. Thus, the archaeologists who worked on the Susquehannock sites divided the objects they recovered into two primary groups: native made and European made. Within each of these groups, they classified items chiefly by material: ceramic, stone, shell, and organic (bone, wood, antler) for native-made goods; brass, iron, pewter, glass, and ceramic for European-made goods. This approach is helpful for studying the penetration of European imports into the Indians' material lives, but it is not without its problems. What about classifying objects by use rather than form? Should a stone pipe be grouped separately from a clay one? Would it be useful to group all weapons together, whether they are stone axes, European guns, iron knives, or wooden war clubs? How you identify, classify, and use such evidence will depend upon the questions you want to answer. Are you interested primarily in the origin of an object or its use? Are you studying its technological role in a culture or its social and ideological significance?

Working with the Source

This table will help you organize your thoughts and reactions to the field notes as you read through them. For each site, try to identify the objects most commonly and least commonly found in burial sites, cultural practices (for example, burial customs, spiritual beliefs, body decoration) indicated from the notes on the burials, and any questions or comments these field notes raise for you.

	Schultz Site	Strickler Site	Conestoga Town Site
Most Common Items Found			
Least Common Items Found			
Evidence of Cultural Practices			
Questions or Comments Arising from the Field Notes			

The Source: Field Notes, Artifacts, and Analysis from Archaeological Excavations of Susquehannock Sites

FIELD NOTES FROM SUSQUEHANNOCK SITES

 Field Notes from the Schultz Site, 1575–1600

Location	Body Position	Culture Group	Sex	Age	Notes/Associations
N4-W4 (2 Bodies)	Extended	Shenk's Ferry	?	Adult	Animal Bone (Possibly Dog)
	Extended	Shenk's Ferry	?	Adult	Quartz Arrow Point
N5-W21	Extended	Shenk's Ferry	?	Child	None
N4-W9	Flexed?	Susquehannock?	?	Adult	Possible Animal Bone
N4-W9	Flexed	Susquehannock	?	Adult	Broken Pot, Seeds
N5-W11	Flexed	Susquehannock	?	Adult	2 Pots, Animal Bone (Deer)
N5-W15	Extended	Shenk's Ferry	?	Infant	None
N4-W10	Flexed	Susquehannock	?	Adult	Ochre[1]
N17-W27	Extended	Shenk's Ferry	?	Adult?	None
N12-W12	Flexed	Susquehannock	?	Adult	3 Pots, Animal Bone
N13-W13	Flexed	Susquehannock	?	Adult	Glass Beads, Ochre, 3 Pots, Animal Bone

[1] Native. Ground hematite, used by Indians for its red pigment as paint.

Source: State Museum of Pennsylvania, Schultz Site, 1575–1600 (36La7), Burial Records, 1969.

2   *Field Notes from the Strickler Site, 1645–1665*

Location	Body Position	Sex	Age	Notes/Associations
N57-W21 (2 Bodies)	Extended	?	Adult	Cache Near Head: Steatite Pipe,[1] Flints, Archaic Projectile Point, Pewter Object, Steel Strike-a-Lite,[2] Knife Cache Near Hips: Gun Parts: Flintlock Pan, Main Spring, Hammer?[3]
	Bundled	?	Adolescent	Strickler Pot, Small Iron Knife under Pot
N57-W23	Flexed	?	Adult	Brass Piece, Brass Kettle with Iron Handle
N58-W19 (2 Bodies)	Extended	M	Adult	Probable Old Male 2 Clay Pipes, Iron Knife, Brass Kettle, Strickler Pot, Pewter Porringer,[4] Silver Medallion and Beads, Apparently on a Necklace
	?	?	Child	Necklace of Red Glass Beads around Skull, Belt of Glass Beads around Mid-Section, Iron Bracelet, 2 Brass Coils
N58-W20 (2 Bodies)	Extended	?	Adult	5 Kettles (One with Pewter Mug and Broken Pot in It), 3 Guns, 3 Axes, Iron Saw Blade **Cache A:** Tulip Bowl Pipe,[5] Flint, Beaver Tooth, Small String Red Straw Beads **Cache B:** Small Axe, Pipe, Knife, Ochre, Lump of Kaolin,[6] Wampum,[7] Pot, Musket Balls, Gunlock **Cache C:** Ladle, Points, Stone Celt,[8] Steatite Pipe Blank,[9] Iron Knife **Cache D:** 2 Tulip Bowl Pipes, Flint, Kaolin Pipe,[10] Musket Ball Three Bead Groups: Red Straw,[11] Red Straw: 5-Strand Wide Belt Pattern, Large Sub-Spherical Red-Striped
	?	?	Child	Teeth Caps[12]
N58-W23	Flexed	?	Adult	Pipe, Sword Blade, Glass Lens, Piece of Iron, Rapier, Chisel, Gun Parts, Ochre, Brass Kettle, Kaolin Lump, Four Balls (2 Stone, 2 Iron): Possible Cannon Balls?
N59-W19	Extended	?	Adult	Gun Flints, Iron Knife, Iron Wedge, Iron Nails, Hone Stone,[13] Lead, Scrap of Pewter, Possible Strike-a-Lite
N60-W22	Flexed	?	Adult	3 Lead Balls, String of White Wampum Beads Woven into a Belt in Area of Hands

[1] Native. Stone pipe.
[2] European. Fire-making tools for striking sparks.
[3] European. The wooden stocks of muskets rotted away quickly underground, but the barrel and other metal parts such as those listed here remained.
[4] European. Small metal bowl.
[5] Native. Indian pipe.
[6] Clay.
[7] Native. Small tubular beads made from marine shell.
[8] Native. Stone axe head.
[9] Native. Unfinished stone pipe block.
[10] European. Clay trade pipe.
[11] European. Small tubular beads.
[12] Child's teeth with undeveloped roots.
[13] Native. Stone sharpening tool.

Source: State Museum of Pennsylvania, Strickler Site, 1645–1665 (36La3), Burial Records, 1974.

Field Notes from the Conestoga Town Site, 1690–1750

Location	Body Position	Sex	Age	Notes/Associations
N6-E14	Extended	F	Adult	Old Female Kettle (Pieces of Turtle Shell and Remnants of Wooden Spoon inside), Axe Head
N7-E9	Extended	?	Child	Beads throughout, Brass Kettle, Iron Hoe, Long Glass Bottle, Cache of Rings, Cache of Beads, Iron Snuff Box,[1] Green Glass Medicine Bottle, Several Knife Blades, Brass Bells, 4 River Pebbles, Tubular Shell Beads, Catlinite[2] Triangles
N7-E10	Extended	?	Adult	Age: 35+ Much Tooth Wear Iron Axe, 2 Brass Kettles, Cache of Beads, Flints, Catlinite, George Medal,[3] Iron Knife, Long Shell Tubes, Coffin Nails, White Seed Beads,[4] Iron, Lead
N7-E11	Extended	M	Adult	Adult Male, Moderate Teeth Wear Rifle, Necklace(s) Containing Blue Faceted Beads, Brass Medals, Brass Rings, Small White Seed Beads, Shell Triangles, 4 Brass Thimbles, Brass Jinglers[5] **Cache 1:** Gun Flints, Brass Jinglers, Red Ochre, Brass Chain, Ash, Brass Wires, Scissors, White Seed Beads, Kaolin Pipe, Iron Jew's Harp,[6] Wampum Beads, Shell Triangles, Long Catlinite Beads, Pocket Knife, Brass Coil, Brass Kettle Containing Hammer Head, Wooden Spoon, Mirror **Cache 2:** Brass Jinglers, White Seed Beads, Brass Bell, Gun Flints, Corner-Notched Arrow Head, Musket Balls, Bark, Axe Head Brass Ring on Right Hand and Left Brass Wires over Right Rib Cage Horse or Cow Pelvis above Right Pelvis **Cache 3:** Gunpowder, Brass Thimbles, Gun Flints, Archaic Arrow Head White Seed Beads, Wampum Bead Bracelet on Lower Left Arm, Wampum Extending under Right Arm, Small White Beads throughout Fill under Left Thorax
N8-E10	Extended	M?	Adult	Probable Male—Erupting Molars, 18–22 **Cache A:** Light Blue and White Seed Beads, Mirror, Knife, Brass Arrowhead, 3 Knives, Gun Flint, 2 Clay Balls (Marbles), Shell Wampum, Coins, Red Ochre, Gunpowder, Musket Balls **Cache B:** Musket Balls, Gun Flints, Hone Stone, Gunpowder **Cache C:** Kaolin Pipe, Iron Box, Numerous Beads, Some Definitely on Necklaces, Brass Spiral, Hair Puller,[7] Rings on Fingers of Right Hand, Wampum Bracelets on Both Arms, Pocket Knife **General Contents:** Gun, 2 Brass Kettles, One Containing a Latteen Spoon[8] Enormous Quantity of Beads in Grave Fill
N15-E18	?	?	Infant	Bracelet of Glass Wampum, Strings of Large Blue Glass Faceted Beads, 2 Brass Springs, Small Black and White Glass Beads, Three Brass Rings, George Medal, Kaolin Pipe, String of Small Brass Beads, Small Earthenware Vessel, Small Quantity of Red Ochre
N16-E13	Extended	M	Adult	Extended Adult Burial, Old Male, Considerable Tooth Wear, Robust Skeleton, Musket Lying along West Side of Grave, Iron Axe, Cache of Musket Balls and Buckshot, Brass Kettle Lying between Lower Legs, Mirror, Kaolin Pipe, Catlinite Pipe, Bear Canine, Gun Flints, Knife, Scissors, Shell Barrel Beads, Brass Points, Bottle, Powderhorn, Rings on Right Hand, Wampum under Rings, Small White Seed Beads

[1] European. Small box with hinged lid for tobacco.
[2] Native. Soft red stone, often used in making pipes.
[3] European. Medallion featuring English kings, George I (1714–1727) or George II (1727–1760).
[4] European. Small, spherical beads.
[5] European and native. Indian jewelry made from refashioned brass.
[6] European. Mouth harp.
[7] Native. Jewelry worn in hair.
[8] European. Metal spoon.

Source: State Museum of Pennsylvania, Conestoga Town Site, 1690–1750 (La52), Field Sheets, 1972.

PHOTOGRAPHS AND ANALYSIS OF ARTIFACTS
RECOVERED FROM SUSQUEHANNOCK SITES

 Native Pottery

This pot is an example of native-made pottery from the Schultz site (1575–1600). Archaeologists use the distinctive patterns of pottery (note the lines incised around the upper half of the pot) to date the site from which it is recovered.

Source: State Museum of Pennsylvania, Pennsylvania Historical and Museum Commission.

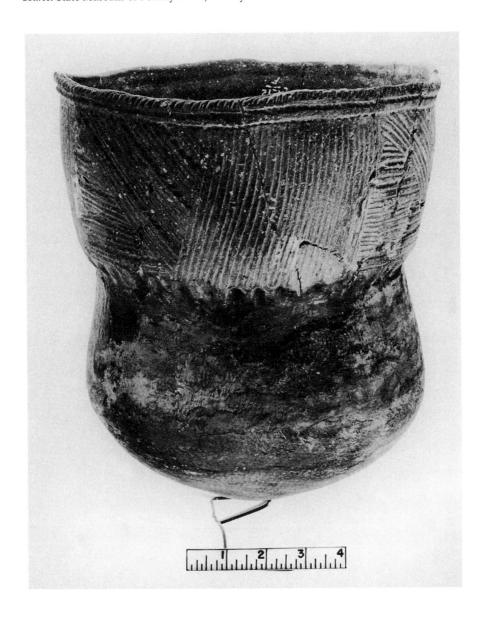

5   *European Ceramic Pitcher*

This stoneware pitcher testifies to the Susquehannocks' contact and exchange with Europeans.
Source: State Museum of Pennsylvania, Pennsylvania Historical and Museum Commission.

6 · *Native Stone Tools*

Archaeologists recovered several different types of stone tools from Susquehannock sites. The two notched disk-shaped tools in the top row were probably used as hoes in the Susquehannocks' cornfields. From left to right on the bottom row are a milling stone (used to process corn) and three celts, used as striking tools.

Source: State Museum of Pennsylvania, Pennsylvania Historical and Museum Commission.

European Iron Axe Heads, side and above views

Iron axe heads were a popular item in the fur trade, and Indians used them as tools and weapons. The axe heads rapidly replaced native stone celts (see Source 6 on p. 15) because they were sharper, more durable, and lighter.

Source: State Museum of Pennsylvania, Pennsylvania Historical and Museum Commission.

8   *European Trade Knives, Blades, and Handles*

Like iron axe heads, iron knives were a popular item in the fur trade because of their technological advantages over stone knives. The broken blades and handles found in archaeological excavations are evidence of their heavy use by Indians, who repaired broken handles by fashioning new ones out of bone or wood. The two objects in the bottom row are clasp knives, in which the blade folded into the handle.

Source: State Museum of Pennsylvania, Pennsylvania Historical and Museum Commission.

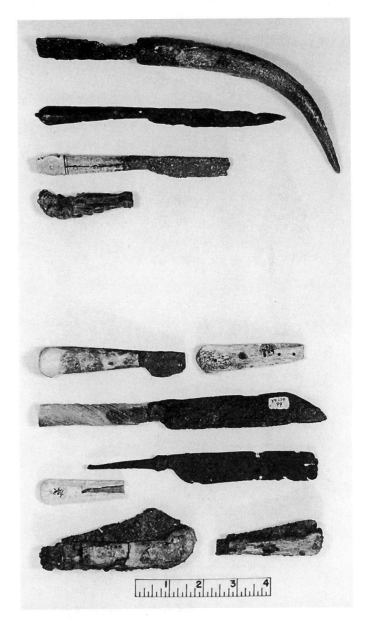

Arrow Points Made from Native and European Materials

The arrow points on the top row are made from brass that Indians refashioned from kettles acquired in the fur trade. Those on the bottom row are traditional native points made from stone.

Source: State Museum of Pennsylvania, Pennsylvania Historical and Museum Commission.

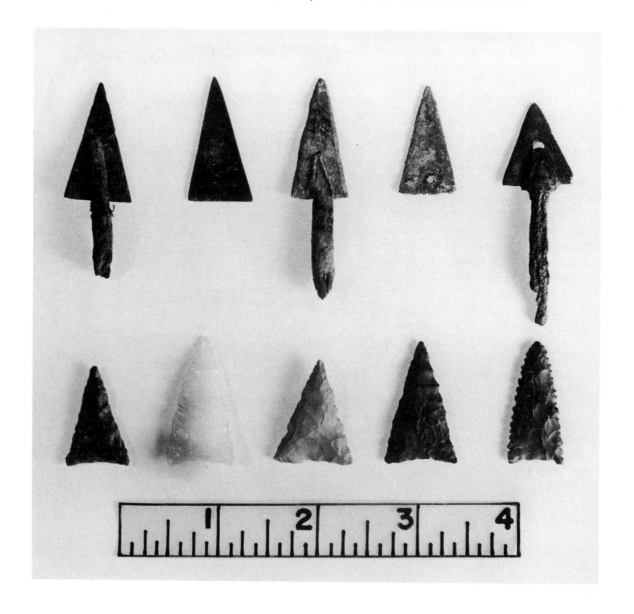

10 *Native Clay Pipes*

Five of these pipes are representative of a Susquehannock form archaeologists have named the tulip bowl pipe, because its rounded bowl resembles the flower. It was most commonly associated with the Strickler site (1645–1665). The pipe on the far right is a Seneca type distinguished from the others by its fluted rather than rounded bowl. It came from the Conestoga Town site (1690–1750) and is evidence of that site's connection to the Seneca Indians of western New York.

Source: State Museum of Pennsylvania, Pennsylvania Historical and Museum Commission.

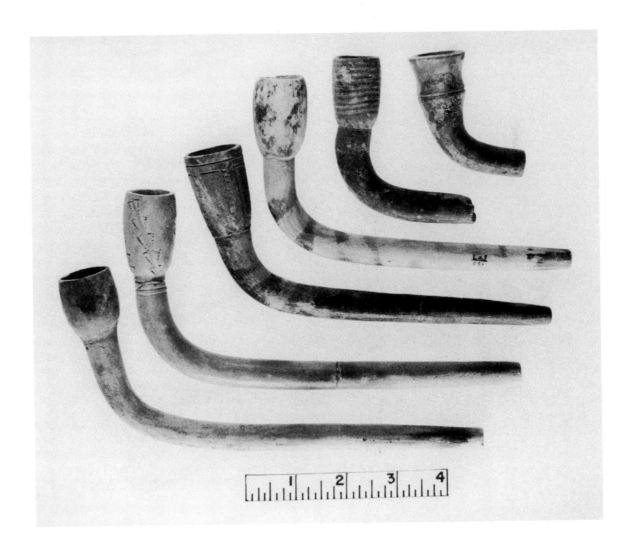

European Kaolin Pipes

Fur traders and colonial officials commonly distributed these pipes with gifts of tobacco to Indians. Note their similarity in form to the native tulip bowl pipe (Source 10 on p. 19). The second pipe from the top has a maker's mark emblazoned on the side of the bowl. Archaeologists used such marks to date the manufacture of the pipe and the site where it was found.

Source: State Museum of Pennsylvania, Pennsylvania Historical and Museum Commission.

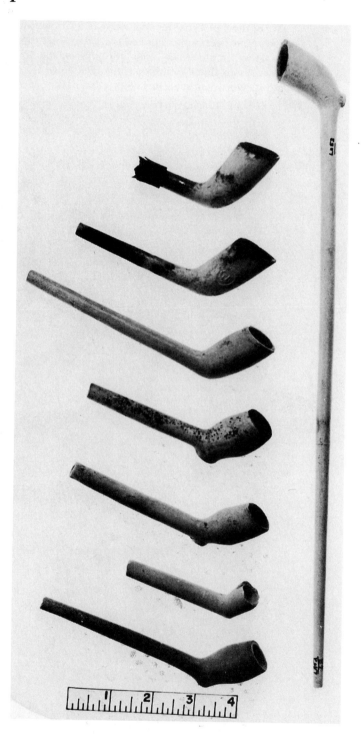

12   *Native Antler Comb with Human Effigies*

Indians used such combs as adornment for their hair. Human and animal effigies were common on them, but this one is noteworthy for the buttons on the clothing of the two figures, which suggest they are either Europeans or Indians attired in European clothing.

Source: State Museum of Pennsylvania, Pennsylvania Historical and Museum Commission.

Native Objects and Jewelry Fashioned from European Materials

These objects were made from the copper and brass found in kettles Indians acquired from Europeans. Indians incorporated these items into their clothing and used them as pendants, necklaces, bracelets, jigglers, and earrings.

Source: State Museum of Pennsylvania, Pennsylvania Historical and Museum Commission.

Comparison of Select Native and European Objects in Susquehannock Burial Sites, 1575–1750

The archaeologists who excavated the Susquehannock sites compiled the data table on the facing page after their work was complete. It allows for an analysis of the shifting composition of grave goods between the sixteenth and eighteenth centuries. The percentages were calculated by dividing the number of items found by the number of interments.

Time	Site	No. of Graves	Stone Celts	Iron Axes	Iron Knives	Iron Hoes	Stone Points	Brass Points	Whole Guns	Native Pots	Brass Kettles	Native Pipes	Kaolin Pipes
1575–1600	Schultz	222	0	5 2%	7 3%	1 <1%	68 31%	0	0	210 95%	1 <1%	2 1%	0
1645–1665	Strickler	307	1 <1%	53 17%	136 44%	41 13%	68 22%	102 33%	36 12%	169 55%	145 47%	130 42%	12 4%
1690–1750	Conestoga Town	69	0	24 35%	74 100%	3 4%	3 4%	11 16%	9 13%	0	42 61%	9 13%	37 54%

Source: Adapted from Barry C. Kent, *Susquehanna's Indians* (Harrisburg: Pennsylvania Historical and Museum Commission, 1989), 292.

Analyzing the Source

REFLECTING ON THE SOURCE

1. Judging from the notes you made in the table on page 9, how did the quantity and types of grave goods differ between the Schultz, Strickler, and Conestoga Town sites? Is there a discernible pattern to how the composition and use of these grave goods changed over time?

2. Using the field notes, photographs, and information in Source 14, describe which European goods replaced native goods in these burial sites. Did such change occur uniformly or were some native goods more or less likely to be supplanted by imported substitutes? What factors do you think most affected the likelihood of such substitution: technological superiority, physical resemblance, or versatility?

3. Where in these sources do you see evidence of Indians altering European goods or making use of them in ways different from the original functions of those goods? What do such alterations in the function or appearance of a good tell you about the value Indians placed upon it?

MAKING CONNECTIONS

4. The field notes from the Schultz and Strickler sites rarely venture a guess as to the sex of a burial site's occupant, yet the field notes from Conestoga Town do. How might the archaeologists at Conestoga Town have used grave goods to make their guesses in this regard? What does a gender difference in the distribution of grave goods tell you about the impact that contact with European colonists had on gender roles in native society?

5. The Schultz, Strickler, and Conestoga sites are all characterized as "Susquehannock," but what evidence do you see here of cultural variation among the peoples who inhabited these sites? How do these differences help illuminate historical change in Indian societies, both before and after European contact?

6. How does archaeology help provide a better sense of the Indians' role in the European-Indian encounter? Based on the evidence you studied in this chapter, how would you describe the course of the Susquehannocks' encounter with Europeans? Is it a story of conquest, adaptation, or resistance?

Beyond the Source

From the very beginning of the European-Indian encounter, the disturbance of Indian burial sites by Europeans has been controversial. In the colonial era, treasure seekers ransacked Indian cemeteries to recover valuable trade goods or "curiosities" (including human remains) that could be sold to wealthy collectors in America and Europe. In the nineteenth and twentieth centuries, that practice continued, with amateur archaeologists and private collectors digging up Indian burial sites to build their own collections of Indian artifacts. In the late nineteenth and early twentieth centuries, many of these private collections moved into museums, where they were placed on public display and became available for scholarly research.

Meanwhile, American Indians protested the disturbance of cemeteries, the desecration of human remains, and the looting of sacred objects by collectors. They viewed this sort of practice, be it by amateurs or professional scholars, as a continuation of the assault on Indian mortuary customs and spiritual beliefs that began with the arrival of the first missionaries in the colonial era. In the 1970s, many Native Americans approached museums about taking human remains and sacred objects off display and returning them to the descendants of the people with whom such remains and objects were associated. In 1990, the federal government passed the Native American Graves Protection and Repatriation Act (NAGPRA), which formalized a legal process for this purpose. NAGPRA mandates that museums must return upon request any human remains, grave goods, sacred objects, or similar items to Indian groups that can prove cultural affiliation with those objects. This legislation has prompted many museums to inventory their Native American collections, review their exhibition procedures, and work much more closely with native peoples in managing and preserving these materials.

The Susquehannock sites you studied in the chapter were excavated in the 1960s and 1970s. Today, the ethical standards of archaeologists no longer condone the excavation of Native American burial sites, unless the sites would otherwise be destroyed without the opportunity to record their existence. Such instances typically happen when earthmoving equipment at a construction site uncovers a previously unknown cemetery or village site. In such instances, the archaeological work can become politically charged as Native Americans and scholars butt heads over access to the materials recovered. While Indians usually advocate the prompt reburial of human remains and mortuary objects recovered in such a manner, archaeologists note that the study of such materials is essential to documenting the Indians' history and can benefit current Native American groups by proving their links to cultural groups of the past. Indeed, the federal government will grant recognition (and thus aid for housing, health care, and education) only to those Indian groups that can prove their historical integrity as a cultural group and their historical association with a particular homeland. Considering the migrations and forced removals that

Indians have faced since the colonial era and the dearth of written documents detailing those moves (especially before 1800), archaeology presents one of the best methods for meeting such federally mandated criteria. Thus, archaeologists and Native Americans remain involved in a tug-of-war over the past, and modern political struggles will continue to shape our recovery and interpretation of the history of the European-Indian encounter.

Finding and Supplementing the Source

The artifacts and field notes associated with archaeological excavations are usually archived and maintained by the universities or museums that sponsor the research. The best way to start your own search for such materials is by consulting the scholarly journals in which archaeologists publish their work. *American Antiquity* is the leading journal for American archaeology, but you may also want to check regional journals, depending upon the areas or cultures in which you are interested. Two useful titles in this category are *Plains Anthropologist* and *Southeastern Archaeology*. For coverage of issues concerning professional standards and ethics in modern archaeology, see the *SAA Bulletin*, published by the Society for American Archaeology, and available online at **saa.org/publications/saabulletin**.

For the fullest scholarly treatment of the Susquehannocks, see Barry C. Kent, *Susquehanna's Indians* (Harrisburg: Pennsylvania Historical and Museum Commission, 1989). For a briefer summary, see Francis Jennings, "Susquehannock," in *Handbook of North American Indians, Volume 15: The Northeast*, edited by Bruce G. Trigger (Washington, D.C.: Smithsonian Institution, 1978), 362–67. The *Handbook of North American Indians* is an excellent research reference for anyone interested in the history and archaeology of the European-Indian encounter, but not all volumes in the series have published yet.

For a good overview of the European-Indian encounter, see Daniel K. Richter, *Facing East from Indian Country: A Native History of Early America* (Cambridge: Harvard University Press, 2001). Two essay collections provide excellent examples of how scholars use archaeological methods and sources to study this topic: *Cultures in Contact: The Impact of European Contacts on Native American Cultural Institutions, A.D. 1000–1800*, edited by William W. Fitzhugh (Washington, D.C.: Smithsonian Institution Press, 1985), and *The Recovery of Meaning: Historical Archaeology in the Eastern United States*, edited by Mark P. Leone and Parker B. Potter Jr. (Washington, D.C.: Smithsonian Institution Press, 1988).

A recent study that addresses modern archaeology's dilemma over the use of Native American burial sites is Patricia E. Rubertone, *Grave Undertakings: An Archaeology of Roger Williams and the Narragansett Indians* (Washington, D.C.: Smithsonian Institution Press, 2001). The most controversial case involving a NAGPRA claim concerns a set of human remains known as Kennewick Man, uncovered in the Columbia River Valley of Washington in the 1990s. Two books that use this case to explore tensions between anthropologists and

Native Americans are David Hurst Thomas, *Skull Wars: Kennewick Man, Archaeology, and the Battle for Native American Identity* (New York: Basic Books, 2000), and Jeff Benedict, *No Bone Unturned: The Adventures of a Top Smithsonian Forensic Scientist and the Legal Battle for America's Oldest Skeletons* (New York: Harper-Collins, 2003). The film *Who Owns the Past?* (directed by N. Jed Riffe, 2000) offers a thought-provoking introduction to the dispute surrounding the Kennewick Man remains.

CHAPTER 2

Coming to America

Passenger Lists from the
1635 London Port Register

Richard Frethorne was one of many thousand English men and women who crossed the Atlantic in the seventeenth century to improve their lives in America. What little we know of his experiences there comes from a single letter to his parents that has survived in the records of the Virginia Company, the merchant company that sponsored the colonization of the Chesapeake Bay.

Frethorne's father had arranged for Richard to go to America as a worker for the Virginia Company, perhaps thinking that this would be a good start for his son as he made his way into the world. Richard went to work on a tobacco plantation called Martin's Hundred, about ten miles from Jamestown. There he encountered horrors that neither he nor his parents could have anticipated. Diseases killed his companions with frightening efficiency, in particular scurvy, caused by a nutritional deficiency, and the "bloody flux," or dysentery, a gastrointestinal ailment caused by contaminated drinking water. Hard work reduced Richard's clothes to rags, and one of his fellow workers stole his cloak, refusing to divulge its whereabouts even as the thief lay dying. The forests were full of deer, but Richard could eat no venison because he was forced to "work hard both early and late for a mess of water gruel and a mouthful of bread and beef." He feared for his life from nearby Indians, against whom the English made war even though the colonists were outnumbered 100 to 1. "There is nothing to be gotten here but sickness and death," Richard wrote on March 20, 1623, begging his parents to buy him out of his service to the Virginia Company. "The answer of this letter will be life or death to me," he implored, before listing the names of seventeen others who had landed with him in Virginia and already perished. We do not know how his parents responded, or if they even saw the letter.

Richard Frethorne is not the kind of character we typically meet in stories about the early colonization of America. Instead, myth and popular culture have reduced the story of England's colonization of the Americas to a parade of caricatures. Every November, schoolchildren dress up as pious Pilgrims and friendly Indians to reenact the first Thanksgiving dinner. Disney's version of the Pocahontas story is the latest in a long line of narrative inventions that have turned the travails suffered by early Virginia colonists like Richard Frethorne into the makings of a romance novel. From the colonial Caribbean, American popular culture has borrowed a few swashbuckling pirates, such as Blackbeard and Henry Morgan, who, if we are to believe the advertising industry, whiled away their days drinking rum and playing miniature golf.

This penchant for turning seventeenth-century colonists into storybook characters hides the complexity and human drama behind the movement of people that gave England its transatlantic colonies. During the seventeenth century, more than five hundred thousand men and women left England to establish new homes in America. The peak years of this movement occurred between 1630 and 1660, a time of great economic and social uncertainty in England marked by religious division, political breakdown, and civil war. The three most common transatlantic destinations in this period were New England, the Chesapeake Bay, and the Caribbean.

This Atlantic migration was an extension of an internal migration already underway in England by 1600. England's population increased from 3 to 4 million between 1550 and 1600; it increased another million by 1650. This rapid growth put pressure on the economy, causing inflation and a decline in real wages that was worsened by periodic harvest failures and recessions in the cloth trade, England's leading industry. Landowners also displaced many of their tenants by enclosing common fields previously used for crop and live-stock production and converting this land to sheep pasturage. Agricultural workers cut loose by these changes drifted into urban areas looking for work. London absorbed approximately 7,000 to 10,000 new residents each year in the seventeenth century, its population increasing from 200,000 in 1600 to 490,000 by 1700.

All of this mobility challenged the social institutions and relations that had governed England since the medieval era. Families that had lived in a particular home, worked the same plot of land, and worshiped among neighbors in a local church for generations fragmented and dispersed. Poverty and unemployment also disrupted traditional patterns of education, marriage, and childbearing because young adults found it harder to start households of their own. Elites complained of increasing crime and vagrancy, which they attributed to "masterless men," individuals who lived free from the authority and government imposed by fathers, ministers, masters, and landlords.

Colonial promoters in England believed that overseas expansion would provide an outlet for this volatile, excess population, and they published pamphlets and broadsides recruiting migrants for their ventures by promising them the opportunities for work and land ownership that were missing at home. Like Richard Frethorne, the people who answered this call tended to be young, male, and single. Many were unskilled because they were unable to find steady employment at a time in their lives when young people gained occupational training as servants or apprentices. Others possessed a craft but could not find gainful employment at home. Although they left England from such urban centers as Bristol and London, many of the migrants had rural origins in the English hinterlands. Their passage to America simply extended a much longer process of migration that had begun many years earlier.

Making the transatlantic voyage required considerable planning and resources. A list published in 1630 detailing the costs of immigration to America estimated that a minimum budget of five pounds for transportation and ten pounds for provisions, clothing, and tools was necessary; providing more than the bare necessities or taking along a family would of course require much more. A typical English husbandman, a tenant farmer working thirty acres of land, might earn a profit of fifteen pounds in a good year. The laboring poor earned considerably less, perhaps an annual income of eight to twelve pounds. The high cost of immigration meant that only a small percentage of the population could fund the voyage themselves. The rest came to the New World as indentured servants. In exchange for the cost of their passage, they agreed to sell their labor for a number of years, typically four to five, to a master who would provide them with food, clothing, and shelter during that time as well as "freedom dues" of new clothing, tools, and sometimes land upon the completion of their service. Servitude was a common form of labor in England, especially for young adults (ages 14 to 24) seeking training in the skills that would allow them to establish their own households. In the New World, servitude became the primary source of labor for plantation colonies in the Chesapeake and Caribbean until it was displaced by African slavery. Overall, historians estimate that 75 to 80 percent of the English men and women who traveled to the Chesapeake and Caribbean colonies in the seventeenth century did so as servants. Servant migration to New England was considerably less than in those other regions, but still substantial: about 35 percent.

Seventeenth-century English observers liked to describe these migrants as the dregs of society. Sir Josiah Child, an economist and commentator on colonial policy, referred to them as "a sort of loose, vagrant People, vicious and destitute of means to live at home, being either unfit for labor, or such as could find none to employ themselves about, or had so misbehaved themselves by Whoring, Thieving, or other Debauchery, that none would set them to work." Travel narratives from early America painted with the same broad brush as Child, describing New England's inhabitants as religious dissidents forced out of England by their zealotry and the Chesapeake's and Caribbean's inhabitants as ne'er-do-wells who immigrated to escape debts, ill repute, or the noose at home.

Such stereotypes, while colorful, do little to advance our knowledge of England's New World colonizers. This problem is compounded by the fact that very few of these seventeenth-century migrants left behind records detailing their reasons for going to America or their experiences once there. Richard Frethorne's sole surviving letter home is exceptional in this regard. Puritan

New England did have a high literacy rate, and many of its settlers kept spiritual journals and wrote letters to family and friends who remained in England, but taken as a whole, English transatlantic migration involved people who lacked the education or motivation to write the story down from their perspective. For most, the only trace they left behind was a name on a ship's passenger list.

These lists, however, are not as limited as they might seem at first glance. Historians have used them to reconstruct patterns of migration over time, including variations in places of origin and destination. The lists also yield important information about the demographics of migration—the sex ratio between male and female passengers, their age distribution, and kinship relations among them—that is useful in comparing colonial development in different regions. By looking at the source in this manner, we can make the passenger lists speak for the migrants, the vast majority of whom left no first-person account of their story. Such analysis requires more effort than simply reading the impressionistic descriptions of a few colonial promoters and policymakers, but the information gleaned in this process can help us explain why the three zones of English colonization in seventeenth-century America developed in such different ways. English men and women sharing a common cultural heritage created vastly different societies in the Caribbean, the Chesapeake, and New England in the seventeenth century. Certainly, differences in the native peoples and environments they encountered can help explain this variation, but the passenger lists from the ships that carried them across the Atlantic also provide important clues about the circumstances that shaped their lives in the New World.

Using Passenger Lists as a Source

By the 1630s, migration from England was in high gear, and the government wanted to keep track of this movement for a number of reasons. The king, Charles I, did not want his wealthier subjects, who paid the lion's share of England's taxes, abandoning him for a foreign realm. Also, in an age of fierce religious and political division, the king wanted to make sure that England's overseas dominions were populated by loyal subjects. Thus, in 1634 Charles I told royal officials in London to record information about individuals sailing abroad. The Crown required oaths of allegiance from adult travelers and proof of their conformity with the English Church (usually referred to as "oaths of allegiance and supremacy" on the passenger lists). Some passengers carried with them letters from justices of the peace and ministers in their hometowns attesting that they met these conditions. Others, particularly those headed for Virginia or the Caribbean, took these oaths as their ships prepared to sail.

The king's order to record the names of travelers going abroad and proof of their oaths of allegiance resulted in the 1635 London Port Register, the most detailed record of English overseas migration from the seventeenth century.

The passenger lists collected in the register recorded the names of 7,507 English men, women, and children who sailed overseas from London in that year. Of these, 1,595 were soldiers going to European posts. Another 1,034 were civilians traveling to Europe. The remaining 4,878 headed across the Atlantic: 1,169 (24 percent) to New England, 2,009 (41 percent) to the Chesapeake, and 1,700 (35 percent) to the Caribbean.

Like any good historical source, these passenger lists seem to raise as many questions as they answer. Jotted down by government officials who were completing a variety of tasks before a ship embarked, the lists offer individual snapshots of migration rather than a motion picture with a clear beginning, middle, and end. Some lists include information on the passengers' hometowns, occupations, and families, but most offer less detail than a modern phone book, recording only names and ages.

Using this source, therefore, requires analysis in several steps. First, the historian must do some counting and calculating to boil down the lists' contents into statistics useful for analysis. In the next step, the historian looks for noteworthy trends or differences in those statistics that are relevant to telling the migrants' story: How old were they? Where did they come from? How many of them were married or related to each other? Finally, the historian considers interpretive questions raised by the lists: What is the significance of whether a migrant's occupation is listed or not? What does the organization of a list tell us about the social status and gender roles of its passengers? What kind of impact will the demographics of migration have on the passengers' fortunes in the New World?

Advantages and Disadvantages of Working with Passenger Lists

The most important advantage to working with this type of source is the raw data it provides on migration. Unlike promotional pamphlets, political tracts, or tell-all narratives aimed at exposing abuses in the servant trade, these passenger lists were not written to persuade an audience to favor or resist migration. Rather, they were government records kept by customs officials charged with the task of inspecting people as they left the country, much as they might have inspected the rest of a ship's cargo. The information they collected in the form of names, ages, and other biographical details provides an important means of checking the general impressions about immigrants left in more subjective narrative sources. In an age before regular government census taking, these lists provide the most complete record of overseas migration from England's busiest port. When used in conjunction with other types of public record keeping from this era, such as church baptismal and marriage registers or wills and probate inventories, they also make it possible to retrace some individuals' movements over a lifetime, from their birthplace in the English countryside to their new homes in colonial America. While such cases are rare, they do help fit the Atlantic crossing into a wider trajectory of movement and resettlement throughout England's domestic and overseas dominions.

Another characteristic of these lists that can be used to the historian's advantage is their uniformity in design and function. These lists were created for the same government-mandated purpose, and at a bare minimum, they recorded the same types of information: passengers' names and ages, ship names, and ports of departure. Therefore, deviations in that basic model often offer important clues about the people on board. For example, consider the headings from the London Port Register that begin the three lists reproduced in this chapter:

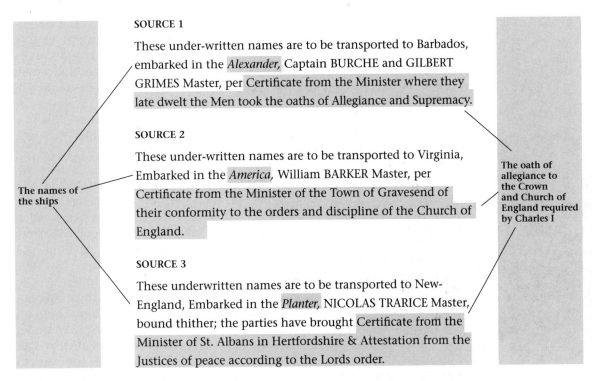

SOURCE 1

These under-written names are to be transported to Barbados, embarked in the *Alexander,* Captain BURCHE and GILBERT GRIMES Master, per Certificate from the Minister where they late dwelt the Men took the oaths of Allegiance and Supremacy.

SOURCE 2

These under-written names are to be transported to Virginia, Embarked in the *America,* William BARKER Master, per Certificate from the Minister of the Town of Gravesend of their conformity to the orders and discipline of the Church of England.

SOURCE 3

These underwritten names are to be transported to New-England, Embarked in the *Planter,* NICOLAS TRARICE Master, bound thither; the parties have brought Certificate from the Minister of St. Albans in Hertfordshire & Attestation from the Justices of peace according to the Lords order.

The names of the ships

The oath of allegiance to the Crown and Church of England required by Charles I

Each heading conveys similar information: the ship's name, captain, and destination, and confirmation that the passengers have taken the necessary oaths. The headings also offer important clues about the passengers' origins. Source 1 refers only to "the Minister where they late dwelt" (bear in mind the ship embarked from London). Source 2 mentions "the Town of Gravesend," a port on the Thames River where ships from London often stopped for customs inspection before heading out to sea. Source 3 notes that the passengers brought proof of their oaths with them from St. Albans, an inland town west of London. For either Source 1 or Source 2, it is easy to imagine that the minister referred to in the heading was administering oaths to people in a busy port city, many of whom were strangers to him and each other, on the eve of the ship's departure. On the other hand, the passengers in Source 3 all seem to have originated in the same inland town, where they swore their oaths before a local minister and magistrates. Appreciating such variations in the lists' headings can help you compare and contrast the passengers' backgrounds.

It is also important to take into account how the lists are organized. In our data-driven modern world, lists of names are usually organized alphabetically (consider again the phone book). That was not the case in 1635, so we must determine what the organizing principle was behind these passenger lists. Sources 1 and 2 share a common structure, dividing the passengers into male and female categories. Source 3 is different, grouping names according to families rather than segregating them according to gender. Recognizing that difference might help solve another riddle presented by the lists: kin relations. In Source 3, it is fairly easy to determine spousal and parent-child relationships. Picking relations out of Sources 1 and 2 is harder, especially for adult men and women sharing the same last name: which are spouses, which are siblings, and which are not even related? Source 1 offers an important clue when it refers to the following individuals:

PHILLIPP LOVELL   34
uxor ELIZABETH LOVELL   33

Uxor is Latin for "wife"; Elizabeth Lovell is also the only woman on Source 1 not listed under the heading *Women*. This piece of evidence suggests that married women were listed under their husbands, while single women, even if traveling with a male relation (consider the Remmingtons in Source 2), were listed separately. In other words, marital status trumped sex in determining a woman's place on these lists, and the royal officials composing these lists gave precedence to the husband-wife relationship over other kin relations.

With proper organization and analysis, the information on these lists can also yield clues about the motives of immigrants. All of the lists in the London Port Register contained information about the passengers' ages. We may render that information more useful by doing an age distribution, to see at what ages individuals were most or least likely to migrate. This task raises the issue of defining categories—such as childhood, adulthood, and old age—appropriate for the historical period in which the lists were generated. By our modern standards, the ages of eighteen (right to vote, end of secondary schooling) and twenty-one (legal drinking age, end of undergraduate education) signify the passage from adolescence to adulthood, but should we use those chronological markers for seventeenth-century immigrants? A dividing line between childhood and young adulthood at age fourteen is more relevant for that era, for that was when children typically passed from their parents' control to that of a master or mistress by entering into servitude or apprenticeship. Likewise, the passage into full adulthood did not come until the midtwenties, when men and women passed out of servitude and became eligible for marriage. Working with those categories in mind, it is easier to comprehend why fourteen- and fifteen-year-olds, and even some twelve- and thirteen-year-olds, show up traveling alone on these passenger lists; in all likelihood, they were going to America as servants, for that was the occupation they would be entering into if they had stayed at home. Also, the presence of so many single twenty-somethings in Sources 1 and 2 suggests that some may have been migrating in search of the employment and resources necessary to improve their marriage prospects.

You must also consider some of the potential limitations of working with these passenger lists. Government record keeping before 1800 was spotty at best. We cannot expect the same degree of detail in these passenger lists that we might from their equivalent in a modern industrialized society, and this lack of thoroughness can frustrate your effort to reconstruct the social background of the passengers. Controlling for this limitation requires taking into account the motives and potential biases of the people recording this information. On first impression, we might assume that the Crown's officials were inclined to record similar information about the passengers they inspected from one ship to the next, just as a department of motor vehicles clerk today will record the same information about each applicant for a driver's license, regardless of the applicant's background. However, even a cursory review of the evidence reveals that this was not the case with the passenger lists. Much more detail is provided about the passengers in Source 3 than about those in Sources 1 or 2. Why? Did the recorders of these lists assign more value and attention to people who traveled as families rather than as individuals? Did they do likewise for people with identifiable occupations versus those with no evident education or skills? On what basis did they make such judgments: a person's appearance, his or her companions, the nature of the ship on which he or she embarked? Remember, one of the reasons the Crown mandated collecting this information was because it did not want its wealthier subjects to leave the realm. That intention bred a bias in recording this information that shortchanges the less fortunate when we use the passenger lists to assemble a social profile of English immigrants to America.

Another disadvantage of this source is the perspective it offers on a person's political or religious identity. Supposedly, the primary purpose of these lists was to make sure that those people leaving England were not renouncing their loyalty to the Crown and Church. Yet, the lists record only the names of those people who took the oaths of allegiance and supremacy; they do not mention the names of anyone about to embark for the Americas who failed to meet this litmus test. We know that many seventeenth-century English colonists were religious dissenters seeking freedom from persecution for their beliefs, yet no passengers on these lists are identified as "Puritans" or by any other dissident religious label. Did such passengers simply cross their fingers when taking the necessary oaths so that they could leave? Or did local officials look the other way when they administered such oaths, so that they could rid themselves of troublesome malcontents? Regardless of the answer, it seems plain that these lists cannot be taken at face value as evidence of a person's political or religious allegiance.

After reading these lists, you may find yourself focusing on what's *not* there. Source 3 includes the occupations of its passengers, but Sources 1 and 2 do not. How should we interpret the absence of occupational information in Sources 1 and 2? None of the lists reproduced here attempt to explain why these people were leaving England. Having now read something about the economic and social problems of early modern England, you may be willing to venture some guesses about those motives, based on what you *do* know from the lists: sex ratios, marital status, age distributions. When you do that, you are thinking like a historian, drawing defensible conclusions from evidence that is often incomplete, fragmentary, and even contradictory.

Working with the Source

As you read through the passenger lists, use the following table to collect some information about their contents.

	1. To Barbados (the Caribbean)	2. To Virginia (Chesapeake)	3. To New England
Total passengers			
Ratio of males to females			
Age distribution: *0–4 (infants)* *5–13 (children)* *14–24 (young adults)* *25–59 (adults)* *60 and over (elderly)*			
Number of married passengers			
Number of passengers traveling with at least one family member			

The Source: Passenger Lists from the 1635 London Port Register

 1 *To Barbados (the Caribbean),* May 2, 1635

THESE under-written names are to be transported to Barbados, embarked in the *Alexander*, Captain BURCHE and GILBERT GRIMES Master, per Certificate from the Minister where they late dwelt the Men took the oaths of Allegiance and Supremacy.

	Years		Years
WILLIAM RAPEN	29	WILLIAM POWELL	19
LEONARD STAPLES	22	RALPH PROWD	26
JOSEPH STANFORD	24	JOSEPH BULLMAN	40
JAMES MANZER	27	JOSEPH WATTS	19
JOSEPH WATTS	25	WILLIAM DENCH	16
THOMAS CLARK	26	FRANCIS PECK	22
MICHELL KIMP	27	JOSEPH BENSTEDD	24
HENRY BROUGHTON	20	SYMON PARLER	24
GEORGE VENTIMER	20	RICHARD HOWSEMAN	19
ROBERT HARDY	18	WALTER JONES	20
THOMAS DABB	25	PHELIX LYNE	25
GEORGE NORTON	22	ARTHUR WRITE	21
WILLIAM HUCKLE	20	LEWES WILLIAMS	21
EDWARD KEMP	19	WILLIAM POTT	18
THOMAS GILSON	21	GEORGE RIDGLIE	17
NICOLAS WATSON	26	DENNIS MACBRIAN	18
OLLIVER HOOKHAM	32	JOSEPH BUSSELL	36
CHRISTOPHER BUCKLAND	25	JAMES DRIVER	27
JOSEPH HILL	23	HUGH JOHNES	22
ANTHONY SKOOLER	20	THOMAS GILDINGWATER	30
JOSEPH ANDERSON	21	JOHN ASHURST	24
WILLIAM PHILLIPPS	17	JAMES PARKINSON	23
JOSEPH BESFORD	18	WILLIAM YOUNG	21
HENRY YATMAN	21	WILLIAM SMITH	18
ROBERT DUCE	18	MORGAN JONES	31
OWEN WILLIAMS	18	JOSEPH RICHARD	30

Source: The passenager lists in Sources 1, 2, and 3 are from John Camden Hotten, editor, *The Original Lists of Persons of Quality; Emigrants; Religious Exiles; Political Rebels; Serving Men Sold for a Term of Years; Apprentices; Children Stolen; Maidens Pressed; and Others Who Went from Great Britain to the American Plantations, 1600–1700* (London: Chatto and Windus, 1874).

	Years		Years
JOSEPH WRITE	24	PETER FLAMING	16
WILLIAM CLARK	19	MILES FARRING	24
EDWARD HALINGWORTH	46	ROBERT ATKINS	23
RICHARD POWELL	32	BENIAMIN MASON	23
HENRY LONGSHA	23	THOMAS RUTTER	22
JOSEPH BUSH	22	JOSEPH HOWSE	41
JONATHAN FRANKLIN	17	JOSEPH COLE	20
JOSEPH PHILLIPPS	20	JAMES WATTS	35
RICHARD CRIBB	19	WILLIAM CROWE	17
THOMAS BROWNE	18	PHILLIPP LOVELL	34
JOSEPH GREENWICH	21	*uxor* ELIZABETH LOVELL	33
JOSEPH NEDSOM	19	ROWLAND MATHEW	27
EDWARD CHURCH	18	ROBERT SPRITE	30
ANTHONY THRELCATT	19	JOSEPH WESTON	41
WILLIAM WILLIS	17	JAMES SMITH	19
CLEMENT HAWKINS	16	JOSEPH SMITH	19
LEWES HUGHES	19	RICHARD LEE	22
JOHN GREENE	22	WILLIAM SEELY	29
RICHARD MARSHALL	36	EDWARD PLUNKETT	20
MATHEW CALLAND	16	THOMAS PLUNKETT	28
LEWES DAVID	28	ROWLAND PLUNKETT	18
GEORGE WHITE	18	TEAGUE NACTON	28
DERMOND O BRYAN	20	RICHARD FANE	15
CHARLES GALLOWAY	19	ROBERT ROBERT'S	18
JAMES MONTGOMERY	19	WILLIAM LAKE	14
JONATHAN McCONRY	28	RICHARD IVESON	16
SAMUELL PRIDAY	20	HUMFREY KERBY	18
SAMUELL FARRON	30	EDWARD COKES	17
EDMOND MONTGOMERY	26	HENRY MORTON	20
OLLIVER BASSETT	14	JAMES BRETT	17
PARRY WY	15	THOMAS DENNIS	18
DANIELL BURCH	14	THOMAS MORE	33
RICHARD STONE	13	JOSEPH LAWRENCE	17
THOMAS TAYLER	27	WILLIAM MARTIN	13
EDMOND NASH	21	RICHARD PHILPE	17
JOSEPH HERRING	28		
WILLIAM BEATON	24	*Women.*	
THOMAS ROE	22	BARBARIE REASON	20
EDWARD BANKS	35	JANE MARSHALL	21
THOMAS FLUDD	21	DIANA DRAKE	19
DAVID COLLINGWORTH	22	MARY INGLISH	17
WILLIAM MATHEWS	30	ANNIS BARRAT	20
TYMOTHIE GOODMAN	27	MARIE LAMBETH	17

	Years		Years
THOMAS PENSON	20	ANN MANN	17
WILLIAM ANDERSON	36	ELIZABETH WARREN	17
GEORGE MERRIMAN	41	ANN SKYNGGLE	18
JOSEPH DELLAHAY	27	ALICE CHUMP	20
ROBERT LEE	33	MATHEW MAY	21
JOSEPH JACKSON	24	ELIZABETH CHAMBERS	20
ALEXANDER DE LA GARDE	27	ELIZABETH FARMER	20
FRANCIS MARSHALL	26	MARGARET CONWAY	20
WALTER LUTTERELL	20	GRACE WALKER	34
JOSEPH WHITE	15	EDITH JONES	21
JOSEPH BURTON	17	ALICE GUY	20
SYMON WOOD	14	MARY SPENDLEY	17
ROBERT MUSSELL	14	ANN GARDNER	36

2   *To Virginia (Chesapeake)*, June 23, 1635

THESE under-written names are to be transported to Virginia, Embarked in the *America*, William BARKER Master, per Certificate from the Minister of the Town of Gravesend of their conformity to the orders and discipline of the Church of England.

	Years		Years
RICHARD SADD	23	RICHARD HERSEY	22
THOMAS WAKEFIELD	17	JOHN ROBINSON	32
THOMAS BENNETT	22	EDMOND CHIPPS	19
STEVEN READ	24	THOMAS PRITCHARD	32
WILLIAM STANBRIDGE	27	JONATHAN BRONSFORD	21
HENRY BARKER	18	WILLIAM COWLEY	20
JAMES FOSTER	21	JOHN SHAWE	16
THOMAS TALBOTT	20	RICHARD GUMMY	21
RICHARD YOUNG	31	BARTHOLOMEW HOLTON	25
ROBERT THOMAS	20	JOHN WHITE	21
JOHN FAREPOYNT	20	THOMAS CHAPPELL	33
ROBERT ASKYN	22	HUGH FOX	24
SAMUELL AWDE	24	DAVIE MORRIS	32
MILES FLETCHER	27	ROWLAND COTTON	22
WILLIAM EVANS	23	WILLIAM THOMAS	22
LAWRENCE FAREBERN	23	JOHN YATES	20
MATHEW ROBINSON	24	RICHARD WOOD	36

	Years		Years
ISACK BULL	27	JAMES SOMERS	22
PHILLIPP REMMINGTON	29	DAVIE BROMLEY	15
RADULPH SPRAGING	37	WALTER BROOKES	15
GEORGE CHAUNDLER	29	SYMON RICHARDSON	23
THOMAS JOHNSON	19	THOMAS BOOMER	13
JOSEPH AVERIE	20	GEORGE DULMARE	8
JOHN CROFTES	20	JOHN UNDERWOOD	19
THOMAS BROUGHTON	19	WILLIAM BERNARD	27
BENIAMIN WRAGG	24	CHARLES WALLINGER	24
HENRY EMBRIE	20	THOMAS DYMMETT	23
ROBERT SABYN	40	RYCE HOOE	36
GEORGE BROOKES	35	JOHN CARTER	54
THOMAS HOLLAND	34		
HUMFREY BELT	20	**_Women._**	
JOHN MACE	20	ELIZABETH REMINGTON	20
WALTER JEWELL	19	KATHERIN HIBBOTTS	20
WILLIAM BUCLAND	19	ELIZABETH WILLIS	18
LAUNCELOT JACKSON	18	JOAN JOBE	18
JOHN WILLIAMSON	12	ANN NASH	22
PHILLIPP PARSONS	10	ELIZABETH PHILLIPS	22
HENRY PARSONS	14	DOROTHY STANDICH	22
ANDREW MORGAN	26	SUZAN DEATH	22
WILLIAM BROOKES	17	ELIZABETH DEATH	3
RICHARD HARRISON	15	ALICE REMMINGTON	26
THOMAS PRATT	17	DOROTHIE BAKER	18
JOHN EELES	16	ELIZABETH BAKER	18
RICHARD MILLER	12	SARA COLEBANK	20
ROBERT LAMB	16	MARY THURROGOOD	19

 ## _To New England,_ April 2, 1635

THESE underwritten names are to be transported to New-England, Embarked in the _Planter_, NICOLAS TRARICE Master, bound thither; the parties have brought Certificate from the Minister of St. Albans in Hertfordshire & Attestation from the Justices of peace according to the Lords order.

	Years		Years
A Mercer JOSEPH TUTTELL	39	Husbandman GEORGE GIDDINS	25
JOAN TUTTELL	42	JANE GIDDINS	20
JOHN LAWRENCE	17	THOMAS SAVAGE, a Tayler	27

	Years		Years
WILLIAM LAWRENCE	12	A Taylor RICHARD HARVIE	22
MARIE LAWRENCE	9	Husbandman FRANCIS	
ABIGALL TUTTELL	6	PEBODDY	21
SYMON TUTTELL	4	Linen weaver WILLIAM	
SARA TUTTELL	2	WILCOCKSON	34
JOSEPH TUTTELL	1	MAGARET WILCOCKSON	24
JOAN ANTROBUSS	65	JOSEPH WILLCOCKSON	2
MARIE WRAST	24	ANN HARVIE	22
THO: GREENE	15	A Mason WILLIAM BEARDSLEY	30
NATHAN HEFORD	16	MARIE BEADSLEY	26
servant to JOSEPH TUTTELL		MARIE BEADSLIE	4
MARIE CHITTWOOD	24	JOHN BEADSLIE	2
Shoemaker. THOMAS OLNEY	35	JOSEPH BEADSLIE	6. mo:
MARIE OLNEY	30	Husbandman ALLIN PERLEY	27
THOMAS OLNEY	3	Shoemaker WILLIAM FELLOE	24
EPENETUS OLNEY	1	A Taylor FRANCIS BAKER	24

	Years
servants to GEORGE GIDDINS:	
THOMAS CARTER	25
MICHELL WILLIAMSON	30
ELIZABETH MORRISON	12

Analyzing the Source

REFLECTING ON THE SOURCE

1. Using the data you have assembled in the table on page 36, briefly describe the "typical" English immigrant to the New World in terms of sex, age, and marital status. How does that portrait change as you move from one list to another?

2. What kinds of assumptions have you made in order to calculate the number of married passengers and those traveling with at least one family member? How have you identified and evaluated evidence in order to determine the nature of kinship between passengers?

3. What information, if any, does each list provide about its passengers' occupations? What do these occupations tell you about their social background, education, wealth? To what social rank would you assign those adult passengers with no occupation listed?

MAKING CONNECTIONS

4. Source 3 (New England) provides much more detail about its passengers than either Sources 1 or 2. Briefly describe the nature of the additional information

provided by Source 3. How might you use it to assess the background and motives of these immigrants? Bearing the detail of Source 3 in mind, what conclusions do you draw from the *lack* of similar information in Sources 1 and 2?

5. Compare and contrast how women are placed on these lists. What advantages or disadvantages do the lists suggest for single women traveling to these destinations?

6. If you were living in England in the 1630s and contemplating the move to the Americas, which one of these lists would you prefer to be on? Support your choice with evidence from your analysis of these passenger lists.

Beyond the Source

An immigrant's fate in the New World could vary widely according to the region to which he or she traveled. Those going to the Caribbean or the Chesapeake faced the most daunting odds but also the greatest payoffs if they succeeded. Barbados and the other Caribbean colonies specialized in the production of sugar, Virginia and Maryland in tobacco. Both of those crops commanded high prices in Europe and made fortunes for New World planters. But making those riches required access to land and labor, which most servants stood little chance of acquiring. Furthermore, all English immigrants, but especially servants, suffered high mortality rates in the plantation colonies. An average servant's life expectancy in the seventeenth-century Chesapeake and Caribbean was about five years. For most servants in those regions, migration was a death sentence served out laboring for someone else.

Immigrants to New England faced circumstances altogether different. Fish and furs offered that region's most profitable exports, but most immigrants preferred to work and live in occupations and towns similar to those that they had left in England. Epidemic disease did not plague New Englanders with the same tenacity as it did those colonists further south, and the Puritans' communal ethos prevented the brutal exploitation of labor found in the plantation colonies. For English men and women, the average life expectancy increased when they moved to New England, and it was not uncommon for children to know their grandparents. These conditions made it possible for New England's population to sustain its growth even when immigration to that region slowed to a trickle after the outbreak of civil war in England in 1641.

European immigration to England's American colonies continued in the eighteenth century, but its character changed. Most immigrants no longer came from England. Instead, the largest groups were Germans, Scots-Irish (descendants of Scottish colonists of northern Ireland), Scots, and Irish. Pennsylvania and the Virginia-Carolina backcountry were the most popular destinations for these immigrants. Servitude remained a popular way of paying for the passage to America, but overall, servants made up a smaller percentage of immigrants and they tended to be better skilled than their seventeenth-century counterparts, which gave them more bargaining power with their masters. Furthermore, African slavery replaced white servitude as the primary form of labor in English plantation colonies between 1650 and 1750. This shift occurred first in the Caribbean, where English planters imitated Portuguese and Dutch sugar planters in their use of slave labor. The transition took longer in the Chesapeake, but between 1680 and 1720, tobacco planters replaced their white indentured servants with African slaves.

As Richard Frethorne's letter home indicated, many factors specific to a region affected the fate of colonists there. Disease, malnutrition, and hostilities with neighboring Indians figured prominently in the development of colonial societies, but the demographics of migration also shaped this process. The data you have culled from the passenger lists in this chapter is indicative of the futures faced by the people on those lists. Age distribution, kinship relations, and sex ratios determined a colonial population's ability to reproduce itself. In those regions marked by family migrations, such as New England and later Pennsylvania, sex ratios tended to be more even, and the colonial population achieved a positive rate of natural reproduction more quickly. In those regions dominated by young, single males, society was marked by high rates of mortality, violence, and transience and had to rely on a constant supply of new arrivals to reproduce itself. In this manner, seventeenth-century English immigrants created colonies in America vastly different from each other despite their common cultural heritage.

Finding and Supplementing the Source

The passenger lists from the 1635 London Port Register were generated by royal officials and archived as government documents. Today they can be found in the Public Records Office in Kew, England. In the nineteenth century, independent scholars and genealogical societies collected, transcribed, and published many of these lists to assist in the reconstruction of family histories. The lists reproduced here are from *The Original Lists of Persons of Quality; Emigrants; Religious Exiles; Political Rebels; Serving Men Sold for a Term of Years; Apprentices; Children Stolen; Maidens Pressed; and Others Who Went from Great Britain to the American Plantations, 1600–1700*, edited by John Camden Hotten (London: Chatto and Windus, 1874). For a look at passenger lists to another zone of seventeenth-century English colonization, see Agnes Leland Baldwin, *First Settlers of South Carolina, 1670–1700* (Easley, S.C.: Southern Historical Press, 1985).

There are many searchable online databases and bibliographies for passenger lists to North America, but bear in mind that most cover the nineteenth and twentieth centuries much more completely than the seventeenth or eighteenth centuries. A research librarian at a university library or in the genealogical section of a public library can help you locate sources for passenger lists appropriate for the period and region in which you are interested. A good Web site for starting such a search is *Sources for Ship Passenger Lists and Emigration Research*, sponsored by the University Libraries of the University of Minnesota (**wilson.lib.umn.edu/reference/shp-gene.html**).

Alison Games uses the 1635 Port Register as the basis for her research in *Migration and the Origins of the English Atlantic World* (Cambridge: Harvard University Press, 1999). David Cressy's *Coming Over: Migration and Communication between England and New England in the Seventeenth Century* (Cambridge: Cambridge University Press, 1987) is useful for its analysis of the mechanics of promoting, recruiting, and supplying migration from England.

Studies that have used the passenger lists to reconstruct the colonization of New England include Virginia DeJohn Anderson, *New England's Generation: The Great Migration and the Formation of Society and Culture in the Seventeenth Century* (Cambridge: Cambridge University Press, 1991), and T. H. Breen and Stephen Foster, "Moving to the New World: The Character of Early Massachusetts Immigration," *William and Mary Quarterly*, third series, 30 (1973): 189–222. For similar studies of the Chesapeake colonies, see James Horn, *Adapting to a New World: English Society in the Seventeenth-Century Chesapeake* (Chapel Hill: University of North Carolina Press, 1994), and Russell R. Menard, "British Migration to the Chesapeake Colonies in the Seventeenth Century," in *Colonial Chesapeake Society,* edited by Lois Green Carr, Philip Morgan, and Jean B. Russo (Chapel Hill: University of North Carolina Press, 1988), 99–132. Jack P. Greene provides a useful perspective on English transatlantic migrations that includes the Caribbean colonies in *Pursuits of Happiness: The Social Development of Early Modern British Colonies and the Formation of American Culture* (Chapel Hill: University of North Carolina Press, 1988). In *Albion's Seed: Four British Folkways in America* (New York: Oxford University Press, 1989), David Hackett Fischer uses colonial-era British migrations to North America to trace the cultural and regional development of the United States into the twentieth century.

Two collections of essays allow comparison of English migration to America with that from other European colonial powers: *"To Make America": European Emigration in the Early Modern Period*, edited by Ida Altman and James Horn (Berkeley: University of California Press, 1991), and *Europeans on the Move: Studies on European Migration, 1500–1800*, edited by Nicholas P. Canny (New York: Oxford University Press, 1994).

CHAPTER 3

Colonial America's Most Wanted

Runaway Advertisements in Colonial Newspapers

Between 1759 and 1766, a man named Bood appeared three times in run-away advertisements placed by his master in the *New-York Gazette*, a colonial newspaper. The first advertisement, from June 21, 1759, described Bood as a "Mulatto" who ran away with "three Negroe Men." The four fugitives took with them extra shirts, breeches, shoes and stockings, two guns, two or three hatchets, and several blankets. William Hunt, who claimed Bood and one of the other runaways as his property, believed that the four men had planned their escape together and would likely head for "the Indian Towns upon the Sasquehannah [Susquehanna River]" in frontier Pennsylvania, because Bood had lived among the Indians there for "several months, some years ago."

Bood showed up next in a runaway advertisement on May 26, 1763. His owner Wilson Hunt (the same William Hunt as before, or perhaps a relative?) described Bood as "of a yellowish Complexion," and this time he ran away without accomplices or goods other than the clothes on his back. Hunt warned anyone who apprehended Bood that he was a "smooth Tongued Fellow" who would surely try to escape again "if not well secured."

On December 25, 1766, Bood made his last appearance in the *New-York Gazette* (see Figure 3.1 on p. 46). This time Wilson Hunt added to his physical description of Bood, noting that the runaway "has had the Small Pox" and "his great Toes have been froze, and have only little Pieces of Nails on them." Hunt repeated his warning about Bood's penchant for evading capture, "as he is a re-markable stout, cunning, artful Fellow."

THIRTY DOLLARS REWARD:

RUN-AWAY from the Subscriber, the 16th of September last, a Negro Man named **BOOD**, about 38 Years old, 5 Feet 10 Inches high, yellow Complexion, thin Visage, has had the Small Pox; his great Toes have been froze, and have only little Pieces of Nails on them : He is much addicted to strong Liquor, and when drunk very noisy and troublesome. Whoever takes up said Slave, and brings him home, or secures him in Gaol, so that his Master may get him again, shall be intitled to the above Reward of THIRTY DOLLARS, paid by   WILSON HUNT.

Any Person who takes up said Negro, is cautioned to be particularly careful that he does not make his Escape, as he is a remarkable stout, cunning, artful Fellow.

Hunterdon-County,
Maidenhead, December 20, 1766.

Figure 3.1 *Runaway Advertisement from the* New-York Gazette *This runaway advertisement appeared in the* New-York Gazette *on December 25, 1766. It is the last one in which Bood, a runaway from New Jersey, appeared. We do not know if he was recaptured or remained free. Source:* Graham Russell Hodges and Alan Edward Brown, editors, *"Pretends to Be Free": Runaway Slave Advertisements from Colonial and Revolutionary New York and New Jersey* (New York: Garland, 1994).

The historical record is silent as to whether Bood was caught again, and we do not know if he lived the rest of his life in bondage or freedom. These three advertisements, however, paint a fascinating portrait of a man who constantly resisted another person's effort to claim him as property. When read in conjunction with similar runaway advertisements, they tell us about the material circumstances of slavery and servitude in colonial America as well as about the physical and psychological tensions between masters and their human property. In Bood's record, we can glimpse instances of collective and individual resistance to a master's authority. The advertisements also tell us something about how masters viewed their human property, what physical characteristics and personality traits they attributed to them, and the techniques they relied upon to recapture runaways and keep them in line.

Most important, Bood's story challenges the typical image of runaway slaves in American history, which depicts them as fugitives from cotton plantations in the Deep South running north to freedom. Nineteenth-century slave narratives and novels such as Harriet Beecher Stowe's *Uncle Tom's Cabin* have indelibly printed this image in the American mind, associating fugitive slaves with the coming of the Civil War. The Underground Railroad, with its secret network of "conductors" and "stations" that ferried runaway slaves to freedom, played an important role in the sectional crisis, but its story belongs to the nineteenth century. Before the American Revolution, slavery and servitude were legal throughout the colonies, and no clear geographic line or barrier separated freedom from bondage. When slaves such as Bood stole themselves, they were just as likely to run east, west, or south as north.

Bood's story also raises questions about the intersection of race, slavery, and servitude in eighteenth-century America. In each of the three advertisements placed for Bood, his master claimed him as property, sometimes referring to him as a slave, other times not. Many people lived and worked in eighteenth-century America in a state of bondage; some were African slaves, but others were white indentured servants, apprentices, or convicted felons transported from the British Isles. The institutions of slavery and servitude were universal, and unfree laborers, whether servants or slaves, dominated the workforce. Black slaves and white servants toiled in the swamps of lowland Georgia, the tobacco fields of Virginia, in workshops and iron forges in Pennsylvania, and in the homes and on the docks of Boston. Both called their bosses "master" and endured whipping as the most common form of discipline.

On the other hand, a clear racial barrier separated black slaves and white servants and made the conditions of their bondage different. Slavery was a hereditary, lifetime status that passed from mother to child. Servitude was contractual, and people entered into it voluntarily, even convicts who chose it over the noose, for a fixed number of years. It was much harder for a runaway slave to pass unmolested into free society, and a suspected runaway slave faced much more severe punishment and fewer legal protections when apprehended. A master could "outlaw" a runaway slave, giving license to others to kill the fugitive, but no such legal sanction existed for the murder of a runaway servant. While the working lives of servants and slaves could be similar in many ways, race made the experience of running away much different for an African slave than for a white servant.

Advertisements for runaway servants and slaves were a common feature of colonial newspapers published from Boston, Massachusetts, to Savannah, Georgia. These advertisements numbered in the thousands. Individually, they provide snapshots of men, women, and children who sought at least temporary respite from a life of working for others. Collectively, these advertisements provide scholars with a database that they can use to quantify the age, sex, place of origin, occupation, and destination of thousands of discontented workers who otherwise left no discernable trace in the historical record. By sampling runaway advertisements from a number of regions, you can recover the dynamics of unfree labor in colonial America: the living and working conditions of the slaves and servants, their relations with each other and their masters, and their masters' efforts to control their lives.

Using Runaway Advertisements as a Source

Few sources offer a more comprehensive or interesting look inside colonial American society than its newspapers. The first colonial newspaper appeared in 1690 in Boston, but it folded after one issue; a successful newspaper did not appear until the *Boston News-Letter* in 1704. Boston sustained its preeminence in newspaper publication throughout the colonial era, but during the 1720s newspapers appeared in New York and Philadelphia as well. The most significant growth in colonial newspapers occurred in the 1760s and 1770s. In 1764, there were twenty-three colonial newspapers; on the eve of the American Revolution, that figure had increased to thirty-eight.

Colonial newspapers were typically published once a week, on long sheets of paper that when folded in half, divided into columns, and printed on both sides, made for four pages stuffed with information. Their publishers included local and international news they copied from other papers or that they received from private correspondents. As with modern newspapers, an important source of the newspaper's revenues was advertising. In columns of notices similar to the modern classifieds section, readers found announcements for the arrival and departure of ships, the importation and sale of goods, public auctions, and the like. Seaports such as Boston, New York, Philadelphia, and Charleston were the nerve centers of colonial trade, and merchants and other business folk relied heavily on newspapers for this information. The smudged and tattered state of surviving editions of colonial newspapers testifies to their wide circulation and readership.

Runaway advertisements in colonial newspapers were found among other advertisements for lost or stolen goods, for debt collections and foreclosures, or for the sale of real estate, servants, slaves, or livestock. One of the great advantages to reading these advertisements in their original context is to comprehend how casually colonial Americans bought and sold human laborers, subjecting them to public inspections and sales in the same way that they traded livestock or any other goods. No one in colonial America thought it out of the ordinary to read an advertisement for a runaway servant or slave alongside one for a stray horse, or to see a monetary reward offered for both.

A review of even a small sample of runaway advertisements reveals a consistent pattern in their composition. This advertisement placed by Virginia slave owner Archibald Cary for three runaways in the *Virginia Gazette* on March 7, 1766, is typical of the style used in such ads. A close reading reveals important clues about the runaways' background, their relationship to each other, and their relationship with their master.

These runaways worked at an iron forge

A skilled slave

RUN away from the subscriber's forge, on the 22d instant, at night, three Negro men; one of them named STEPHEN, by trade a carpenter, Virginia born, a black fellow, about 5 feet 8 or 9 inches high, very brisk and active, speaks quick, has a

Born into slavery in North America and therefore assimilated into colonial society

Born in coastal West Africa and therefore less familiar with colonial society

The physical hazards these slaves faced in their work may have motivated their flight

Cary believes these slaves may have intended to run far from home

pleasant countenance, and walks very nimbly. Also NED, a fellow fire-man, a black fellow, remarkably well made for strength, about 5 feet 7 or 8 inches high, generally laughs when he speaks, has a large mouth, which is seldom shut, Virginia born, inclinable to be fat, has a sluggish walk, and broad shoulders. Also BRUMALL, a Gold Coast Negro, about the size and height of Ned; he is a fire-man, has remarkable broad shoulders, a roll in his walk, and had a hurt on his knee lately, from which he was lame a day or two before he went off; but whether any scar on it, I know not. Both the last mentioned fellows, have scars on their arms, from burns which they got by melted cinders flying on them when at work. Brumall is a yellow Negro, and has a very pleasant countenance. I can give no particular description of their clothes; I do not know of their carrying any more than their suits of cotton and osnabrugs. I will give £5 reward for each slave, if taken up in Virginia, and delivered to me; if in Carolina, £10 for each.

ARCHIBALD CARY

Runaway advertisements often included details about the speech patterns of runaways, such as their proficiency with English or foreign languages, accents, or speech impediments

Suggests biracial parentage

Suggests that someone other than Cary supervised these slaves

Details commonly found in runaway advertisements included the name, age, sex, ethnicity, and race of the fugitive, along with a description of his or her physical appearance and disposition followed by a description of the clothing he or she was wearing when last seen. Advertisements typically concluded with the offer of a reward for the return of the fugitive and a warning against assisting the person in flight. More detailed advertisements provided a wealth of other information: occupations and skills; aliases, disguises, motivations for running away; potential destinations or plans; distinctive habits or vices.

Advantages and Disadvantages of Working with Runaway Advertisements

There are many advantages to working with runaway advertisements when studying slaves and servants in colonial America. First, the detailed descriptions of the runaways' physical appearance offer important clues about the day-to-day lives and material circumstances of the "lower sort" in colonial society: slaves and servants who lived and worked under the authority of someone else. The coarseness of the clothing these runaways wore serves as a metaphor for the hand-to-mouth existence so many of them endured. Likewise, descriptions of scars and physical disabilities are evidence of the dangers they endured from the elements, disease, malnutrition, hazardous working conditions, and brutal discipline meted out by their masters.

Runaway advertisements also offer a glimpse into the runaways' strategies and motives for resisting their masters. In many such advertisements, the master speculates as to why the slave or servant ran away. Was the fugitive seeking a reunion with family members or perhaps trying to preserve a family that was about to be driven apart by the sale of a spouse or child? Labor was very scarce in colonial America. Many runaway advertisements hint that a servant or slave with a marketable skill—such as blacksmithing, woodworking, or seafaring—left to find more satisfactory work, perhaps at the instigation of another potential employer. Some advertisements, such as the one for Bood from the June 21, 1759, edition of the *New-York Gazette,* also indicate that runaways found living among neighboring Indians or backcountry settlements more appealing; others suggest that runaways headed for seaports where they hoped to find work in shops or on ships.

One of the disadvantages of working with runaway advertisements derives in part from the medium in which they appeared. Relatively few colonial newspapers existed before 1760, and those that did tended to be in northern seaports, such as Boston, New York, and Philadelphia. Southern newspapers lagged behind northern ones in their founding and readership because the southern colonies lacked the urban centers and printshops necessary to sustain newspapers. New England had few servants and slaves but many newspapers; the colonies of the Chesapeake and Lower South had many slaves but few newspapers. The middle colonies had many servants and slaves as well as an active printing industry. Thus, historians interested in runaway advertisements have often focused their attention on New York, New Jersey, and Pennsylvania. While this geographic bias shortchanges the southern colonies, especially before 1760, it does help shed light on the experience of northern and urban slaves and servants.

Another disadvantage is that runaway advertisements accounted for only a small portion of slaves and servants who ran away. Placing a newspaper advertisement cost money and required a master to post a reward and pay the charges of anyone who apprehended the runaway. Capturing a fugitive slave or servant was an expensive proposition, and many masters chose to wait a considerable period before placing a runaway advertisement in hopes that they would recover their property by some other means. Some slaves and servants used running away for short periods of time as a way of protesting their treatment or negotiating better working and living conditions. Such fugitives were less likely to be documented in runaway advertisements than those who absconded with stolen goods or left evidence that they were seeking permanent freedom. Masters were also less likely to post advertisements for runaways that they did not consider worthy of the expense of retrieving. Therefore, runaway advertisements were more likely to describe valuable, skilled slaves and servants than old, sick, or unskilled ones.

Finally, in considering the disadvantages of this source, the historian must bear in mind that the advertisements' descriptions of the runaways came from the masters rather than the fugitives themselves. In composing advertisements, masters were anxious to dismiss any suggestion that a runaway's actions reflected mistreatment or abuse on their part. They were also inclined to attribute negative personality traits to the runaways in question. In the master's eyes, any servant or slave who ran away was by definition a person of questionable moral character. The standard words and phrases that masters used to describe runaways' personalities sound like a roll call of seven dwarfs Snow White would not want to meet: Surly, Insolent, Cunning, Lusty, Sour, Impudent, and Artful. In this respect, the advertisements do not tell us about the runaways themselves so much as they tell us about what their masters thought of them.

Working with the Source

The table on page 52 will help you organize your notes on the advertisements as you read them. It includes information drawn from the first two advertisements as examples.

Source	Number of Runaways	Runaway's Name	Servant or Slave	Ethnicity or Race	Sex	Age	Physical Features, Personality Traits, Occupational Skills, or Other Significant Information	Notes
Source 1	1	Quomino	servant	African	M	21	head half-shaved; speaks good English; carried away clothes and a scythe	carrying scythe as a weapon?
Source 2	1	Cuff	?	African	M	45	facial scars in "Negro Fashion"; could be carrying a forged pass	born in Africa?
Source 3								
Source 4								
Source 5								
Source 6								
Source 7								
Source 8								
Source 9								
Source 10								
Source 11								
Source 12								
Source 13								
Source 14								
Source 15								
Source 16								

The Source: Runaway Advertisements from Colonial Newspapers, 1747–1770

These runaway advertisements are reprinted in their entirety. They are arranged by region: New England, the Middle Colonies, the Chesapeake, and the Lower South.

As you will see, all runaway advertisements promised rewards, but it is hard to convert eighteenth-century values into their modern equivalents. The colonies used a bewildering combination of monetary units they borrowed from British and Spanish precedents, not to mention their own paper currencies. Exchange rates varied substantially over time and between regions. The table below offers a roughly estimated conversion guide to help you get a sense of the modern equivalent of the reward amount most commonly cited in the advertisements you will read.

In 1766	1 pound (£) = in 1991 Dollars	£5 Reward = in 1991 Dollars
New England	$ 43.25	$216.25
Middle Colonies	$ 28.38	$141.90
Chesapeake	$ 48.54	$242.70
Lower South	$153.52	$767.60

Table based on values of local currency in 1766–1772 for Massachusetts, Pennsylvania, Virginia, and South Carolina listed in Table A-3 in John J. McCusker, *How Much Is That in Real Money? A Historical Price Index for Use as a Deflator of Money Values in the Economy of the United States* (Worcester, Mass.: American Antiquarian Society, 1992).

NEW ENGLAND

 Boston Evening-Post, August 1, 1748

RAN away from his Master, John Allen, Merchant of Newton, a Negro Man named Quomino, about 21 Years of Age, a likely Fellow, of middling Stature, his Head shav'd half over, and speaks good English. Carried away with him, an Olive coloured Cloth Coat with Buttons of the same Colour, a new Jacket and Breeches, dark Cloth Colour, homespun, with Pewter Buttons on, two pair of Trousers, two Tow[1] Shirts, two Linnen Shirts, an old Bever Hat, and large Brass Buckles in his Shoes, &c. He also carried with him a Scythe.

Whoever shall take him up and return him to his said Master, shall receive of him the Sum of Five Pounds, and all necessary Charges, in Old Tenor

---

[1] Fabric made from flax or hemp fibers.

Money;[2] and all Masters of Vessels are upon their Peril forbid concealing or carrying off said Servant.

NEWTON, JULY 26, 1748.

[2] Paper currency used in Massachusetts.

Boston Evening-Post, May 19, 1755

RAN away from his Master William Bucknam, a Negro Man named Cuff, about 45 Years old, and pretty tall and slender, and has Scars on each Side of his Face, Negro Fashion,[1] and had on a streaked blue and white woollen Shirt, an under Jacket and Breeches, homespun woollen Cloth, streaked black and white about an Inch wide, mill'd Cloth; outside Jacket, homespun Kersey[2] grey colour'd, and grey yarn-Stockings, thick [illegible], worsted Cap, Felt Hat, and is suspected to have a forged Pass or Freedom for his Protection with him. Any Person that shall take up said Negro, and commit him to Gaol,[3] and secure the Papers, if any, and send me Tidings of the same, or to Messieurs Samuel Hewes and Son, Merchants in Boston, shall have Five Dollars Reward, and all necessary Charges paid. This likewise is to forbid all Masters of Vessels from carrying said Negro away.

FALMOUTH, APRIL 22. 1755   WILLIAM BUCKNAM

[1] A reference to ritual scarification found on slaves born in West Africa (also described as "country marks" in Source 14 on p. 60).
[2] Coarse woolen cloth from Yorkshire, England.
[3] Jail.

Boston Evening-Post, March 29, 1762

SIXTY DOLLARS Reward

RUN-away from Messi'rs Bodkin & Ferrall, of the Island of St. Croix,[1] on the 1st Day of July, 1760, a Negro Man named Norton Minors, is by Trade a Caulker and Ship-Carpenter, was born & bred up at Capt. Marquand's at Newbury,[2] who sold him to Mr. Craddock of Nevis,[3] from whom the above Gentleman

[1] A Caribbean island.
[2] A Massachusetts port town.
[3] A Caribbean island.

bought him, is about 5 Feet 10 Inches high, about 30 Years of Age, speaks good English, can read and write, is a very sensible, smart, spry Fellow, has a remarkable bright Eye, he has been seen at and about Newbury sundry Times since his Elopement. Whoever takes up and secures the said Negro Man, so that he may be delivered to the Subscriber,[4] shall receive SIXTY DOLLARS Reward, and all necessary Charges paid by

BOSTON, MARCH 29, 1762   HENRY LLOYD

N.B. All Persons whatever are cautioned against harbouring or concealing said Negro, or carrying him off, as they may depend on being prosecuted with the utmost Rigour of the Law.

[4] The person placing the advertisement.

MIDDLE COLONIES

Pennsylvania Gazette, November 26, 1747

RUN away the 22d instant, from James Greenfield, of Newlin township, Chester county, an Irish servant man named Robert Clinton, a weaver by trade. He is of middle stature, with black curled hair, swarthy complexion, and about twenty years of age. Had on when he went away, a new felt hat, a dark brown coat, green jacket, flaxen shirt, and fine stock, tow trowsers, black stockings, footed with brown worsted,[1] old brass shoes, with large brass buckles. He was enticed away by one Sylvester Eagon, an Irishman, by trade a weaver, and speaks very brogueish, but no servant. Whoever secures said servant, and sends word to his master, so as he may have him again, shall have Five Pounds reward, and reasonable charges, paid by

JAMES GREENFIELD

[1] Woolen fabric made in Worstead, England.

Pennsylvania Gazette, July 8, 1756

RUN away on the 23rd of June last, from the subscriber, living in Vincent township, Chester county two Dutch[1] servants, husband and wife; the man named Jacob Hakaliver, about 24 years of age, 5 feet 4 inches high, has a pale complexion, and a down look: Had on and took with him, a coarse shirt and

[1] When used in runaway advertisements from the eighteenth century, this ethnic designation usually refers to German-speaking servants from the Rhine River Valley.

trowsers, a black coat, with white metal buttons on it, the fore skirts lined with red, an old blue jacket, old felt hat, and has no shoes; he has brown bushy hair. His wife is named Magdalen, a lusty woman, about 30 years of age, has fair hair and a sour look: Had on and took with her, an orange coloured linsey[2] bed-gown, three petticoats, one of linsey, striped red and brown, another of brown cloth, bound about the tail with black, and the third of black linen, a coarse shirt and apron, three black Dutch laced caps. She has with her a male child, named Michael, five months old, little of his age. They carried with them some bed clothes, and some Dutch books. Whoever takes up and secures said servants, so as their master may have them again, shall have Forty Shillings reward, and reasonable charges, paid by

ABRAHAM SMITH

[2] A wool-flax blend.

6   *Pennsylvania Gazette,* July 22, 1756

RUN away from the subscriber, living in Kent County, Maryland, two convict servant men; the one named Benjamin Shotton, a shoemaker by trade, about 5 feet 8 or 9 inches high, of a tawney complexion, large black beard, and curled hair; he is a talkative, pert, well-made fellow: Had on when he went away, An ozenbrigs[1] shirt, coarse country made trowsers, old brown cloth coat, with a cuff and slash sleeve, and broad metal buttons, old swanskin jacket, with red stripes, and an old beaver hat. He also got with him a pair of old fine blue broadcloth breeches, and probably has other clothes with him. He is a notorious villain, and this is the third time he has run away without the least reason. The other one is a young fellow, named Edward Phelps, about 22 years of age, a smooth faced fellow, about 5 feet ten inches high, slim made and thin faced, has light colour'd short hair, and a down look: Had on when he went away, An old white linen shirt, a country kersey jacket, a half-worn, dark colour'd, and almost black coat, trimmed with brass buttons with wood bottoms, ozenbrigs trowsers, and a pair of old pumps[2] much too big for him. He also took with him two new shirts, made of country linen. They have forged two passes; probably will change their names and cut their hair. Whoever takes up and secures abovesaid fellows, shall have Four Pistoles[3] reward, or two for each, paid by

THOMAS SMYTH.

[1] Cheap linen made in Oznaburg, Germany.
[2] Thin-soled shoes.
[3] A Spanish coin commonly used in colonial North America.

Pennsylvania Gazette, August 11, 1757

Middletown, Monmouth County, East New Jersey, Aug. 1. 1757.
RUN away from the Subscriber the First of January, twelve Months past, a Negroe Man, named Cato, who has since his Elopement changed his Name several times: Had on when he went away, a Pair of Buckskin Breeches, fine brown Linen Shirt, a plain made whitish Camblet[1] Coat, dark Yarn Stockings, new Shoes, and a Wool Hat. He is a stout well set Fellow, understands Husbandry in all its Parts, an excellent Hand with a Scythe in Grass or Grain, speaks English as well as if Country born, and pretends to be free. Underneath his right-shoulder Blade he was branded in Jamaica when a Boy with the Letters BC, which are plain to be seen. He plays poorly on the Fiddle, and pretends to tell Fortunes. It is supposed he has a forged Pass. Whoever secures the said Negroe, so that his Master may have him again, shall receive a Reward of FIVE POUNDS and reasonable Charges, paid by

RICHARD STILLWELL.

[1] A fabric made from different materials, including wool and silk.

 ### *Pennsylvania Gazette,* November 29, 1764

RUN away from the Subscriber, in King and Queen, Virginia, two white indented Servants, a Man and his Wife. The Man is English, about 5 Feet 5 Inches high, of a red Complexion, wears his Hair, is much Sun-burnt, steps short and quick in his Walk, is a Brickmaker by Trade, and has a sett of Shoemaker's Tools; had a short red Coat, red Breeches with Metal Buttons, an old green lapelled Jacket, a Flannel Jacket with red Stripes, new Osenbrigs Trowsers, with other Clothes, as he stole Part of mine; his Name is James Marrington. His Wife is about 30 Years of Age, about 5 Feet high, very thick, looks well, and has got good Clothes; she is an Irish Woman, and her Name is Mary Marrington.

Run away likewise 4 Negroes, viz. Jack, a black thick Fellow, about 30 Years old, about 5 Feet 6 Inches high, speaks broken English, has been used to go by Water, but of late to Plantation Business; had on a blue Cotton Jacket and Breeches, Petticoat Trowsers, Stockings, Shoes with Buckles, and has a Whitemetal Button in his Hat. Dick, a dark Mulattoe, very lusty, about 25 Years old, about 5 Feet 8 Inches high, a Carpenter and Painter by Trade; had on Cotton Clothes, with Petticoat Trowsers, and he has got a red Jacket and Breeches, a good Felt Hat, and Buckles in his Shoes. Daniel, a well set black Fellow, about 5 Feet 10 Inches high, has been used to Plantation Business, and had on Cotton Clothes. Dorcas, a small Wench, about 5 Feet high, has been used to House Business, has got a new brown Linen Jacket and Petticoat, and sundry other Things that she stole. They have all large Bundles, as they stole several

Sheets and Blankets, with other Things. They are supposed to be seen crossing from Point Comfort to Little River, in a small Boat, with a Blanket Sail, Last Saturday Morning, and I imagine will make for North-Carolina. Whoever apprehends the above Servants and Slaves, and delivers them to me, shall have Ten Pounds Reward, if taken in Virginia, if out thereof Twenty Pounds.

EDWARD VOSS.

If the above Runaways are taken in Pennsylvania, and conveyed to Philadelphia, the above Reward will be paid by RITCHIE and CLYMER.

CHESAPEAKE

 Virginia Gazette, **April 11, 1766**

WARWICK county,
April 8, 1766.
RUN away from the subscriber, on or about the 10th of February last, a Virginia born Negro man named GEORGE AMERICA, about 5 feet 8 or 9 inches high, about 30 years old, of a yellow complexion, is a tolerable good shoemaker, and can do something of the house carpenters work, walks quick and upright, and has a scar on the back of his left hand; had on a cotton waistcoat and breeches osnbrugs shirt, and yarn stockings. As the said slave is outlawed,[1] I do hereby offer a reward of £5 to any person that will kill and destroy him, and 40s.[2] if taken alive.

THOMAS WATKINS

[1] An "outlawed" runaway slave was considered a threat to public safety, and he or she could be killed by another person without fear of legal prosecution.
[2] 20 shillings (s.) equaled 1 pound (£). Thus, in this advertisement, the reward for returning the runaway slave alive is £2, but the reward for killing him is £5.

 Virginia Gazette, **April 25, 1766**

RUN away from the subscriber in Louisa county, the 24th of February last, 2 Negroes viz. POMPEY, a short thick fellow, 36 years old, Virginia born, very apt to wink his eyes quick, contract one corner of his mouth, and stammer in his speech when under any apprehension of fear; had on when he went away a cotton waistcoat and breeches, died of 2 brown colour, Virginia shoes and stockings; he carried with him some other clothes, but of what sort is not known; he pretends to something of the tailor's business, and sews well. ALICE, a tall slim wench, about 20 years old, and clothed in Negro cotton when she went away. Whoever secures them, or either of them, shall have 20s. reward, besides what the law allows, if taken in the colony and if out thereof 40s. They are both outlawed.

R. ARMISTEAD

 ## Virginia Gazette, August 10, 1769

RUN away from the subscriber, in King & Queen county, a Negro man named BEN about six feet high, a very black fellow, his right knee so much bent in, that when he walks it knocks much against the other. Also, a Negro woman named ALICE, about five feet eight inches high, of a yellow complexion; and has remarkable large eyes. A few years ago she made an elopement, and passed for a free woman, in Williamsburg, and I suspect she may now do the like, or both of them attempt to get on board some vessel; if [this] should be the case, I beg of all persons they may apply to, to forward them (or either of them) to the most convenient gaol, and the gaoler is also begged to send an express immediately to the subscriber, which he will defray. As neither of those slaves have been ill used at my hands, I have had them outlawed in this county, and for their bodies without hurt, or a proper certificate of their death, a proper reward will be given; the fellow I suppose (for many reasons) will not be taken easily, as he has formerly made several overseers fear him.

EDWARD CARY

 ## Virginia Gazette, May 31, 1770

RUN away from the subscriber, the first day of November last, (under pretence of suing for his freedom) a likely young fellow, named Bob, of a yellow complexion, slim made, near six feet high, has a remarkable down look, is a very good blacksmith, and, as supposed, is harboured by some white man of that trade. Whoever will bring the said fellow to my house in Dinwiddie county, near the court-house, shall receive a reward of FIVE POUNDS.

JOHN HARDAWAY

LOWER SOUTH

 ## Georgia Gazette, May 26, 1763

Run away in January last, from my plantation near Savannah,
A NEGROE called Primus, belonging to James Skirving, Esq; of Ponpon. As he has not been heard of since, I am apprehensive he might have gone away with

a gang of Creek Indians which were down at that time, or that he may be taken up by some of the back settlers, who, I am informed, frequently conceal runaway Negroes, and work them in their own fields, or change them in some of the northern colonies for horses; whoever delivers the said negroe to me, or gives information of his being concealed, shall be well rewarded; and whoever conceals him may expect to be prosecuted by

JOSEPH GIBBONS.

N.B. He is a slim fellow, speaks tolerable good English, and had when he went away a new blanket, jacket and breeches.

 ### *Georgia Gazette,* March 7, 1765

RUN AWAY FROM THE SUBSCRIBER
A YOUNG NEW NEGROE WENCH, named SIDNEY, has her country marks[1] on her breast and arms, and a mole under her left eye, talks no English, wore a blue negroe cloth gown and coat, a new oznaburg shirt, a cheque handkerchief on her head and another about her neck. A reward of TEN SHILLINGS will be given to any person who takes her up and delivers her in Savannah to

ELIZABETH ANDERSON

[1] See note 1 with Source 2, p. 54.

 ### *Georgia Gazette,* January 14, 1767

RUN AWAY from the subscriber's brick-yard, the 19th August last, ONE NEW NEGROE MAN, named DAVID, of the Gambia country, about 5 feet nine inches high, can speak no English, has a large hole in each ear, had on when he went away a blanket, a hat, a pair of broad, cheque trowsers, and an old cheque shirt. Whoever takes up said negroe, and delivers him to me, or to the warden of the work-house, shall receive 40s. reward.

THOMAS LEE

 ### *Georgia Gazette,* August 31, 1768

RUN AWAY from Mr. Robert Bradley's plantation at Pansacola, THREE NEW NEGROE MEN, called NEPTUNE, BACCHUS, and APOLLO, that can speak no

English, and one STOUT SEASONED FELLOW called LIMERICK, speaks good English, and is very much marked on the back, &c. by severe whipping. It is imagined he has taken the conduct of the rest, and that they may have found their way through the Creek nation. Whoever takes up and will deliver the said Negroes, or any of them, to the Warden of the Work-House in Savannah, shall receive TWENTY SHILLINGS STERLING REWARD for each over and above all reasonable charges for bringing them any considerable distance from Savannah.

11TH AUGUST, 1768   T. NETHERCLIFT

Analyzing the Source

REFLECTING ON THE SOURCE

1. One striking feature of these advertisements is the detail they devoted to the physical appearance and dress of the runaways. Describe the composite portraits these advertisements paint of slaves and servants. What were the typical visual or spoken clues that indicated a person's status (slave, servant, or free)?

2. What evidence do these advertisements present of the techniques and strategies runaways used to make their way into free society? What skills or traits were helpful for doing so? Judging from the information conveyed in Sources 4, 12, and 13, who was likely to assist a runaway slave or servant, and why?

3. What types of racial and ethnic diversity are evident in the slaves and servants described in these advertisements? How does information about a runaway's place of origin (that is, born in America or elsewhere?) contribute to your understanding of his or her motive and method for running away?

MAKING CONNECTIONS

4. Are there any significant differences in the structure and content of runaway advertisements from one region to another? If so, what do these differences tell you about regional variations in slavery and servitude in colonial America?

5. Where in these advertisements do you see evidence of different methods used to apprehend runaway slaves versus runaway servants? How was a runaway's race likely to affect the punishment he or she faced if caught?

6. Compare the servants and slaves in these advertisements to the servants you studied in Chapter 2, "Coming to America: Passenger Lists from the 1635 London Port Register." How did the experience of labor in colonial America change from the seventeenth to the eighteenth centuries? What role did race and ethnicity play in those changes?

Beyond the Source

The American Revolution changed the nature of unfree labor in North America. Indentured servitude gradually fell out of use in all regions after independence from Britain, in part because it was considered contrary to the democratic values of the new nation. Also, after 1790 the economy of the northern states began to industrialize, and wage labor gradually replaced other forms of labor in urban areas. Apprentices and journeymen, who in the colonial era typically received room, board, and clothing from their masters, now received cash payments instead. These wages allowed apprentices and journeymen to live outside of their masters' homes and independently of their authority when not at work, but the wage economy also led to greater social and geographic segregation between employers and workers in the cities of nineteenth-century America.

The nature of slavery in the new nation also changed dramatically. Between 1780 and 1830, every state north of the Mason-Dixon Line, which divided Maryland and Pennsylvania, prohibited slavery within its borders. New York and New Jersey were the slowest in this regard, passing gradual emancipation laws that freed only slaves born after a certain date. As late as 1840, advertisements appeared in New Jersey newspapers for runaway slaves. Nevertheless, in the wake of the Revolution, slavery receded along with indentured servitude in the North.

Labor relations took a different course in the South. Southern states experienced a hemorrhaging of runaway slaves during the Revolution, but the invention of the cotton gin and expansion into new western territories after the war reinvigorated the plantation system. Rather than melting away as it had in the North, unfree labor in the South became the cornerstone of the economy. Runaway slaves remained a problem for their masters, who continued to place runaway advertisements in southern newspapers through the era of the Civil War.

During the 1840s and 1850s, runaway slaves became a political wedge between North and South. Free blacks and abolitionists encouraged Southern slaves to seek their freedom by fleeing north, and slave owners insisted that the federal government help them recover such human contraband. The Constitution included a fugitive slave clause (Article IV, Section 2) that prohibited states from passing laws that would confer freedom upon runaways from other states. In 1850, the federal Fugitive Slave Law strengthened the hand of slaveholders by denying accused runaways the right to trial by jury and by requiring U.S. citizens to assist federal marshals in apprehending runaways. Abolitionists and free blacks decried this law as a blatant violation of civil liberties, and even people unsympathetic to the plight of slaves found the law's extension of federal power repugnant. Yet, so long as there was slavery in America, slaves continued to challenge the institution by stealing themselves. While the decision to run away was as singular as the person making it, the collective impact of runaways on the slave system is undeniable. Runaways made slavery less efficient and more costly, and their masters' efforts to recover them caused political repercussions that were not resolved until the Civil War.

Finding and Supplementing the Source

Students wishing to conduct research in colonial newspapers should begin with Clarence Brigham, *History and Bibliography of American Newspapers, 1690–1820*, two volumes (Worcester, Mass.: American Antiquarian Society, 1947), a reference work that can help identify a newspaper appropriate to the region and period you wish to study. Original copies of colonial newspapers are very rare and fragile, making it hard for researchers to access them unless they live near a rare books library, but several colonial newspapers are available on microfilm, which can be accessed at university libraries or via interlibrary loan. The online database Accessible Archives (**accessible.com**) provides full-text articles from eighteenth- and nineteenth-century American newspapers, including the *Pennsylvania Gazette*. This database is available by subscription only, so you will want to check with a reference librarian to see if you can gain access to it.

If you cannot access a colonial newspaper but still want to research runaway advertisements, there are several published collections. For the Middle Colonies, see Graham Russell Hodges and Alan Edward Brown, editors, *"Pretends to Be Free": Runaway Slave Advertisements from Colonial and Revolutionary New York and New Jersey* (New York: Garland, 1994), and Billy G. Smith and Richard Wojtowicz, editors, *Blacks Who Stole Themselves: Advertisements for Runaways in the Pennsylvania Gazette, 1728–1790* (Philadelphia: University of Pennsylvania Press, 1989). For the southern colonies, see Lathan A. Windley, editor, *Runaway Slave Advertisements: A Documentary History from the 1730s to 1790*, four volumes (Westport, Conn.: Greenwood, 1983). As their titles indicate, these collections focus on runaway advertisements for slaves, but *Blacks Who Stole Themselves* contains a small selection of runaway advertisements for servants.

Noteworthy studies of colonial slavery that make use of runaway advertisements include Edgar J. McManus, *Black Bondage in the North* (Syracuse, N.Y.: Syracuse University Press, 1973); Gerald W. Mullin, *Flight and Rebellion: Slave Resistance in Eighteenth-Century Virginia* (New York: Oxford University Press, 1972); and Michael A. Gomez, *Exchanging Our Country Marks: The Transformation of African Identities in the Colonial and Antebellum South* (Chapel Hill: University of North Carolina Press, 1998). For a study of runaway advertisements that focuses on their production and significance as part of colonial print culture, see David Waldstreicher, "Reading the Runaways: Self-Fashioning, Print Culture, and Confidence in Slavery in the Eighteenth-Century Mid-Atlantic," *William and Mary Quarterly*, third series, 56 (April 1999): 243–72. For studies that focus on the experience of servants, see Sharon V. Salinger, *To Serve Well and Faithfully: Labor and Indentured Servants in Pennsylvania, 1682–1800* (Cambridge: Cambridge University Press, 1987), and Jonathan Prude, "To Look upon the 'Lower Sort': Runaway Ads and the Appearance of Unfree Laborers in America, 1750–1800," *Journal of American History* 78, no. 1 (1991): 124–59.

Sylvia Frey discusses the impact of runaways on the southern states during the American Revolution in *Water from the Rock: Black Resistance in a Revolution-*

ary Age (Princeton, N.J.: Princeton University Press, 1991). For studies that look at runaway advertisements from the American South in the nineteenth century, see Daniel Meaders, editor, *Advertisements for Runaway Slaves in Virginia, 1801–1820* (New York: Garland, 1997), and John Hope Franklin and Loren Schweninger, *Runaway Slaves: Rebels on the Plantation, 1790–1860* (New York: Oxford University Press, 1999).

CHAPTER 4

Germ Warfare on the Colonial Frontier

An Article from the Journal of American History

During the summer of 1763, the northern colonial frontier erupted in a paroxysm of violence known as Pontiac's War. Three years earlier, the British had conquered Canada and taken over forts surrendered by the French in the Great Lakes and Ohio Country. The Indians who lived in this region were not pleased with the manner in which the British newcomers conducted themselves. The commander in chief, General Jeffery Amherst, ordered his officers to stop giving presents of material goods to Indians who had traditionally received such gifts from the French. Amherst also severely curtailed the gunpowder and ammunition available to Indians who needed these supplies for hunting. In May 1763, Ottawa Indians led by the war chief Pontiac laid siege to Fort Detroit to protest the British presence there. A month later, Delawares, Shawnee, and Iroquois did the same to Fort Pitt at the headwaters of the Ohio River, where the British had built fortifications despite their promise to leave the area after they had dislodged the French.

As Fort Pitt endured its siege, Amherst corresponded with one of his subordinates about the possibility of using smallpox as a weapon against the Indians. Amherst wrote from his headquarters in New York City to Colonel Henry Bouquet, who was marching west from Philadelphia with an army to relieve Fort Pitt. In their letters, Amherst and Bouquet discussed the latest news from the Ohio Country, and with each succeeding exchange, their rhetoric in regard to the Indians grew more vicious, declaring (in Bouquet's words) their intention to "extirpate that Vermine from a Country they have forfeited."

In a postscript to a letter he sent to Bouquet on July 7, Amherst raised the possibility of using germ warfare against the Indians: "Could it not be contrived to Send the *Small Pox* among those Disaffected Tribes of Indians? We must, on this occasion, Use Every Stratagem in our power to Reduce them." Bouquet's reply came in a postscript to a letter he wrote on July 13, while still en route to Fort Pitt: "I will try to innocculate the Indians by means of Blankets that may fall in their hands, taking care however not to get the disease myself." An undated postscript found among Bouquet's papers appears to be Amherst's response to Bouquet's idea: "You will Do well to try to Innoculate the Indians by means of Blanketts, as well as to try Every other method that can serve to Extirpate this Execreble Race."

While Amherst and Bouquet were exchanging these letters, the civilians and soldiers inside Fort Pitt had already taken matters into their own hands. Six hundred people, practically the entire population of the new town of Pittsburgh, had sought refuge in the fort. Smallpox soon broke out among them, and the fort's commander, Captain Simeon Ecuyer, ordered a hospital built to quarantine the victims. On June 24, several weeks before Bouquet arrived with his force at Fort Pitt in early August, a trader at the fort named William Trent recorded in his journal that a parley had occurred between Ecuyer and two Delaware Indians. The Indians had asked for the customary diplomatic presents before leaving, and according to Trent, "we gave them two Blankets and an Handkerchief out of the Small Pox Hospital. I hope it will have the desired effect." In an account entry, Ecuyer approved reimbursing Trent for two blankets and two handkerchiefs "taken from people in the Hospital to Convey the Small-pox to the Indians."

Smallpox was a deadly disease feared by colonists and Indians alike in the eighteenth century. It spread quickly, especially among previously unexposed populations, and killed with frightening efficiency, as many as one-third of those infected. The most common method of dealing with smallpox was to quarantine its victims. Inoculation, a medical procedure in which a person was deliberately infected with the smallpox virus, was also used; if successful, it caused a milder form of the disease that resulted in lifelong immunity. However, people who were inoculated had to be quarantined during their treatment; otherwise, they could spread the disease among the general population. Despite such measures, the disease spread easily among neighboring populations. In April 1764, a former Indian captive named Gershom Hicks described for British officers at Fort Pitt smallpox cases he had witnessed among his captors in the Ohio Country the previous year. Whether this outbreak was related to Trent's infected blankets and handkerchiefs is impossible to tell, but it is evidence of smallpox's presence among the Indians who lived in that area.

Historians have been in general agreement about this reconstruction of what has become known as the Fort Pitt incident since the 1950s, but they continue to argue about what it means. Were Amherst and Bouquet aware that Trent and Ecuyer had given infected goods to their Delaware guests on June 24, or did they conduct their correspondence without any knowledge of this exchange? Did Bouquet act upon the ideas he had discussed with Amherst once he arrived at Fort Pitt in August 1763? Did the blankets and handkerchiefs that

Trent retrieved from the hospital cause the smallpox cases observed by Hicks, or did the contagion come from another source? Was this an isolated incident, or was it symptomatic of a wider use of smallpox as a biological weapon?

The Fort Pitt incident drives home an important point about how historians go about their work. Facts do not write history; historians do. And they don't just organize the facts; they interpret them. Historians will, and often do, come to different conclusions based upon their interpretation of the same evidence. When you read a book or an article written by a historian, it is important to bear in mind this relationship between facts and interpretation. What evidence is the historian presenting to support the argument? Based upon that evidence, does the historian's interpretation appear sound and reasonable or speculative and unwarranted? How should you weigh and compare contradictory interpretations? All history is an interpretation of the past, but not all interpretations are equally valid. When you encounter a historian's interpretation of the facts, what methods or standards will you apply to determine its worth?

Using a Journal Article as a Source

Within the historical profession, journals have long served the role of featuring the "breaking news" of the field, highlighting new scholarship, calling attention to new books, and providing a forum for current debates. Most of these journals are quarterlies, meaning that they are published four times a year. They typically feature two to three articles, book reviews, and sometimes roundtables in which historians offer opinions about a common topic. Articles in scholarly journals are the front lines of new historical interpretations, and a provocative article can often generate more excitement and controversy in the profession than a book, which takes much longer to reach its intended readership. If you want to jump into the middle of an argument between historians or to learn what the most recent scholarship has to say about a long-standing topic, reading an article in a history journal is a great place to start.

The article excerpted in this chapter first appeared in the *Journal of American History* in March 2000. Its author, Elizabeth A. Fenn, uses the Fort Pitt incident to explore the role that smallpox played in eighteenth-century warfare. Fenn's work is an excellent example of how a historian uses a journal article to push the analysis of a controversial topic forward, not by settling it once and for all, but by asking new questions and taking new approaches to old sources.

Fenn's article also illustrates the features that make a journal article a "secondary source." "Primary sources" are the raw materials historians use to interpret the past. Any source providing firsthand information about the topic you are studying is a primary source (you have already encountered some of these in the form of archaeological artifacts, passenger lists, and runaway advertisements). "Secondary sources" are the result of a historian's interpretation of those primary materials, and they are most commonly found in the form of books and journal articles. Several components make up a successful journal article: it has an introduction that presents a research question and thesis, a body that advances a persuasive argument based on the evidence at hand, footnotes that document that evidence, and a conclusion that summarizes the argument and describes its broader significance.

A journal article offers an excellent model for writing about history, and students can improve their own writing by paying close attention to how historians organize and present their arguments in such articles. For example, the introduction to any piece of persuasive writing must complete certain tasks. It must acquaint the reader with the topic at hand and provide necessary background information, articulate the author's research question, and present the thesis, a brief statement of the argument the author intends to prove. The following introduction from Fenn's article is only two paragraphs long, yet it manages to accomplish all of these jobs, making it a model of concise historical prose.

The opening paragraph introduces the topic, supplies background information, and summarizes the debate over the Fort Pitt incident

Did he or didn't he? For generations, the Amherst–smallpox blanket episode has elicited animated debate both within and beyond academic circles. In books, journals, and now in Internet discussion groups, historians, folklorists, and lay people have argued the nuances of the case. Some have contended that at Gen. Jeffery Amherst's orders, British subordinates at Fort Pitt in 1763 did indeed infect local Indians with items taken from a nearby smallpox hospital. Others have argued that they did not, that the British lacked the knowledge, the ability, or the desire to do so. Still others have claimed that regardless of intent, the timing is wrong, that the Indians around Fort Pitt came down with smallpox well before the damning exchange of letters between Jeffery Amherst and his subordinate Henry Bouquet, and that in fact they were sick even before they received "two Blankets and an Handkerchief" out of the post's smallpox hospital. Finally, and perhaps predictably, a recent article has focused on the incident's genesis as a highly mutable cross-cultural legend that reflects deep anxieties about encounters with the "other."[1]

The author defines the purpose of this article in part by stating explicitly what the article is *not* about

What follows is not an attempt to condemn or exonerate Jeffery Amherst. The man's documentary record speaks loudly enough regarding his character, if not regarding his ultimate culpability for the smallpox that struck Indians near Fort Pitt in 1763 and 1764. Nor is this essay an exhaustive accounting of all the accusations and incidents of biological warfare in late-eighteenth-century North America. It is, however, an attempt to broaden the debate and to place it in context. Our preoccupation with Amherst has kept us from

What is this article's research question and thesis?

recognizing that accusations of what we now call biological warfare—the military use of smallpox in particular—arose frequently in eighteenth-century America. Native Americans, moreover, were not the only accusers. By the second half of the century, many of the combatants in America's wars of empire had the knowledge and technology to attempt biological warfare with the smallpox virus. Many also adhered to a code of ethics that did not constrain them from doing so. Seen in this light, the Amherst affair becomes not so much an aberration as part of a larger continuum in which accusations and discussions of biological warfare were common, and actual incidents may have occurred more frequently than scholars have previously acknowledged.

> What is this article's research question and thesis?

[1]William Trent, "William Trent's Journal at Fort Pitt, 1763," ed. A. T. Volwiler, *Mississippi Valley Historical Review*, 11 (Dec. 1924), 400. For an excellent appraisal of the Fort Pitt episode that places it in the context of the larger and more complicated struggle for control of the Ohio Valley, see Michael N. McConnell, *A Country Between: The Upper Ohio Valley and Its Peoples, 1724–1774* (Lincoln, 1992), 194–96. For an example of an Internet discussion devoted to biological warfare and smallpox, see the H-OIEAHC discussion log for April 1995, available at http://www.h-net.msu.edu/logs/. For the contention that the attempt at biological warfare was "unquestionably effective at Fort Pitt," see Francis Jennings, *Empire of Fortune: Crowns, Colonies, & Tribes in the Seven Years War in America* (New York, 1990), 447–48, 447n26. On the issue of timing, see Bernhard Knollenberg, "General Amherst and Germ Warfare," *Mississippi Valley Historical Review*, 41 (Dec. 1954), 489–94; Bernhard Knollenberg to editor, "Communications," *Mississippi Valley Historical Review*, 41 (March 1955), 762; and Donald H. Kent, to editor, *ibid.*, 762–63. For a cross-cultural analysis of the incident's place in a pantheon of other such "legends," see Adrienne Mayor, "The Nessus Shirt in the New World: Smallpox Blankets in History and Legend," *Journal of American Folklore*, 108 (Winter 1995), 54–77.

> Practically every journal article has one key footnote in the opening pages that demonstrates the author's familiarity with the existing scholarship on the topic

Advantages and Disadvantages of Working with Journal Articles

The rise of Internet listservs, discussion boards, and Web sites devoted to historical topics has made the four-times-a-year publication schedule of most history journals seem slow and antiquated. In our fast-paced society, it may seem strange that historians rely on journals as a method of engaging each other in conversation about the latest research in their fields. But the scholarly journal persists because it has important advantages over other forms of organizing and publishing historical scholarship.

First and most important, scholarly journals are peer-reviewed. What that means is that articles published by historians in scholarly journals undergo a rigorous editing process in which the author of the piece and the reviewers who decide if it merits publication remain anonymous to each other. This process is designed to make sure that all articles published in the journal are evaluated by experts in the field, working as freely as possible from the prejudices and biases that might result if they knew the author's identity. While no review process is foolproof, this method does allow readers of a scholarly journal to assume that any article published in that journal has met professional standards about research, documentation, and writing. This assurance stands in stark contrast to the Internet, where people with the technical ability to build a Web site can do so, fill it with whatever content they choose, and label it "history."

A second advantage to working with scholarly articles is that they are concise. Generally, an article published in a history journal will run between 20 to

30 pages. Books written by historians, on the other hand, might run anywhere between 150 to 1,000 pages. Historians write articles and books to accomplish different things: an article is brief and to the point, focused on illuminating a particular question or topic; a book allows room for developing a narrative or synthesizing material with far greater chronological breadth or analytical depth. A good researcher will recognize the merits of each format and use articles and books accordingly. Scholarly articles, because of their brevity and focus, can be especially helpful to you in the early stages of your research, when you are casting your net for potential sources widely and trying to decide what to keep and what to throw back.

This point brings us to the third advantage of using journal articles in your research: their documentation can lead you to the sources you will want to look at next. The quality of documentation on a Web site claiming to contain historical scholarship can vary widely, depending upon the creator of the site. All scholarly journals, on the other hand, insist that their authors document their work. The footnotes that accompany a journal article offer you a road map to other sources that might be helpful in your own research. Part of the architecture of any article in a history journal is a review of the relevant scholarship that has preceded it. Within the first few footnotes of an article, its author will identify the most significant previous articles or books on the topic and then situate his or her work in relation to it. Professional historians are avid footnote readers: they are always interested in seeing what new sources the author has identified or what previous interpretations the author is trying to refine or discredit. If you take the time to pay attention to an article's documentation, you will identify the interpretive issues that occupy historians on any given topic more quickly.

The chief disadvantage to working with a journal article or any other secondary source is that someone else is interpreting the facts for you. In one sense, the author has done the reader a service by identifying, collecting, and reading the relevant materials—no small task, even for a thirty-page article—and synthesizing them into a persuasive argument. However, the author has done that in response to his or her own research question; you in all likelihood have a different one. Whenever you read an article, it is important to ask yourself about the author's motives for writing the piece: What is the research question and thesis? How have that question and thesis shaped the interpretation of the materials? Where do you see flaws or weaknesses in the argument based upon your own analysis of the evidence and documentation provided in the article?

One other disadvantage of working with journal articles is that they often assume that the reader is already familiar with the topic at hand. Historians publish articles in scholarly journals to engage in conversation with each other, not a popular audience with only a passing interest in history. The authors of journal articles will assume that their readers bring some prior knowledge to the topic and are ready to plunge into finer points of interpretation and analysis. If you find yourself reading an article that has not provided you with enough background information, you may want to read up on the topic first in a textbook, encyclopedia, or other reference work.

Working with the Source

Every journal article begins with an introduction that presents a research question and thesis. Oftentimes, the argument and evidence to prove that thesis are subdivided into sections marked by subtitles or headings. The table below will assist you in identifying the major points and evidence used in each section of Elizabeth Fenn's article. First, write down the research question and thesis. Then, in the left column note the main point of each section, followed by the evidence used to support it in the middle column, and any comments or questions you have about that evidence in the right column.

Introduction (pp. 72–73) Research Question: Thesis:		
Section	**Evidence Used to Support It**	**Comments or Questions on the Use of That Evidence**
Fort Pitt, 1763 (pp. 73–76) *Main Point:*		
Other Accusations and Incidents (pp. 76–82) *Main Point:*		
Biological Weapons and the Ethics of War (pp. 83–86) *Main Point:*		

The Source: An Article from the *Journal of American History*, March 2000

 Biological Warfare in Eighteenth-Century North America: Beyond Jeffery Amherst

ELIZABETH A. FENN

Did he or didn't he? For generations, the Amherst–smallpox blanket episode has elicited animated debate both within and beyond academic circles. In books, journals, and now in Internet discussion groups, historians, folklorists, and lay people have argued the nuances of the case. Some have contended that at Gen. Jeffery Amherst's orders, British subordinates at Fort Pitt in 1763 did indeed infect local Indians with items taken from a nearby smallpox hospital. Others have argued that they did not, that the British lacked the knowledge, the ability, or the desire to do so. Still others have claimed that regardless of intent, the timing is wrong, that the Indians around Fort Pitt came down with smallpox well before the damning exchange of letters between Jeffery Amherst and his subordinate Henry Bouquet, and that in fact they were sick even before they received "two Blankets and an Handkerchief" out of the post's smallpox hospital. Finally, and perhaps predictably, a recent article has focused on the incident's genesis as a highly mutable cross-cultural legend that reflects deep anxieties about encounters with the "other."[1]

What follows is not an attempt to condemn or exonerate Jeffery Amherst. The man's documentary record speaks loudly enough regarding his character, if

[1] William Trent, "William Trent's Journal at Fort Pitt, 1763," ed. A. T. Volwiler, *Mississippi Valley Historical Review,* 11 (Dec. 1924), 400. For an excellent appraisal of the Fort Pitt episode that places it in the context of the larger and more complicated struggle for control of the Ohio Valley, see Michael N. McConnell, *A Country Between: The Upper Ohio Valley and Its Peoples, 1724–1774* (Lincoln, 1992), 194–96. For an example of an Internet discussion devoted to biological warfare and smallpox, see the H-OIEAHC discussion log for April 1995, available at http://www.h-net.msu.edu/logs/. For the contention that the attempt at biological warfare was "unquestionably effective at Fort Pitt," see Francis Jennings, *Empire of Fortune: Crowns, Colonies, & Tribes in the Seven Years War in America* (New York, 1990), 447–48, 447n26. On the issue of timing, see Bernhard Knollenberg, "General Amherst and Germ Warfare," *Mississippi Valley Historical Review,* 41 (Dec. 1954), 489–94; Bernhard Knollenberg to editor, "Communications," *Mississippi Valley Historical Review,* 41 (March 1955), 762; and Donald H. Kent, to editor, *ibid.,* 762–63. For a cross-cultural analysis of the incident's place in a pantheon of other such "legends," see Adrienne Mayor, "The Nessus Shirt in the New World: Smallpox Blankets in History and Legend," *Journal of American Folklore,* 108 (Winter 1995), 54–77.

Source: Elizabeth A. Fenn, "Biological Warfare in Eighteenth-Century North America: Beyond Jeffery Amherst," *Journal of American History* 86, no. 4 (March 2000): 1552–80. (To save space, some text and footnotes have been edited.)

not regarding his ultimate culpability for the smallpox that struck Indians near Fort Pitt in 1763 and 1764. Nor is this essay an exhaustive accounting of all the accusations and incidents of biological warfare in late-eighteenth-century North America. It is, however, an attempt to broaden the debate and to place it in context.[2] Our preoccupation with Amherst has kept us from recognizing that accusations of what we now call biological warfare—the military use of smallpox in particular—arose frequently in eighteenth-century America. Native Americans, moreover, were not the only accusers. By the second half of the century, many of the combatants in America's wars of empire had the knowledge and technology to attempt biological warfare with the smallpox virus. Many also adhered to a code of ethics that did not constrain them from doing so. Seen in this light, the Amherst affair becomes not so much an aberration as part of a larger continuum in which accusations and discussions of biological warfare were common, and actual incidents may have occurred more frequently than scholars have previously acknowledged.

Fort Pitt, 1763

The most famous "smallpox blanket" incident in American history took place in the midst of Pontiac's Rebellion in 1763. In May and June of that year, a loose confederation of tribes inspired by the Ottawa war leader Pontiac launched attacks on British-held posts throughout the Great Lakes and Midwest. On May 29, 1763, they began a siege of Fort Pitt, located in western Pennsylvania at the confluence of the Allegheny and Monongahela rivers. The officer in charge at Fort Pitt was the Swiss-born captain Simeon Ecuyer. On June 16, 1763, Ecuyer reported to Col. Henry Bouquet at Philadelphia that the frontier outpost's situation had taken a turn for the worse. Local Indians had escalated the hostilities, burning nearby houses and attempting to lure Ecuyer into an engagement beyond the walls of the well-protected post, where traders and colonists, interlopers on Indian lands, had taken refuge. "We are so crowded in the fort that I fear disease," wrote Ecuyer, "for in spite of all my care I cannot keep the place as clean as I should like; moreover, the small pox is among us. For this reason I have had a hospital built under the bridge beyond musketfire." Henry Bouquet, in a letter dated June 23, passed the news on to Jeffery Amherst, the British commander in chief, at New York. "Fort Pitt is in good State of Defence against all attempts from Savages," Bouquet reported, but "Unluckily the small Pox has broken out in the Garrison."[3] By June 16, then,

---

[2] A thorough appraisal of the use of biological warfare in the prescientific era can be found in Mark Wheelis, "Biological Warfare before 1914," in *Biological and Toxin Weapons: Research, Development, and Use from the Middle Ages to 1945,* ed. Erhard Geissler and John van Courtland Moon (Oxford, 1999), 8–34.

[3] For a summary of the documentation of this incident, see Knollenberg, "General Amherst and Germ Warfare," 489–94; and Kent to editor, "Communications," 762–63. While my conclusions differ from Knollenberg's, much of the evidence consulted is the same. Simeon Ecuyer to Henry Bouquet, June 16, 1763 [translation], in *The Papers of Col. Henry Bouquet,* ed. Sylvester K. Stevens and Donald H. Kent (30 series, Harrisburg, 1940–1943), series 21649, part 1, p. 153. . . . Bouquet to Jeffery Amherst, June 23, 1763, *ibid.,* ser. 21634, p. 196.

from sources unknown, smallpox had established itself at Fort Pitt. It is likely that Amherst knew of the situation by the end of June.

But it was not Amherst, apparently, who first proposed the use of smallpox against the Delaware, Shawnee, and Mingo Indians surrounding Fort Pitt. Nor was it Amherst who executed the scheme. While the actual provenance of the plan remains unclear, a brief description of the deed itself appears in the diary of William Trent, a trader and land speculator with ties to the more prominent George Croghan. On June 23, the very day that Bouquet penned his letter to Amherst from Philadelphia, Trent reported that two Delaware dignitaries, Turtle's Heart and Mamaltee, visited Fort Pitt late at night and asked to speak with post officials. A conference took place the following day, June 24, in which the Indians urged the British to abandon the fort, and the British, for their part, refused. The parleys came to a close, and the Indians asked for "a little Provisions and Liquor, to carry us Home." The British obliged their request. "Out of our regard to them," wrote William Trent, "we gave them two Blankets and an Handkerchief out of the Small Pox Hospital. I hope it will have the desired effect."[4] He does not mention who conceived the plan, and he likewise does not mention who carried it out, but Fort Pitt account books make it clear that the British military both sanctioned and paid for the deed. The records for June 1763 include this invoice submitted by Levy, Trent and Company:

> To Sundries got to Replace in kind those which were taken from people in the Hospital to Convey the Smallpox to the Indians Viz:
>
> | | | | | |
> |---|---|---|---|---|
> | 2 Blankets | @20/ | £2" | 0" | 0 |
> | 1 Silk Handkerchef | 10/ | | | |
> | & 1 linnen do: | 3/6 | 0" | 13" | 6 |

Captain Ecuyer certified that the items "were had for the uses above mentioned," and Gen. Thomas Gage ultimately approved the invoice for payment, endorsing it with a comment and his signature.[5]

Had Jeffery Amherst known of these actions, he certainly would have approved. From the safety of his New York headquarters, he laid forth his own strategy for biological warfare in early July, prompted no doubt by Bouquet's letter of June 23 informing him that smallpox had broken out at the Monongahela post. In an undated memorandum that is apparently a postscript to a letter of July 7, 1763, Amherst proposed the following to Bouquet: "Could it not be contrived to Send the *Small Pox* among those Disaffected Tribes of Indians? We must, on this occasion, Use Every Stratagem in our power to Reduce them." Bouquet, now at Carlisle en route to Fort Pitt with reinforcements, replied on July 13, also in postscript: "I will try to innoculate the Indians by

---

[4] . . . Trent, "William Trent's Journal at Fort Pitt," ed. Volwiler, 400.

[5] Levy, Trent and Company: Account against the Crown, Aug. 13, 1763, in *Papers of Col. Henry Bouquet,* ed. Stevens and Kent, ser. 21654, pp. 218–19. While the account was submitted for payment in August, the items in it are all listed under the date "1763 June." As Mark Wheelis has pointed out, readers should note that William Trent refers to a single handkerchief in his journal, while the invoice is for two: one silk, one linen. Wheelis, "Biological Warfare before 1914," 23n73.

means of Blankets that may fall in their hands, taking care however not to get the disease myself." To this Amherst responded approvingly on July 16. "You will Do well to try to Innoculate the Indians by means of Blanketts, as well as to try Every other method that can serve to Extirpate this Execreble Race."[6] Unbeknownst to both Bouquet and his commander in chief, their subordinates at Fort Pitt had already conceived and executed the very plan proposed. If the garrison at Fort Pitt perpetrated a second, later act of biological warfare at Amherst's behest, the documents currently available make no mention of it.

What the documents do show, however, is that smallpox struck hard among the Indians around Fort Pitt in the spring and summer of 1763. On April 14, 1764, a man named Gershom Hicks arrived at the British post, having escaped from the Shawnee and Delaware Indians who had held him captive since May 1763. In a deposition taken the day of his arrival, Hicks reported "that the Small pox has been very general & raging amongst the Indians since last spring and that 30 or 40 Mingoes, as many Delawares and some Shawneese Died all of the Small pox since that time, that it still continues amongst them." Five months later, in September 1764, the epidemic continued to wreak havoc among the Shawnees. "Y^e poor Rascals are Dieing very fast with ye small pox," reported Col. Andrew Lewis from Virginia's Blue Ridge Mountains; "they can make but Little Resistance and when Routed must parish in great Numbers by ye Disordere." . . . As the historian Michael McConnell has pointed out, it is possible and perhaps likely that the epidemic stemmed from multiple sources of infection. John M'Cullough, a fifteen-year-old captive among the Indians, reported that the disease took hold after an attack on some settlers sick with the smallpox along central Pennsylvania's Juniata River. The timing, however, is uncanny: the eruption of epidemic smallpox in the Ohio country coincided closely with the distribution of infected articles by individuals at Fort Pitt.[7] While blame for this outbreak cannot be placed squarely in the British camp, the circumstantial evidence is nevertheless suggestive.

[6] Memorandum by Sir Jeffery Amherst, [July 7, 1763], in *Papers of Col. Henry Bouquet,* ed. Stevens and Kent, ser. 21634, p. 161. . . . Bouquet to Amherst, Aug. 11, 1763, *ibid.,* 243; Bouquet to Amherst, July 13, 1763, in Jeffery Amherst, *Official Papers, 1740–1783* (microfilm, 202 reels, World Microfilms Publications, 1979), reel 32, frame 305. The published typescript of this last document deviates in important ways from the original. See Bouquet to Amherst, July 13, 1763, in *Papers of Col. Henry Bouquet,* ed. Stevens and Kent, ser. 21634, p. 214. For the July 16 letter, see Amherst to Bouquet, July 16, 1763, in Amherst, *Official Papers,* reel 33, frame 114. . . . See Memorandum by Sir Jeffery Amherst, [July 16, 1763], in *Papers of Col. Henry Bouquet,* ed. Stevens and Kent, ser. 21634, p. 161. . . .

[7] Deposition of Gershom Hicks, April 14, 1764, in *Papers of Col. Henry Bouquet,* ed. Stevens and Kent, ser. 21650, part 1, p. 102. Five days later, under pressure from Fort Pitt officials, Hicks recanted much of his testimony and de-emphasized the Indians' martial intentions. He apparently made no reference to smallpox in his second deposition. William Grant, Re-Examination of Gershom Hicks, in *Papers of Col. Henry Bouquet,* ed. Stevens and Kent, ser. 21651, pp. 7–10. . . . On the Virginia Indians, see Andrew Lewis to Bouquet, Sept. 10, 1764, in *Papers of Col. Henry Bouquet,* ed. Stevens and Kent, ser. 21650, part 2, p. 127. . . . On the possibility of multiple sources of infection, see McConnell, *Country Between,* 195–96. M'Cullough's report is in Archibald Loudon, ed., *A Selection, of Some of the Most Interesting Narratives, of Outrages, Committed by the Indians, in Their Wars, with the White People* (1808; 2 vols., New York, 1977), I, 331. . . .

Usually treated as an isolated anomaly, the Fort Pitt episode itself points to the possibility that biological warfare was not as rare as it might seem. It is conceivable, of course, that when Fort Pitt personnel gave infected articles to their Delaware visitors on June 24, 1763, they acted on some earlier communication from Amherst that does not survive today.[8] The sequence of events, however, makes it more likely that Amherst and Fort Pitt authorities conceived of the idea independently. In each case, the availability of contagious material (thanks to the smallpox epidemic at the post itself) seems to have triggered the plan of infection. Ecuyer reported the outbreak at Fort Pitt on June 16, and the attempt to communicate the disease took place eight days later. Amherst learned of the outbreak in Bouquet's letter of June 23, and the commander in chief proposed his own scheme on July 7. The fact that a single wartime outbreak could prompt two independent plans of contagion suggests that the Fort Pitt incident may not have been an anomaly. Evidence from other fields of battle indicates that in the minds of many, smallpox had an established, if irregular, place in late-eighteenth-century warfare. . . .

Other Accusations and Incidents

Eighteenth-century biological warfare is at best a slippery topic of inquiry. (The term "biological warfare" is itself anachronistic, but it remains well suited for describing what eighteenth-century Americans clearly viewed as a distinctive category of acts and allegations.) The long-standing debate over the Fort Pitt episode — easily the best-documented incident in the period — reveals how very treacherous the historical landscape can be. Even contemporaries could rarely prove culpability beyond refute in a suspicious outbreak of disease; for historians, the task is next to impossible. Accidents happened, and unintentional contagion was common, particularly in wartime. Moreover, in those rare cases where malicious intent was evident, as at Fort Pitt in 1763, the actual effectiveness of an attempt to spread smallpox remains impossible to ascertain: the possibility always exists that infection occurred by some "natural" route.

While all of this complicates the historian's task, it may nevertheless have enhanced smallpox's appeal as a weapon. For unlike rape, pillage, and other atrocities in which the intent and identity of the perpetrator could be made clear, the propagation of smallpox had the advantage of deniability. In the honor-bound world in which eighteenth-century military officials lived, this may well have been biological warfare's greatest attribute. It is possible, given the dearth of ironclad evidence, that biological warfare did not occur beyond the Fort Pitt incident. But another perspective also seems warranted, particularly when smallpox's deniability is taken into account: the shortage of conclusive documentation may simply indicate that perpetrators did not record their deeds.

The surviving evidence is rife with ambiguity. Some accusations served propaganda purposes in situations of social or military stress. Others come

---

[8] Such a communication might have been either written or oral in form. It is also possible that documents relating to such a plan were deliberately destroyed.

from oral traditions, at times recorded long after the alleged incidents took place. Many allegations are unsubstantiated, and some are weakly substantiated at best. Nevertheless, the sheer weight of the evidence that follows points to the distinct possibility that eighteenth-century biological warfare was more common than historians have previously believed.

It may well have been Indians, not whites, who used the strategy first. In his voluminous *History and Description of New France,* Pierre-François-Xavier de Charlevoix recounts an Iroquois act of biological sabotage against the English during Queen Anne's War in the early 1700s. The English army, Charlevoix writes, "was encamped on the banks of a little river; the Iroquois, who spent almost all the time hunting, threw into it, just above the camp, all the skins of the animals they flayed, and the water was thus soon all corrupted." The army, Charlevoix continued, suspected nothing. Soldiers "continued to drink this water, and it carried off so many, that Father de Mareuil, and two officers . . . observing the graves where the dead were buried, estimated the number at over a thousand." This account is remarkable not only because it seems to be the only eighteenth-century American incident that did not involve smallpox but also because the perpetrators were Indians. In this regard, the fact that smallpox was *not* the weapon of choice is hardly surprising. Already decimated by repeated epidemics, American Indians everywhere more likely viewed smallpox as a enemy in its own right than as a weapon that might bring down their adversaries.[9] The years that followed would show how true this was.

Amherst aside, smallpox seemed to be everywhere during the Seven Years' War. D. Peter MacLeod has demonstrated elegantly how Indian participation in the conflict with the British waxed and waned according to their simultaneous struggle against smallpox. In 1755–1756 and again in 1757–1758, the disease wreaked havoc among the Indians allied with the French. After the Lake George campaign of 1757, the French-allied Potawatomis suffered greatly in a smallpox outbreak that they believed stemmed from deliberate infection by the British. In July 1767, the British Indian superintendent William Johnson interviewed a man named Cornelius Van Slyke, held prisoner among the Chippewas and the Potawatomis for four years. Van Slyke told Johnson the Potawatomis believed "that the great Number they lost of their People at & returning from Lake George in 1757, was owing to y^e. English poisoning the Rum, & giving them the Small Pox, for which they owe them an everlasting ill will." The innuendo here is that the infection was willful, and it is possible that biological warfare occurred. But it is far more likely that the source of the contagion that ravaged the

[9] Even the Aztecs may have tried to utilize such a strategy during the Spanish conquest from 1519 to 1521. Motecuhzoma reportedly asked his magicians to work "some charm" against the Spaniards that might "cause them to break out in sores" or even "cause them to fall sick, or die, or return to their own land." Ironically, it was the Aztecs, not the Spaniards, who succumbed en masse to smallpox. Miguel-Leon Portilla, ed., *The Broken Spears: The Aztec Account of the Conquest of Mexico* (Boston, 1966), 34. On Queen Anne's War, see Pierre-François-Xavier de Charlevoix, *History and General Description of New France,* ed. and trans. John Dawson Gilmary Shea (6 vols., New York, 1900), V, 221–22. . . .

Potawatomis was the famous attack (fictionalized in James Fenimore Cooper's *Last of the Mohicans,* 1826) on unarmed prisoners leaving Fort William Henry on August 10, 1757.[10] Many of those prisoners were sick with smallpox.

By the nineteenth century, intentional smallpox infection turned up regularly in Native American oral histories. The Ottawa Indians suffered from smallpox after the 1757 campaign, and their tradition held that the disease came from Montreal, ironically in the possession of the Indians' French allies at the time of the outbreak. "This smallpox," according to Andrew Blackbird's account, "was sold to them shut up in a showy tin box, with the strict injunction not to open the box on their way homeward." When they arrived at their village on the shores of Lake Michigan, the Indians opened the box only to find another box and then another inside. In the end, Blackbird says, the Ottawas "found nothing but mouldy particles in this last little box." Many inspected it, and shortly thereafter, smallpox broke out. According to the story, an enormous Ottawa village, extending for miles west of Mackinac, "was entirely depopulated and laid waste." It is unlikely that the French would have knowingly passed smallpox on to their Indian supporters at this crucial juncture in the Seven Years' War. But the accusation may well reflect a Native American perception that since they had caught the disease while fighting for the French, the French were therefore responsible for the devastation it caused. Eager to retain and appease their Indian allies, French officials laid the blame for the epidemic in the British camp.[11] If further documentation for this alleged incident exists, it remains undiscovered. Nor is it clear how, if at all, this tradition might be linked to the Fort Pitt episode six years later. . . .

The next great conflict to shake the continent was the Revolutionary War. Once again, smallpox erupted repeatedly, and once again, those on the receiving end believed that the outbreaks were not all accidental. Allegations of biological warfare arose in the course of confrontations at Quebec, Boston, and Yorktown, as well as during the mobilization of the Earl of Dunmore's Ethiopian Regiment on the Chesapeake. At Boston, charges of deliberate smallpox propagation by the British cropped up even before the outbreak of hostilities at Lexington and Concord. "The [British] soldiers try all they can to spread the *smallpox,*" wrote an unnamed Bostonian in January 1775. "One of their Officers inoculated his whole family without letting any person know it,—there was a man, his wife, and seven children, under the same roof, and not one of them ever had it." When the American siege of Boston began in April, the dis-

---

[10] D. Peter MacLeod, "Microbes and Muskets: Smallpox and the Participation of the Amerindian Allies of New France in the Seven Years' War," *Ethnohistory,* 39 (Winter 1992), 42–64. On the epidemic among the Potawatomis, see *ibid.,* 49; R. David Edmunds, *The Potawatomis: Keepers of the Fire* (Norman, 1978), 55–56; and James A. Clifton, *The Prairie People: Continuity and Change in Potawatomi Indian Culture, 1665–1965* (Lawrence, 1977), 102. . . . For a valuable appraisal of the Fort William Henry affair, see Ian K. Steele, *Betrayals: Fort William Henry & the "Massacre"* (New York, 1990).

[11] Andrew J. Blackbird, *Complete Both Early and Late History of the Ottawa and Chippewa Indians of Michigan, a Grammar of Their Language, Personal and Family History of the Author* (Harbor Springs, Mich., 1897), 2–3. . . . On the French blaming the British, see MacLeod, "Microbes and Muskets," 50–51.

ease became epidemic among British soldiers and other residents of the city. "The small pox rages all over the Town," wrote George Washington from his headquarters in nearby Cambridge on December 14. "Such of the [British] Military as had it not before, are now under innoculation—this I apprehend is a weapon of Defence, they Are useing against us."[12]

In fact, Washington already suspected that the British, in an effort to infect the vulnerable Continental Army, had inoculated some of the refugees leaving the city. On December 3, 1775, four deserters had arrived at the American headquarters "giving an account that several persons are to be sent out of *Boston,* this evening or to-morrow, that have been lately inoculated with the small-pox, with design, probably, to spread the infection, in order to distress us as much as possible." It was, according to Washington's aide-de-camp, an "unheard-of and diabolical scheme." Washington at first regarded the report with disbelief. "There is one part of the information that I Can hardly give Credit to," he wrote. "A Sailor Says that a number of these Comeing out have been inoculated, with design of Spreading the Smallpox through this Country & Camp."[13]

A week later, however, as the pox erupted among the refugees, the American commander in chief changed his mind. In a letter to John Hancock on December 11, 1775, he explained his reappraisal: "The information I received that the enemy intended Spreading the Small pox amongst us, I could not Suppose them Capable of—I now must give Some Credit to it, as it has made its appearance on Severall of those who Last Came out of Boston." The Americans controlled the outbreak through careful quarantine and disinfection of both refugees and their effects. In the aftermath, the *Boston Gazette* carried a sworn declaration from one refugee, a servant, saying that he had been inoculated and then, as the pustules broke out, ordered by his master to embark on a crowded vessel leaving the city. There he could not avoid communicating the infection to "A Number of said Passengers," as the boat's departure was delayed more than two weeks. According to another report, a Boston physician named Dr. Rand had admitted "that he had effectually given the distemper among those people" quitting the city.[14] . . .

[12] Extract of a letter from Boston, author unknown, *London Evening Post,* March 25–28, 1775, reprinted in Margaret W. Willard, ed., *Letters on the American Revolution, 1774–1776* (Boston, 1925), 57–58; George Washington to John Hancock, Dec. 14, 1775, in *The Papers of George Washington: Revolutionary War Series,* ed. W. W. Abbot and Dorothy Twohig (26 vols., Charlottesville, 1983–), II, 548.

[13] Robert H. Harrison to Council of Massachusetts, Dec. 3, 1775, in *American Archives,* ed. Peter Force, 4th ser. (6 vols., Washington, 1837–1853), IV, 168; Washington to Hancock, Dec. 4, 1775, in *Papers of George Washington: Revolutionary War Series,* ed. Abbot and Twohig, II, 486.

[14] Washington to Hancock, Dec. 11, 1775, in *Papers of George Washington: Revolutionary War Series,* ed. Abbot and Twohig, II, 533; Washington to Hancock, Nov. 28, 1775, *ibid.,* 447; Samuel Bixby, "Diary of Samuel Bixby," *Proceedings of the Massachusetts Historical Society,* 14 (March 1876), 297; Washington to James Otis Sr. [Mass. General Court], Dec. 10, 1775, in *Papers of George Washington: Revolutionary War Series,* ed. Abbot and Twohig, II, 526; John Morgan to Washington, Dec. 12, 1775, *ibid.,* 541–42; Washington to Joseph Reed, Dec. 15, 1775, *ibid.,* 553. On the servant refugee, see *Boston Gazette and Country Journal,* Feb. 12, 1776, p. 4. On Dr. Rand, see Ezekiel Price, "Diary of Ezekiel Price, 1775–1776," *Proceedings of the Massachusetts Historical Society,* 7 (Nov. 1863), 220.

Boston was not the only city besieged by American troops through the winter of 1775–1776. At Quebec another siege was underway, and here again, smallpox emerged as a major player in military affairs. While the American efforts to keep the Continental Army free of smallpox were generally successful at Boston, they failed dismally at Quebec. Here the disease erupted almost immediately upon the Americans' arrival outside the walled city in late November and early December of 1775. What followed was one of the great disasters in American military history. An American attempt on the city failed in a blizzard on the night of December 31, and the army settled in for a miserable, snowbound siege that lasted until the first week of May 1776, when British reinforcements arrived. Riddled with smallpox, the Americans retreated, first to the town of Sorel, where the Richelieu River joins the Saint Lawrence, and then, in midsummer, southward to Ticonderoga and Crown Point. . . .

Many accused the British general, Sir Guy Carleton, of willfully infecting the American camp during the wintry siege of the Canadian city. In the deathbed diary he dictated in 1811, the Pennsylvania rifleman John Joseph Henry recalled that smallpox had been "introduced into our cantonments by the indecorous, yet fascinating arts of the enemy." The Continental Congress held hearings on the debacle even as the Northern Army still suffered from smallpox at Ticonderoga. Thomas Jefferson's abbreviated notes of the testimony reveal that several of the witnesses believed the epidemic was no accident. Capt. Hector McNeal, for example, said "the small pox was sent out of Quebeck by Carleton, inoculating the poor people at government expence for the purpose of giving it to our army." Likewise, according to another witness, it "was said but no proof that Carleton had sent it into the suburbs of St. Roc where some of our men were quartered." The testimony of a Dr. Coates reiterated the theme: "Was supposed Carlton sent out people with it," Jefferson noted in his shorthand. Jefferson, for one, found the testimony credible. "I have been informed by officers who were on the spot, and whom I believe myself," he wrote to the French historian François Soulés, "that this disorder was sent into our army designedly by the commanding officer in Quebec. It answered his purposes effectually."[15]

Smallpox was present at Quebec when the American army arrived, and it seems probable, as they mingled with *habitants* outside the city, that the troops would have picked up the *Variola* virus regardless of any actions on Carleton's part. "The small pox is all around us, and there is great danger of its spreading in the army," wrote the soldier Caleb Haskell on December 6, 1775, shortly after the siege began. "We have long had that disorder in town," observed a British officer on December 9, as the disease made its first appearance among the Americans. Carleton's humane treatment of American smallpox victims

[15] John Joseph Henry, "Campaign against Quebec," in *March to Quebec: Journals of the Members of Arnold's Expedition,* ed. Kenneth Roberts (New York, 1940), 374–75; Thomas Jefferson, "Notes of Witnesses' Testimony concerning the Canadian Campaign, July 1–27, 1776," in *Papers of Thomas Jefferson,* ed. Boyd, I, 435, 437, 447–48; Thomas Jefferson, "Comments on Soulés' *Histoire,* August 8, 1786," *ibid.,* X, 373, 377n24. . . .

taken prisoner when the siege ended would seem to undermine the argument that he deliberately infected the American lines.[16] Nevertheless, it remains possible. By providing a ready supply of inoculees and other contagious patients, the ongoing presence of smallpox in Quebec might in fact have made deliberate infection easier to disguise.

Meanwhile, farther south, more accusations of willful contagion surfaced in Virginia, where some eight hundred African American refugees from slavery had rallied to the British cause in response to a promise of freedom from the colony's royal governor, John Murray, Earl of Dunmore. Written on November 7, 1775, and issued a week later, Dunmore's limited emancipation proclamation inspired African Americans and terrified the slaveholding revolutionaries who spearheaded the American revolt. By May 1776, however, smallpox had infested the governor's little band of freedom fighters in their precarious waterfront camp near Norfolk. Dunmore decided to move to a safe spot and inoculate his men. "His Lordship," according to a rumor in the *Virginia Gazette*, "before the departure of the fleet from Norfolk harbour, had two of those wretches inoculated and sent ashore, in order to spread the infection, but it was happily prevented."[17]

In the end, it was Dunmore's black regiment that suffered most from the disease, dwindling under its impact to 150 effective men and eventually withdrawing from Virginia entirely. "Had it not been for this horrid disorder," wrote Dunmore, "I should have had two thousand blacks; with whom I should have had no doubt of penetrating into the heart of this Colony." When the American rebels questioned one eyewitness to the ravages of smallpox and to Dunmore's final withdrawal, they broached the topic of biological warfare directly: "How long were they inocul[ated] & was it done to communicate it to the People on shore[?]" asked the interrogators. "By no means," was the vague response, "every one in the Fleet was inoculated, that had it not."[18] . . .

---

[16] Caleb Haskell, "Diary at the Siege of Boston and on the March to Quebec," in *March to Quebec*, ed. Roberts, 482–83. . . . When the Americans fled on May 6, 1776, many of the sick were left behind on the Plains of Abraham. Noting "that many of his Majesty's deluded subjects of the neighbouring provinces, labouring under wounds and diverse disorders," were "in great danger of perishing for want of proper assistance," Carleton ordered his men "to make diligent search for all such distressed persons, and afford them all necessary relief, and convey them to the general hospital, where proper care shall be taken of them." Carleton's orders are reprinted in Andrew Parke, *An Authentic Narrative of Facts Relating to the Exchange of Prisoners Taken at the Cedars* (London, 1777), 4–5.

[17] The best account of Dunmore's Ethiopian Regiment remains Benjamin Quarles, *The Negro in the American Revolution* (Chapel Hill, 1961), 19–32. The accusation can be found in Dixon and Hunter's *Virginia Gazette*, June 15, 1776, quoted in *Naval Documents of the American Revolution*, ed. William Bell Clark, William James Morgan, and Michael J. Crawford (10 vols., Washington, D.C., 1964–1996), V, 554. . . .

[18] John Murray, Earl of Dunmore, to the Secretary of State, June 26,1776, in George W. Williams, *History of the Negro Race in America from 1619–1800* (New York, 1885), 342, quoted in Gerald W. Mullin, *Flight and Rebellion: Slave Resistance in Eighteenth-Century Virginia* (New York, 1972), 132; "[James] Cunningham's Examination 18th July 1776," in *Naval Documents of the American Revolution*, ed. Clark, Morgan, and Crawford, V, 1136. . . .

Additional accusations surfaced in 1781, as Gen. Charles Cornwallis's southern campaign came to a close. The British retreat to Yorktown in many ways echoed Lord Dunmore's Virginia campaign five years earlier. Again, African American slaves flocked to British lines seeking freedom from their revolutionary masters. And again smallpox cut them down, for African Americans, like all other Americans, were far more likely to be susceptible to the disease than were troops from Europe.[19]

As early as June 1781, American soldiers in Virginia suspected Cornwallis's army of using smallpox-infected blacks to propagate disease. "Here I must take notice of some vilany," wrote Josiah Atkins as his regiment pursued the British near Richmond. "Within these days past, I have marched by 18 or 20 Negroes that lay dead by the way-side, putrifying with the small pox." Cornwallis, Atkins believed, had "inoculated 4 or 500 in order to spread smallpox thro' the country, & sent them out for that purpose." A Pennsylvania soldier, William Feltman, found a "negro man with the small-pox lying on the road side" on June 25, supposedly left by a British cavalry unit "in order to prevent the Virginia militia from pursuing them." By October, with surrender looming on the horizon, Cornwallis had become desperate. "The British," noted James Thacher in his diary, "have sent from Yorktown a large number of negroes, sick with the small pox, probably for the purpose of communicating the infection to our army." Writing three days after the capitulation, Robert Livingston hoped that reports of such conduct would sway Europeans to the American side. "In Virginia," he wrote, "they took the greatest pains to communicate the Small Pox to the Country; by exposing the dead bodies of those who had died with it, in the most frequented places." Benjamin Franklin later reiterated the charge in his "Retort Courteous."[20]

It may be tempting to dismiss such accusations as so much American hyperbole. But evidence indicates that in fact the British did exactly what the Americans charged. At Portsmouth, Virginia, in July 1781, Gen. Alexander Leslie outlined his plan for biological warfare in a letter to Cornwallis. "Above 700 Negroes are come down the River in the Small Pox," he wrote. "I shall distribute them about the Rebell Plantations." Even if they pardoned their actions by saying they could no longer support so many camp followers, the fact that sick African Americans might communicate smallpox to the enemy could not have been lost on British commanders.[21]

---

[19] . . . S. R. Duncan, Susan Scott, and C. J. Duncan, "The Dynamics of Smallpox Epidemics in Britain, 1550–1800," *Demography,* 30 (Aug. 1993), 405–23.

[20] Josiah Atkins, *The Diary of Josiah Atkins,* ed. Steven E. Kagle (New York, 1975), 32–33; William Feltman, *The Journal of Lt. William Feltman 1781–82* (1853; New York, 1969), 6; Thacher, *Military Journal of the American Revolution,* 337; Robert R. Livingston to Francis Dana, Oct. 22, 1781 (reel 102, item 78, vol. 21, p. 99), Papers of the Continental Congress. . . . Benjamin Franklin, "The Retort Courteous," in *Writings: Benjamin Franklin,* ed. J. A. Leo Lemay (New York, 1987), 1126–27.

[21] Alexander Leslie to Charles Cornwallis, July 13, 1781 (microfilm: frames 280–81, reel 4), Cornwallis Papers, P.R.O. 30/11/6 (Public Record Office, London, Eng.). . . .

Biological Weapons and the Ethics of War

. . . In the seventeenth and eighteenth centuries, many of the widely accepted rules of European warfare had seen codification in Hugo Grotius's *De jure belli ac pacis,* first published in 1625, and Emmerich de Vattel's *The Law of Nations,* published in 1758. Both works established theoretical protections in war for women and children and for the elderly and infirm. They addressed the issue of surrender, and they determined when soldiers should give "quarter" to their enemies. Beyond all this, they also included strictures against the use of poison weapons and "the poisoning of streams, springs, and wells." In an era before microbiology, in which deadly toxins and infectious microbes were hardly distinguishable, it is nearly inconceivable that either Grotius or Vattel would have excluded communicable disease from the general category of poisons."[22] All of these rules applied, theoretically at least, to "civilized" nations engaged in what were termed "just" wars.

For our purposes, ironically, the most important corollary to these customarily determined rules was that in certain situations, they did not apply. Cases in point included not only "unjust" wars but also rebellions, wars against enemies who themselves violated the laws of war, and wars against "savage" or "heathen" people. Vattel used the Turks and Mongols as his example, but his general point is clear: "nations are justified in uniting together as a body with the object of punishing, and even exterminating, such savage peoples." An earlier formulation of this philosophy had allowed the English to pursue brutal policies in Ireland, on the grounds that the Irish were not just rebels but (despite their professed Christianity) barbarians as well. More than one historian has argued that Ireland provided the English with a convenient ideological precedent for their actions in the New World. And colonists did indeed justify their own savage conduct in New England's seventeenth-century Indian wars by touting the "savagery" of the natives they brutalized.[23] In conflicts with "heathen" Indians, European rules of war gave license to unfettered violence, complete annihilation, and, yes, biological warfare. . . .

---

[22] Hugo Grotius, *De jure belli ac pacis libris tres,* ed. James Brown Scott, trans. Francis W. Kelsey (1646; 3 vols., New York, 1964), III, 734–36, 739–40; Emmerich de Vattel, *The Law of Nations: or, Principles of the Law of Nature; Applied to the Conduct and Affairs of Nations and Sovereigns* (1758; New York, 1964), 280, 282–83, 289; Barbara Donagan, "Atrocity, War Crime, and Treason in the English Civil War," *American Historical Review,* 99 (Oct. 1994), 1149–51. . . .

[23] Vattel, *Law of Nations,* 246. . . . On Ireland, see Nicholas Canny, "The Ideology of English Colonization: From Ireland to America," *William and Mary Quarterly,* 30 (Oct. 1973), 575–98; Barbara Donagan, "Codes and Conduct in the English Civil War," *Past and Present* (no. 118, Feb. 1988), 70–71; Donagan, "Atrocity, War Crime, and Treason in the English Civil War," 1139, 1148–49; and Howard Mumford Jones, "Origins of the Colonial Ideal in England," *Proceedings of the American Philosophical Society,* 85 (Sept. 1942), 448–65. On New England, see Jill Lepore, *The Name of War: King Philip's War and the Origins of American Identity* (New York, 1998), 112; Ronald Dale Karr, "'Why Should You Be So Furious?': The Violence of the Pequot War," *Journal of American History,* 85 (Dec. 1998), 888–89, 899–909; and Adam J. Hirsch, "The Collision of Military Cultures in Seventeenth-Century New England," *Journal of American History,* 74 (March 1988), 1187–1212.

Far more ambiguity surrounded the use of smallpox against Americans of European descent—the allegation that surfaced repeatedly during the Revolutionary War. Nothing captured these moral tensions so clearly as a little book titled *Military Collections and Remarks,* published in British-occupied New York in 1777. Written by a British officer named Robert Donkin, the book proposed a variety of strategies the British might use to gain the upper hand in the American conflict. Among them was biological warfare. In a footnote to a two-page section on the use of bows and arrows, Major Donkin made the following suggestion: "Dip arrows in matter of smallpox, and twang them at the American rebels, in order to inoculate them; This would sooner disband these stubborn, ignorant, enthusiastic savages, than any other compulsive measures. Such is their dread and fear of that disorder!"[24]

Such ideas may have been common in verbal banter, but they rarely made it into print. What happened next is therefore revealing, for it shows how controversial the topic of biological warfare was during the American Revolution: Donkin's provocative footnote survives in only three known copies of his book. In all others, it has been carefully excised. The person responsible for this act is unknown, as is the timing. But the fact that only three known copies survived intact seems to indicate that the excision took place close to the time of publication, before the volume was widely distributed.[25] Likely perpetrators include the author, the publisher, or an agent acting on behalf of British high command. Someone may well have found the suggestion morally offensive; or, in the battle for the "hearts and minds" of the American people, someone may have realized that explicit calls for biological warfare could only make enemies.

If the strategy was controversial, those who sought sanction for biological terror could nevertheless find it in customary codes of conduct. Donkin himself called the Americans "savages," and this alone countenanced the repudiation of behavioral constraints in war. The colonists, in fact, even cultivated a symbolic "Indian" identity in episodes such as the Boston Tea Party. But beyond this, the Americans were also "rebels." Sentiments regarding rebellion were changing, but popular insurrection, like savagery, could legitimate a war of unrestrained destruction—a war in which conventional strictures against biological warfare would not apply. . . . But there was no consensus on this among British officers. While some took a conciliatory stance early in the war, it appears that by 1779 a majority of British officers had become what one scholar has termed "hard-liners"—men who believed that "nothing but the Bayonet & Torch" could quell the colonial revolt. Included among them were men such as Banastre Tarleton, notorious for terrorizing the Carolina backcountry, and Charles Grey, famous for two nighttime bayonet attacks on

---

[24] Robert Donkin, *Military Collections and Remarks* (New York, 1777), 190–91, insert.

[25] Some copies of the book contain an engraved insert replicating the missing text. For an example of both the excision and the insert, see the copy of Donkin, *Military Collections and Remarks,* 190n., in the Clements Library, University of Michigan, Ann Arbor. I am grateful to John Dann of the Clements Library for bringing Donkin's book to my attention and for informing me of the recent discovery of a third intact copy.

sleeping American soldiers. In one of these attacks, Grey's men shouted "No Quarters to rebels" as they leapt upon their slumbering foes.[26]

If the mere fact of rebellion was grounds enough for such an attitude, the difficulties presented by long sieges and the Americans' unconventional fighting methods provided additional justification. In the view of many British soldiers, the Americans had themselves violated the rules of war many times over. Some took offense at the effective Patriot sniping during the retreat from Lexington. Others resented the withering musket fire at Bunker Hill, where General Gage's men believed "the Enemy Poisoned some of their Balls." Confronted by rebellion and frustrated by atrocities committed by a "savage" American enemy who often refused to face off head-to-head on the field of battle, British officers may well have believed the propagation of smallpox was justified and put this belief into practice, especially given the fact that the law of nations apparently permitted it. It is worth recalling that Jeffery Amherst, who had found biological warfare so unabashedly justifiable in 1763, was an extremely popular figure in England. According to the historian Robert Middlekauff, he was "probably the most admired military leader in the nation" during the era of the American Revolution.[27] That General Leslie and other British officers may have thought and acted as Amherst did should come as no surprise. . . .

. . . While Native Americans suffered most from smallpox, they were neither the only targets of its use on the battlefield nor the only ones who leveled the charge against others. The Fort Pitt incident, despite its notoriety, does not stand alone in the annals of early American history. Accusations of deliberate smallpox propagation arose frequently in times of war, and they appear to have had merit on at least one occasion—the Yorktown campaign—during the American Revolution. Elsewhere the evidence is often ambiguous. But it nevertheless indicates that the famous Fort Pitt incident was one in a string of

---

[26] On Indian-as-America symbolism, see Hugh Honour, *The New Golden Land: European Images of America from the Discoveries to the Present Time* (New York, 1975), 84–117, 138–60. . . . On views within the British military, see Stephen Conway, "'The Great Mischief Complain'd of': Reflections on the Misconduct of British Soldiers in the Revolutionary War," *William and Mary Quarterly,* 47 (July 1990), 378–79; Stephen Conway, "To Subdue America: British Army Officers and the Conduct of the Revolutionary War," *William and Mary Quarterly,* 43 (July 1986), 396–97; and Armstrong Starkey, "Paoli to Stony Point: Military Ethics and Weaponry during the American Revolution," *Journal of Military History,* 58 (Jan. 1994), 18. The "Bayonet & Torch" quotation is from Patrick Campbell to Alexander Campbell, July 8, 1778, Campbell of Barcaldine Muniments, G.D. 170/1711/17, S.R.O., quoted in Conway, "To Subdue America," 392. On "hard-liners," see *ibid.,* 404–5; and Conway, "'The Great Mischief Complain'd of,'" 370–90. On Banastre Tarleton and Charles Grey, see Harold E. Selesky, "Colonial America," in *The Laws of War: Constraints on Warfare in the Western World,* ed. Michael Howard, George J. Andreopoulos, and Mark R. Shulman (New Haven, 1994), 80–83.

[27] Selesky, "Colonial America," 81–83. On the poisoned musket balls, see Thomas Sullivan, "The Common British Soldier—From the Journal of Thomas Sullivan, 49th Regiment of Foot," ed. S. Sydney Bradford, *Maryland Historical Magazine,* 62 (Sept. 1967), 236. On Amherst, see Robert Middlekauff, *The Glorious Cause: The American Revolution, 1763–1789* (New York, 1982), 406.

episodes in which military officials in North America may have wielded *Variola* against their enemies. Justification for doing so could be found in codes of war that legitimated excesses even as they defined constraints. Biological warfare was therefore a reality in eighteenth-century North America, not a distant, abstract threat as it is today. Its use was aimed, as one patriot writer accusingly put it in the year of Yorktown, "at the ruin of a whole Country, involving the indiscriminate murder of Women and Children."[28]

Analyzing the Source

REFLECTING ON THE SOURCE

1. Briefly describe the incidents of smallpox during the American Revolution that raised suspicions of its use as a weapon. Who made such accusations, and who did they accuse?

2. By her own admission, much of Fenn's evidence is "rife with ambiguity." Where in this article's argument does the evidence consist of rumors or accusations rather than documented cases of the use of smallpox as a weapon? Does Fenn make this distinction clear?

3. Judging from the notes you made in the table on page 71, are any parts of the argument weakened by questionable evidence? Historians often interpret an *absence* of evidence in their primary sources to their advantage; has Fenn done so here?

MAKING CONNECTIONS

4. Any piece of persuasive writing relies on the author's command of argument, evidence, and organization. How does the organization of this article reinforce its argument? How has Fenn's evidence shaped the organization and presentation of her argument?

5. Fenn states in the introduction that one of her objectives is to "broaden the debate" over the Fort Pitt incident and "place it in context." Does the article succeed in this regard? If so, explain how Fenn has redefined the significance of the Fort Pitt incident.

6. How did the debate over the use of smallpox as a weapon in the eighteenth century parallel or diverge from debates over the use of weapons of mass destruction (both biological and nuclear) today? Have modern technology and warfare increased or decreased the likelihood of smallpox's use as a weapon?

---

[28] Robert R. Livingston to Francis Dana, Oct. 22, 1781 (reel 102, item 78, vol. 21, p. 99), Papers of the Continental Congress.

Beyond the Source

Shortly after Fenn's article appeared in the March 2000 edition of the *Journal of American History*, historian Philip Ranlet published "The British, the Indians, and Smallpox: What Actually Happened at Fort Pitt in 1763?" in *Pennsylvania History* 67 (2000): 427–41. Ranlet's article is much more skeptical than Fenn's about the use of smallpox as a biological weapon in the eighteenth century, as is evident from his thesis: "Logic, a better understanding of smallpox itself, and another look at the evidence call into question much of the standard rendition of the story and the ways that historians for more than a century have misrepresented the evidence."

Ranlet exonerated Amherst and Bouquet from complicity in the distribution of the infected goods at Fort Pitt, not out of humanitarian or moral principles they may have held dear, but because Bouquet was unwilling to expose himself to the disease (ironically, Bouquet died of yellow fever a few weeks after moving to a British post in Florida in 1765). Ranlet also questioned whether the goods that Trent and Ecuyer gave the Indians on June 24 had their intended effect. Reviewing the available evidence on the reported outbreak of smallpox in the vicinity of Fort Pitt in 1763, Ranlet concluded that the contagion had already been present among the Indians before June 24, most likely as a result of unintentional transmission from their colonial neighbors in the area. By his reading of the same sources used by Fenn, Ranlet found that the "[Fort Pitt] smallpox incident has been blown out of all proportion" by historians.

Fenn further developed her argument about smallpox and biological warfare in the book *Pox Americana: The Great Smallpox Epidemic of 1775–82* (New York: Hill and Wang, 2001). Building on themes found in her article, Fenn's book describes an increasing willingness by the British to use smallpox as a weapon against enemy armies, civilian noncombatants, and Native Americans during the Revolutionary era. Historians who reviewed *Pox Americana* for scholarly journals praised the breadth of her research but varied in their assessment of her conclusions. The reviewer for the *William and Mary Quarterly*, a journal of early American history, heaped praise on the book for "reconstituting the pandemic [of smallpox] for us to behold through a meticulous and imaginative assembly of fragmentary sources." The reviewer for the *Journal of American History* was less impressed, finding the book "great as a story but flawed as historical epidemiology" because in its rush to prove a continental smallpox epidemic, it failed to convey the disease's "early modern profile and narrower geopolitical contexts." Such a range of opinions in book reviews is not uncommon in history journals. Historians are trained to approach evidence and arguments critically, whether their own or those assembled by their peers.

The Fort Pitt incident has become a fixture in American folklore and has been retold countless times in such popular media as movies, television shows, and comic books. Historians still grapple with it because they are constantly reinterpreting the past through the lens of the present. The use of smallpox as a biological weapon raised a host of questions about the ethics of warfare in the eighteenth century. It is no wonder that this particular story retains its hold on our historical consciousness, as modern society deals with similar questions raised by the spread of intercontinental epidemics such as AIDS and SARS and the manufacture of biological and nuclear weapons of mass destruction.

Finding and Supplementing the Source

The Internet has made using scholarly journals much easier than it used to be. A good reference librarian can show you any number of online databases that can help you research articles by author, title, subject, keyword, or a variety of other parameters. Two that are particularly well suited for research in American history are *Humanities Abstracts* and *America: History and Life*. Both of these databases will provide a citation and a brief summary, or abstract, of an article's content to help you decide if it is relevant to your research. Once you find a citation for an article in one of these databases, you can check to see if the journal is on shelf in your library or if you need to order it via interlibrary loan. If a journal you want to use is not available in your library, check to see if your library subscribes to *JSTOR* (**jstor.org**), an online database that offers full-text articles from a host of scholarly journals. However, the most recent years of a journal are not usually available on *JSTOR* (for example, the *Journal of American History* lags behind the present date by about three years). In such cases, you can consult the paper copy of the journal on shelf if your library carries it or try a search in another online database.

The footnotes to Fenn's article provide the relevant citations to scholarship on the Fort Pitt incident before 2000. For an excellent recent study of Pontiac's War, see Gregory Evans Dowd, *War under Heaven: Pontiac, the Indian Nations, and the British Empire* (Baltimore, Md.: Johns Hopkins University Press, 2002). For broader discussions of disease and its role in European expansion in the New World, see Alfred W. Crosby, *Ecological Imperialism: The Biological Expansion of Europe, 900–1900* (Cambridge: Cambridge University Press, 1986), and Noble David Cook, *Born to Die: Disease and New World Conquest, 1492–1650* (Cambridge: Cambridge University Press, 1998).

CHAPTER 5

Toasting Rebellion

Songs and Toasts in Revolutionary America

In May 1766, the inhabitants of Philadelphia celebrated the repeal of the much despised Stamp Act in grand fashion. Shortly after the ship *Minerva* arrived from England with a copy of the official act of repeal, a local resident "instantly proclaimed the News" by reading the act "aloud at the London Coffee House," a popular haunt of Philadelphia's merchants. The crowd that gathered for this performance expressed its approval by raising "three loud Huzzas [cheers]" and sending a "Deputation from their Number" to escort the captain of the *Minerva* back to the coffeehouse, where a "large Bowl of Punch" awaited them. The crowd and the captain raised their glasses in toasting "Prosperity to America," and then the appreciative colonists presented the captain with a gold-laced hat "for having brought the first certain Account of the Stamp Act being totally repealed."

The celebration was far from over. Philadelphia's leading citizens "appointed the next Evening to illuminate the City," a popular form of civic celebration in which residents placed lighted candles in their windows. According to the newspaper report of this event, the "Ladies" of the city were especially creative in "the different Manner of Placing Lights, Devices, etc." in their windows, adding to the beauty of the event. That same evening, the city's inhabitants enjoyed a bonfire and consumed "many Barrels of Beer," yet no "Riot or Mob" disturbed the peace.

A few days later, Philadelphia's celebration culminated when the "principal Inhabitants" of the city attended "an elegant Entertainment at the State House." Among the three hundred guests were Pennsylvania's governor, military and naval officers, and the city's mayor and aldermen, all of whom conducted themselves with the "greatest Elegance and Decorum." These same guests drank twenty-one toasts, each one punctuated by a cannon salute. The first four toasts honored the king, the queen, the Prince of Wales; most of the remaining ones honored members of Parliament, the king's ministry, or the British Empire. The seventeenth toast was typical in its patriotic sentiments: "May the Interest of Great Britain and her Colonies be always united." The evening concluded with more bonfires, bell-ringing, and "Strong Beer to the Populace."

Seventeen years later, in 1783, Philadelphia witnessed another grand celebration, this one in honor of the Continental Army. Once again, the city's most prominent citizens took the lead, sponsoring a dinner attended by civilian and military officers of the United States. After dinner, Pennsylvania's governor (now styled the "President of the State" according to its new constitution) led the crowd in thirteen toasts, the first several of which honored the United States Congress, the new nation's allies France and Holland, and George Washington and the Continental Army, respectively. Between each toast, a military band played music and soldiers fired salutes. According to the newspaper report of this celebration, everyone conducted themselves "with the utmost order, good honour, and good breeding," and even though the company included people from "every State in the union," they all regarded each other "like members of one great and happy family."

Although separated by seventeen years of political upheaval and revolution, these two events shared elements common to festive culture in eighteenth-century America. Celebration was a full sensory experience. Illuminations and bonfires created spectacles of sight; cannon salutes loudly announced the occasion to all within earshot; the smell and taste of food delighted noses and filled stomachs; and alcohol flowed freely. While reports from both celebrations emphasized widespread participation, distinctions of gender and social rank determined where and how people experienced these events. Prominent male citizens and their guests occupied center stage, attending dinners in taverns or other public buildings. Elite women appeared at public celebrations only fleetingly or in their homes, where the "Ladies" of the city illuminated their windows. The rest of the populace celebrated out-of-doors, in the streets and at bonfires.

Two important features of this festive culture were drink and music. Eighteenth-century Americans—regardless of their race, gender, or class—consumed alcohol regularly and considered it part of a healthy diet. Public drinking, however, followed certain culturally sanctioned patterns that defined who could participate and in what ways. Generally, only free adult white men joined in the communal drinking that occurred at such civic celebrations. Elite women might raise glasses of wine at a toast made during a ball or dinner, but the rules of social decorum would not allow them to indulge in rounds of toasting or public consumption of barrels of beer. Laws passed by local and colonial governments regulated the consumption of alcohol by servants, slaves, Indians, and apprentices, limiting the amount of time they could spend in taverns and the size of the groups in which they could gather for social drinking.

To indulge in drink publicly, in other words, was one of the ways in which free white men in eighteenth-century America expressed their shared identity and set themselves apart from others. Taverns and coffeehouses provided their male customers with social centers and an arena for exchanging news and discussing politics. When the *Minerva* arrived in Philadelphia with word of the Stamp Act's repeal, a crowd of colonists immediately took the captain to the London Coffee House to share the news. In a busy commercial seaport like Philadelphia, such establishments served as a kind of emergency broadcast network, the easiest way to reach an audience as quickly as possible. Likewise, by reading or listening to someone read the newspapers from home and abroad kept at coffeehouses and taverns, patrons could acquaint themselves with current events in the world around them.

Music and song also filled the air at coffeehouses, taverns, and public festivities. Colonial Americans brought a rich musical heritage with them from Europe, and of course, Africans and Indians had their own traditions of music,

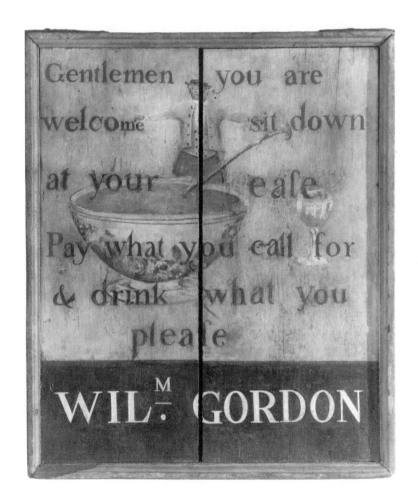

Figure 5.1 Sign for Gordon's Inn, c. 1790–1830 *Tavern and inn signs in early America announced their businesses to potential customers on busy streets and often offered visual cues as to what went on inside their doors. This sign, from an inn of unknown location, reveals much about the social significance of drinking in Revolutionary America. The verses read,*

> Gentlemen you are welcome
> sit down at your ease
> Pay what you call for &
> drink what you please

The bowl and glass suggest plenty of good drink and companionship, but the figure and verses limit that invitation to indulgence to only well-to-do males.

Source: The Connecticut Historical Society, Hartford.

song, and dance associated with communal celebration. Drinking songs were a part of the folk music tradition in the colonies, and anyone with a knack for rhyming and satire might compose one, often by grafting new lyrics onto a familiar tune. "Yankee Doodle," regarded by subsequent generations as the quintessential patriot song, actually originated in the British army and was sung by redcoats marching toward Lexington, Massachusetts, on the fateful morning of April 19, 1775. It became an American standard only after a parody of it appeared satirizing the British retreat from Lexington and Concord. Singing was also more inclusive during public occasions than drinking: those social groups whose access to alcohol was limited by legal and cultural restraints could nevertheless participate in public gatherings by listening to and joining in the music and song going on around them.

For many eighteenth-century Americans, rituals of public celebration shaped and defined their experience of the Revolution. History books often tell the story of the coming of the Revolution as a series of violent public confrontations between raucous crowds and British soldiers or officials: the Stamp Act riots, the tarring and feathering of customs officials, the Boston Massacre, the Boston Tea Party. However, much more common were crowds that assembled in a peaceful, celebratory fashion to support the patriot cause, their participants more likely to be found carrying wine glasses and punch bowls than clubs and torches. Until the eve of independence, they expressed their political opinions in songs and toasts that venerated the British monarchy and proudly proclaimed their membership in the British Empire. During the Revolutionary era, Americans made changes, some obvious and some subtle, in the way they conducted such celebrations, but the social and political purposes of these events remained much the same. Public festivities were the primary way in which people affirmed their political identity and displayed their notion of the social order. On such occasions, drink and song conveyed important political messages and served as one of the chief ways in which Americans expressed their transformation from loyal British subjects into citizens of a new nation.

Using Songs and Toasts as a Source

Drinking songs and toasts were part of the masculine drinking culture of eighteenth-century America. Oral tradition transmitted songs and toasts from one generation to the next, and both found their way into printed sources as well. Booksellers in Britain and America published collections of popular toasts, so that the shy and tongue-tied could be prepared to deliver one when in polite company. The association of toasting with refined behavior struck some observers as absurd, considering how the practice encouraged drunkenness. Bumpers, toasts in which each drinker emptied a full glass, were especially damaging to the group's composure but embodied the male bravado associated with drinking. Most toasts were never written down and disappeared along with the alcohol that accompanied them, but newspapers often published in detail the toasts made by prominent men at public celebrations.

Like toasts, drinking songs could be found in book collections or newspapers. Printers also disseminated them on broadsides (also known as ballad sheets), large single sheets of paper that could be shared by a group or posted in public places, such as taverns and coffeehouses. Patriotic songs proclaiming the martial spirit and triumphs of the British were popular among colonial drinkers, but satirical ballads aimed at unpopular public figures also enjoyed a wide audience. Some songs were set to familiar tunes that a crowd would readily recognize. New lyrics could turn the meaning of a popular tune on its head, such as when a New York woman in the 1790s set lyrics titled "The Rights of Women" to the patriotic British anthem "God Save the King." Other songs were little more than poorly metered attempts at patriotic drum-beating, published in newspapers as "curiosities" that reflected the spirit of the times.

While many traditional songs and toasts in eighteenth-century America were too vague and general in the sentiments they expressed to be controversial or confrontational, those with more pointed political content could disrupt the unity of the drinkers who recited them. A drinker who declined to join in a toast or song broke the fellowship symbolized by the communal punch bowl out of which the company drank. Onlookers in a crowded tavern or street might interpret this passive act of refusal as an aggressive challenge to the values and opinions expressed by the group. Toasts and songs could also be an effective way of exerting pressure on a reluctant participant to show solidarity with the rest of the crowd. Consider the case of the captain of the *Minerva*, described on page 89. Did he join enthusiastically or reluctantly in the toasts made in his honor at the coffeehouse? Much of the description provided of this occasion suggests a not-so-subtle form of coercion: a deputation from the crowd retrieved him from his ship, brought him to the coffeehouse, and placed a glass in his hand. What would the consequences have been if he had refused their hospitality and failed to drink to the Stamp Act's repeal?

Using songs and toasts as a source requires being attentive not just to the words used but also the way in which they were arranged to express the singers' and drinkers' notions of solidarity, allegiance, and social order. Calls to resistance against the king or Parliament were naturally inflammatory, and many eighteenth-century Americans defined political rebellion as a sin, a violation of the biblical commandment to honor your father and mother. Therefore, words and actions taken against Britain's controversial tax policies in the 1760s had to be distanced from outright rebellion by professions of loyalty to the Crown and empire. Notice how the toasts and song lyrics reproduced on pages 94–95 engage in this balancing act.

As recounted in the May 26, 1766, edition of the *Pennsylvania Gazette,* these toasts were made with "flowing glasses" at the Philadelphia dinner in celebration of the repeal of the Stamp Act. As you read them, pay careful attention to the sequence in which they were made.

These opening toasts affirm the colonists' loyalty as British subjects

1. The King

2. The Queen

3. Prince of Wales, and Royal Family

4. May the Illustrious House of Hanover preside over the United British Empire, to the End of Time

Express gratitude to the British Parliament and the king's ministry for repealing the Stamp Act

5. The House of Lords

6. The House of Commons

7. The present Worthy Ministry

8. The Glorious and Immortal Mr. Pitt

9. That Lover and Supporter of Justice, Lord Camden

Honor British merchants who exerted pressure on the Crown and Parliament to repeal the Stamp Act

10. The London Committee of Merchants

11. America's Friends in Great Britain

Toasts to other British colonists in North America and the Caribbean who have resisted the Stamp Act

12. The Virginia Assembly

13. All other Assemblies on the Continent, actuated by the like Zeal for the Liberties of their Country

14. Prosperity to the Spirited Inhabitants of St. Christophers

Formulaic tributes to the prosperity of the colony and the British Empire

15. The Navy and Army

16. Daniel Dulany, Esquire

17. May the Interest of Great Britain and her Colonies be always United

18. Trade and Navigation

19. America's Friends in Ireland

20. Prosperity to the Province of Pennsylvania

21. The Liberty of the Press in America

Potentially controversial tributes to an anti–Stamp Act pamphleteer (16), the printers who published such tracts (21), and political radicals in Ireland sympathetic to the American cause (19)

Like the toasts you just read, the following song lyrics delicately balance the colonists' assertion of their rights with professions of their loyalty as subjects. They are excerpted from "The Liberty Song," written by Pennsylvania patriot John Dickinson and published in the *Boston Gazette* on July 18, 1768 (reprinted in Frank Moore, ed., *Songs and Ballads of the American Revolution* [1856; repr., New York: Arno Press, 1969], 36–40). Dickinson wrote this song to rally support for nonimportation, a boycott movement in which patriots refused to buy goods they thought were unjustly taxed by Parliament.

Song begins with very strong language, equating new taxes with tyranny and enslavement

Come join hand in hand, brave Americans all,

And rouse your bold hearts at fair Liberty's call;

No tyrannous acts, shall suppress your just claims,

Or stain with dishonor America's name.

 In freedom we're born, and in freedom we'll live;

  Our purses are ready,

  Steady, Friends, steady,

 Not as *slaves*, but as *freemen* our money we'll give. . . .

Swarms of placemen and pensioners[1] soon will appear,
Like locusts deforming the charms of the year:
Suns vainly will rise, showers vainly descend,
If we are to drudge[2] for what others shall spend.

Then join hand in hand, brave Americans all,
By uniting we stand, by dividing we fall;
In so righteous a cause let us hope to succeed,
For Heaven approves of each generous deed. . . .

This bumper[3] I crown for our sovereign's health,
And this for Britannia's glory and wealth;
That wealth, and that glory immortal may be,
If she is but just, and we are but free.

> Raises specter of British tax collectors and customs officers robbing colonists of their property

> Calls colonists to united resistance

> Ends, like many drinking songs, by calling singers to a toast, in this case one affirming loyalty to Britain

Advantages and Disadvantages of Working with Songs and Toasts

Toasts and songs tell us much about popular political culture in Revolutionary America. In an age before universal adult suffrage or organized political parties, most people expressed their political opinions in ways that did not involve casting votes or supporting particular candidates for office. Unlike the elite males who sat in council chambers and assembly halls to pass laws or draft petitions, most folks practiced their politics out-of-doors, by assembling in crowds to celebrate, commemorate, or protest specific events or policies. A crowd might burn a despised political figure in effigy or bury a hated law, such as the Stamp Act, in a mock funeral procession. A crowd's attendance at a public celebration also lent legitimacy to the political authority of the elites who sponsored it. The toasts and songs that accompanied public events were a part of the experiential nature of politics in Revolutionary America for a much wider cross-section of the population than that represented in the official channels of government.

In toasts and songs people also expressed their vision of a well-ordered body politic, in which each part of society occupied a particular place and played a particular role in promoting the unity and welfare of the whole. Multiple toasts, in which participants drank to individuals or groups in descending order of importance, illustrated this hierarchy of political and social relations. Songs likewise celebrated ideal roles and virtues for different groups. By analyzing their lyrics, we can glimpse how patriots mobilized these different groups—women and men, soldiers and civilians—for their cause.

---

[1] "Placemen" and "pensioners" were derogatory terms for customs officials, military officers, and other officeholders who profited from royal appointments in the colonies.

[2] Labor.

[3] A type of toast in which all drinkers were expected to empty their glasses.

Songs and toasts also offer insights into the origins and development of American nationalism. At the outbreak of the Revolution, regional and cultural differences separated the thirteen colonies. Somehow, the patriots overcame these differences to forge a single nation that withstood not only the war with Britain but also the divisive politics of the postwar period. Songs and toasts of the era allow us to see how the former colonists created a shared political identity in the wake of independence. They tell us much about how colonists formerly connected only by their common status as British subjects manufactured a new inventory of public symbols and rituals to express their new identity as Americans.

The disadvantages of using songs and toasts to study the patriot movement arise from the formulaic and idealized nature of these forms of political expression. Songs and toasts seldom described the world as it was; rather, they described the world as it ought to be, in the eyes of the people who composed them. In toasts, political unity and social harmony always prevailed; in songs, soldiers were always brave, women virtuous, and civilians self-sacrificing. Songs and toasts that promoted social cohesion naturally understated social conflict and political opposition. Whenever studying these sources, it is important to ask, who was making the toast or singing the song and what motivation did they have for emphasizing unity and ignoring division?

One other disadvantage to using toasts and songs has to do with the context in which they were made, sung, and printed. As noted earlier, public drinking in eighteenth-century America was a prerogative of free adult males. We know that women, slaves, and laboring peoples drank, but it is much harder to find descriptions of what political opinions they may have expressed during their consumption. Newspapers did not report songs or toasts associated with these groups. Society did not condone their public consumption of alcohol, associating it with disorder and violence rather than political solidarity and social cohesion. Thus, while songs and toasts associated with the patriot movement claimed to state universally held sentiments, substantial elements of the social order were not invited to join in this form of expression. If those left out did engage in such activity on their own, it was rarely recorded in a way historians can retrieve. The songs and toasts that have survived carry a distinct bias in favor of white, urban men from the middle and upper ranks of society.

Working with the Source

The table on page 97 will help you organize your notes on the toasts and songs you will read. For the toasts, be attentive to how the occasions, methods, and subjects of celebration changed or remained constant over time. For the songs, try to determine what values or ideas they were transmitting to their intended audiences.

Toasts	The Occasion of Celebration	The Method of Celebration	The Subjects of the Toasts
1. Wilmington, N.C., 1765			
2. Charlestown, S.C., 1777			
3. Annapolis, Md., 1788			

Songs	Topic	What group(s) are addressed in the lyrics?	What values or ideas are the lyrics promoting?
4. "To the Ladies"			
5. "The New Recruit"			
6. "The Epilogue"			
7. "The Dance"			

The Source: Toasts and Songs of the Patriot Movement, 1765–1788

TOASTS

 Wilmington, North Carolina, 1765

> Following the passage of the Stamp Act in early 1765, the Crown appointed a stamp distributor for each of its North American colonies to oversee the collection of the new tax. Colonists used a variety of means to convince these stamp distributors to resign from their posts. The newspaper item below reports on one such instance in North Carolina, in which the stamp distributor was first intimidated and then toasted by a colonial mob.

WILMINGTON, in North Carolina, Nov. 20.—On Saturday, the 16th of this Instant,[1] WILLIAM HUSTON, Esq; Distributor of STAMPS for this Province, came to this Town; upon which three or four Hundred People immediately gathered together, with Drums beating, and Colours flying, and repaired to the House the said STAMP OFFICER put up at, and insisted upon knowing, "Whether he intended to execute the said Office, or not." He told them, "He should be very sorry to execute any Office disagreeable to the People of the Province." But they, not content with such a Declaration, carried him into the Court House, where he signed a Resignation Satisfactory to the Whole.

As soon as the STAMP OFFICER had complied with their Desire, they placed him in an Arm Chair, carried him first round the Court House, giving three Huzzas[2] at every Corner, and then proceeded with him round one of the Squares of the Town, and set him down at the Door of his Lodgings, formed themselves in a large Circle round him, and gave him three Cheers. They then escorted him into the House, where was prepared the best Liquors to be had, and treated him very genteelly. In the Evening a large Bonfire was made, and no Person appeared in the Streets without having LIBERTY, in large Capital Letters, in his Hat. They had a large Table near the Bonfire, well furnished with several Sorts of Liquors, where they drank in great Form, all the favourite AMERICAN Toasts, giving three Cheers at the Conclusion of each. The whole was conducted with great Decorum, and not the least Insult offered to any person.

[1] This month (November).
[2] Three cheers.
Source: Pennsylvania Gazette, January 2, 1766.

2 *Charlestown, South Carolina,* 1777

After the Second Continental Congress declared independence, the American patriots abandoned a calendar of British civic holidays, such as the monarch's birthday or royal weddings. Instead, the new nation created its own civic holidays, aimed at celebrating the break from Britain. The following newspaper item reports on a public celebration of the first anniversary of American independence in Charlestown (Charleston), South Carolina.

CHARLESTOWN, July 19.—Friday last being the first anniversary of the glorious formation of the American Empire, when Thirteen Colonies, driven by necessity, threw off the yoke, and rejected the tyranny of Great Britain, by declaring themselves Free, Independent and Sovereign States, the same was commemorated by every demonstration of joy.

Ringing of bells ushered in the day. At sunrise, American colours were displayed from all the forts and batteries and vessels in the harbour. The Charlestown regiment of militia, commanded by the Hon. Col. Charles Pinckney, and the Charlestown Artillery Company, commanded by Capt. Thomas Grimball, were assembled upon the Parade, and reviewed by his Excellency the President, who was attended, upon this occasion, by his Honour the Vice-President, and the Hon. Members of the Privy Council.[1] At one o'clock the several forts, beginning at Fort Moultrie on Sullivan Island, discharged 76 pieces of cannon, alluding to the glorious year 1776, and the militia and artillery fired three general vollies.

His Excellency the President then gave a most elegant entertainment in the Council Chamber, at which were present all the members of the Legislature then in town, all the public officers, civil and military; the clergy and many strangers of note, to the amount of more than double the number that ever observed the birthday of the present misguided and unfortunate King of Great Britain. After dinner the following toasts were drank, viz.

1. The Free, Independent and Sovereign States of America. 2. The Great Council[2] of America—may wisdom preside in all its deliberations. 3. General Washington. 4. The American army and navy—may they be victorious and invincible. 5. The nations in friendship or alliance with America. 6. The American Ambassadors at foreign courts. 7. The 4th of July, 1776. 8. The memory of the officers and soldiers who have bravely fallen in defence of America. 9. South Carolina. 10. May only those Americans enjoy Freedom, who are ready to die for its defence. 11. Liberty triumphant. 12. Confusion, shame and disgrace to our enemies—may the foes to America (slaves to tyranny) humble and fall before her. 13. May the rising States of America reach the summit of human power and grandeur, and enjoy every blessing.

[1] References to the governor, lieutenant governor, and council of the state of South Carolina.
[2] Second Continental Congress.
Source: Pennsylvania Gazette, July 30, 1777.

Each toast being succeeded by a salute of 13 guns, which were fired by Capt. Grimball's company from their two field pieces with admirable regularity. The day having been spent in festivity and the most conspicuous joy and harmony; the evening was concluded with illuminations, &c. far exceeding any that had ever been exhibited before.

 ## *Annapolis, Maryland,* 1788

The battle over ratifying the Constitution (discussed in Chapter 7) threatened to split the new nation apart. In an effort to mobilize public opinion behind the Constitution, supporters sponsored public celebrations of ratification as it occurred in each state. The following news item reports on one such celebration in Maryland.

ANNAPOLIS, April 30.—Monday the 28th instant being the day appointed by the honorable convention of this State, for the ratification of the Federal Government, that solemn, and happy event accordingly took place at Three o'clock in the afternoon.

The Members present at this ceremony amounted to seventy-four, of which number the names of sixty-three were subscribed to the instrument of ratification. The great and important business being completed, the members, preceded by the honorable the President of that body, in consequence of an invitation from the citizens of Annapolis, retired to Mr. Mann's Tavern, where an elegant entertainment was provided, at which were also present many strangers of distinction, and several respectable inhabitants of the city. The company consisted of nearly Two Hundred Persons. The cordiality, and festivity that appeared in the countenance, and conduct of each guest, were the strongest testimonies of the general satisfaction felt on this happy occasion.

After dinner the following Toasts, with a discharge of Thirteen Cannon to each, were given:

1. The United States and Congress.
2. Louis the XVI King of France, and the friendly powers in Europe.
3. The State of Maryland and the present Convention.
4. The late Federal Convention.[1]
5. General Washington.
6. Marquis La Fayette.[2]

[1] The Convention that had drafted the Constitution in Philadelphia in summer 1787.
[2] A French officer and close associate of George Washington who joined the patriot cause.
Source: Pennsylvania Gazette, May 14, 1788.

7. To the memory of the brave officers and soldiers who fell defending America during the late war.

8. May Agriculture, Manufactures and Commerce flourish in the United States.

9. Success to useful Learning and the Arts and Sciences.

10. The late American Army and Navy.

11. The Count Rochambeau,[3] and the French Army and Navy which served in America.

12. May our public councils ever be actuated by wisdom and patriotism.

13. May all the States of America join heartily in adopting and making effectual the proposed Federal Government.

When the fifth toast was proclaimed by the President, a portrait of the Hero, in respect, and in honor to whom that toast was announced, and which had been artfully concealed behind a curtain at the head of the room, was suddenly displayed. The powers of the pen, or the pencil, are inadequate to the description of those feelings that animated the hearts, and glowed in the countenances of the spectators. A general burst of applause testified at once the strong remembrance of past services, and an ardent gratitude for present endeavours and patriotic perseverance.

The entertainment was concluded with a ball at the Assembly-Room, at which the Ladies appeared to partake of the general joy in an equal proportion with the Gentlemen. In a word, all classes of people gave the strongest proofs of their satisfaction on this joyful event.

[3] Commander of French troops at the Battle of Yorktown.

SONGS

 ## To the Ladies

> This song appeared in the *Boston News-Letter* in 1769. It rallied support for the nonimportation movement aimed at overturning the Townshend Duties, a series of taxes imposed by Parliament on colonial imports in 1767.

Young ladies in our town, and those that live round,
Let a friend at this season advise you;
Since money's so scarce, and times are growing worse,
Strange things may soon hap and surprise you.

Source: Frank Moore, editor, *Songs and Ballads of the American Revolution* (1856; repr., New York: Arno Press, 1969), 48–50.

First, then, throw aside your topknots[1] of pride;
Wear none but your own country linen;
Of economy boast, let your pride be the most
To show clothes of your own make and spinning.

What if homespun they say is not quite so gay
As brocades, yet be not in a passion,
For when once it is known this is much worn in town,
One and all will cry out — 'Tis the fashion!

And, as one, all agree, that you'll not married be
To such as will wear London factory,
But at first sight refuse, tell 'em such you will choose
As encourage our own manufactory.

No more ribbons wear, nor in rich silks appear;
Love your country much better than fine things;
Begin without passion, 'twill soon be the fashion
To grace you smooth lock with a twine of string.

Throw aside your Bohea, and your Green Hyson[2] tea,
And all things with a new-fashion duty;
Procure a good store of the choice Labrador,[3]
For there'll soon be enough here to suit you.

These do without fear, and to all you'll appear,
Fair, charming, true, lovely and clever;
Though the times remain darkish; young men may be sparkish,
And love you much stronger than ever.

Then make yourselves easy, for no one will teaze ye,
Nor *tax* you, if chancing to sneer
At the sense-ridden tools, who think all us fools;
But they'll find the reverse far and near.

---

[1] Fancy headdresses worn by women of fashion.

[2] Bohea and Green Hyson were types of tea imported to the colonies.

[3] An alternative to foreign tea, made from the red-root bush native to New England.

5

The New Recruit, or the Gallant Volunteer, A New Song

Recruitment was a constant problem for the Continental Army after the disastrous campaign of 1776. Drink and song helped facilitate the process, especially when recruiters appeared at taverns or other public places. It is easy to imagine this song being sung on such an occasion.

Come on my hearts of tempered steel,
And leave your girls and farms,
Your sports and plays and holidays,
And hark, away to arms!
And to conquest we will go, will go, will go,
And to conquest we will go.

A Soldier is a gentleman,
His honour is his life,
And he that won't stand to his post,
Will never stand by his wife,
And to conquest we will go, &c.

For love and honour are the same,
Or else so near an ally,
That neither can exist alone,
But flourish side by side.
And to conquest we will go, &c.

So fare you well sweethearts a while,
You smiling girls adieu;
And when we drub the dogs away,[1]
We kiss it out with you.
And to conquest we will go, &c.

The spring is up, the winter flies,
The hills are green and gay,
And all inviting honour calls,
Away, my boys, away.
And to conquest we will go, &c.

In shady tents, by cooling streams,
With hearts all firm and free,
We chase the cares of life away,
In songs of liberty.
And to conquest we will go, &c.

[1] Send the redcoats retreating.
Source: Pennsylvania Packet, April 8, 1778.

No foreign slaves shall give us law,
No British tyrants reign;
Tis Independence made us free;
And freedom we maintain.
And to conquest we will go, &c.

We charge the foe from post to post,
Attack their works and lines,
Or by some well laid stratagem,
We make them all Burgoynes.[2]
And to conquest we will go, &c.

And when the war is over, boys,
Then down we sit at ease,
And plow and sow and reap and mow,
And live just as we please.
When from conquest we shall go, &c.

Each hearty lad shall take his lass,
And beaming like a star,
And in her softer arms forget,
The dangers of the war.
When to conquest we did go, &c.

The rising world shall sing of us,
A thousand years to come,
And to their children's children tell,
The Wonders we have done.
When to conquest we did go, &c.

So my honest fellows here's my hand,
My heart, my very soul,
With all the joys of Liberty,
Good fortune and a bowl.[3]
And to conquest we will go, &c.

[2] British general John Burgoyne suffered a humiliating defeat at the Battle of Saratoga in 1777.

[3] A punch bowl.

The Epilogue

Loyalists also used toasts and songs to express their political opinions, as this song attests. It appeared in October 1778 on ballad sheets published in British-occupied Philadelphia and New York. Its title suggests that the songwriter thought the war almost over and decided in the British favor. The tune is borrowed from the popular British song "Derry Down."

Our farce is now finish'd, your sport's at an end,
But ere you depart, let the voice of a friend
By way of a chorus, the evening crown
With a song to the tune of a hey derry down,
Derry down, down, hey derry down . . .

Let Washington now from his mountains descend,
Who knows but in George[1] he may still find a friend;
A Briton, altho' he loves bottle and wench,
Is an honester fellow than parle vous French.

Our great Independence we give to the wind,
And pray that Great Britain may once more be kind.
In this jovial song all hostility ends,
And Britons and we will for ever be friends.

Boys fill me a bumper! now join in the chorus!
There is happiness still in the prospect before us,
In this sparkling glass, all hostility ends,
And Britons and we will for ever be friends.

Good night! my good people, retire to your houses,
Fair ladies, I beg you, convince your dear spouses
That Britons and we are united in bliss,
And ratify all with a conjugal kiss.

Once more, here's a health[2] to the king and queen!
Confusion to him, who on rancor and spleen,
Refuses to drink with an English friend,
Immutable amity to the world's end.

[1] King George III of Britain.
[2] A toast.
Source: Moore, *Songs and Ballads of the American Revolution,* 220–23.

The Dance

This song from 1781 celebrates the American victory at Yorktown, Virginia, the last major battle of the war. Like many songs celebrating military victories, it incorporates the names of each army's commanding officers, lionizing the victors and lampooning the defeated. It is set to the tune of "Yankee Doodle," a popular British song that the patriots adapted to their cause.

Cornwallis[1] led a country dance,
The like was never seen, sir,
Much retrograde and much advance,
And all with General Greene,[2] sir.

They rambled up and rambled down,
Join'd hands, then off they run, sir,
Our General Greene to Charlestown,[3]
The earl to Wilmington,[4] sir.

Greene, in the South, then danc'd a set,
And got a mighty name, sir.
Cornwallis jigg'd with young Fayette,[5]
But suffer'd in his fame, sir.

Then down he figur'd to the shore,
Most like a lordly dancer,
And on his courtly honor swore,
He would no more advance, sir.

Quoth he, my guards are weary grown
With footing country dances,
They never at St. James's[6] shone,
At capers, kick or prances.

Though men so gallant ne'er were seen,
While sauntering on parade, sir,
Or wriggling o'er the park's smooth green,
Or at a masquerade, sir.

[1] The British commander at Yorktown.

[2] The commander of the Continental troops who lured Cornwallis into Virginia from the Carolinas.

[3] Charleston, South Carolina.

[4] North Carolina.

[5] The Marquis de Lafayette.

[6] St. James Palace in Britain (i.e., they were never skilled dancers at home).

Source: Moore, *Songs and Ballads of the American Revolution,* 363–66.

Yet are red heels and long-lac'd skirts,
For stumps and briars meet, sir?
Or stand they chance with hunting-shirts,
Or hardy veteran feet, sir? . . .

And Washington, Columbia's son,
Who's easy nature taught, sir,
That grace which can't by pains be won,
Or Plutus'[7] gold be bought, sir.

Now hand in hand they circle round,
This ever-dancing peer, sir;
Their gentle movements, soon confound
The earl, as they draw near, sir.

His music soon forgets to play—
His feet can no more move, sir,
And all his bands now curse the day,
They jigged to our shore, sir.

Now Tories all, what can ye say?
Come—is not this a griper,[8]
That while your hopes are danc'd away,
'Tis you must pay the piper.

[7] Greek god of the underworld.
[8] A cause for complaint.

Analyzing the Source

REFLECTING ON THE SOURCE

1. Using your notes from the table on page 97, what were the most significant changes in the occasions and methods of public toast making between 1765 and 1788? Which elements of these rituals remained essentially unchanged?

2. Which of the songs reproduced here invoke social drinking (both alcoholic and nonalcoholic) in their lyrics? How is that drinking defined by gender, and what political significance is attached to it in these songs?

3. How did references to King George III and other symbols of British power change over time or according to audience in these toasts and songs? Who or what replaced the king as the new focal points of American patriotism?

MAKING CONNECTIONS

4. Do you think these songs and toasts describe mostly change or stability in American society during the Revolutionary era? How does your answer to that

question differ if you look at specific social groups referred to in these sources, such as women, soldiers, or political leaders?

5. Using your notes from the table on page 97, what do these songs tell you about this society's definitions of male and female roles in public life? How did these songs attempt to mobilize men and women for the patriot cause, and did their messages challenge or reinforce traditional gender roles?

6. Eighteenth-century Americans used toasts and songs to describe who they were as well as who they were not. What individuals or groups were marked as outsiders or exiles from the body politic in these sources? Do you see any evidence here of how rituals of public celebration also intimidated or coerced the reluctant or neutral into supporting a particular cause?

Beyond the Source

The necessity of mobilizing and maintaining support for the patriot cause during the American Revolution did much to politicize drinking culture in the new nation. During the 1760s and 1770s, patriot leaders were quite liberal with the punch bowl and strong beer during public festivities meant to draw support to their cause. Once the war was over, the Fourth of July and George Washington's birthday became new public holidays that called for parades, illuminations, bonfires, fireworks, military parades, and of course, drink and song. The rivalry between the Federalists and Democratic Republicans during the 1790s intensified the political partisanship associated with such events, as each side scrambled to use the new symbols and rituals of American civic culture to its own advantage. As the 1790s gave way to the nineteenth century, marginalized groups such as free blacks and women asserted their place in the new nation's political and social order by appropriating the rites of public celebration for their own purposes. In 1796, a group of women in York, Pennsylvania, attending an outdoor tea party made eight toasts honoring President Washington and the federal government, but ended with one to "The Rights of Women." In 1810, free blacks in Boston celebrating the American ban on the transatlantic slave trade made nine toasts to individuals, groups, and nations who supported the abolitionist cause. Interspersed in their list were the names of several honorees probably not typically cited in toasts printed in American newspapers:

> 2. *Mr. Wilberforce*, and other members who advocated the abolition of the slave trade in the British Parliament. . . .
> 4. The Trustees of the African School in *Boston*. . . .
> 8. Liberty to our African brethren in *St. Domingo* [Haiti, the site of a successful slave revolution in the 1790s], and elsewhere.

These African American celebrants had appropriated one of the most common practices in American popular politics to express their own revolutionary cause: the end of slavery.

The political activism associated with public drinking in the new nation put some social reformers ill at ease. They associated tavern going with disorder and contention and demonized public drinking as socially aberrant behavior. Nevertheless, drinking songs and toasts remained fixtures of nineteenth-century American politics, and both survive in modified forms today. Patriotic songs are still an important part of our civic rituals, as anyone who has stood for the performance of "The Star-Spangled Banner" at the start of a sporting event can attest. In the wake of the September 11, 2001, terrorist attacks on the United States, patriotic songs became an important part of how Americans communally acknowledged the tragedy.

Most people encounter formal toasts today only at wedding celebrations, but toasting remains a part of modern politics in the rarefied world of state dinners and diplomatic protocol. In those contexts, the practice can still generate controversy. During a trip to China in March 1997, Vice President Al Gore came under fire in the American press for engaging in toasts with his host, Prime Minister Li Peng, the person responsible for the massacre of prodemocracy demonstrators in Tiananmen Square several years earlier. When photos of this toast appeared in American newspapers, many critics used the occasion to chastise the Clinton administration for placing trade concessions above human rights in its China policy.

Finding and Supplementing the Source

Songs and toasts from the Revolutionary era that addressed the political issues of the day were often reproduced in newspapers. A useful resource for tracking down such items is the online database *Accessible Archives* (**accessible.com**), which provides full-text articles from eighteenth- and nineteenth-century American newspapers. This database is available by subscription only, so you will want to check with a reference librarian to see if you can gain access to it. For more information on using eighteenth-century newspapers, see "Finding and Supplementing the Source" in Chapter 3 (p. 63).

An important nineteenth-century collection of popular political songs from the Revolutionary era is available in a modern edition: Frank Moore, editor, *Songs and Ballads of the American Revolution* (1856; New York: Arno Press, 1969). Researchers interested in ballad sheets will also want to consult the Library of Congress's Web site, *An American Time Capsule: Three Centuries of Broadsides and Other Political Ephemera* (**memory.loc.gov/ammem/rbpehtml/pehome.html**), which includes some examples of Revolutionary era songs. Travel narratives provide some of the best descriptions of public drinking in early America. Especially useful in this regard are the narratives of Sarah Kemble Knight and Dr. Alexander Hamilton, both of which can be found in Wendy Martin, editor, *Colonial American Travel Narratives* (New York: Penguin Books, 1994).

Two classic articles on the roles of drink and song respectively in the coming of the Revolution are Richard J. Hooker, "The American Revolution Seen through a Wine Glass," *William and Mary Quarterly,* third series, 11 (1954): 52–77, and Arthur M. Schlesinger, "A Note on Songs as Patriot Propaganda, 1765–1776," *William and Mary Quarterly,* third series, 11 (1954): 78–88. More recently, historians have used drinking and tavern going to explore social and political relationships in early American society. See for example Sharon V. Salinger, *Taverns and Drinking in Early America* (Baltimore, Md.: Johns Hopkins University Press, 2002); Peter Thompson, *Rum Punch and Revolution: Tavern-going and Public Life in Eighteenth-Century Philadelphia* (Philadelphia: University of Pennsylvania Press, 1999); and David W. Conroy, *In Public Houses: Drink and the Revolution of Authority in Colonial Massachusetts* (Chapel Hill: University of North Carolina Press, 1995). For drinking and gender roles in early America, see Jessica Kross, "'If you will not drink with me, you must fight me': The Sociology of Drinking in the Middle Colonies," *Pennsylvania History* 64 (1997): 28–55, and Bruce Dorsey, *Reforming Men and Women: Gender in the Antebellum City* (Ithaca, N.Y.: Cornell University Press, 2002).

A good introduction to the festive culture of the colonial era is Richard L. Bushman, *King and People in Provincial Massachusetts* (Chapel Hill: University of North Carolina Press, 1985). Two studies of the political meaning of festive culture in the early United States are Simon P. Newman, *Parades and Politics of the Streets: Festive Culture in the Early American Republic* (Philadelphia: University of Pennsylvania Press, 1997), and David Waldstreicher, *In the Midst of Perpetual Fetes: The Making of American Nationalism, 1776–1820* (Chapel Hill: University of North Carolina Press, 1997).

CHAPTER 6

The Question of Female Citizenship

Court Records from the New Nation

William and Anna Martin left home in a hurry. William was an artillery officer in the British army, and when it evacuated Boston in early 1776, he and Anna went with it. They left behind a substantial amount of property. Most of the family's wealth came from Anna, the daughter of a prosperous Boston merchant. When her father died in 1770, she had inherited a house with a wharf and stables in Boston, a farm in Braintree, and more than eight hundred acres of land in Massachusetts and New Hampshire.

The Martins were just two of the thousands of Americans who went into exile in Britain, Canada, or the West Indies as a result of the Revolution. Many loyalists tried to sit out the war by avoiding public life or military service, but the patriots did not make that easy to do. Local and state governments demanded loyalty oaths from those people they considered suspect and expected adult males to serve in the militia. Many loyalists left home for what they hoped would be temporary stays abroad until the rebellion ended. Others were forced out by neighbors and enemies anxious to seize their property. By the war's end, about eighty thousand loyalists had left the United States. They ranged from some of the wealthiest families in British North America to slaves who did not even own the clothes on their backs.

We do not know whether William and Anna Martin intended for their exile to be permanent, but they never returned to Boston. They followed the British Army to Nova Scotia and then to New York City, where they stayed until the army evacuated in 1783. From there the Martins resettled in England. In the eyes of the revolutionary government of Massachusetts, the Martins were "absentees," people who had expressed their political allegiance with their feet by leaving the state after the War for Independence broke out on April 19,

1775. Under a law passed in 1779, Massachusetts claimed the right to confiscate the property left behind by such absentees, and the state did so with the Martins' estate in 1781, selling the land and buildings to raise money for the Massachusetts treasury.

In 1801 James Martin, the son and heir of William and Anna (both of whom had since died), sued the state of Massachusetts for restoration of the confiscated property. After losing his case in a lower court, he appealed it to the Massachusetts Supreme Court, which heard the case in 1805. Such legal cases were not uncommon in the aftermath of the Revolution. The peace treaty that ended the war recommended that the states allow loyalists to recover lost property. The novelty of *Martin v. Massachusetts* rested in its focus on the political and legal status of Anna Martin. Both sides agreed that the property in question had belonged to Anna by right of her inheritance from her father. James Martin's attorneys argued that because Anna was a wife, she had no choice but to follow her husband into exile, and therefore, she was not subject to the state's confiscation law. The state's attorneys argued that the law's wording explicitly extended its authority over women as well as men, and therefore, the confiscation was legal and binding. Each side also argued other points about legal jurisdiction and due process, but the case ultimately hinged on the question of Anna Martin's status as a wife and citizen: did she voluntarily renounce her allegiance to Massachusetts when she left the state, or was she, as a woman and wife, a person who could exercise no option other than to obey her husband's wishes?

Martin v. Massachusetts tells us much about the limits and possibilities of change in women's legal status during the Revolutionary era. In a famous exchange of letters in 1776, Abigail and John Adams debated the extent to which political independence from Great Britain should affect gender relations in the new nation. Abigail urged her husband and his fellow delegates at the Second Continental Congress to "remember the Ladies" in the "new code of laws" they would pass after declaring independence, and she warned him that if they did not, women would not "hold ourselves bound by any laws in which we have no voice, or Representation." John replied dismissively to Abigail's request, noting that the patriots' cause against Britain had "loosened the bands of government everywhere," so that children, apprentices, students, slaves, Indians, and now even wives challenged the authority of their rightful masters. Historians have long used this exchange to illustrate dissension within American society over the meaning of independence. Many Americans previously excluded from the political process hoped that the Revolution would make possible an expansion in their rights and liberties, but many patriot leaders worked to limit the impact that independence from Britain had on the people over whom they claimed authority.

The legal dispute over Anna Martin's property illustrates the questions the Revolution raised about female citizenship. Before the Revolution, the colonists were subjects of the British Crown. A person became a subject to the Crown upon birth, and as the word implies, subjecthood entailed obligations of submission, obedience, and loyalty. When the American patriots declared independence, they disavowed their status as subjects and redefined themselves as citizens of a republic. Then, as now, citizenship implied choice and equality: a person became a citizen by entering into a social contract with others and voluntarily assenting to the laws their government created. This social contract equated property ownership with citizenship: only those individuals who held property had the economic and political independence necessary to enter into the social contract. People without property—children, servants, slaves, the laboring poor—were by definition too dependent upon others to live and act independently as fully enfranchised citizens. Under the old system of monarchy, subjecthood was hierarchical and authoritarian, but also inclusive; the British Crown claimed all sorts of people as its subjects, regardless of their race, sex, or ethnic origin. Citizenship in the new nation was egalitarian and contractual, but also exclusive; some people possessed the attributes necessary to become citizens while others lacked them entirely.

In *Martin v. Massachusetts*, attorneys and judges debated the nature of female citizenship. The case raised all sorts of nettlesome questions about the intersection of property, gender, and a woman's allegiance to her husband and country. The fact that the property in question had belonged to Anna Martin suggested that she had the means to act independently when she chose to give her allegiance to Britain. On the other hand, she was also a wife, bound by personal vows, religious principles, and the law to submit to the will of her husband. The lawyers' arguments and judges' opinions in *Martin v. Massachusetts* raised a host of questions about citizenship in the new nation. What possible obligations could a woman owe to the republic, and could those obligations take precedence over marriage vows? Did independence turn *all* of the former British subjects in the thirteen colonies—or only some of them—into citizens of the new nation? And, if only some subjects became citizens, how did gender figure into that equation?

Using Court Records as a Source

Court cases can be difficult to read because lawyers and judges speak and write in their own specialized language. This problem is compounded when a researcher confronts historical court cases that deal with legal principles and terms no longer commonly used today. Thus, the best place to start when analyzing a source such as *Martin v. Massachusetts* is with making sure you understand the key legal concepts and language involved in the case.

A married woman in eighteenth-century Anglo-American law was known as a "feme-covert" (the plural "femes-covert" is often used in the source on pp. 114–15). This term meant a wife was literally covered by her husband: she could not buy, sell, or own property independently of him; she could not write her own will or enter into contracts; she could not sue or be sued in a court of law; and she could not vote, serve on juries, or hold public office. In short, a woman had no recognized legal identity because the law assumed that her husband spoke and acted for her.

A married woman's status as a feme-covert severely restricted her access to property, yet Anglo-American legal custom did provide certain protections to women in this regard. A woman such as Anna Martin who inherited real estate surrendered its management to her husband upon marriage but retained an interest in it. In legal terms, a husband acquired only a "life estate" in such property: he could lease or rent it and enjoy the profits it generated, but he did not own the property in "fee simple," that is, with no restrictions on transfer of ownership. He could not permanently sell or bequeath the property in question to someone else without his wife's consent. When he died, the management of the property reverted to his wife or her heirs. This legal custom ensured that property the wife brought to the marriage would remain in her family line; her husband could not divert it to the children of a previous or subsequent marriage.

Another important custom that governed female access to property was a woman's "dower right." Anglo-American probate courts, which settled estates when a property owner died without a will, set aside one-third of the estate (both real estate and personal property) to support the widow of the deceased. This reservation was known as a "dower right" or "widow's thirds." Its purpose was to provide for a woman's subsistence during her widowhood. It did not grant her full possession of that property, only the right to the revenues it produced. Upon her remarriage or death, full possession of the property in question reverted to the heirs of her deceased husband.

The legal definitions of a feme-covert and dower right figured prominently in the deliberation of *Martin v. Massachusetts,* as is evident in the following excerpt from the court case. In this passage, Massachusetts Solicitor General Daniel Davis is referring to both a wife's status as a feme-covert and her dower right. Note how he interprets the wording of the Confiscation Act to mean that it applies to absentee women as well as men.

Asks whether a wife can commit any of the offenses that the law identifies as causes for confiscation

Wording of the Confiscation Act that protects the dower right of women who remained in the United States after their loyalist husbands left the country

The question then is: whether a *feme-covert* is capable of committing the offences, or any *one* of the offenses specified in the statute?[1] For if a *feme-covert* could commit any one of the offences mentioned, and that offence be well laid in the information, the judgment ought to be affirmed.[2] That a *feme-covert* could perform *one,* at least, of the acts described, that of withdrawing herself from the State into parts and places under the dominion of the King of *Great Britain,* &c. is proved by the *seventh section*—which provides, "that when the *wife* or widow of any of the persons aforedescribed, *shall have remained* within the jurisdiction of any of the said United States &c. she shall be entitled to the improvements and income of one third part of her husband's real and personal estate, after payment of debts, during her life *and continuance within* the said United States; and her dower therein shall be set

---

[1] The Massachusetts Confiscation Act of 1779.

[2] The judgment of the lower court upholding the confiscation should stand.

off to her by the judge of probate in like manner as it might have been if her husband had *died intestate*,[3] within the jurisdiction of this State." The exception proves the rule. *Wives* who *remained here* are mentioned as an exception—the statute therefore embraced all persons who did not remain—who withdrew. The very supposition that *some* persons of this description, some *femes-covert* might remain, implies that all had the *power* of remaining or withdrawing as they pleased—and if *femes-covert* had not been *intended* to be included under the previous *general words* of the statute there could have been no necessity of making the exception in favour of those who remained behind.

> Argues that the Confiscation Act subjects to confiscation all property held by women who chose to follow their husbands into exile

The Massachusetts Confiscation Act of 1779 penalized loyalists by seizing the property they left behind when they fled the state. The preamble of the Confiscation Act legitimized such confiscations by claiming that the absentees had broken the social contract by failing to provide assistance to the state during wartime. By fleeing its borders, they renounced their citizenship, freeing the state from its obligation to protect their property and allowing the government to dispose of the abandoned property as it saw fit. This logic became much murkier when applied to women. Most of the states recognized a woman's dower right when they confiscated loyalist estates, preserving one-third of the property to support the dependent women and children of absentees. The Massachusetts Confiscation Act specifically preserved the dower right of loyalist wives who stayed in America, but what about a woman such as Anna Martin who followed her husband into exile? Was she also guilty of breaking the social contract?

In debating this question, the lawyers and judges involved in *Martin v. Massachusetts* had two choices. If the court upheld the confiscation of Anna Martin's property, then it would endorse the idea that a married woman could choose her political allegiance and be held accountable for it independently of her husband. Such a decision would seriously undermine the legal notion of a feme-covert. If the court overturned the confiscation, it would uphold the more traditional view of married women as femes-covert, but it would also give land back to loyalists (or in this case, their heirs), which would undoubtedly prove a politically unpopular decision.

Advantages and Disadvantages of Working with Court Records

Popular images of the law present it as something divinely ordained, neutral, and unchanging, literally carved in stone like the commandments Moses carried down from a mountaintop. The architecture of American courthouses, built in the style of ancient Greek temples and adorned with statues of blindfolded female figures holding the scales of justice, certainly encourage such

---

[3] Without a will.

associations. Legal historians, however, emphasize the social and political context within which laws are made and enforced. Just as Abigail Adams recognized that declaring independence would make necessary a "new code of laws," legal historians find in the law a way of examining how society responds to changing political or social conditions. Legal decisions, from landmark Supreme Court cases such as *Roe v. Wade* to more obscure cases heard in local and state courts, provide a mirror on the critical issues of their day.

Examining court cases also helps historians see how legal abstractions get put into practice. Take for example the republican rhetoric of the American Revolution. The patriots enshrined liberty, equality, and independence as the founding principles of the new nation, but how did these ideas actually affect social relations within the United States, and how did people react when these principles conflicted with traditional ideas about how society should work? In *Martin v. Massachusetts*, the court had to reconsider the meaning of citizenship in light of a clash between a Revolutionary commitment to equality and traditional gender roles that accorded women second-class status to men.

Another advantage to working with court cases and legal documents is their narrative structure. Each court case tells a story with a clear beginning, middle, and end. Anglo-American legal culture emphasizes precedent and logic; lawyers build cases and judges render decisions based upon what previous cases have said and the evidence before them. Anyone who has ever watched a film or television show based on a court trial is familiar with the adversarial nature of the American legal process; each side gets to present its case, countering the evidence and arguments presented by the other. Once you comprehend the vocabulary and procedure used in such court cases, you will find that they often render complex ideas in a concise, concrete manner.

Of course, the logic and order evident in a court case can also be a disadvantage if you do not approach the source with a critical eye. It is always important to ask of this type of source, who made the law in question and why? Who is controlling its interpretation and execution? Legal decisions do not take place in a vacuum; all sorts of external factors influence how lawyers, witnesses, juries, and judges present and interpret evidence. Racism, prejudice, or outright bribery can and do corrupt the legal process. Legal historians must also be aware of more subtle biases that affect the administration of the law.

Consider for example the political affiliations involved in the *Martin v. Massachusetts* case. All four of the judges who rendered written opinions in this case belonged to the Federalist Party, which generally attracted social and political conservatives. As a group, these judges were probably not particularly interested in using this case to rewrite the law on women's rights. James Sullivan, the attorney general of Massachusetts and chief spokesman for the state's case, belonged to the Democratic-Republican Party, which advocated more radical ideas about social and political equality. His argument makes a case for redefining female citizenship in light of the Revolution's commitment to contractual government. At the time of the trial, he was also Massachusetts's Democratic-Republican candidate for governor. How likely do you think it was that the judges listened to Sullivan's arguments without being prejudiced by their opposition to his politics? One does not have to accuse the judges of corruption to recognize that their decision may have been influenced by factors other than the evidence and arguments before them.

Gender bias may also have influenced the decision in the *Martin v. Massachusetts* case. This case was initiated, argued, and decided entirely by men, as was consistent with legal practices at that time. Anna Martin, the central figure in the legal arguments presented, remains mute throughout the entire proceedings. She was of course dead at the time, but neither side in the case seemed particularly interested in trying to retrieve what she thought about her loyalism, property, or status as a wife. Even if she had been alive, the legal system as it was then constructed would have offered her little opportunity to speak for herself in court. You must take into consideration the obvious gender bias built into the legal system that decided this case when determining its usefulness as a source.

Working with the Source

As you read the *Martin v. Massachusetts* case, use the tables on page 118 to organize your notes on the lawyers' and judges' interpretations of the Massachusetts Confiscation Act of 1779.

	The Lawyers' Arguments
Representing the Plaintiff, James Martin *George Blake* *Theophilus Parsons*	
Representing the Defendant (Commonwealth of Massachusetts) *Daniel Davis* *James Sullivan*	

	The Judges' Opinions
Justice Sedgwick	
Justice Strong	
Justice Dana	

The Source: *James Martin (Plaintiff in Error) v. The Commonwealth and William Bosson and Other Ter-tenants*, 1805

James Martin is identified in the case's name as the "plaintiff in error," because he was arguing that he was wronged by an error made in the lower court's decision. "The Commonwealth" identifies the state of Massachusetts as a codefendant in the suit. William Bosson and the other "ter-tenants" were the owners and/or occupants of the property at the time James Martin filed suit. "Ter" means three; thus, Bosson and three other owners and/or occupants were named as codefendants in the suit.

THE LAWYERS' ARGUMENTS

James Martin's lawsuit began in 1801 in a lower court, which upheld the confiscation of his mother's property. He appealed that decision to the Supreme Judicial Court of Massachusetts, which heard the case in 1805. His attorneys argued that the lower court had made four errors in its judgment. These "errors" were the points on which Martin made his case to the state's Supreme Court. The first three dealt with issues of the original right of ownership in the land, due process, and the lower court's jurisdiction. The fourth (referred to in the source text as the "fourth error") concerned whether Anna Martin's status as a feme-covert made her property liable for confiscation under the Massachusetts Confiscation Act of 1779. These excerpts follow the arguments of both sides on this point.

 ## The Fourth Error Identified by James Martin's Attorneys in Their Appeal

Fourthly. Because, by the information and complaint aforesaid, it doth appear that the said *William Martin* was owner of the estates aforesaid during his natural life only, and that the fee-simple[1] thereof belonged to the said *Anna Martin*, the said *William's* wife, who by the act or law aforesaid, referred to in said information, was not liable to have her estates confiscated as aforesaid, and against whom the process and judgment aforesaid could not by law extend.

---

[1] Right of ownership.

Source: All of the arguments and opinions reprinted in this chapter are excerpted from *Reports of Cases Argued and Determined in the Supreme Judicial Court of the State of Massachusetts from September 1804 to June 1805 — Both Inclusive,* volume 1 (Boston: S. & E. Butler, 1805): 347–99.

2   *George Blake, Attorney for James Martin*

As to the *fourth* error assigned. *Femes-covert* are not within the statute.[1] They are not within the *letter* of the act—almost all the provisions of the act are masculine—nothing is said about females, excepting where provision is made for their dower. It is admitted that there are cases where statutes will extend to females, where the expressions are similar to those used in this act. But it is manifest from the act itself that women were not *intended* to be included under the general description of persons mentioned.

The first *section* of the act says "that every inhabitant and member of the State who &c." Upon the strict principles of law a *feme-covert* is not a member—[she] has no *political* relation to the State any more than an alien—upon the most rigid and illiberal construction of the words she cannot be a member within the meaning of the statute. . . . The legislation[2] *intended* to exclude *femes-covert* and infants from the operation of the act—otherwise the word *inhabitant* would have been used alone, and not coupled with the word *member*. This construction is strengthened by the provision in the same (*the first*) section of the act respecting an oath of allegiance. A *feme-covert* was never holden to take an oath of allegiance. The statute is highly penal—the court therefore will not extend it beyond the express words, or obvious meaning, by an equitable construction. The preamble is a key to unlock the meaning. What says the preamble?

> "Whereas every government has a right to command the personal services of all its members, whenever the exigencies of the State shall require it, especially in times of an impending or actual invasion, no member thereof can then withdraw himself from the jurisdiction of the government, and thereby deprive it of *his personal service,*[3] without justly incurring the forfeiture of all *his* property, rights and liberties holden under and derived from that conclusion of government, to the support of which *he* hath refused to afford *his* aid and assistance: and whereas the King of *Great Britain* did cause &c. &c. whereupon it became the indispensable duty of all the *people* of said States forthwith to *unite in defence* of their common freedom, and *by arms* to oppose the fleets and armies of the said King; yet, nevertheless, divers[4] of the *members* of this and the other United States of America, evilly disposed, or regardless of their duty towards their country, did withdraw themselves &c. &c. *aiding* or giving encouragement and countenance to the operations of the fleets and armies of the said King against the United States aforesaid."

It is impossible to read the preamble to the statute without seeing the object and intention of the act. The object was not to punish, but to retain the

---

[1] The Massachusetts Confiscation Act of 1779.

[2] The Confiscation Act.

[3] Military service.

[4] Many.

physical force of the state, as is evident from the expressions, *personal services in times of actual invasion*—opposing *by arms*—*aiding* the enemy, &c. How much physical force is retained by retaining married women? What are the *personal services* they are to render in opposing by *force* an actual invasion? What *aid* can they give to an enemy? So far are women from being of service in the defence of a country against the attacks of an enemy that it is frequently thought expedient to send them out of the way, lest they impede the operations of their own party.

In construing statutes[5] no rule is better established than that *general expressions* shall be *restrained* by the manifest intent of the legislature to be collected from the whole act taken together.

. . . And can it be supposed, in the case before the court, that the legislature contemplated the case of a wife withdrawing with her husband? It ought not to be, and surely was not, intended that she should be exposed to the loss of all her property for withdrawing from the government with her husband. If he commanded it she was bound to obey him, by a law paramount to all other laws—the law of God.

[5] In interpreting laws.

3 *Daniel Davis, Solicitor General for Massachusetts*

As to the *fourth original* error. It is contended by the counsel for the plaintiff in error, that the statute does not extend to *femes-covert*, that women are not named, are not mentioned in the statute. The *first section* says, *every* inhabitant and member. *Anna Martin* was an inhabitant, and appears by the record to have been so. She is therefore within the statute. The *third section* says, any *person*—this is certainly sufficiently comprehensive to include all persons who could commit any of the offences mentioned in the act. The question then is: whether a *feme-covert* is capable of committing the offences, or any *one* of the offences specified in the statute? For if a *feme-covert* could commit any one of the offences mentioned, and that offence be well laid in the information, the judgment ought to be affirmed. That a *feme-covert* could perform *one*, at least, of the acts described, that of withdrawing herself from the State into parts and places under the dominion of the King of *Great Britain*, &c. is proved by the *seventh section*—which provides, "that when the *wife* or widow of any of the persons afore-described, *shall have remained* within the jurisdiction of any of the said United States &c. she shall be entitled to the improvements and income of one third part of her husband's real and personal estate, after payment of debts, during her life *and continuance within* the said United States; and her dower therein shall be set off to her by the judge of probate in like manner as it might have been if her husband had *died intestate,*[1] within the jurisdiction of this State." The exception proves the rule. *Wives* who *remained here* are mentioned as an exception—the statute therefore embraced all persons who did not remain—who withdrew. The very supposition that *some* persons of this description, some *femes-covert* might remain, implies that all had the *power* of remaining or withdrawing as they pleased—and if *femes-covert* had not been *intended* to be included under the previous *general words* of the statute there could have been no necessity of making the exception in favour of those who remained behind. If this be not so, still there is another reason. Where the husband has abjured[2] the realm the relation is dissolved between the husband and wife. This act of the husband, *William Martin*, amounts to an abjuration of the realm—and the consequence is that she became sole seized.[3] If this consequence is not liked, then they may both be considered as having abjured, which is in itself treason—which a *feme-covert* can certainly commit, and by which she forfeits her estate—and this process is sufficient to confiscate her estate for her act of treason.

[1] Without a will.
[2] Renounced his allegiance.
[3] Sole owner of the property.

4 *James Sullivan, Attorney General for Massachusetts*

Under the *fourth* error *originally* assigned it has been contended by the counsel for the plaintiff that the statute did not extend to *femes-covert*. And it is said that the *words* of the act do not include them because the words are in the masculine gender—that they are *him, his,* &c. The same reasoning would go to prove that the *Constitution* of the Commonwealth[1] does not extend to women—secures to them no rights, no privileges—for it has no words in the feminine gender: it would prove that a great variety of crimes, made so by statute, could not be committed by women, because the statutes had used only the words *him* and *his*. It is also said that a *feme-covert* is not an *inhabitant* and *member* of the State. Surely a *feme-covert* can be an inhabitant, in every sense of the word. Who are members of the body-politic? Are not all the *citizens,* members; infants, idiots, insane or whatever may be their *relative* situations in society? Cannot a *feme-covert* levy war and conspire to levy war? She certainly can commit treason—and if so, there is no one act mentioned in the statute which she is not capable of performing. In the case before the court she was defaulted[2]—this, as in common civil actions, which may be brought against a *feme-covert*, confesses the facts alleged.

[1] Massachusetts.
[2] Failed to appear in court to contest the original confiscation.

Theophilus Parsons, Attorney for James Martin

The real question is whether the statute was intended to include persons who have, by law, no wills of their own. The statute extends to persons who have *freely* renounced their relation to the State. Infants, insane, *femes-covert*, all of whom the law considers as having no will, cannot act *freely*. Can they freely renounce? The statute meant such, and such only, as could. Is the State entitled to the *personal* services of a *femes-covert* to defend it in war? Can she render any? What aid and comfort can she give to an invading enemy? Has she the control of property? Is she ever required to take the oath of allegiance? — As to the provision in the statute for dower; that has no relation to *her* property — it is merely the donation of the State, giving to her a part of that which was absolutely its own. . . . It has been said that the husband abjured the realm, and that this dissolved the marriage contract — this is a strange consequence, and one till now unheard of.

THE JUSTICES' OPINIONS

Like the Supreme Court of the United States, the Supreme Judicial Court of Massachusetts did not use a jury. Rather, it was made up of five justices who heard each case and rendered a decision by vote. The justices then issued written opinions explaining their votes. Five justices heard *Martin v. Massachusetts,* and four of those wrote opinions. Justice George Thacher called for reversing the confiscation because of a procedural error in the lower court, but he did not address the issue of Anne Martin's status as a feme-covert in his opinion. The three remaining written opinions all addressed the "fourth error" concerning Anne Martin's status as a feme-covert, and they are excerpted below.

Justice Theodore Sedgwick

. . . By the record before us it appears that *William Martin* and *Anna Martin,* the father and mother of the plaintiff in error, are *jointly* charged with the several acts which are alleged in the libel[1] of the Attorney-General as incurring the forfeiture for which he sued — that, since the 19th day of *April* 1775, they had levied war and conspired to levy war against the provinces, or colonies, or United States: that they had, adhered[2] to the king of *Great Britain* his fleets and armies and had given to them aid and comfort; that since that time they had,

[1] Statement of charges against the Martins.
[2] Pledged their allegiance.

without permission of the legislative or executive authority of any of the United States, withdrawn themselves therefrom into parts and places under the acknowledged authority of the king of *Great Britain*—all these charged as done jointly by the husband and wife—and we are called upon, by matter apparent on the record and by one of the errors expressly assigned, to say whether a *feme-covert* for *any* of these acts, *performed with her husband*, is within the intention of the statute: and I think that she is not.

In construing statutes the great object is to discover from the words, the subject-matter, the mischiefs contemplated and the remedies proposed, what was the true meaning and design of the legislature. In the relation of husband and wife the law makes, in her behalf, such an allowance for the authority of the husband and her duty of obedience, that guilt is not imputed to *her* for actions performed jointly by them, unless of the most heinous and aggravated nature. For instance—the law says, whoever steals shall be punished, and yet if the wife participates in a theft with her husband she is not punishable. Innumerable other instances might be given. She is exempted from punishment, not because she is within the letter of the law if she had sufficient will to be considered as acting voluntarily and as moral agent but, because she is viewed in such a state of subjection and so under the control of her husband that she acts merely as his instrument, and that no guilt is imputable[3] to her.

Compare this with the case under consideration. In a case of great political interest, in which men of great powers and equal integrity, as said by the Attorney-General, divided; and where a *feme-covert* is not expressly included, shall we suppose her to be so by general words? Can we believe that a wife for so respecting the understanding of her husband as to submit her own opinions to his, on a subject so all-important as this, should lose her own property and forfeit the inheritance of her children? Was she to be considered as criminal because she permitted her husband to elect his own and her place of residence? Because she did not, in violation of her marriage vows, rebel against the will of her husband? So hard and cruel a construction, against the general and known principles of law on this subject, could be justified by none but strong and unequivocal expressions. So far is this from being the case in this statute, that it seems to me understood that such was the intention of the legislature—but the contrary. The preamble of the statute has described the persons whom it intended to bring within it. It is that member who "withdraws himself from the jurisdiction of the government and thereby deprives it of the benefit of his personal services." A *wife* who left the country in the company of her husband did not *withdraw* herself—but was, if I may so express it, withdrawn by him. She did not deprive the government of the benefit of her personal services—she had none to render—none were exacted of her. "The member who so withdraws, incurs," says the preamble, "the forfeiture of all his property, right and liberties holden under and delivered from that constitution of government, to the support of which he has refused to afford his aid and assistance." Can any one believe it was the intention of the legislature to demand of *femes-covert*

---

[3] Assignable.

their *aid and assistance* in the support of their constitution and government? The preamble then goes on to particularize the violation of our rights by our former sovereign, and proceeds to declare that it thereupon "became the indispensable duty of all the *people* of said states forthwith to unite in defense of their common freedom, and *by arms* to oppose the fleets and armies of the said King; yet, nevertheless, divers of the *members* of this, and of the other United States of *America*, evilly disposed or regardless of their duty towards their country did withdraw themselves, &c." Now it is unquestionably true that the *members* here spoken of as "evilly disposed" are included in the *people* above-mentioned. What then was the duty of these evilly disposed persons, for a violation of which they were to be cut off from the community to which they had belonged, and rendered aliens to it? It was "to unite in defense of their common freedom and *by arms* to oppose" an invading enemy. And can it be supposed to have been the intention of the legislature to exact the performance of this duty from *wives* in opposition to the will and command of their husbands? Can it be believed that an humane and just legislature ever intended that wives should be subjected to the horrid alternative of, either on the one hand, separating from their husbands and disobeying them, or, on the other, of sacrificing their property? It is impossible for me to suppose that such was ever their intention.

The conclusion of the preamble speaks of those who withdrew as thereby "aiding or giving encouragement and countenance to the operations" of the enemy. Were *femes-covert*, accompanying their husbands, thus considered by the legislature? I believe not. So far from believing that *wives* are within the statute, for any acts by them done jointly with their husbands, that a fair construction of the whole *act* together does, to my judgment, clearly exclude them. And I do not discern that the 7th *section* which has been cited to prove that *femes-covert*, for withdrawing with their husbands, were within the act, has the least tendency to that purpose.—This *section* does not contemplate those who withdrew with their husbands, but those who staid behind. The provision which it makes for them is not from their own estates, but from those of their husbands. And I cannot perceive that any inference is to be drawn from the one case which tends to illustrate the other. On the whole I am clearly of opinion that for this error the judgment must be reversed.

 ## 7   *Justice Simeon Strong*

. . . Upon the question whether the estates of *femes-covert* were, by this statute, liable to confiscation, I am of opinion that they were not. The *act* was intended to take the estates of those persons who had voluntarily withdrawn themselves from the country and joined the fleets and armies of *Great Britain* with whom we were then at war. Could a *feme-covert* in any reasonable sense of the words of the *act* do this? I think not. The law considers a *feme-covert* as having no will— she is under the direction and control of her husband—is bound to obey his commands—and in many cases which might be mentioned, indeed in all cases except perhaps treason and murder cannot jointly with her husband act at all—or at least so as to make herself liable to punishment. She could not even have conveyed this very estate during the coverture[1]—her husband could not have conveyed it so as to have bound her—and therefore I think that she could not forfeit it by any thing which she did or could do against the statute—and that no act of her husband could incur the forfeiture of *her* estate.—I am clearly of opinion that the statute does not extend to *femes-covert*. As to the other points in the cause I give no opinion—it not being necessary for the decision of the case now before us—but for the reasons already given I think that the judgment of the inferior[2] court ought to be reversed.

[1] Time of her marriage.

[2] Lower.

 ### *Chief Justice Francis Dana*

. . . Another objection is, that "the statue does not extend to a *feme-covert* leaving the country with her husband." In a former stage of the cause I gave an opinion on this point, (a) and I see no reason to alter it. The words of the statute are general—*femes-covert* are not named—if the statute extends to them it must be by implication.—The statute does not charge a crime—every person had a right to take which side he pleased, in the contest in which we were then engaged. The statute rests on another principle. It is this—that every subject held his lands mediately[1] or immediately[2] from the *Crown*. Then it became a question whether all the *real* property[3] in the country was not holden under the authority of the states. And it was here adopted as a principle of the law that it was so holden. The consequence was that those persons who withdrew themselves from the country, for the purposes mentioned in the statute, lost the right of holding in the manner they would have been entitled to hold if the empire had not been divided. It was not thought fit and right that they should continue to possess and enjoy their property let the issue be what it might. The language of this statute was—go if you please—but if you withdraw we will not protect your property—we will take it. This was fair—they were not to be punished as criminal—but their property was considered as abandoned; and of course, that it belonged to the State. This was a consequence resulting from division of the empire.

    . . . I am clearly of opinion that the judgment ought to be reversed . . . because *femes-covert*, having no will, could not incur the forfeiture. And that the

[1] Through an intermediary landholder.

[2] Directly.

[3] Real estate.

statute never was intended to include them—and oblige them either to lose their property or to be guilty of a breach of the duties which by the laws of their country and the law of God they owed to their husbands.

JUDGMENT REVERSED.

[Justice] *Sewall* absent—but the Chief Justice said that he perfectly concurred with the rest of the court, on the ground that the statute did not extend to *femes-covert.*

Analyzing the Source

REFLECTING ON THE SOURCE

1. Using your notes from the tables on page 118, summarize the arguments on each side of the case. On what principles or ideas do Martin's attorneys make their case, and how do the attorneys for Massachusetts counter those points? Do the same for the judges' opinions.

2. The lawyers in this case argued about the purposes and uses of the Massachusetts Confiscation Act, but they agreed on certain ideas about the nature of citizenship. According to them, what were the duties of a citizen, and what members of society were fit or unfit to perform them?

3. What are some of the contradictions or tensions between a woman's status as a feme-covert and her role as a citizen that are made evident in this case? How did the judges resolve these contradictions in their decision? How would that resolution have differed if the judges had decided in the state's favor?

MAKING CONNECTIONS

4. At several points in this case, lawyers and judges referred to marriage as a relationship governed by law. Which law? How could a woman's adherence to the laws of marriage conflict with her adherence to the laws of the state? Which of the two did these lawyers and judges recognize as the higher law?

5. What implicit or explicit comparisons did the lawyers and judges in this case make between the British king's relationship to his subjects and a husband's relationship to his wife? What does their reasoning in this regard tell you about the impact the patriots' declaration of political independence from Britain had on other patriarchal relationships in American society?

6. Compare this source to the songs and toasts you examined in Chapter 5. How can historians use both to examine gender roles in Revolutionary America? Do these sources suggest a changing role for women in American society or a commitment to the status quo in gender relations?

Beyond the Source

In rendering its decision in *Martin v. Massachusetts*, the court failed to challenge or reinterpret a woman's legal status as a feme-covert in post–Revolutionary America. By reversing the confiscation of Anna Martin's property, the judges endorsed the notion that a married woman could not act independently of her husband in political or economic matters. In the court's view, Anna Martin was bound by her marriage vows to obey her husband and follow him into exile. She could not therefore be subject to the state's confiscation law because she could exercise no choice in her political allegiance independently of her husband.

As this case illustrates, gender and citizenship intersected over the issue of property. In the Declaration of Independence, Thomas Jefferson had changed John Locke's enumeration of natural rights from "life, liberty, and property" to "life, liberty, and the pursuit of happiness." In the nation that Jefferson and his contemporaries created, a person's freedom to pursue happiness depended in a large part on that person's access to property. Adult male property holders could vote, hold office, and dispose of their labor as they wished. All others — women, children, slaves, servants — were defined legally as dependents ruled over by husbands, parents, or masters.

Some changes occurred in marriage and property laws after the Revolution, but the impact of such changes on women were limited so long as they remained femes-covert. In the 1780s and 1790s, many states liberalized their divorce laws, making it easier for women to divorce husbands who abused or deserted them. State legislatures also abolished primogeniture laws, which favored firstborn sons over daughters and younger sons in settling probate cases. But these changes did not substantially alter a married woman's ability to own property.

Significant changes did not occur in laws governing female property ownership until the Jacksonian era. In the 1830s and 1840s, states passed laws that allowed married women to own and dispose of property independently of their husbands. These new laws originated in circumstances created by the rapidly expanding and highly volatile American economy. As more husbands found themselves entangled in debt, they warmed to the idea of transferring property to their wives, where it would be shielded from creditors in the event of bankruptcy or default. The expansion of industrial production and wage earning in the early nineteenth century also eroded the economic significance of a woman's dower right, and some states reduced or eliminated it altogether. In the face of such economic uncertainty, married women sought greater access and control over a family's real estate and personal property to provide financial stability for themselves and their children. Women's rights advocates supported such legal reforms because they regarded female property rights as one of the foundations of gender equality.

The American Revolution, in short, did not alter women's status as citizens or property holders as dramatically as Abigail Adams had hoped for in 1776.

Despite the "new code of laws" drafted by her husband and his peers, the principles and practices behind the feme-covert remained embedded in the legal system. In the American republic, control over property was fundamental to defining citizenship, and the law defined both in masculine terms.

Finding and Supplementing the Source

Court records from the colonial and Revolutionary eras are sometimes available in modern editions. For cases from New England, a good place to start is David Thomas Konig and William Edward Nelson, editors, *Plymouth Court Records, 1686–1859,* 16 volumes (Wilmington, Del.: M. Glazier, 1978–1981). The records of federal courts are deposited in the National Archives in Washington, D.C. State court records are likewise maintained by state archives. Two works that will help you untangle the legal intricacies of inheritance and property laws in early America are Marylynn Salmon, *Women and the Law of Property in Early America* (Chapel Hill: University of North Carolina Press, 1986), and Carole Shammas, Marylynn Salmon, and Michael Dahlin, *Inheritance in America: From Colonial Times to the Present* (New Brunswick, N.J.: Rutgers University Press, 1987). A standard reference work for the meaning of legal terms is Bryan A. Garner, editor, *Black's Law Dictionary,* 7th edition (St. Paul, Minn.: West Group, 1999).

Historians interested in the effects that the American Revolution had on women's lives in the United States have found property law a very fruitful avenue of inquiry. Linda K. Kerber provided a compelling analysis of the legal and political significance of *Martin v. Massachusetts* in the first chapter of *No Constitutional Right to Be Ladies: Women and the Obligations of Citizenship* (New York: Hill and Wang, 1998). See also her article, "The Paradox of Women's Citizenship in the Early Republic: The Case of *Martin v. Massachusetts,* 1805," *American Historical Review* 97 (1992): 349–78. Two useful essays on women's property rights in the Revolutionary era are Carole Shammas, "Early American Women and Control over Capital," and Marylynn Salmon, "Republican Sentiment, Economic Change, and the Property Rights of Women in American Law," both in *Women in the Age of the American Revolution,* edited by Ronald Hoffman and Peter J. Albert (Charlottesville: United States Capitol Historical Society and the University Press of Virginia, 1989), 134–54, and 447–75, respectively. Two studies that focus on women and the law at the state level are Cornelia Hughes Dayton, *Women before the Bar: Gender, Law, and Society in Connecticut, 1639–1789* (Chapel Hill: University of North Carolina Press, 1995), and Norma Basch, *In the Eyes of the Law: Women, Marriage, and Property in Nineteenth-Century New York* (Ithaca, N.Y.: Cornell University Press, 1982).

The case of *Martin v. Massachusetts* also brings to light the difficulties faced by female loyalists, many of whom, like Anna Martin, endured exile and confiscation of property. Two articles that focus on loyalist women are Mary Beth Norton, "Eighteenth-Century American Women in Peace and War: The Case of the Loyalists," *William and Mary Quarterly*, third series, 33 (1976): 386–409, and Wayne Bodle, "Jane Bartram's 'Application': Her Struggle for Survival, Stability, and Self-Determination in Revolutionary Pennsylvania," *Pennsylvania Magazine of History and Biography* 115 (1991): 185–220. For more on loyalist confiscations in Massachusetts, see Richard D. Brown, "The Confiscation and Disposition of Loyalists' Estates in Suffolk County, Massachusetts," *William and Mary Quarterly*, third series, 21 (1964): 534–50. A good general history of the loyalists is Wallace Brown, *The Good Americans: The Loyalists in the American Revolution* (New York: William Morrow and Company, 1969).

CHAPTER 7

Debating the Constitution

Speeches from the New York Ratification Convention

The delegates who attended the Federal Convention in Philadelphia in the summer of 1787 knew that the result of their meeting would be controversial. During the months that followed, as the states organized special conventions to ratify or reject the new plan for a federal government, supporters of the Constitution watched anxiously, like bettors trying to handicap a horse race. One such observer was George Washington, who had come out of his retirement at Mount Vernon to preside over the Federal Convention. Writing to his friend and fellow Federalist Henry Knox in January 1788, Washington noted that of all the states, "the determinations of new York . . . seem the most problematical."

Washington had a gift for understatement. New York had sent three delegates to the Federal Convention, but two of them—Robert Yates and John Lansing—left a few weeks into the proceedings when it became clear that the convention intended to replace rather than revise the Articles of Confederation. Yates and Lansing reported their misgivings to New York governor George Clinton, who shared their displeasure with what was happening at the Federal Convention. A New York City newspaper, the *Daily Advertiser*, printed the first copy of the Constitution in the state on September 21. Other printers quickly followed, even printing the Constitution in translation, so that Dutch-speaking inhabitants could read it in their native language. The Constitution's rapid dissemination throughout the state ensured that it would be the subject of a spirited public debate.

By the time Washington wrote his letter to Knox in early 1788, New York had become a battleground over ratification, with well-organized factions on each side raising money and calling in outside support to make their case.

Supporters of ratification were known as Federalists. As was the case in other states, they came chiefly from urban and commercial backgrounds and favored the Constitution because they believed it would create a more centralized and stable union between the states. They wanted a stronger federal government, one capable of acting independently of the states, so that the United States could pursue its economic and diplomatic interests more effectively with foreign powers and Indian nations. They also wanted the federal government to have its own taxation power, so that it could be financially independent of the states and pay off its debts at home and abroad. The most famous published commentary on the Constitution, a series of eighty-five editorials in New York's newspapers known collectively as *The Federalist*, was a product of their propaganda campaign on behalf of the Constitution in New York.

The Antifederalists, or opponents of the Constitution, met fire with fire, churning out their own editorials and pamphlets in the battle over ratification. As in other states, New York's Antifederalists tended to come from backgrounds more rural and less wealthy than the Federalists. They were more likely than Federalists to be debtors instead of creditors and to be engaged in subsistence agriculture rather than commercial food or craft production. They opposed the Constitution because a strong central government reminded them too much of the government they had rebelled against in 1776. The proposed federal government looked too much like the British Crown and Parliament, distant from and unrepresentative of the common people. They feared that the rich and well-connected could easily monopolize power in such a government, shifting the burden of taxation to the lower and middle classes. Worst of all, the proposed Constitution did not even have a bill of rights, a common feature of the state constitutions, that guaranteed the civil liberties such as freedom of speech and religion that Americans had fought and died for during the Revolution.

When New York's ratification convention finally met in the Hudson River town of Poughkeepsie on June 17, 1788, the Constitution appeared dead on arrival. Governor Clinton, whose Antifederalist sympathies were already well known, chaired the proceedings. More importantly, of the sixty-five delegates in attendance, forty-six were Antifederalists, a better than two-to-one margin over the Constitution's supporters. The only counties to send Federalist delegations to Poughkeepsie were centered around New York City; every county north of the lower Hudson Valley was represented by Antifederalists. This geographic distribution reflected a division of interests within the state. While lawyers, merchants, and large landowners could be found on each side of the ratification debate, they made up a much larger proportion of the Federalist delegates at the convention (79 percent to 50 percent). One historian who analyzed the occupational status and wealth of the delegates to New York's ratification convention summarized the division this way: "most of the wealthy landowners and merchants, in and out of the convention, were Federalists and . . . the Antifederalists, while drawing some of their leaders from this class, were on the whole men of lesser means." From the outset, the New York ratification convention pitted a minority of wealthy, urban Federalists against a majority of Antifederalists from rural counties and more middling social backgrounds.

New York's vote on the Constitution had profound implications for the rest of the United States. When the convention opened, eight of the nine state ratifications necessary for the new government to take effect had already occurred, while contests too close to call were being fought in New Hampshire and Virginia. Regardless of how the votes in New Hampshire and Virginia turned out, the new federal government would not fare well if New York stood apart from the union. New York City had the best harbor in the country and played a central role in the nation's overseas trade. Furthermore, the Hudson and Mohawk rivers provided the nation with its most important route into the continent's interior, and New York was a vital communications link between New England and the South. Without New York, no one expected the new federal government to prosper or endure.

Despite their numerical superiority at the convention, New York's Antifederalists could not afford to reject the Constitution out of hand. Eight states had already ratified, and the Antifederalist delegates were no more interested in seeing their state stand apart from the union than their opponents were. There was even some talk among the Federalists of splitting the state in two, so that the lower Hudson Valley, New York City, and Long Island could join the new federal union if the delegations from the northern counties refused to budge. When news arrived in Poughkeepsie on June 25 that New Hampshire had ratified, it became apparent to all concerned that some version of the Constitution would go into effect, regardless of what the New Yorkers decided. The chief goal of the Antifederalist leadership at that point became securing a conditional ratification, contingent upon the acceptance of amendments to the Constitution before it went into effect. The Federalists opposed this strategy, because conditional ratification would require convening another interstate convention, thereby delaying and perhaps jeopardizing the installation of the new government. Worse yet, the new federal government might form without the New Yorkers onboard, locking them out of key decisions on such matters as the location of the new federal capital.

Once deliberations got underway in Poughkeepsie, leaders emerged on both sides of the debate. As presiding officer, Governor Clinton needed to maintain an air of impartiality, so he spoke rarely. Instead, the Antifederalists' most effective speaker was Melancton Smith, a self-educated merchant and lawyer who lived mostly in New York City but attended the convention as a delegate from upstate Dutchess County, where he owned a large estate. Smith's wealth did not make him a typical Antifederalist, but his unpolished manner and firm commitment to democratic principles made him suspicious of privilege and power and naturally sympathetic to the Antifederalist cause. His chief opponent was Alexander Hamilton, a former aide-de-camp to George Washington who had married into one of the state's wealthiest families. Hamilton had been New York's third delegate to the Federal Convention the previous year, but unlike Yates and Lansing, he supported the convention's designs and signed the Constitution when it was finished. With James Madison and John Jay, he coauthored the *Federalist* newspaper editorials in 1787–1788. Observers at the ratification convention recognized the talents and energy of Smith and Hamilton. Poughkeepsie lawyer James Kent called Smith "the most prominent and responsible speaker on the party of the anti-federalist majority . . . Hamilton's most persevering and formidable antagonist." Smith himself described Hamilton as the "champion" of the Federalists: "he speaks frequently, very long and very vehemently." The fate of the Constitution in New York and the nation hinged upon the standoff between these two men and their political allies in a Hudson River courthouse.

Using the Ratification Debates as a Source

The Federal Convention that drafted the Constitution took place in secrecy. The delegates cloistered themselves behind closed doors and did not speak a word to anyone about their proceedings until they presented a completed draft to the public in September 1787. The process of ratification was different. Each state called a special convention solely for the purpose of passing judgment on the document. These conventions were as open and public as the Federal Convention had been closed and secret. New York's ratification convention was no exception: the Poughkeepsie courthouse accommodated two hundred spectators in addition to the sixty-five delegates. For the first two weeks of the convention, the *Daily Advertiser* printed each day's debates in full; after July 2 (when news of Virginia's ratification arrived), it printed summaries of each day's proceedings. Like the other state ratification conventions, New York's convention left a substantial public record that has captivated historians ever since.

Each state determined the time and place of its ratification convention and the means by which delegates would be selected for it. Most states held special elections for delegates to their conventions, using the same eligibility requirements for voting that they did for elections to the state legislature. New York differed from this practice by temporarily expanding its franchise, allowing all free adult males to vote for delegates to the ratification convention. This move actually had little impact on the number of votes cast, because the state's 1777 constitution had already significantly lowered the amount of property a man had to own in order to vote, but it did indicate the pervasive belief among Federalists and Antifederalists alike that the power of the proposed federal government would derive directly from the people, and, therefore, they would have to be the ultimate arbiters on ratification. Of course, this definition also reflected their consensus that the "people" did not include women, slaves, or other groups traditionally excluded from the political process.

Advantages and Disadvantages of Working with the Ratification Debates

The great advantage to studying the proceedings of the ratification conventions is that they provide the fullest record available to historians of how Americans interpreted the Constitution at the time it was adopted. In other words, this is a source that speaks directly to one of the guiding principles of constitutional interpretation: what was the original intent of the framers of the Constitution? Strict constructionists, those scholars and judges who believe that the power of the federal government should extend no farther than is explicitly stated in the Constitution, place great emphasis on original intent and argue that the purposes and ideas of those men who adopted the Constitution should guide our interpretation of the document. Loose constructionists, on the other hand, believe that the Constitution is a "living document" that needs to be reinterpreted by each generation if it is to meet the needs of a changing society. They place less importance on original intent but still argue with strict constructionists about what the framers had in mind when they wrote and ratified the Constitution. Some of the most hotly debated constitutional issues of today, such as gay rights and affirmative action, testify to how far removed our modern society is from the world of Alexander Hamilton and Melancton Smith. Yet, the words they spoke in Poughkeepsie in 1788 are an important part of the textual record lawyers and judges use to interpret the Constitution in our courtrooms.

In arguing over original intent, strict and loose constructionists invariably refer to the same set of sources: the notes kept by James Madison during the Federal Convention, editorials and pamphlets published during the ratification process in 1787–1788, and the proceedings of the state ratification conventions. Madison's notes are important because he was the primary author of the Constitution, and he left the most complete account of what occurred during the Federal Convention in Philadelphia. The political tracts published during 1787–1788 convey the visceral intensity of the debate over ratification. Neither of these sources, however, compares to the proceedings of the state ratification conventions in presenting the range and depth of the Federalist and Antifederalist positions. Even a cursory review of the state convention records reveals that the debate over original intent should really be one over "original intents," because there was such a variety of opinions expressed among the delegates who decided the ratification issue.

The proceedings of the ratification conventions also illustrate the nature of political expression and ideology in post–Revolutionary America. In our age of modern media politics, in which politicians speak on the evening news in sound bites that are measured in seconds, we may find it strange that convention delegates gave speeches that lasted for hours and commanded the rapt attention of their audiences. As indicated by the following excerpt from a June 21, 1788, speech by Alexander Hamilton, the delegates sprinkled their debates liberally with references to the republics of ancient Greece and Rome.

It was remarked yesterday, that a numerous representation was necessary to obtain the confidence of the people. This is not generally true. The confidence of the people will easily be gained by a good administration. This is the true touchstone. I could illustrate the position by a variety of historical examples, both ancient and modern. In Sparta, the ephori were a body of magistrates, instituted as a check upon the senate, and representing the people. They consisted of only five men; but they were able to protect their rights, and therefore enjoyed their confidence and attachment. In Rome, the people were represented by three tribunes, who were afterwards increased to ten. Every one acquainted with the history of that republic will recollect how powerful a check to the senatorial encroachments this small body proved; how unlimited a confidence was placed in them by the people, whose guardians they were; and to what a conspicuous station in the government their influence at length elevated the plebeians.

One of the city-states of ancient Greece

Representatives of the common people in the Roman republic, who possessed a veto power over other magistrates

The common people of ancient Rome

Elected annually as overseers of Sparta's kings, whom they could impeach and depose if the kings acted contrary to the law

What assumption is Hamilton making here about the education of his audience?

Refers to the Roman Senate, which represented the aristocracy

These references may strike us now as haughty and obscure, but this political language resonated among their listeners. By reading these speeches and trying to unlock their persuasive power, we can gain insight into the political culture and ideology that generated the Constitution in the first place.

A disadvantage arising from the use of this source is the difficulty of measuring how much impact public speeches and debates had on the votes cast at the ratification conventions. Delegates got elected to the New York ratification convention in part because their constituents already knew how they would vote. Then, as now, political debate made for good public theater, but did the eloquence of Alexander Hamilton or Melancton Smith actually convince any of the delegates to change their minds? We know from the final vote tally that some of the Antifederalist delegates did end up voting for ratification, but we do not know if they did so because of the persuasive power of the speeches they heard or because of some other motivation.

Certainly, factors external to New York influenced the proceedings. After news of Virginia's ratification reached Poughkeepsie on July 2, the proceedings changed markedly. As the ratification of the Constitution was now a foregone conclusion, delegates gave fewer speeches and spent most of their time negotiating the wording of proposed amendments and ratification resolutions. How should historians weigh this change in circumstances when trying to determine the impact of the speeches made before July 2? In fathoming the motivations behind the final vote, we must also consider the possibility that some delegates voted for unstated reasons of personal interest, such as the desire for public office in the new federal government, or because of compromises struck with their rivals behind closed doors.

In other words, the ratification debates are a great source for reconstructing the public arguments Federalists and Antifederalists made for and against the Constitution, but we cannot rely on them solely if we wish to reconstruct the thoughts behind the votes cast in the ratification conventions. That is why historians usually supplement their work on the debates with research into the backgrounds and personal writings of the convention delegates. In private letters or recollections, the men who decided the fate of the Constitution were often more plainspoken about the delicate balancing of ideology and interests that determined their votes. Also, research into the economic and social background of the delegates helps to uncover patterns in the voting on ratification that may confirm or contradict the delegates' public statements about the Constitution.

Working with the Source

As you read through the source, use this table to help organize your notes and summarize the Federalist and Antifederalist positions on the following issues.

	Federalists	Antifederalists
Representation in Congress		
Sources of Corruption		
Constitution's Impact on the States		

The Source: Speeches Debating the Constitution from the New York Ratification Convention, June 21–28, 1788

The passages that follow are from debates that occurred between June 21 and June 28, when delegates on both sides gave long speeches detailing their contrasting opinions on the Constitution. You will notice that the style of presentation varies from one speech to the next. Some read like verbatim transcriptions, while others read like an editor's narrative summary of the speech's content. These differences resulted from day-to-day variances in how the proceedings were recorded by a newspaper editor who published them in the *Daily Advertiser,* a New York newspaper.

REPRESENTATION IN CONGRESS

One of the Antifederalists' chief objections to the Constitution was that the House of Representatives was not representative enough. The House would be limited in size to no more than one representative for every thirty thousand people. Antifederalists believed this would lead to electoral districts much too large to represent the people adequately and that election would be out of the reach for any candidate not rich or famous enough to command reputation over such a wide area. Federalists responded to this argument by questioning whether more representatives actually meant better representation.

 Melancton Smith, June 21, 1788

To determine whether the number of representatives proposed by this Constitution is sufficient, it is proper to examine the qualifications which this house[1] ought to possess, in order to exercise their power discreetly for the happiness of the people. The idea that naturally suggests itself to our minds, when we speak of representatives, is, that they resemble those they represent. They should be a true picture of the people, possess a knowledge of their circumstances and their wants, sympathize in all their distresses, and be disposed to seek their true interests. The knowledge necessary for the representative of a free people not only comprehends extensive political and commercial information, such as is

---

[1] The House of Representatives.

Source: All of the debate passages reprinted in this chapter are excerpted from Bernard Bailyn, editor, *The Debate on the Constitution: Federalist and Anti-Federalist Speeches, Articles, and Letters during the Struggle over Ratification* (New York: Library of America, 1993), 2:759–835.

acquired by men of refined education, who have leisure to attain to high degrees of improvement, but it should also comprehend that kind of acquaintance with the common concerns and occupations of the people, which men of the middling class of life are, in general, more competent to, than those of a superior class. To understand the true commercial interests of a country, not only requires just ideas of the general commerce of the world, but also, and principally, a knowledge of the productions of your own country, and their value, what your soil is capable of producing, the nature of your manufactures, and the capacity of the country to increase both. To exercise the power of laying taxes, duties, and excises, with discretion, requires something more than an acquaintance with the abstruse[2] parts of the system of finance. It calls for a knowledge of the circumstances and ability of the people in general—a discernment how the burdens imposed will bear upon the different classes.

From these observations results this conclusion—that the number of representatives should be so large, as that, while it embraces the men of the first class, it should admit those of the middling class of life. I am convinced that this government[3] is so constituted that the representatives will generally be composed of the first class in the community, which I shall distinguish by the name of the natural aristocracy of the country. I do not mean to give offence by using this term. I am sensible this idea is treated by many gentlemen as chimerical.[4] I shall be asked what is meant by the natural aristocracy, and told that no such distinction of classes of men exists among us. It is true, it is our singular felicity that we have no legal or hereditary distinctions of this kind; but still there are real differences. Every society naturally divides itself into classes. The Author of nature[5] has bestowed on some greater capacities than others; birth, education, talents, and wealth, create distinctions among men as visible, and of as much influence, as titles, stars, and garters. In every society, men of this class will command a superior degree of respect; and if the government is so constituted as to admit but few to exercise the powers of it, it will, according to the natural course of things, be in their hands. Men in the middling class, who are qualified as representatives, will not be so anxious to be chosen as those of the first. When the number is so small, the office will be highly elevated and distinguished; the style in which the members live will probably be high; circumstances of this kind will render the place of a representative not a desirable one to sensible, substantial men, who have been used to walk in the plain and frugal paths of life.

. . . A substantial yeoman,[6] of sense and discernment, will hardly ever be chosen. From these remarks, it appears that the government will fall into the hands of the few and the great. This will be a government of oppression. I do not mean to declaim against the great, and charge them indiscriminately with

---

[2] Difficult to comprehend.

[3] The new federal government proposed by the Constitution.

[4] Imaginary.

[5] God.

[6] A middle-class farmer.

want of principle and honesty. The same passions and prejudices govern all men. The circumstances in which men are placed in a great measure give a cast to the human character. Those in middling circumstances have less temptation; they are inclined by habit, and the company with whom they associate, to set bounds to their passions and appetites. If this is not sufficient, the want of means to gratify them will be a restraint: they are obliged to employ their time in their respective callings; hence the substantial yeomanry of the country are more temperate, of better morals, and less ambition, than the great. The latter do not feel for the poor and middling class; the reasons are obvious—they are not obliged to use the same pains and labor to procure property as the other. They feel not the inconveniences arising from the payment of small sums. The great consider themselves above the common people, entitled to more respect, do not associate with them; they fancy themselves to have a right of preeminence in every thing. In short, they possess the same feelings, and are under the influence of the same motives, as an hereditary nobility. I know the idea that such a distinction exists in this country is ridiculed by some; but I am not the less apprehensive of danger from their influence on this account. . . .

 Alexander Hamilton, June 21, 1788

Mr. *Hamilton* then reassumed his argument. . . .

It has been observed, by an honorable gentleman,[1] that a pure democracy, if it were practicable, would be the most perfect government. Experience has proved that no position in politics is more false than this. The ancient democracies, in which the people themselves deliberated, never possessed one feature of good government. Their very character was tyranny; their figure, deformity. When they assembled, the field of debate presented an ungovernable mob, not only incapable of deliberation, but prepared for every enormity.[2] In these assemblies, the enemies of the people brought forward their plans of ambition systematically. They were opposed by their enemies of another party; and it became a matter of contingency, whether the people subjected themselves to be led blindly by one tyrant or by another.

It was remarked yesterday, that a numerous representation was necessary to obtain the confidence of the people. This is not generally true. The confidence of the people will easily be gained by a good administration. This is the true touchstone. I could illustrate the position by a variety of historical examples, both ancient and modern. In Sparta, the ephori were a body of magistrates, instituted as a check upon the senate, and representing the people. They consisted of only five men; but they were able to protect their rights, and there-

[1] Melancton Smith.
[2] Outrage.

fore enjoyed their confidence and attachment. In Rome, the people were represented by three tribunes, who were afterwards increased to ten. Every one acquainted with the history of that republic will recollect how powerful a check
to the senatorial encroachments this small body proved; how unlimited a confidence was placed in them by the people, whose guardians they were; and to
what a conspicuous station in the government their influence at length elevated the plebeians. Massachusetts has three hundred representatives; New
York has sixty-five. Have the people in this state less confidence in their representation than the people of that? Delaware has twenty-one. Do the inhabitants of New York feel a higher confidence than those of Delaware? I have
stated these examples to prove that the gentleman's principle is not just. The
popular confidence depends on circumstances very distinct from considerations of number. Probably the public attachment is more strongly secured by a
train of prosperous events, which are the result of wise deliberation and vigor-
ous execution, and to which large bodies are much less competent than small
ones. . . .

It has been further, by the gentlemen in the opposition,[3] observed, that a
large representation is necessary to understand the interests of the people. This
principle is by no means true in the extent to which the gentlemen seem to
carry it. I would ask, Why may not a man understand the interests of thirty as
well as of twenty? The position appears to be made upon the unfounded pre-
sumption that all the interests of all parts of the community must be represented. No idea is more erroneous than this. Only such interests are proper to
be represented as are involved in the powers of the general[4] government. These
interests come completely under the observation of one or a few men; and the
requisite information is by no means augmented in proportion to the increase
of number. . . .

Sir, we hear constantly a great deal which is rather calculated to awake our
passions, and create prejudices, than to conduct us to the truth, and teach us
our real interests. I do not suppose this to be the design of the gentlemen. Why,
then, are we told so often of an aristocracy? For my part, I hardly know the
meaning of this word, as it is applied. If all we hear be true, this government is
really a very bad one. But who are the aristocracy among us? Where do we find
men elevated to a perpetual rank above their fellow-citizens, and possessing
powers entirely independent of them? The arguments of the gentlemen only
go to prove that there are men who are rich, men who are poor, some who are
wise, and others who are not; that, indeed, every distinguished man is an aristocrat. This reminds me of a description of the aristocrats I have seen in a late
publication styled the *Federal Farmer*.[5] The author reckons in the aristocracy all
governors of states, members of Congress, chief magistrates, and all officers of

---

[3] The Antifederalists.

[4] Federal.

[5] A widely circulated Antifederalist pamphlet.

the militia. This description, I presume to say, is ridiculous. The image is a phantom. Does the new government render a rich man more eligible than a poor one? No. It requires no such qualification. . . .

It is a harsh doctrine that men grow wicked in proportion as they improve and enlighten their minds. Experience has by no means justified us in the supposition that there is more virtue in one class of men than in another. Look through the rich and the poor of the community, the learned and the ignorant. Where does virtue predominate? The difference indeed consists, not in the quantity, but kind, of vices which are incident to various classes; and here the advantage of character belongs to the wealthy. Their vices are probably more favorable to the prosperity of the state than those of the indigent, and partake less of moral depravity. . . .

 ### *Melancton Smith,* June 21, 1788

The honorable *Melancton Smith* rose, and observed, that the gentleman[1] might have spared many of his remarks in answer to the ideas he had advanced. The only way to remedy and correct the faults in the proposed Constitution was, he imagined, to increase the representation and limit the powers. He admitted that no precise number could be fixed upon. His object only was to augment the number in such a degree as to render the government more favorable to liberty. . . .

The honorable member[2] had observed, that the confidence of the people was not necessarily connected with the number of their rulers, and had cited the ephori of Sparta, and the tribunes in Rome, as examples. But it ought to be considered, that, in those places, the people were to contend with a body of hereditary nobles; they would, therefore, naturally have confidence in a few men who were their leaders in the constant struggle for liberty. The comparison between the representations of several states did not better apply. New York had but sixty-five representatives in Assembly. But because sixty-five was a proper representation of two hundred and forty thousand, did it follow that it was also sufficient for three millions? The state legislatures had not the powers of the general government, and were not competent to those important regulations which might endanger liberty.

The gentleman, continued Mr. *Smith,* had ridiculed his idea of an aristocracy, and had entered into a definition of the word. He himself agreed to this definition, but the dispute was not of words, but things. He was convinced that in every society there were certain men exalted above the rest. These men he did not consider as destitute of morality or virtue. He only insisted that they could not feel sympathetically the wants of the people.

[1] Alexander Hamilton.
[2] Hamilton.

SOURCES OF CORRUPTION

Both Federalists and Antifederalists believed that corruption in government resulted from the pursuit of individual ambitions for wealth, fame, and power. They disagreed over who was more or less likely to fall prey to such ambitions. The Antifederalists believed that the Constitution gave free rein to the ambitions of the rich and powerful. The Federalists believed that under the Constitution, those seeking office in the federal government were more likely to do so out of a sense of public spiritedness than personal gain.

 ### *Robert R. Livingston*, June 23, 1788

Robert R. Livingston was a Federalist delegate and chancellor of the New York State Supreme Court.

The honorable gentleman from Dutchess,[1] who has so copiously declaimed against all declamation,[2] has pointed his artillery against the rich and the great. I am not interested in defending rich men: but what does he mean by telling us that the rich are vicious and intemperate?[3] Will he presume to point out to us the class of men in which intemperance is not to be found? Is there less intemperance in feeding on beef than on turtle?[4] or in drinking rum than wine? I think the gentleman does not reason from facts. If he will look round among the rich men of his acquaintance, I fancy he will find them as honest and virtuous as any class in the community. He says the rich are unfeeling; I believe they are less so than the poor; for it seems to me probable that those who are most occupied by their own cares and distresses have the least sympathy with the distresses of others. The sympathy of the poor is generally selfish, that of the rich a more disinterested[5] emotion.

The gentleman further observes, that ambition is peculiarly the vice of the wealthy. But have not all classes of men their objects of ambition? Will not a poor man contend for a constable's staff with as much assiduity and eagerness as a man of rank will aspire to the chief magistracy? The great offices in the state are beyond the view of the poor and ignorant man: he will therefore contemplate an humbler office as the highest alluring object of ambition; he will look with equal envy on a successful competitor, and will equally sacrifice to the attainment of his wishes the duty he owes to his friends or to the public. But, says the gentleman, the rich will be always brought forward; they will exclusively enjoy the suffrages of the people. For my own part, I believe that, if

[1] Melancton Smith.

[2] Spoken pompously against pompous speech.

[3] Prone to excess, especially in drink.

[4] Turtle was considered a delicacy of the rich.

[5] Concerned for the well-being of others.

two men of equal abilities set out together in life, one rich, the other of small fortune, the latter will generally take the lead in your government. The rich are ever objects of envy; and this, more or less, operates as a bar to their advancement. What is the fact? Let us look around us: I might mention gentlemen in office who have not been advanced for their wealth; I might instance, in particular, the honorable gentleman who presides over this state,[6] who was not promoted to the chief magistracy[7] for his riches, but his virtue.

. . . We are told that, in every country, there is a natural aristocracy, and that this aristocracy consists of the rich and the great: nay, the gentleman goes further, and ranks in this class of men the wise, the learned, and those eminent for their talents or great virtues. Does a man possess the confidence of his fellow-citizens for having done them important services? He is an aristocrat. Has he great integrity? Such a man will be greatly trusted: he is an aristocrat. Indeed, to determine that one is an aristocrat, we need only be assured he is a man of merit. But I hope we have many such. I hope, sir, we are all aristocrats. So sensible am I of that gentleman's[8] talents, integrity, and virtue, that we might at once hail him the first of the nobles, the very prince of the Senate. But whom, in the name of common sense, will we have to represent us? Not the rich, for they are sheer aristocrats. Not the learned, the wise, the virtuous, for they are all aristocrats. Whom then? Why, those who are not virtuous; those who are not wise; those who are not learned: these are the men to whom alone we can trust our liberties. He says further, we ought not to choose these aristocrats, because the people will not have confidence in them; that is, the people will not have confidence in those who best deserve and most possess their confidence. He would have his government composed of other classes of men: where will we find them? Why, he must go out into the highways, and pick up the rogue and the robber; he must go to the hedges and ditches, and bring in the poor, the blind, and the lame. As the gentleman has thus settled the definition of aristocracy, I trust that no man will think it a term of reproach; for who among us would not be wise? Who would not be virtuous? Who would not be above want? How, again, would he have us to guard against aristocracy? Clearly by doubling the representation, and sending twelve aristocrats instead of six. The truth is, in these republican governments, we know no such ideal distinctions. We are all equally aristocrats. Offices, emoluments,[9] honors, are open to all.

---

[6] Governor George Clinton, chair of the ratification convention.

[7] Governorship.

[8] Smith's.

[9] The profits of office.

Melancton Smith, June 23, 1788

The gentleman[1] wishes me to describe what I meant by representing the feelings of the people. If I recollect right, I said the representative ought to understand and govern his conduct by the true interest of the people. I believe I stated this idea precisely. When he attempts to explain my ideas, he explains them away to nothing; and, instead of answering, he distorts, and then sports with them. But he may rest assured that, in the present spirit of the Convention, to irritate is not the way to conciliate. The gentleman, by the false gloss[2] he has given to my argument, makes me an enemy to the rich: this is not true. All I said was, that mankind were influenced, in a great degree, by interests and prejudices; that men, in different ranks of life, were exposed to different temptations, and that ambition was more peculiarly the passion of the rich and great. The gentleman supposes the poor have less sympathy with the sufferings of their fellow-creatures, for that those who feel most distress themselves, have the least regard to the misfortunes of others. Whether this be reasoning or declamation, let all who hear us determine. I observed, that the rich were more exposed to those temptations which rank and power hold out to view; that they were more luxurious and intemperate, because they had more fully the means of enjoyment; that they were more ambitious, because more in the hope of success. The gentleman says my principle is not true, for that a poor man will be as ambitious to be a constable as a rich man to be a governor; but he will not injure his country so much by the party he creates to support his ambition.

The next object of the gentleman's ridicule is my idea of an aristocracy; and, indeed, he has done me the honor to rank me in the order. If, then, I am an aristocrat, and yet publicly caution my countrymen against the encroachments of the aristocrats, they will surely consider me as one of their most disinterested friends.

[1] Robert R. Livingston.
[2] Explanation.

THE CONSTITUTION'S IMPACT ON THE STATES

One of the chief topics of debate at the New York ratification convention was the impact that the Constitution would have on the powers of the state governments. The Federalists believed the Constitution would elevate the federal government above the state governments, allowing it to operate independently in such realms as international relations, interstate commerce, and taxation. Antifederalists balked at reducing the influence of the state governments within the federal union, because they believed those governments were more democratic and less prone to corruption than the federal one proposed by the Constitution.

Melancton Smith, June 27, 1788

Sir, I contemplate the abolition of the state constitutions as an event fatal to the liberties of America. These liberties will not be violently wrested from the people; they will be undermined and gradually consumed. On subjects of the kind we cannot be too critical. The investigation is difficult, because we have no examples to serve as guides. The world has never seen such a government over such a country. If we consult authorities in this matter, they will declare the impracticability of governing a free people on such an extensive plan. In a country where a portion of the people live more than twelve hundred miles from the centre, I think that one body cannot possibly legislate for the whole. Can the legislature frame a system of taxation that will operate with uniform advantages? Can they carry any system into execution? Will it not give occasion for an innumerable swarm of officers, to infest our country and consume our substance? People will be subject to impositions[1] which they cannot support, and of which their complaints can never reach the government.

Another idea is in my mind, which I think conclusive against a simple government for the United States. It is not possible to collect a set of representatives who are acquainted with all parts of the continent. Can you find men in Georgia who are acquainted with the situation of New Hampshire, who know what taxes will best suit the inhabitants, and how much they are able to bear? Can the best men make laws for the people of whom they are entirely ignorant? Sir, we have no reason to hold our state governments in contempt, or to suppose them incapable of acting wisely. I believe they have operated more beneficially than most people expected, who considered that those governments were erected in a time of war and confusion, when they were very liable to errors in their structure. It will be a matter of astonishment to all unprejudiced men hereafter, who shall reflect upon our situation, to observe to what a great degree good government has prevailed. It is true some bad laws have been passed in most of the states; but they arose from the difficulty of the times rather than from any want of honesty or wisdom. Perhaps there never was a government which, in the course of ten years, did not do something to be repented of. . . . We all agree that a general government is necessary; but it ought not to go so far as to destroy the authority of the members. We shall be unwise to make a new experiment, in so important a matter, without some known and sure grounds to go upon. The state constitutions should be the guardians of our domestic rights and interests, and should be both the support and the check of the federal government.

[1] Taxes.

7   *Alexander Hamilton,* June 28, 1788

The gentleman[1] has made a declaration of his wishes for a strong federal government. I hope this is the wish of all. But why has he not given us his ideas of the nature of this government, which is the object of his wishes? Why does he not describe it? We have proposed a system which we supposed would answer the purposes of strength and safety.—The gentleman objects to it, without pointing out the grounds, on which his objections are founded, or shewing[2] us a better form. These general surmises never lead to the discovery of truth. It is to be desired, that the gentleman would explain particularly the errors in this system, and furnish us with their proper remedies. . . .

The gentleman says, that the operation of the taxes[3] will exclude the states, on this ground, that the demands of the community are always equal to its resources; that Congress will find a use for all the money the people can pay. This observation, if designed as a general rule, is in every view unjust. Does he suppose the general government will want all the money the people can furnish; and also that the state governments will want all the money the people can furnish? What contradiction is this? But if this maxim be true, how does the wealth of a country ever increase? How are the people enabled to accumulate fortunes? Do the burthens regularly augment,[4] as its inhabitants grow prosperous and happy? But if indeed all the resources are required for the protection of the people, it follows that the protecting power should have access to them. The only difficulty lies in the want of resources: If they are adequate, the operation will be easy. If they are not, taxation must be restrained: Will this be the fate of the state tax alone? Certainly not. The people will say no. What will be the conduct of the national rulers? The consideration will not be, that our imposing the tax will destroy the states, for this cannot be effected; but that it will distress the people, whom we represent, and whose protectors we are. It is unjust to suppose that they[5] will be altogether destitute of virtue and prudence. It is unfair to presume that the representatives of the people will be disposed to tyrannize, in one government more than in another. If we are convinced that the national legislature will pursue a system of measures unfavorable to the interests of the people, we ought to have no general government at all. But if we unite, it will be for the accomplishment of great purposes. . . .

I shall conclude with a few remarks by way of apology. I am apprehensive, sir, that, in the warmth of my feelings, I may have uttered expressions which were too vehement. If such has been my language, it was from the habit of using strong phrases to express my ideas; and, above all, from the interesting nature of the subject. I have ever condemned those cold, unfeeling hearts,

[1] Melancton Smith.

[2] Showing.

[3] Taxes levied by the new federal government.

[4] Burdens regularly increase.

[5] Federal officeholders.

which no object can animate. I condemn those indifferent mortals, who either never form opinions, or never make them known. I confess, sir, that on no subject has my breast been filled with stronger emotions, or more anxious concern. If any thing has escaped me, which may be construed into a personal reflection, I beg the gentlemen,[6] once for all, to be assured that I have no design to wound the feelings of any one who is opposed to me.

While I am making these observations, I cannot but take notice of some expressions which have fallen in the course of the debate. It has been said that ingenious men may say ingenious things, and that those who are interested in raising the few upon the ruins of the many, may give to every cause an appearance of justice. I know not whether these insinuations allude to the characters of any who are present, or to any of the reasonings in this house. I presume that the gentlemen would not ungenerously impute such motives to those who differ from themselves. I declare I know not any set of men who are to derive peculiar advantages from this Constitution. Were any permanent honors or emoluments to be secured to the families of those who have been active in this cause, there might be some grounds for suspicion. But what reasonable man, for the precarious enjoyment of rank and power, would establish a system which would reduce his nearest friends and his posterity to slavery and ruin? If the gentlemen reckon me amongst the obnoxious few, if they imagine that I contemplate with ambitious eye the immediate honors of the government, yet let them consider that I have my friends, my family; my children, to whom ties of nature and of habit have attached me. If, to-day, I am among the favored few, my children, tomorrow, may be among the oppressed; these dear pledges of my patriotism may, at a future day, be suffering the severe distresses to which my ambition has reduced them. The changes in the human condition are uncertain and frequent: many, on whom Fortune has bestowed her favors, may trace their family to a more unprosperous station; and many, who are now in obscurity, may look back upon the affluence and exalted rank of their ancestors. But I will no longer trespass on your indulgence. I have troubled the committee with these observations, to show that it cannot be the wish of any reasonable man to establish a government unfriendly to the liberties of the people. Gentlemen ought not, then, to presume that the advocates of this Constitution are influenced by ambitious views. The suspicion, sir, is unjust; the charge is uncharitable.

Analyzing the Source

REFLECTING ON THE SOURCE

1. Using your notes from the table on page 137, briefly explain the principles upon which Antifederalists objected to the Constitution. How did Federalists answer those objections? How did Antifederalists envision the future of the nation if the Constitution was ratified?

[6] His fellow convention delegates.

2. In Sources 1–5 (pp. 138–45), what meanings did the delegates attach to the following words and phrases: *natural aristocracy, ambition, passions,* and *interests*? Did the meanings of these words change depending upon whether a Federalist or Antifederalist uttered them?

3. What, if anything, do these passages tell you about the delegates who remained silent during the proceedings? What sort of evidence would you want to see before assuming that they shared the views expressed by their leaders on the floor?

MAKING CONNECTIONS

4. Some historians describe the clash between Federalists and Antifederalists as a struggle between economic classes; others emphasize differences in political ideology. Having read these excerpts from the ratification debates, what do you think was the most distinguishing characteristic of the divide between Federalists and Antifederalists? Was the struggle over ratification ultimately about differences in economic interests or political ideas?

5. How should scholars and judges trying to interpret original intent make use of the ratification convention proceedings? Antifederalists were present at the creation of the Constitution, yet spoke—and sometimes voted—against it. How then should modern scholars regard the opinions of the Antifederalists when trying to reconstruct original intent?

6. Having read Federalist and Antifederalist predictions of how the Constitution would work, who do you think was right? Have any of the Antifederalists' fears come true? If you had attended the New York ratification convention, which side do you think you would have taken?

Beyond the Source

New York ratified the Constitution by a vote of 30–27, the narrowest margin of victory in any of the state ratification conventions that met in 1787–1788 (Rhode Island, which initially refused to call a ratification convention, finally did so in spring 1790 and ratified the Constitution by an even closer vote of 32–30). If we consider New York along with two other key states, we can get a clearer picture of how narrowly the Constitution passed through the ratification process. Convention delegates in New York, Virginia, and Massachusetts cast a total of 580 votes; the margin of victory in each of those states was 3, 10, and 19 votes respectively. In other words, 32 votes out of 580 cast in those states tilted the balance in favor of ratification, a margin of only 5.5 percent.

In some respects, it might be said that New York's Antifederalists lost the battle but won the war. None of them ever seriously considered making New York an independent republic; after news of ratification in New Hampshire and Virginia reached them, they pegged their hopes on amending the Constitution after it went into effect. As was the case in several other states, the New York

Antifederalists thought that the Constitution needed to have a bill of rights that would protect the people's liberties from the power of the new federal government. Alexander Hamilton answered on behalf of the Federalists, calling a federal bill of rights unnecessary because the Constitution did not grant the federal government powers over the rights in question and the state constitutions already guaranteed such rights to their citizens.

The delegates at the New York convention broke their impasse by drafting a resolution that voted for ratification "in full confidence" that a federal convention would be called after the formation of the new government to give "early and mature Consideration" to amendments recommended by the Antifederalists. When Smith and other leading Antifederalist delegates made clear their support for this phrasing, the vote for ratification passed, albeit by only three votes. Smith and his allies formed a political society in the fall of 1788 to pursue a second federal convention, but their objective was preempted by James Madison, who introduced to the first Congress a list of twelve amendments to the Constitution that distilled many of the recommendations made by Antifederalists at the state ratification conventions, including New York's. Madison's proposed amendments dealt chiefly with the civil liberties the Antifederalists were so concerned about protecting: freedom of religion and freedom of the press; the rights to assembly, to bear arms, and to trial by jury; and prohibitions on excessive bail, cruel and unusual punishments, and unreasonable search and seizures. The states ratified ten of those amendments in 1791, and they became known collectively as the Bill of Rights. It is ironic that today, the one part of the Constitution with which Americans are most familiar (who among us has not "taken the Fifth" when faced with an unpleasant question?) would not be there if the Antifederalists had not been so persistent in their demands for a more perfect union.

Finding and Supplementing the Source

The proceedings of the New York ratification convention were first published in the newspaper *The Daily Advertiser* and then as *Debates and Proceedings of the Convention of the State of New-York* (1788; repr., Poughkeepsie, N.Y.: Vassar Brothers Institute, 1905). Nineteenth-century historian Jonathan Elliot included them in his collection of documents related to the state ratification conventions, available in a five-volume reprint as *The Debates in the Several State Conventions on the Adoption of the Federal Constitution* (New York: B. Franklin, 1968). Two other useful reference works on the ratification conventions are Bernard Bailyn, editor, *The Debate on the Constitution: Federalist and Anti-Federalist Speeches, Articles, and Letters during the Struggle over Ratification,* 2 volumes (New York: Library of America, 1993), and Merrill Jensen, John P. Kaminski, and Gaspare J. Saladino, editors, *The Documentary History of the Ratification of the Constitution,* 18 volumes (Madison: State Historical Society of Wisconsin, 1976–). The Avalon Project at the Yale Law School is a Web site that contains an online archive of documents related to the drafting and ratification of the Constitution (see *The American Constitution—A Documentary Record* at **yale.edu/lawweb/avalon/constpap.htm**).

Linda Grant De Pauw provided a complete and engaging retelling of ratification in New York in *The Eleventh Pillar: New York State and the Federal Constitution* (Ithaca, N.Y.: Cornell University Press, 1966). Students looking for a concise retelling of the Constitution's origins might try Carl Van Doren's *The Great Rehearsal: The Story of the Making and Ratifying of the Constitution of the United States* (1948; repr., New York: Penguin Books, 1986), although its bias in favor of the Federalists is quite clear. A good antidote to Van Doren's triumphant tale is Jackson Turner Main's *The Anti-Federalists: Critics of the Constitution, 1781–1788* (Chapel Hill: University of North Carolina Press, 1961).

Three more recent books have added new vigor to the scholarly debate over ratification. David J. Siemers's *Ratifying the Republic: Antifederalists and Federalists in Constitutional Time* (Stanford, Calif.: Stanford University Press, 2002) and Saul Cornell's *The Other Founders: Anti-Federalism and the Dissenting Tradition in America, 1788–1828* (Chapel Hill: University of North Carolina Press, 1999) reconsider the political thought of the Antifederalists and their enduring influence on American politics. Jack N. Rakove's *Original Meanings: Politics and Ideas in the Making of the Constitution* (New York: Vintage Books, 1996) illuminates the question of original intent by examining the diversity of opinion on several key issues surrounding the Constitution's drafting and ratification.

For an offbeat retelling of the New York ratification convention on film, see *An Empire of Reason*, directed by Muffie Meyer (1988), which recreates the convention as if it were being covered by the modern news media. Actors playing Alexander Hamilton and Melancton Smith express opinions drawn from the original ratification convention proceedings but in the context of television talk shows and news programs. This imaginative film merits viewing, especially for the questions it raises about how our modern media and political system might handle the ratification process if it took place today.

CHAPTER 8

Family Values

*Advice Literature for Parents and
Children in the Early Republic*

In Philadelphia in 1783, twenty-year-old Nancy Shippen took some time out of her busy day to record how she wanted to raise her seventeen-month-old daughter Peggy. The child was her first, and Shippen, like many new parents, wanted to have some purposeful design behind her parenting. Starting from the premise that her daughter's upbringing should in "some particulars . . . differ from mine," Shippen recorded in her journal a list of points "Concerning a Daughter's Education":

1st.   Study well her constitution and genius.
2nd.   Follow nature and proceed patiently.
3rd.   Suffer not servants to terrify her with stories of ghosts and goblins.
4th.   Give her a fine pleasing idea of good, and an ugly frightful one of evil.
5th.   Keep her to a good and natural regimen of diet.
6th.   Observe strictly the little seeds of reason in her, and cultivate the first appearance of it diligently.

Shippen listed thirty-five points in all. She ended her list with this thought: "When wisdom enters into her heart, and knowledge is made pleasant to her soul, 'discretion shall preserve her, and understanding shall keep her.'"

Almost fifty years later, in 1831, another parent paused to record his thoughts about child rearing. The Reverend Francis Wayland was a New England minister and the father of a fifteen-month-old son named Heman. One Friday morning, Heman began to cry. Francis took from the child a piece of bread, "intending to give it to him again after he became quiet." Heman quieted down, but when his father offered him the bread, the child threw it away in anger. Displeased by this fit of temper, Francis decided it was time to teach his son a lesson. He left the child alone in a room and gave orders that no one was to speak to Heman or give him food or drink until further notice. Every hour or two throughout the day, Francis visited his son, "offering him the bread and putting out my arms to take him," but the child refused to take any food or drink or to embrace him. Heman went to bed that night without having had anything to eat since the previous day; the next morning, the test of wills continued. At 10:00 A.M., Heman took some bread and milk from his father but still refused to embrace him, so Francis continued the child's confinement. Finally, around 3:00 P.M., Heman capitulated and came to his father, "completely subdued." Francis Wayland was so proud of his method of disciplining Heman, which had rendered the child so much more "mild and obedient," that he published a summary of the episode in the *American Baptist Magazine* to serve as a model for other parents.

Between 1780 and 1830, middle-class Americans made child rearing a national project, devoting an enormous amount of time and energy to raising the first generation born after independence. Of course, parents of all times and places have always contemplated the best way to raise their children, and every culture produces a prescribed set of rules for doing so. Shippen and Wayland, however, were representatives of a conscious effort by American parents in the wake of the Revolution to reexamine and experiment with child-rearing practices. Parents such as Shippen and Wayland became self-consciously reflective about their child rearing, often writing about their experiences with an air of scientific observation and detachment. They also felt the urge to share their thoughts on child rearing with others, to read books published by self-appointed experts, or even (as in Wayland's case) to announce their own expertise. Along with this advice literature for parents came a steady flow of books and magazines aimed at children. By 1830, a homegrown genre of children's literature had emerged in America, offering not only instruction in reading and writing but also stories meant to instill habits and values in their young readers appropriate to the gender roles they would assume as adults.

This focus on child rearing and childhood in the early republic had its roots in several important cultural trends associated with American independence. First, the political ideology of the American Revolution, grounded in the scientific and intellectual movement known as the Enlightenment, challenged patriarchal power in all forms, whether it was held by kings or fathers. As a model of family government, patriarchy equated the father's power over the family with a king's power over his subjects: both were absolute and ordained by God. When the colonies disavowed their allegiance to the British Crown, they also dealt a blow to the unlimited power of the father within the family. A significant figure in this regard was the Enlightenment philosopher John Locke, whose *Second Treatise of Government* had inspired Jefferson's language in the Declaration of Independence. Locke also authored two works, *Essay Concerning Human Understanding* (1690) and *Some Thoughts Concerning Education* (1693), that influenced American attitudes about child rearing. Locke posited that an infant's mind was a tabula rasa, or blank slate; children learned and developed personalities according to the circumstances in which they were raised. Locke's ideas challenged long-held beliefs about original sin and the inherent depravity of children, and they were popular among many parents in eighteenth-century America, as evidenced in Nancy Shippen's emphasis on controlling her daughter's environment and nurturing her reason.

Evangelical Protestantism also encouraged a reexamination of child rearing in the new nation, although often on principles much different from those associated with John Locke. When Francis Wayland waged battle with fifteen-month-old Heman, he was following a time-honored practice among many Anglo-American Protestants: "breaking the will" of the child. The Calvinist theology of many Protestant denominations (especially Congregationalists, Presbyterians, and Baptists) taught that original sin corrupted human nature. Left to their own devices, children would follow their natural inclination to do evil rather than good. A parent's job was to break the child of this predisposition early in life, so that a temperament more submissive and obedient to parental and godly authority could be molded in its place. Wayland's episode with his son perfectly illustrates this process and the reasoning behind it. During the early nineteenth century, a wave of religious revivals known as the Second Great Awakening reinvigorated evangelical religion in America, adding to the old Calvinist emphasis on original sin a new message of spiritual perfectionism made possible by God's grace. The evangelists' metaphor of being "born again" into salvation in Christ drew a parallel between spiritual redemption and childhood, inspiring many parents like Wayland to redouble their efforts to raise children who would be fit to respond obediently to God's call when it came.

Economic change and political ideas also influenced family roles and child rearing in the early republic, especially in the Northeast, where urbanization and industrialization were separating the home from the workplace. As fathers took jobs outside the home, the mother's role in child rearing became more pronounced, and the family's domestic life came increasingly under her authority. Middle- and upper-class women redefined their role in society as "republican mothers," charged with the task of raising children capable of governing themselves as productive citizens of the new nation. The notion of Republican Motherhood encouraged female education because mothers had to be capable of instructing their children not only in reading, writing, and arithmetic but also in the moral habits and virtues of a free citizenry: industry, frugality, trustworthiness, public duty, and piety. The "Cult of Domesticity," a phrase used by historians to describe nineteenth-century America's celebration of the home as a refuge from the cold, impersonal world outside, elevated mothers as the central figure in the household. Society praised them for the loving nurture and wise counsel they dispensed to their children. Unlike the patriarchal family model so evident in Francis Wayland's disciplining of his son, Republican Motherhood and the Cult of Domesticity made affection and sentiment, not duty and obedience, the primary bonds of family life. In the South, where slavery persisted after the American Revolution and industrialization occurred much more slowly, patriarchy remained the defining principle behind family roles in white society.

The transformation of child rearing and childhood in the early republic had important ramifications for family and gender roles in American society. Many of the ideas and images associated with our modern debates over family values—the nuclear family, the stay-at-home mother, the "breadwinner" father—have their origins in the world of Nancy Shippen and Francis Wayland. In the half-century after the American Revolution, they made a purposeful effort to redefine the meaning and purpose of family in a democratic society, and their efforts left a lasting imprint on our culture.

Using Advice Literature as a Source

Before 1800, Anglo-Americans imported their advice on child rearing from Britain or wrote their own imitations of popular English works. Rising literacy rates in eighteenth-century Britain produced a consumer market for children's books in which colonial Americans participated as well. The market for these English works decreased during the Revolutionary era, when Americans rejected much of their cultural patrimony from Britain. Just as many artists thought it important for the new nation to create its own art rather than slavishly imitate Europe's, so too did prominent intellectuals such as Noah Webster, the author of the first American dictionary, urge Americans to reinvent their methods of raising and educating children. By 1830, this impulse had led to a significant surge in magazines and books published by American authors for American parents and children.

Advantages and Disadvantages of Working with Advice Literature

Reading advice literature for parents and children is one of the best ways to reconstruct cultural expectations about roles within the family. All advice literature tells its readers how things ought to be, and parenting literature is no exception. Consider for example this excerpt from a popular parenting book, *The Mother at Home, or, the Principles of Maternal Duty Familiarly Illustrated* by John S. C. Abbott (1833; repr., New York: Harper & Brothers, 1852), in which the author uses the occasion of a boy's question about a pot of boiling coffee to advise parents on how to deal with a child's curiosity:

> "Mother," says the little boy, "what makes the coffee bubble up so?"
> Here the motive is good, and the occasion is proper.[1] And one of the parents explains to the child the chemical process which we call the boiling. The

Note the scientific, experimental tone of author's language

[1] For the child to ask a question.

The author states a rule of child rearing

Note which parent intercedes

The rule is expressed to the child

parents have reason to be gratified at the observation of the child, and the explanation communicates to him valuable knowledge. But perhaps a stranger is present, with whom the father is engaged in interesting conversation. Under these circumstances, the child asks the same question. It is, however, now unseasonable.[2] He ought to be silent when company is present. The mother accordingly replies, "My son, you should not interrupt your father. You must be perfectly silent and listen to what he is saying."

This passage calls to mind the adage, "children should be seen and not heard," but closer reading also reveals assumptions the author is making about gender and the division of power within the family. The father is present in this scene, but the mother intercedes when the child speaks before company. What does this vignette tell you about the author's notion of how authority ought to be ordered within a family?

Even children's literature, which at first glance might seem formulaic and transparent in its purposes, reflects the wider cultural currents in which it is produced. Consider the famous illustrated alphabet from *The New-England Primer* (see Figure 8.1), the most commonly used book for teaching spelling and reading to American children before 1850. The images and rhyming couplets that accompany the letters are meant to focus the children's attention as they memorize their ABCs, in much the same way that the "Alphabet Song" is used today. These images and couplets also convey messages that teach moral lessons and proper behavior.

Another advantage to using advice literature to study the family and childhood in the early republic is their inclusion of both male and female voices. Before 1800, advice literature on child rearing was written overwhelmingly by men, usually ministers concerned with the moral instruction of youth. The notion of Republican Motherhood, however, gave women the social authority to write and publish their own opinions on the family and domestic life. Indeed, several of nineteenth-century America's most prominent female public figures first gained recognition for their advice literature on the home and child rearing. By comparing male and female authorship of such works, historians can get a sense of how women reshaped their private and public lives during the early nineteenth century.

When working with these sources, it is also important to bear in mind their shortcomings. First, advice literature on child rearing is prescriptive: its purpose is to tell people what to do, and if they need to be told, then they probably are not doing what the literature recommends. No one should assume, for example, from the glut of diet books available in modern American bookstores that we are a society in which everyone eats right and gets enough exercise. Likewise, nineteenth-century advice literature on parenting does not necessarily reflect how people raised their children, only what certain authors

---

[2] Untimely.

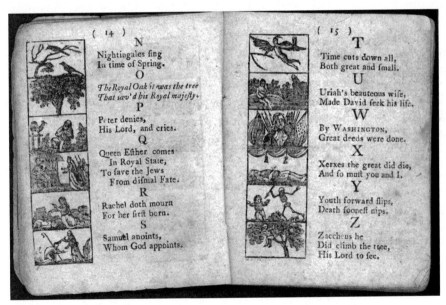

Figure 8.1 Illustrated Alphabet from **The New-England Primer** *This illustrated alphabet from an early nineteenth-century edition of* The New-England Primer *shows how children learned lessons about morality and proper behavior as they learned to read and write. The letters B, H, I, and S teach submission to the authority of God and parents. A, F, and P warn of the punishments that follow of bad behavior. G, R, T, X, and Y remind children of their own mortality: death can come at any time, to the old or young, weak or strong.*

Source: The New-England Primer Improved, Being an Essay Method to Teach Young Children the English Language *(New York: Daniel D. Smith, 1807), 12–15.*

thought about the way people should raise their children. Historians always approach prescriptive literature with skepticism, assuming that if everyone acted according to the instructions contained in such books, their authors would not have felt compelled to write them in the first place. It is useful to ask yourself when you read such sources, "what behavior and ideas is the author criticizing, and who does he or she suspect of practicing them?"

You should also look for regional, class, or racial biases that may be evident in these sources. The authors often presume to speak for everyone, but who actually reads these books? Obviously, the authors wrote for a literate audience, but literacy rates varied widely in early nineteenth-century America. Men were more likely to be literate than women, although this gap closed considerably in the Northeast, the center of the nation's publishing industry. Protestants were more likely to be literate than Catholics, many of whom were poor Irish immigrants working in urban centers, and African American slaves suffered from legal prohibitions against teaching them to read. Literacy also reflected a person's social class, and works on childhood and child rearing enshrined an ideal image of the family that was distinctively middle class, in which fathers were breadwinners, mothers were homemakers, and the nuclear family (parents and children living together under one roof) was the norm. Such an image held little meaning to many working-class, immigrant, and African American families.

This last point brings to mind another caveat about using these sources. Change in family roles and child-rearing practices was hardly uniform in the early republic, even for people living in the same region or in similar material circumstances. If you observe parents and their children at a playground today, you will not have to wait long to witness sharply different models of child rearing practiced by people who in many respects seem alike. The same is true for people of the past. Nancy Shippen and Francis Wayland both lived in northern cities and came from privileged backgrounds, yet each took a very different approach to raising children. As you read these sources, rather than thinking in terms of one type of family or approach to child rearing replacing another, try to identify the different types and approaches that coexisted and influenced each other.

Working with the Source

The sources you will read describe the characteristics of parents and children in an ideal family. Use the table on page 159 as a guide in organizing your notes on how the sources describe the ideal father, mother, son, and daughter, bearing in mind that not every source will address each one of these roles.

	Ideal Father	Ideal Mother	Ideal Son	Ideal Daughter
1. John S. C. Abbott, *The Mother at Home*				
2. Lydia Maria Child, *The Mother's Book*				
3. *The New-England Primer*				
4. *The Busy Bee*				
5. *The Life of George Washington*				

The Source: Advice Literature on Child Rearing and Children's Literature, 1807–1833

ADVICE LITERATURE ON CHILD REARING

 ### *The Mother at Home* by John S. C. Abbott, 1833

John S. C. Abbott was a New England minister who published two of the most widely read books on child rearing in early nineteenth-century America: *The Child at Home* and *The Mother at Home.* These excerpts, from the latter book, concern a topic commonly addressed in such literature: the proper method of disciplining children.

Never Give a Command Which You Do Not Intend Shall Be Obeyed.

There is no more effectual way of teaching a child disobedience, than by giving commands which you have no intention of enforcing. A child is thus habituated to disregard its mother; and in a short time the habit becomes so strong, and the child's contempt for the mother so confirmed, that entreaties and threats are alike unheeded. . . .

Sometimes a child gets its passions excited and its will determined, and it can not be subdued but by a very great effort. Almost every faithful mother is acquainted with such contests, and she knows that they often form a *crisis* in the character of the child. If the child then obtain the victory, it is almost impossible for the mother afterward to regain her authority . . . when once entered upon, they[1] must be continued till the child is subdued. It is not safe, on *any account*, for the parent to give up and retire vanquished.

The following instance of such a contest is one which really occurred. A gentleman, sitting by his fireside one evening, with his family around him, took the spelling-book and called upon one of his little sons to come and read. John was about four years old. He knew all the letters of the alphabet perfectly, but happened at that moment to be in a rather sullen humor, and was not at all disposed to gratify his father. Very reluctantly he came as he was bid, but when his father pointed with his pencil to the first letter of the alphabet, and said, "What letter is that, John?" he could get no answer. John looked upon the book, sulky and silent.

"My son," said the father pleasantly, "you know the letter *A.*"

---

[1] Such contests.

Source: John S. C. Abbott, *The Mother at Home, or, the Principles of Maternal Duty Familiarly Illustrated* (1833; repr., New York: Harper & Brothers, 1852), 47, 60–66.

"I can not say *A*," said John.

"You must," said the father, in a serious and decided tone. "What letter is that?"

John refused to answer. The contest was now fairly commenced. John was willful, and determined that he would not read. His father knew that it would be ruinous to his son to allow him to conquer. He felt that he must, at all hazards, subdue him. He took him into another room, and punished him. He then returned, and again showed John the letter. But John still refused to name it. The father again retired with his son, and punished him more severely. But it was unavailing; the stubborn child still refused to name the letter, and when told that it was *A*, declared that he could not say *A*. Again the father inflicted punishment as severely as he dared to do it, and still the child, with his whole frame in agitation, refused to yield. The father was suffering from the most intense solicitude. He regretted exceedingly that he had been drawn into the contest. He had already punished his child with a severity which he feared to exceed. And yet the willful sufferer stood before him, sobbing and trembling, but apparently as unyielding as a rock. I have often heard that parent mention the acuteness of his feelings at that moment. His heart was bleeding at the pain which he had been compelled to inflict upon his son. He knew that the question was now to be settled, who should be master. And after his son had withstood so long and so much, he greatly feared the result. The mother sat by, suffering, of course, most acutely, but perfectly satisfied that it was their duty to subdue the child, and that in such a trying hour a mother's feelings must not interfere. With a heavy heart the father again took the hand of his son to lead him out of the room for farther punishment. But, to his inconceivable joy, the child shrunk from enduring any more suffering, and cried, "Father, I'll tell the letter." The father, with feelings not easily conceived, took the book and pointed to the letter.

"*A*," said John, distinctly and fully.

"And what is that?" said the father, pointing to the next letter.

"*B*," said John.

"And what is that?"

"*C*," he continued.

"And what is that?" pointing again to the first letter.

"*A*," said the now humble child.

"Now carry the book to your mother, and tell her what the letter is."

"What letter is that, my son?" said the mother.

"*A*," said John. He was evidently perfectly subdued. The rest of the children were sitting by, and they saw the contest, and they saw where was the victory. And John learnt a lesson which he never forgot—that his father had an arm too strong for him. He learned never again to wage such an unequal warfare. He learnt that it was the safest and happiest course for him to obey.

But perhaps some one says it was cruel to punish the child so severely. Cruel! It was mercy and love. It would indeed have been cruel had the father, in that hour, been unfaithful, and shrunk from his painful duty. The passions which he was then, with so much self-sacrifice, striving to subdue, if left unchecked, would, in all probability, have been a curse to their possessor, and have made him a curse to his friends. It is by no means improbable that upon the decisions of that hour depended the character and happiness of that child for life, and even for eternity. It is far from improbable that, had he then conquered, all future efforts to subdue him would have been in vain, and that he would have broken away from all restraint, and have been miserable in life, and lost in death. Cruelty! The Lord preserve children from the *tender mercies* of those who so regard such self-denying kindness.

The Mother's Book by Lydia Maria Child, 1831

Lydia Maria Child was one of the most distinguished women authors of nineteenth-century America, an outspoken advocate for the rights of women, Indians, and African Americans. Early in her career, she edited a successful children's magazine called *Juvenile Miscellany* and published *The Mother's Book*, a best-selling volume of child-rearing advice literature. The excerpts below are from Child's recommendations for dealing with teenaged daughters.

The period of twelve to sixteen years of age is extremely critical in the formation of character, particularly with regard to daughters. The imagination is then all alive, and the affections in full vigor, while the judgment is unstrengthened by observation, and enthusiasm has never learned moderation of experience. During this important period, a mother cannot be too watchful. As much as possible, she should keep her daughter *under her own eye;* and above all things she should encourage *entire confidence towards herself.* This can be done by a ready sympathy with youthful feelings, and by avoiding all unnecessary restraint and harshness. I believe it is extremely natural to choose a mother in preference to all other friends and confidants; but if a daughter, by harshness, indifference, or unwillingness to make allowance for youthful feeling, is driven from the holy resting place, which nature has provided for her security, the greatest danger is to be apprehended. Nevertheless, I would not have mothers too indulgent, for fear of weaning the affections of children. This is not the way to gain the perfect love of young people; a judicious parent is always better loved, and more respected, than a foolishly indulgent one. The real secret is, for a mother never to sanction the slightest error, or imprudence, but at the same time to keep her heart warm and fresh, ready to sympathize with all the innocent gayety and enthusiasm of youth. . . .

I would make it an object so to educate children that they could in case of necessity support themselves respectably. For this reason, if a child discovered a

Source: Mrs. [Lydia Maria] Child, *The Mother's Book* (Boston: Carter, Hendee, and Babcock, 1831), 129–30, 136–40, 145–47, 150–53.

decided talent for any accomplishment, I would cultivate it, if my income would possibly allow it. Everything we add to our knowledge, adds to our means of usefulness. If a girl has a decided taste for drawing, for example, and it is encouraged, it is a pleasant resource which will make her home agreeable, and lessen the desire for company and amusements; if she marries, it will enable her to teach her children without the expense of a master; if she lives unmarried, she may gain a livelihood by teaching the art she at first learned as a mere gratification of taste. The same thing may be said of music, and a variety of other things, not generally deemed *necessary* in education. In all cases it is best that what is learned should be learned well. In order to do this, good masters should be preferred to cheap ones. Bad habits once learned, are not easily corrected. It is far better that children should learn one thing thoroughly, than many things superficially. . . .

My idea is this—First, be sure that children are familiar with all the duties of their present situation; at the same time, by schools, by reading, by conversation, give them as much *solid* knowledge as you can, no matter how much, or of what kind; it will come in use some time or other; and lastly, if your circumstances are easy, and you can afford to indulge your children in any matter of taste, do it fearlessly, without any idea that it will unfit them for more important duties. Neither learning nor accomplishments do any harm to man or woman if the *motive* for acquiring them be a proper one. . . . I believe a variety of knowledge (acquired from such views as I have stated) would make a man a better servant, as well as a better president; and make a woman a better wife, as well as a better teacher. . . .

It is certainly very desirable to fit children for the station they are likely to fill, as far as a parent can judge what that station will be. In this country, it is a difficult point to decide; for half our people are in a totally different situation from what might have been expected in their childhood. However, one maxim is as safe, as it is true: A well-informed mind is the happiest and the most useful in all situations. Every new acquirement is something added to a solid capital. . . .

A knowledge of domestic duties is beyond all price to a woman. Every one ought to know how to sew, and knit, and mend, and cook, and superintend a household. In every situation of life, high or low, this sort of knowledge is a great advantage. There is no necessity that the gaining of such information should interfere with intellectual acquirement, or even with elegant accomplishments. A well regulated mind can find time to attend to all. When a girl is nine or ten years old, she should be accustomed to take some regular share in household duties, and to feel responsible for the manner in which it is done, such as doing her own mending and making, washing the cups and putting them in place, cleaning the silver, dusting the parlor, etc. This should not be done occasionally, and neglected whenever she finds it convenient; she should consider it her department. When they are older than twelve, girls should begin to take turns in superintending the household, keeping an account of weekly expenses, cooking puddings and pies, etc. To learn anything effectually, they should actually do these things themselves, not stand by and see others do them. It is a great mistake in mothers to make such slaves of themselves, rather than divide their cares with daughters. A variety of employment, and a feeling of trust and responsibility add very much to the real happiness of young people. . . .

There is one subject on which I am very anxious to say a great deal; but on which, for obvious reasons, I can say very little. Judging by my own observation, I believe it to be the greatest evil now existing in education. I mean the want of confidence between mothers and daughters on delicate subjects.[1] Children from books, and from their own observation, soon have their curiosity excited on such subjects; this is perfectly natural and innocent, and if frankly met by a mother, it would never do harm. But on these occasions it is customary to either put young people off with lies, or still further to excite their curiosity by mystery and embarrassment. Information being refused them at the only proper source, they immediately have recourse to domestics,[2] or immodest school-companions; and very often their young minds are polluted with filthy anecdotes of vice and vulgarity. This ought not to be. Mothers are the only proper persons to convey such knowledge to a child's mind. They can do it without throwing the slightest stain upon youthful purity; and it is an imperious duty that they should do it. A girl who receives her first ideas on these subjects from the shameless stories and indecent jokes of vulgar associates, has in fact prostituted her mind by familiarity with vice. A diseased curiosity is excited, and undue importance given to subjects, which those she has been taught to respect think it necessary to envelope in so much mystery; she learns to think a great deal about them, and to ask a great many questions. This does not spring from any natural impurity; the same restless curiosity would be excited by any subject treated in the same manner. On the contrary, a well-educated girl of twelve years old would be perfectly satisfied with a frank, rational explanation from a mother. It would set her mind at rest upon the subject; and instinctive modesty would prevent her recurring to it unnecessarily, or making it a theme of conversation with others. . . .

It is a bad plan for young girls to sleep with nursery maids, unless you have the utmost confidence in the good principles and modesty of your domestics. There is a strong love among vulgar people of telling secrets, and talking on forbidden subjects. From a large proportion of domestics this danger is so great, that I apprehend a prudent mother will very rarely, under any circumstances, place her daughter in the same sleeping apartment with a domestic, until her character is so much formed, that her own dignity will lead her to reject all improper conversation.

[1] Sexuality.
[2] Household servants.

CHILDREN'S LITERATURE

 The New-England Primer, 1807

> *The New-England Primer* was first published in the late seventeenth century,
> but it remained the most common textbook for teaching children basic
> lessons in reading, writing, and religion throughout the first half of the
> nineteenth century. No author was ascribed to it, but the first editions were
> published by Boston printer Benjamin Harris in the 1690s. Over the next
> one hundred fifty years, many other printers published versions of it,
> varying the content little from one edition to the next. These excerpts
> illustrate *The New-England Primer's* moral instructions to boys and girls.
> Note how the material addressed to boys is rendered in prose form, while
> that to girls is in verse.

Description of a Good Boy

A Good boy is dutiful to his father and mother, obedient to his master, and loving to all his play fellows. He is diligent in learning his book, and takes a pleasure in improving his mind in every thing which is worthy of praise: he rises
early in the morning, makes himself clean and decent, and says his prayers. If
he has done a fault, he confesses, and is sorry for it, and scorns to tell a lie,
though he might by that means conceal it. He never swears, nor calls names,
nor uses any ill words to his companions. He is never peevish nor fretful, but
always cheerful and good-humoured; he scorns to steal or pilfer any thing from
his companions, and would rather suffer wrong, than to do wrong to any of
them. He is always ready to answer when a question is asked of him — to do
what he is bidden, and to mind what is said to him. He is not a wrangler nor
quarrelsome, and refrains from all sorts of mischief into which other boys run.
By this means he becomes, as he grows up, a man of sense and virtue, he is
beloved and respected by all who know him; he lives in the world with credit
and reputation, and when he dies, is lamented by all his acquaintances.

Description of a Bad Boy

A Bad boy is undutiful to his father and mother, disobedient and stubborn to
his master, and ill natured to all his play fellows. He hates his book, and takes
no pleasure in improving in any thing. He is sleepy and slothful in the morning, too idle to clean himself, and too wicked to say his prayers. He is always in
mischief, and when he has done a fault, will tell twenty lies, in hopes to conceal it. He hates that any body should give him good advice, and when they are
out of his sight, will laugh at them. He swears, wrangles, and quarrels with his
companions. He will steal whatever comes his way, and if he is not caught,

*Source: The New-England Primer Improved, Being an Easy Method to Teach Young Children the En-
glish Language* (New York: Daniel D. Smith, 1807), 17–20.

thinks it no crime, not considering that God sees what he does. He is frequently out of humour, sullen and obstinate, so he will neither do what he is bid, nor answer any question which is asked him. In short, he neglects every thing which he should learn, and minds nothing but play or mischief, by which means he becomes as he grows up, a confirmed blockhead, incapable of any thing but wickedness or folly, despised by all men, and generally dies a beggar.

The Good Girl

So pretty Miss Prudence,
You've come to the Fair;
And a very good girl
They tell me you are:
Here take this fine Orange,
This Watch and this Knot;
You're welcome my dear,
To all we have got:
For a girl who is good,
And so pretty as you,
May have what she pleases,
Your servant, Miss Prue.

The Naughty Girls

So pert misses, prate-apace, how came you here?
There's nobody wants to see you at the fair;
No Oranges, Apples, Cakes, or Nuts,
Will any one give to such saucy sluts.
For such naughty girls, we here have no room,
You're proud and ill-natur'd—Go hussies, go home.

The Busy Bee, 1831

The American Sunday School Union, a voluntary association formed by several Protestant denominations in 1824 to promote children's religious education, published thousands of short children's stories aimed at teaching proper values and habits. Like *The New-England Primer,* these stories usually appeared without any attribution to authorship. This typical story features the characters of Fanny and Jane, two eight-year-old orphans who live with a pious old woman, referred to in the story as their mother.

Source: The Busy Bee (Philadelphia: American Sunday School Union, 1831), 11–13, 15–17, 19–24.

The kind lady took the same pains with Fanny as she did with Jane, and taught both these little girls all those things which she thought necessary for children in their station. She endeavoured to teach them to read and write well, to cipher, and to do neatly all kinds of plain work, as well as to understand household business: but though, as I before said, she bestowed the same labour on both children, yet there was great difference in their improvement. Little Jane took every opportunity of profiting, not only by the instructions of her mother, as she called the lady, but like the busy bee, who gathers honey from every flower which comes her way, she strove to gain some good thing, some useful piece of knowledge, from every person she became acquainted with.

Her mother kept only one servant, whose name was Nanny. Nanny was a clever servant, and understood many useful things, though she was often rude and ill-tempered, and spoke in a vulgar manner. But little Jane had sense to know, that although she was not to imitate the manners of Nanny, and her improper way of speaking, yet she might learn many useful things from her: therefore, when she went into the kitchen with the lady, she shut her ears against Nanny's disagreeable way of speaking, and gave her whole mind to learn how to iron, or to make pies and puddings, or whatever useful thing she might be doing.

When any ladies came to drink tea with her mother, Jane would take notice what work they were doing; and if it was pretty or useful, she would try to do something like it for her doll: and thus she taught herself many useful works. . . .

But while Jane was thus daily learning all that is good, Fanny, in the mean time, was gathering all that is evil. Into whatever company she might chance to fall, she always first took notice of what each person was saying or doing wrong, and afterwards tried to do the same. Whenever she went into the kitchen with her mother, instead of learning to do any thing which might be useful from Nanny, she noticed her way of talking or moving, and then tried to do like her. . . .

But I can scarcely tell you (and indeed it would only give you pain if I could) how many naughty things Fanny learned from the young people she met with, when she went with her mother to pay a visit in the town. She came home, I am sorry to say, much worse than she went, and that indeed was bad enough. . . .

One afternoon, at tea, she[1] said to the little girls, "To-morrow will be my birth day, and I mean to give you a feast, in which I intend to consult the taste of each of you."

The little girls said they were very glad to hear it, and the lady told them to come the next evening into her dressing room, where she said the feast would be set out.

When Fanny and Jane came, at the hour which the lady had fixed upon, to the dressing room, they found their mother sitting reading by the fire, and two little round tables were placed in the middle of the room. One of these tables

---

[1] The old woman.

was covered with a neat white napkin and a little dessert set out upon it in doll's dishes, made of white china with blue edges. There were four little dishes on this table: one contained an orange, another a few yellow apples, another a roasted apple, and a fourth a few biscuits; and in the middle was a little covered china cup, made in the shape of a bee-hive, which contained honey in the honey-comb.

The little girls had scarcely time to examine this table, so neatly laid out, before their eyes were caught by the other table, which was set out in a manner so strange, that they stood still with surprise, and were not able to move. This second table was covered with straw instead of a table cloth, and instead of dishes, there was a great empty wooden bowl.

The lady got up when the little girls came in, and, drawing her chair between the two tables, she said, "Come, Fanny, come Jane; come and enjoy yourselves. I have been trying to make a feast suitable to the tastes of each of you." She then pointed to the table neatly set out with china and fine linen, and invited Jane to seat herself at it, and directed Fanny to place herself by the other table. . . .

"And now," said the lady, as soon as they were seated, "I will divide the feast." So saying, she began to peel the oranges, pare the apples, take the roasted apple out of its skin, and pour the honey from the comb. And, as she went on doing these things, she threw the rind of the orange, the parings of the apple, and the other refuse of the feast, into the wooden bowl, while she placed the best parts on the dishes before Jane. When all this was done, she invited the children to begin to eat. . . . Fanny looked very red, and at last, broke into a violent fit of crying.

"What do you cry for?" said the lady. "I know that you heartily love, and have for a long time sought after every thing that is hateful, filthy, and bad; and like a pig, you have delighted in wallowing in mire. I therefore am resolved to indulge you. As you love what is filthy, you shall enjoy it, and shall be treated like a pig."

Fanny looked very much ashamed; and throwing herself on her knees before her mother, begged her to forgive her, and promised that she would never again seek after wickedness, and delight in it, as she had done.

"Fanny," said the lady, "it is very easy for little girls to make fine promises, and to say, 'I will be good,' and 'I am sorry I have behaved ill.' But I am not a person who will be satisfied with words, any more than you can be with orange-peel and skins of apples. I must have deeds, not words. Turn away from your sins, and call upon your God to help you to repent your past evil life. If you do not wish to partake of the portion of dogs and swine and unclean creatures in the world to come, you must learn to hate sin in the present world." . . .

I am happy to say, that this day was the beginning of better things to Fanny: for she at once forsook her evil habits, and, with God's blessing upon her endeavours, and the care of the good old lady, she so far overcame her faults, as to be allowed, by the next birth-day, to feast with little Jane.

The Life of George Washington, 1832

George Washington was a fixture in nineteenth-century children's literature, and his life was used to teach moral lessons about honesty and piety as well as civic lessons about patriotism and citizenship. In children's biographies of Washington, his mother also played a prominent role and served as an exemplar of motherhood for the new nation.

Mrs. Washington was an affectionate parent; but she did not encourage in herself that imprudent tenderness, which so often causes a mother to foster the passions of her children by foolish indulgences, and which seldom fails to destroy the respect which every child should feel for a parent. George was early made to understand that he must obey his mother, and therefore he respected as well as loved her. She was kind to his young companions, but they thought her stern, because they always felt that they must behave correctly in her presence. The character of the mother, as well as that of the son, are shown in the following incident.

Mrs. Washington owned a remarkably fine colt, which she valued very much; but which though old enough for use, had never been mounted; no one would venture to ride it, or attempt to break its wild and vicious spirit. George proposed to some of his young companions, that they should assist him to secure the colt until he could mount it, as he had determined that he would try to tame it. Soon after sunrise one morning, they drove the wild animal into an enclosure, and with great difficulty succeeded in placing a bridle on it. George then sprang upon its back, and the vexed colt bounded over the open fields, prancing and plunging to get rid of its burden. The bold rider kept his seat firmly, and the struggle between them became alarming to his companions, who were watching him. The speed of the colt increased, until at length, in making a furious effort to throw his conqueror, he burst a large blood-vessel, and instantly died.

George was unhurt, but was much troubled by the unexpected result of his exploit. His companions soon joined him, and when they saw the beautiful colt lifeless, the first words they spoke were: "What will your mother say—who can tell her?" They were called to breakfast, and soon after they were seated at the table, Mrs. Washington said, "Well, young gentlemen, have you seen my fine sorrel colt in your rambles?" No answer was given, and the question was repeated; her son George then replied, "Your sorrel colt is dead, mother." He gave her an exact account of the event. The flush of displeasure which first rose on her cheek, soon passed away; and she said calmly, "While I regret the loss of my favourite, *I rejoice in my son, who always speaks the truth.*"

In his fifteenth year, he had so strong a desire to be actively employed, that he applied for a place as a midshipman in the English navy, (for our country

Source: The Life of George Washington (Philadelphia: American Sunday School Union, 1832), 21–24.

was then under the government of Great Britain,) and succeeded in obtaining it. Full of youthful expectations of enjoyment in a new scene, he prepared ardently to engage in it, when he became convinced that by doing so, he would severely wound the heart of an anxious parent; and with a true spirit of heroism, he denied himself, and in obedience to the command, "Honour thy mother," he gave up his fondly cherished plan, and yielded his own inclinations, to promote her comfort. Thus, while his manly superiority to companions of his own age caused admiration, his filial tenderness was an example to them of compliance with the direction which is given to children in the word of God. "Let them learn first to show piety at home, and to requite their parents," and they are assured that "this is good and acceptable to the Lord." Washington proved the truth of this assurance; for, to the act of filial regard which "requited" the anxious cares of his mother, may be traced his usefulness to his country, and the glory of his character. If he had crossed his mother's wish, and entered the British navy as a midshipman, it is not probable, that he would ever have deserved, or obtained, the title of "Father of his country."

Analyzing the Source

REFLECTING ON THE SOURCE

1. Using your notes from the table on page 159, compare and contrast the different types of ideal fathers, mothers, sons, and daughters depicted in these sources. How do these ideals complement or contradict each other? How do the parenting philosophies depicted in these sources compare to those of Nancy Shippen and Francis Wayland?

2. How do these sources depict parental discipline? How do the methods of discipline differ between fathers and mothers, and what do those differences tell you about assumptions these sources make about the distribution of power and authority within the family?

3. What sorts of positive and negative examples do these sources present for the behavior of boys and girls? Compare and contrast the language and plots of *The Busy Bee* (Source 4) and *The Life of George Washington* (Source 5): how do they define virtue and character differently for girls and boys? In what ways are the shortcomings of bad boys and bad girls gender specific? For example, compare Child's discussion of sexuality in *The Mother's Book* (Source 2) with *The New-England Primer*'s descriptions of bad behavior (Source 3).

MAKING CONNECTIONS

4. What clues do these sources offer about the economic class of their intended audience? How do they depict members of the household who are not biologically related to the parents or children? Where in these sources do you perceive any biases or assumptions that would limit their usefulness for studying the domestic life and family roles of immigrants, slaves, or the urban working class?

5. Compare how the sources in this chapter depict marriage and female citizenship with the sources discussed in Chapter 6, "The Question of Female Citizenship: Court Records from the New Nation." How did the legal definition of a wife's place within society parallel or contradict the social roles associated with Republican Motherhood and the Cult of Domesticity?

6. How do *The New-England Primer* (Source 3), *The Busy Bee* (Source 4), and *The Life of George Washington* (Source 5) compare to the books and stories you read as a child? What does this comparison tell you about the cultural construction of childhood in early nineteenth-century America versus present-day America? What role has television taken in the moral and civic education of present-day American children, and how does it compare in that respect to the efforts of the American Sunday School Union?

Beyond the Source

In the two decades after 1830, the changes that Republican Motherhood and the Cult of Domesticity wrought in the middle-class American family came into full bloom. Capitalizing on the influence and moral authority that society ascribed to them as mothers and household managers, women stepped out of the home and into public roles by forming female benevolent societies and maternal associations that embraced such causes as Christian missionary work and temperance reform. Lydia Maria Child was on the vanguard of this transformation, giving up her writing on domestic and family topics in the 1830s to promote the antislavery cause. Men continued to publish advice literature on family government and child rearing, but the tone of this literature gradually shifted from its roots in evangelical Protestantism to a more scientific concern for controlling the early childhood environment and promoting public education. A significant work in this regard was Horace Bushnell's *Christian Nurture* (1847), which attacked the practice of breaking the child's will and recommended instead "bending the will" through loving and mild nurture. Bushnell's approach assigned even greater importance to the role of the mother as a teacher and disciplinarian, because it discounted the impact of grand confrontations between parent and child, such as that between Francis and Heman Wayland, in favor of a mother's constant surveillance of children in their earliest years.

As the nineteenth century progressed, American children's literature diverged into gender-specific themes that reflected the boundary between the female world of the household and the male world beyond it. While the exemplary lessons in honesty and manly virtue from George Washington's boyhood remained a mainstay of schoolbooks, young boys in the mid-nineteenth century could also indulge in the tales of a fictional world traveler named Peter Parley or the rags-to-riches stories of Horatio Alger. Young girls were expected to read books that celebrated the roles they would assume as wives and mothers. Women fiction writers dominated the genre of the domestic novel, which featured female characters and mother-child relationships at the center of the plot. Perhaps the most enduring work in this genre is Louisa May Alcott's *Little Women* (1868), the tale of a temporarily fatherless family of four girls and their mother during the Civil War. Harriett Beecher Stowe's *Uncle Tom's Cabin* (1852) was not originally published for young readers, although it did appear in storybook editions for children. Its remarkable influence on its mostly female readership rested in a large part on its sympathetic portrayal of a slave family and its condemnation of slaveholders for violating middle-class domestic values.

The model of family that emerged in middle-class American culture in the early nineteenth century perpetuated itself in future generations through literature that prepared children to assume gender-specific roles as adults. Boys' adventure stories anticipated the ups and downs and geographic mobility they would experience in the competitive marketplace of industrial America, while girls learned the joys and duties of domestic life from idealized fictional versions of themselves. Yet, as the careers of Lydia Maria Child and Harriett Beecher Stowe suggest, society's elevation of women as mothers also gave them an entrée into the public sphere as writers, reformers, and advocates for the political and social causes they embraced.

Finding and Supplementing the Source

Several good documentary collections provide a starting point for research on American childhood and child rearing. Philip J. Greven Jr., editor, *Child-Rearing Concepts, 1628–1861: Historical Sources* (Itasca, Ill.: F. E. Peacock Publishers, 1973), focuses on the colonial era but includes selections from significant nineteenth-century authors. Paula S. Fass and Mary Ann Mason, editors, *Childhood in America* (New York: New York University Press, 2000), deftly combines primary documents and secondary sources. Robert H. Bremner, editor, *Children and Youth in America: A Documentary History, Volume I: 1600–1865* (Cambridge: Harvard University Press, 1970), is comprehensive in its coverage of such topics as labor, health, and delinquency. Two editions (1805 and 1807) of *The New-England Primer* can be found online at **gettysburg.edu/~tshannon/his341/colonialamer.htm**.

Some of the most influential works on child rearing and childhood in the early republic have been written by social historians interested in the domestic life of American families. See especially Nancy F. Cott, *The Bonds of Womanhood: "Woman's Sphere" in New England, 1780–1835* (New Haven, Conn.: Yale University Press, 1977); Philip Greven, *The Protestant Temperament: Patterns of Child-Rearing, Religious Experience, and the Self in Early America* (New York: Alfred A. Knopf, 1977); Jan Lewis, *The Pursuit of Happiness: Family and Values in Jefferson's Virginia* (Cambridge: Cambridge University Press, 1983); and Mary P. Ryan, *Cradle of the Middle Class: The Family in Oneida County, New York, 1790–1865* (Cambridge: Cambridge University Press, 1981). Linda Kerber explains the meaning of Republican Motherhood in *Women of the Republic: Intellect and Ideology in Revolutionary America* (Chapel Hill: University of North Carolina Press, 1980). E. Anthony Rotundo describes male gender roles in the nineteenth-century family in *American Manhood: Transformations in Masculinity from the Revolution to the Modern Era* (New York: Basic Books, 1993).

For a recent survey of childhood and child rearing in the period discussed in this chapter, see Jacqueline S. Reinier, *From Virtue to Character: American Childhood, 1775–1850* (New York: Twayne Publishers, 1996). Another recent survey notable for its attention to childhood outside of the white middle-class experience is Joseph E. Illick, *American Childhoods* (Philadelphia: University of Pennsylvania Press, 2002). Two noteworthy articles on changing child-rearing practices in the nineteenth century are Charles Strickland, "A Transcendentalist Father: The Child-Rearing Practices of Bronson Alcott," *History of Childhood Quarterly* 1 (1973): 4–51, and Daniel T. Rodgers, "Socializing Middle-Class Children: Institutions, Fables, and Work Values in Nineteenth-Century America," *Journal of Social History* 13 (1980): 354–67. For a survey of child-rearing advice literature in the twentieth century, see Ann Hulbert, *Raising America: Experts, Parents, and a Century of Advice about Children* (New York: Alfred A. Knopf, 2003). For historical studies of American children's literature, see Gail Schmunk Murray, *American Children's Literature and the Construction of Childhood* (New York: Twayne Publishers, 1998), and Gillian Avery, *Behold the Child: American Children and Their Books, 1621–1922* (Baltimore, Md.: Johns Hopkins University Press, 1994).

CHAPTER 9

King Cotton

Economic Data on Slavery in the Antebellum South

Hinton R. Helper had failed as a storekeeper and gold prospector when he tried his hand as an economist in his book *The Impending Crisis of the South: How to Meet It* in 1857. For more than twenty years, Americans had been reading attacks on slavery written by abolitionists and runaway slaves, but Helper's book was different. In the first place, he was a white Southerner, born and educated in backcountry North Carolina before moving to New York and then California to pursue his fortune. Second, his book did not invoke any of the standard arguments found in abolitionist tracts and slave narratives to condemn the South's "peculiar institution." He did not indict masters for the cruelty they inflicted upon their slaves, nor did he appeal to Christian morals or divine judgment to convince them to change their ways. He did not sentimentalize slave families as they struggled against forced separations and their masters' sexual abuse. In fact, Helper did not seem particularly concerned with the plight of the slaves at all. Rather, he addressed himself to the nonslaveholding whites of the South, who needed to be liberated from "the secondary degree of slavery" imposed on them by a labor system that cut off their access to opportunity, retarded their economic progress, and kept them mired in poverty and backwardness.

To make his case against slavery, Helper employed a new kind of evidence: economic data he culled from the seventh U.S. census in 1850. As one reviewer of *The Impending Crisis* put it, Helper fired at the walls of slavery with the "heavy artillery of statistics." In table after table of data, he compared free states and slave states in their wealth, mortality rates, mileage of canals and railroads, crops, livestock, farm machinery, and bank capital. He compared Northern and Southern numbers on literacy, public schools, churches, post offices, newspapers, and libraries. "All the free States are alike, and all the slave States are alike," Helper concluded. "In the former, wealth, intelligence, power, progress, and prosperity are the prominent characteristics; in the latter poverty, ignorance, embecility [sic], inertia, and extravagance, are the distinguishing features. To be convinced it is only necessary for us to open our eyes and look at the facts, to examine the *statistics* of the country . . . [and] let figures be the umpire."

Helper's critics had statistics of their own. "Cotton *is* king," proclaimed South Carolina senator James Hammond, and trade figures backed him up. Cotton grown on Southern plantations dominated the world market in the mid-nineteenth century and accounted for more than 50 percent of U.S. exports. The world's leading industrial nation of the time, Great Britain, imported more than 70 percent of the cotton used in its textile mills from the American South. Slave prices rose steadily between 1800 and 1860, testimony to the continuing profitability and investment potential of this type of labor. Southern planters, taking their cue from Helper, compared the health, diets, and material circumstances of their slaves with those of free wage laborers in the North and found their slaves to be ahead in all categories. Southern agriculture was vital and expansive in the antebellum era, and Southern farmers moved into new western territories at a rate that outpaced their Northern contemporaries.

Ever since Helper and his critics leveled their statistical artillery at each other, historians have been doing the same, compiling data and crunching numbers in an effort to determine whether slavery had a detrimental or beneficial effect on the South's economic development. Some historians have followed in Helper's footsteps and argued that slavery retarded progress in the South because coerced labor was less efficient than free labor. Masters had to rely on constant supervision to make slaves work, and the slaves had an incentive to sabotage that work by performing it slowly or poorly. Slave owners spent their capital on the purchase of more slaves and land, diverting it from investment in technological improvements that could have increased their productivity.

On the other hand (and in economics, there is always the other hand), some historians have challenged the idea that slavery was inherently inefficient. While not endorsing slavery or the racism it spawned, they have argued that the antebellum Southern economy was more diversified and wealthier than Helper and likeminded critics were willing to admit. Slave prices rose during the antebellum era because slaveholders earned a return on their investment at least on par with that of Northern capitalists investing in textile mills. Slavery also gave slaveholders a distinct advantage over Northern farmers when it came to acquiring labor in an agricultural economy. Northern farmers relied on family members and seasonal hired hands to produce their crops. In the North, where land was plentiful and labor scarce, no free adult male would work for someone else if he could acquire his own farm. Slaveholders, however, controlled a dependent labor force that was constantly growing. The seven hundred thousand slaves counted in the first U.S. census in 1790 had increased to a population of four million by 1860. Two factors contributed to that increase. First, the North American slave population achieved a positive rate of natural reproduction during the mid-eighteenth century. Second, the United States continued to import slaves from overseas until Congress banned the international slave trade in 1808 (smuggling meant that the trade did not effectively cease until 1820). With no upward limit on the size of their labor force, slaveholders could specialize in a profitable cash crop and realize economies of scale—that is, increases in production above proportional increases in the inputs of land and labor—that Northern farmers could only dream of.

As Helper did in *The Impending Crisis*, economic historians have compared the economic output of the South and North before the Civil War in an effort to measure the efficiency of slave versus free labor. Efficiency is not the same as profitability. Profitability is a measure of income in excess of outlay; we know slavery was profitable at least in the short run because slaveholders earned enough money to buy more slaves and land. Efficiency is much more difficult to measure. From Helper to the present day, researchers have typically measured the efficiency of slavery relative to that of free labor by trying to determine which of the two labor systems produced more output or higher rates of income. Approaching slavery in this manner may strike you as misleading and unfeeling. After all, this was a racist labor system that brutalized slaves and treated them as property rather than human beings. Asking questions about the economic efficiency of slave labor may seem to minimize or ignore the suffering of those who had to endure this kind of exploitation. Nevertheless, approaching slavery in this manner helps answer important questions about how the economies of the South and North diverged in the decades before the Civil War and why the resources commanded by each during that conflict differed so substantially.

By no means does this approach exhaust the methods or sources economic historians have used to study slavery, but it does offer a way to frame the questions historians must bring to the evidence. Like all investigators, historians tend to find what they are looking for. In other words, the way in which they approach their evidence profoundly affects what they find. Helper and his critics knew that numbers are not neutral. The way a researcher presents data determines in a large part its persuasive power.

Using Economic Data as a Source

Mark Twain once wrote, "There are three kinds of lies: lies, damned lies, and statistics." Historians have typically shared Twain's distrust of statistical data, preferring instead to rely on the more familiar types of textual sources that you have encountered in previous chapters of this book. However, after World War II, the invention of computers that could process enormous quantities of data inspired economic historians to embrace applied mathematics in their reevaluation of American slavery. These scholars described their research methods as "econometrics" or "cliometrics" (Clio was the Muse of history in ancient Greece), a name that signified their emphasis on bringing scientific quantification and precision to the study of history.

Historians who use econometrics to study slavery rely on three main types of evidence. First, they have returned to the census data first used by Helper in 1857 to attack slavery, but rather than simply tallying up totals from the official U.S. census reports, they have gone back into the original manuscript schedules of the census takers and mined them for information as diverse as farm acreage, wealth distribution, and slave birth and marriage patterns. In the same manner, they have used probate records such as wills and estate inventories from county courthouses throughout the South to reconstruct the human and material dimensions of a typical slaveholder's household. The third category of evidence they have used includes textual sources such as slave narratives, travel narratives, and plantation account books and journals. None of these sources were particularly new to historians in the 1950s; previous historians had used them for generations to build their portrait of slavery. But armed with new computer technology, econometricians used these sources differently, bringing a mathematical rigor to their work that rendered in statistical form all sorts of details about day-to-day life in the antebellum South, from the caloric value of the slaves' diet to the average rate of return a planter could expect on his cotton crop.

Some of the evidence and language used in econometrics may be difficult to understand without specialized training in mathematics, but you should confront this data with the same healthy skepticism that you would bring to a more familiar textual source. The mathematics used in compiling the data you will examine in this chapter rarely involved anything more complicated than long division. Even if the mathematical techniques used to compile the data are unfamiliar, you can still ask this source the same questions you would bring to any other source: What is the argument that the author of this data is trying to make? What potential biases or prejudices are evident in that data? Consider for example the two tables on page 178, both of which present data concerning the impact slavery had on the development of technology in the South. The first table, from Helper's *The Impending Crisis,* compares the number of patents issued by the federal government for new inventions in free and slave states during 1856. The second table, from econometrician Gavin Wright's *The Political Economy of the Cotton South* (1978), organizes its data on patents in a different manner. Both authors are making a similar point—that slavery retarded technological innovation in the South—but note how Wright's table overcomes some of the problems inherent in Helper's presentation of his evidence.

There is a tendency among people to assume a degree of truthfulness in statistics that they do not automatically grant to written words, but just because the data is generated by someone with knowledge more specialized than yours does not mean you should presume it to be correct and accurate. As Mark Twain knew, numbers as well as words are used to make arguments, and you do not have to be an expert mathematician to approach statistics with a critical eye.

Patents Issued on New Inventions in the Free and Slave States, 1856

Free States		Slave States	
California	13	Alabama	11
Connecticut	142	Arkansas	0
Illinois	93	Delaware	8
Indiana	67	Florida	3
Iowa	14	Georgia	13
Maine	42	Kentucky	26
Mass.	331	Louisiana	30
Michigan	22	Maryland	49
N. Hampshire	43	Mississippi	8
N. Jersey	78	Missouri	32
New York	592	N. Carolina	9
Ohio	139	S. Carolina	10
Pennsylvania	267	Tennessee	23
Rhode Island	18	Texas	4
Vermont	35	Virginia	42
Wisconsin	33		
Total	**1,929**		**268**

Is the use of patent data for one year only a suitable method for collecting information about the antebellum era? Why should the reader assume 1856 was a representative year for such data?

More people lived in the North than in the South in 1856. Should that matter in explaining this discrepancy in patents issued?

Data is divided into two columns, one for free states and one for slave states. The column totals at bottom show a clear discrepancy between the number of patents issued.

Where did Helper get his data? Presumably, he looked at the records of the U.S. Patent Office for 1856, but the table lists no source.

Patents Granted per Year for Mechanical Devices for Grain and Corn Harvesting, Threshing, and Cutting and for Cotton Harvesting, Picking, and Cutting

	Corn	Grain	Cotton
1837–1849	3.5	6.5	0.2
1850–1860	18.5	10.5	2.6
1866–1879	39.5	38.5	13.2
1880–1890	44.2	59.5	30.5
1891–1900	53.9	56.0	22.9
1901–1914	69.1	52.2	53.6

Source: Jacob Schmookler, *Patents, Inventions, and Economic Change* (Cambridge, Massachusetts: Harvard University Press, 1972), 100–03.

This table tells the reader that farmers who grew cotton (grown overwhelmingly in the South with slave labor before 1860) were much less likely to invest in new technologies than farmers who grew corn or grain (mainstays of the North's agriculture)

Wright's table focuses more specifically on patents issued for technology related to agriculture

Presents patent information from 1837 to 1914, allowing the reader to compare data before and after the Civil War

Citation allows readers to go to Wright's source for the data and check Wright's numbers

Advantages and Disadvantages of Working with Economic Data

One of the advantages to working with statistical data is that it allows researchers to organize and process vast quantities of information in a consistent manner. Census data is a good example. The Constitution mandates a census by the federal government every ten years. This process collects information about the U.S. population that is a treasure trove for historians, but working with it requires a researcher to design a consistent method of evaluating the evidence that can be followed by others. Sampling, in which a researcher constructs a small, representative sample for statistical analysis from a much larger pool of evidence, provides one such method. By following commonly accepted formulas and rules for such analysis, econometricians make sure that the results of one researcher can be replicated by others, a standard commonly used by scientists to judge the integrity of each other's work.

Statistical analysis also enables economic historians to circumvent some of the biases found in the traditional textual sources on slavery. Travel narratives written by Northern abolitionists or slave narratives written by runaways appealed to readers in part because of the eyewitness accounts they gave of slavery, but their evidence was by nature anecdotal and subjective. For example, a runaway's slave narrative might tell a harrowing first-person story about a slave auction, but it cannot tell us how many slaves were sold at such auctions over a given period. To answer that sort of question, econometricians have analyzed data from other sources, such as the records of slave sales maintained by the city government of New Orleans between 1804 and 1862, which included thousands of such transactions.

Statistical analysis also helps recover the experience of marginalized groups who left behind few textual sources. The vast majority of slaves in the antebellum South were illiterate because the law prohibited them from learning to read or write. They could not keep journals or write letters detailing their lives for historians to read. Census data and probate records can be used to recover much information about the material circumstances in which they lived: the size of the farms on which they worked, their average marriage ages and family size, their likelihood of being sold and separated from family during their lifetime.

Disadvantages involved in working with statistical data stem from a number of different sources. First, the researcher must determine if the data he or she has on hand is sufficiently complete to produce meaningful conclusions. A sample that is too small or unrepresentative will not produce results that can be easily replicated. Certainly, the U.S. census provided the most complete and reliable record of such data, but it occurred only every ten years and concerned itself chiefly with the vital statistics and material wealth of free whites rather than enslaved African Americans. Recordkeeping by state, county, and municipal governments varied widely in the antebellum era, and such evidence was also susceptible to destruction by fire or flood. Whether they like it or not, econometricians often have to rely on evidence that is fragmentary and incomplete, forcing them to make judgments about the applicability of their conclusions across state or regional boundaries. For example, can conclusions drawn from the New Orleans records on slave sales be applied to slave markets elsewhere in the South? Econometricians may produce very reliable results from analysis of that particular set of data but find their conclusions challenged when they attempt to apply them across the board.

One other disadvantage commonly associated with using statistical data is that it cannot convey the interpersonal and psychological dimensions of slavery. Statistics can provide a wealth of information about a slave's diet, work productivity, and life expectancy, but they cannot plumb the depths of the master-slave relationship. Some econometricians admit this limitation up front, but it does impinge upon their work in a number of significant ways. For example, the question of whether masters relied chiefly on positive or negative incentives to coerce labor from their slaves cannot be fully answered without due consideration of the emotions generated by this relationship. Masters may have been profit seekers, but they were also human beings prone to passions of anger and hostility that affected their use of discipline. Likewise, slaves may have valued rewards offered for their work, but they may have also had non-monetary motives for their behavior, such as solidarity with their kin and friends. In general, statistics can tell us much about the material circumstances of life in the antebellum South, but they cannot explain human behavior within the institution of slavery.

Working with the Source

A good way to approach the analysis of economic data is to ask, "what point is the author of this data trying to make?" When you comprehend the argument behind a table of data, you may then ask critical questions about the methods or sources used to compile that information. As you read through the sources in the next section, use this table as an aid in recording your answers to these questions.

	What is the point of this data?	What questions do you have about how it was collected and presented?
Output		
1. *Agricultural Bushel-Measure Products*		
2. *Value of Farms and Domestic Animals*		
3. *Crops per Acre*		
Technology		
4. *Patents Issued on New Inventions*		
5. *Patents Granted per Year for Mechanical Devices*		
Wealth and Income		
6. *Wealth Per Capita of Cities*		
7. *Per Capita Income by Region*		
8. *The Relative Level of the Per Capita Income*		
Urbanization and Manufacturing		
9. *Product of Manufactures*		
10. *Regional Patterns of Manufacturing*		
11. *Regional Patterns of Urbanization*		

The Source: Data Measuring the Economic Efficiency of Slavery in the Antebellum South

Historians have tried to measure the efficiency of slave labor in the antebellum South in a number of ways: output (how much Southern farms produced), technology (how intensively those farms used tools and machines to improve their production), wealth and income (how much that production earned for the South's free and enslaved populations), and urbanization and manufacturing (how rapidly nonagricultural sectors of the economy grew). All of these measures involve comparing the South to other states, regions, or nations, most typically to the free states of the North.

OUTPUT

In *The Impending Crisis*, Hinton Helper included more than fifty tables comparing the economic output of the North and South. His primary source of data for these tables was the U.S. census of 1850. The following three tables offer examples of how he organized his data to emphasize the difference in outputs between free labor in the North and slave labor in the South.

Agricultural Bushel-Measure Products of Free and Slave States, 1850

Source: The tables in Sources 1, 2, and 3 are from Hinton R. Helper, *The Impending Crisis of the South: How to Meet It* (New York: Burdick Brothers, 1857), 39.

Free States	Bushels	Price per Bushel	Value
Wheat	72,157,486	1.50	$ 108,236,229
Oats	96,590,371	0.40	38,636,148
Indian Corn	242,618,650	0.60	145,571,190
Potatoes (Irish[1] & Sweet)	59,033,170	0.38	22,432,604
Rye	12,574,623	1.00	12,574,623
Barley	5,002,013	0.90	4,501,811
Buckwheat	8,550,245	0.50	4,275,122
Beans & Peas	1,542,295	1.75	2,699,015
Clover & Grass Seeds	762,265	3.00	2,286,795
Flax Seeds	358,923	1.25	448,647
Garden Products			3,714,605
Orchard Products			6,332,914
Total	**499,190,041**		**$ 351,709,703**

Slave States	Bushels	Price per Bushel	Value
Wheat	27,904,476	1.50	$ 41,856,714
Oats	49,822,799	0.40	19,953,191
Indian Corn	348,992,282	0.60	209,395,369
Potatoes (Irish & Sweet)	44,847,420	0.38	17,042,019
Rye	1,608,240	1.00	1,608,240
Barley	161,907	0.90	145,716
Buckwheat	405,357	0.50	202,678
Beans & Peas	7,637,227	1.75	13,365,147
Clover & Grass Seeds	123,517	3.00	370,551
Flax Seeds	203,484	1.25	254,355
Garden Products			1,377,260
Orchard Products			1,355,827
Total	**481,766,889**		**$ 306,927,067**

[1] White.

Value of Farms and Domestic Animals in Free and Slave States, 1850

Free States	Value of Livestock	Value of Animals Slaughtered	Cash Value of Farms, Farm Implements, and Machines
California	$ 3,351,058	$ 107,178	$ 3,977,524
Connecticut	7,467,490	2,202,266	74,618,963
Illinois	24,209,258	4,972,286	102,538,851
Indiana	22,478,555	6,567,935	143,089,617
Iowa	3,689,275	821,164	17,830,436
Maine	9,705,726	1,646,773	57,146,305
Mass.	9,647,710	2,500,924	112,285,931
Michigan	8,008,734	1,328,327	54,763,817
N. Hampshire	8,871,901	1,522,873	57,560,122
N. Jersey	10,679,291	2,638,552	124,663,014
New York	73,570,499	13,573,883	576,631,568
Ohio	44,121,741	7,439,243	371,509,188
Pennsylvania	41,500,053	8,219,848	422,598,640
Rhode Island	1,532,637	667,486	17,568,003
Vermont	12,643,228	1,861,336	66,106,509
Wisconsin	4,897,385	920,178	30,170,131
Total	**$ 286,376,541**	**$ 56,990,237**	**$ 2,233,058,619**

Slave States	Value of Livestock	Value of Animals Slaughtered	Cash Value of Farms, Farm Implements, and Machines
Alabama	$ 21,690,112	$ 4,823,485	$ 69,448,887
Arkansas	6,647,969	1,163,313	16,866,541
Delaware	1,849,281	373,665	19,390,310
Florida	2,880,058	514,685	6,981,904
Georgia	25,728,416	6,339,762	101,647,595
Kentucky	29,661,436	6,462,598	160,190,299
Louisiana	11,152,275	1,458,990	87,391,336
Maryland	7,997,634	1,954,800	89,641,988
Mississippi	19,403,662	3,636,582	60,501,561
Missouri	19,887,580	3,367,106	67,207,068
N. Carolina	17,717,647	5,767,866	71,823,298
S. Carolina	15,060,015	3,502,637	86,568,038
Tennessee	29,978,016	6,401,765	103,211,422
Texas	10,412,927	1,116,137	18,701,712
Virginia	33,656,659	7,502,986	223,423,315
Total	**$ 253,723,687**	**$ 54,388,377**	**$ 1,183,995,274**

Crops per Acre on the Average in Free and Slave States, 1850

Free States	Wheat	Oats	Rye	Indian Corn	Irish Potatoes
Connecticut	0	21	0	40	85
Illinois	11	29	14	33	115
Indiana	12	20	18	33	100
Iowa	14	36	0	32	100
Maine	10	0	0	27	120
Massachusetts	16	26	13	31	170
Michigan	10	26	0	32	140
N. Hampshire	11	30	0	30	220
N. Jersey	11	26	0	33	0
New York	12	25	17	27	100
Ohio	12	21	25	36	0
Pennsylvania	15	0	0	20	75
Rhode Island	0	30	0	0	100
Vermont	13	0	20	32	178
Wisconsin	14	35	0	30	0
Total	**161**	**325**	**107**	**436**	**1503**

Slave States	Wheat	Oats	Rye	Indian Corn	Irish Potatoes
Alabama	5	12	0	15	60
Arkansas	0	18	0	22	0
Delaware	11	20	0	20	175
Florida	15	0	0	0	125
Georgia	5	18	7	16	125
Kentucky	8	18	11	24	130
Louisiana	0	0	0	16	0
Maryland	13	21	18	23	75
Mississippi	9	12	0	18	105
Missouri	11	26	0	34	110
N. Carolina	7	10	15	17	65
S. Carolina	8	12	0	11	70
Tennessee	7	19	7	21	120
Texas	15	0	0	20	250
Virginia	7	13	5	18	75
Total	**121**	**199**	**63**	**275**	**1360**

Recapitulation of Crops per Acre on the Average, 1850

Free States		Slave States	
Wheat	12 bushels per acre	Wheat	9 bushels per acre
Oats	27 bushels per acre	Oats	17 bushels per acre
Rye	18 bushels per acre	Rye	11 bushels per acre
Indian Corn	31 bushels per acre	Indian Corn	20 bushels per acre
Irish Potatoes	125 bushels per acre	Irish Potatoes	113 bushels per acre

TECHNOLOGY

In addition to buying more land and hiring more labor, a farmer may try to increase production through technological innovation. One way historians have tried to measure such change in the nineteenth century is by looking at patent information. The following tables, from Helper's *The Impending Crisis* and historian Gavin Wright's 1978 book *The Political Economy of the Cotton South*, provide comparative data on patents granted in the North and South. Wright, one of the leading econometricians to study the nineteenth-century South, came to many of the same conclusions as Helper about the negative impact slavery had on technological investment and innovation in the South.

Patents Issued on New Inventions in the Free and Slave States, 1856

Source: Helper, *The Impending Crisis*, 294.

Free States		Slave States	
California	13	Alabama	11
Connecticut	142	Arkansas	0
Illinois	93	Delaware	8
Indiana	67	Florida	3
Iowa	14	Georgia	13
Maine	42	Kentucky	26
Mass.	331	Louisiana	30
Michigan	22	Maryland	49
N. Hampshire	43	Mississippi	8
N. Jersey	78	Missouri	32
New York	592	N. Carolina	9
Ohio	139	S. Carolina	10
Pennsylvania	267	Tennessee	23
Rhode Island	18	Texas	4
Vermont	35	Virginia	42
Wisconsin	33		
Total	**1,929**	**Total**	**268**

Patents Granted per Year for Mechanical Devices for Grain and Corn Harvesting, Threshing, and Cutting and for Cotton Harvesting, Picking, and Cutting

Source: Gavin Wright, *The Political Economy of the Cotton South: Households, Markets, and Wealth in the Nineteenth Century* (New York: W.W. Norton, 1978), 108.

	Corn	Grain	Cotton
1837–1849	3.5	6.5	0.2
1850–1860	18.5	10.5	2.6
1866–1879	39.5	38.5	13.2
1880–1890	44.2	59.5	30.5
1891–1900	53.9	56.0	22.9
1901–1914	69.1	52.2	53.6

Source: Jacob Schmookler, *Patents, Inventions, and Economic Change* (Cambridge, Massachusetts: Harvard University Press, 1972), 100–03.

WEALTH AND INCOME

The following tables compare per capita wealth and income in the South with that of other regions or nations. ("Per capita" means "per person.") The first table is from Helper's *The Impending Crisis*. The second and third tables are the work of econometricians Robert William Fogel and Stanley L. Engerman, whose 1974 book *Time on the Cross: The Economics of American Negro Slavery* challenged many of Helper's conclusions about the inefficiency of slave labor and ignited a controversy among historians about using econometrics to study American slavery.

6   *Wealth Per Capita of Nine Free and Slave Cities*

Source: Helper, *The Impending Crisis,* 347.

Nine Free Cities	Population	Wealth	Wealth Per Capita
New York	700,000	$ 511,740,492	$ 731
Philadelphia	500,000	325,000,000	650
Boston	165,000	249,162,500	1,150
Brooklyn	225,000	95,800,440	425
Cincinnati	210,000	88,810,734	422
Chicago	112,000	171,000,000	1,527
Providence	60,000	58,064,516	967
Buffalo	90,000	45,474,476	505
New Bedford	21,000	27,047,000	1,288
Total	**2,083,000**	**$ 1,572,100,158**	**$ 754**

Nine Slave Cities	Population	Wealth	Wealth Per Capita
Baltimore	250,000	$ 102,053,839	$ 408
New Orleans	175,000	91,188,195	521
St. Louis	140,000	63,000,000	450
Charleston	60,000	36,127,751	602
Louisville	70,000	31,500,000	450
Richmond	40,000	20,143,520	503
Norfolk	17,000	12,000,000	705
Savannah	25,000	11,999,015	480
Wilmington	10,000	7,850,000	785
Total	**787,000**	**$ 375,862,320**	**$ 477**

Per Capita Income by Region for 1840 and 1860 in 1860 Prices

This table shows the growth in per capita income in several regions of the United States. The reference to 1860 prices in the table's title means that Fogel and Engerman have adjusted the figures in the 1840 column to reflect the dollar's value in 1860. This adjustment eliminates inflation as a factor in explaining the growth of these figures between 1840 and 1860. Fogel and Engerman also noted that their per capita income figures for the South included free and enslaved persons. In other words, if they had calculated per capita income for whites only, the South's would have been much higher than the North's.

Source: The tables in Sources 7 and 8 are from Robert William Fogel and Stanley L. Engerman, *Time on the Cross: The Economics of American Negro Slavery*, 2 volumes (Boston: Little, Brown and Company, 1974), 1:248.

	1840	1860	Average Annual Rates of Change (Percent)
National Average	$ 96	$ 128	1.4
North	109	141	1.3
Northeast	129	181	1.7
North Central	65	89	1.6
South	74	103	1.7
South Atlantic	66	84	1.2
East South Central	69	89	1.3
West South Central	151	184	1.0

Northeast: ME, NH, VT, MA, RI, CT, NY, NJ, PA
North Central: MI, OH, IN, IL, WI, MO, IA, MN, ND, SD, NE, KS
South Atlantic: VA, MD, DE, DC, NC, SC, GA, FL
East South Central: KY, TN, AL, MS
West South Central: OK, AR, LA, TX

The Relative Level of the Per Capita Income of the South in 1860

Economists use "relative" measures as a way of creating a common yard-stick for comparing data from different sources. In this case, Fogel and Engerman converted per capita income figures from different nations into U.S. dollars. They assigned the South's per capita income the value of $100 and measured the North's and other nations' per capita incomes relative to it. In other words, think of the $100 value assigned to the South as a bar, the distance over which or under which indicates how another region's or nation's per capita income compared to that of the South in 1860.

Southern Per Capita Income Level = 100

Australia	$144
North	140
Great Britain	126
South	100
Switzerland	100
Canada	96
Netherlands	93
Belgium	92
France	82
Ireland	71
Denmark	70
Germany	67
Norway	54
Italy	49
Austria	41
Sweden	41
Japan	14
Mexico	10
India	9

URBANIZATION AND MANUFACTURING

Economists interested in measuring the efficiency of the South's slave labor system have also studied sectors of the economy other than agriculture. In particular, they have compared the rate of industrialization between the North and South by looking at each region's production of manufactured goods. They have also used urbanization, or the growth of city populations, as a measure of nonagricultural economic activity, because city dwellers typically earned their living in ways others than farming. These tables, from *The Impending Crisis* and *The Political Economy of the Cotton South,* provide data on such trends.

9 *Product of Manufactures in the Free and Slave States, 1850*

Source: Helper, *The Impending Crisis,* 284.

Free States	Value of Annual Products	Capital Invested	Hands Employed
California	$ 12,862,522	$ 1,006,197	3,964
Connecticut	45,110,102	23,890,348	47,770
Illinois	17,236,073	6,385,387	12,065
Indiana	18,922,651	7,941,602	14,342
Iowa	3,551,783	1,292,875	1,707
Maine	24,664,135	14,700,452	28,078
Mass.	151,137,145	83,357,642	165,938
Michigan	10,976,894	6,534,250	9,290
N. Hampshire	23,164,503	18,242,114	27,092
N. Jersey	39,713,586	22,184,730	37,311
New York	237,597,249	99,904,405	199,349
Ohio	62,647,259	29,019,538	51,489
Pennsylvania	155,044,910	94,473,810	146,766
Rhode Island	22,093,258	12,923,176	20,881
Vermont	8,570,920	5,001,377	8,445
Wisconsin	9,923,068	3,382,148	6,089
Total	**$ 842,586,058**	**$ 430,240,051**	**780,576**

Slave States	Value of Annual Products	Capital Invested	Hands Employed
Alabama	$ 4,538,878	$ 3,450,606	4,936
Arkansas	607,436	324,065	903
Delaware	4,649,296	2,978,945	3,888
Florida	668,338	547,060	991
Georgia	7,086,525	5,460,483	8,378
Kentucky	24,588,483	12,350,734	24,386
Louisiana	7,320,948	5,318,074	6,437
Maryland	32,477,702	14,753,143	30,124
Mississippi	2,972,038	1,833,420	3,173
Missouri	23,749,265	9,079,695	16,850
N. Carolina	9,111,245	7,252,225	12,444
S. Carolina	7,063,513	6,056,865	7,009
Tennessee	9,728,438	6,975,279	12,032
Texas	1,165,538	539,290	1,066
Virginia	29,705,387	18,109,993	29,108
Total	**$ 165,413,027**	**$ 95,029,879**	**161,738**

Regional Patterns of Manufacturing

This table provides regional comparisons of two measures of manufacturing: the per capita (per person) investment in manufacturing and the per capita output of manufacturing. In this table, the "South" includes all slaveholding states. The "Cotton South" refers to a smaller interstate region in which cotton production dominated the economy, primarily South Carolina, Georgia, Alabama, Mississippi, Louisiana, Arkansas, and Texas.

Source: Wright, *The Political Economy of the Cotton South,* 110.

	Capital Invested by Manufacturing per Capita		Value of Manufacturing Output per Capita	
	1850	1860	1850	1860
New England	$57.96	$82.13	$100.71	$149.97
Middle States	$35.50	$52.21	$ 71.24	$ 96.28
Northwest	$11.70	$18.95	$ 26.32	$ 37.33
Pacific States	$10.39	$42.35	$ 84.83	$129.04
South	$ 7.60	$10.54	$ 10.88	$ 17.09
Cotton South	$ 5.11	$ 7.20	$ 6.83	$ 10.47
U.S.	$22.73	$32.12	$ 43.69	$ 59.98

Source: U.S. Bureau of the Census, *Compendium of 1850 Census,* 179; Eight U.S. Census, *Manufactures,* 725; Ninth Census, *Compendium,* 799.

Regional Patterns of Urbanization by Percent of Population

This table shows the growth in the urban population in different regions of the United States between 1820 and 1860.

Source: Wright, *The Political Economy of the Cotton South,* 110.

	1820	1830	1840	1850	1860
New England	10.5	14.0	19.4	28.8	36.6
Middle Atlantic	11.3	14.2	18.1	25.5	35.4
East North Central	1.2	2.5	3.9	9.0	14.1
West North Central	0	3.5	3.9	10.3	13.4
South Atlantic	5.5	6.2	7.7	9.8	11.5
East South Central	0.8	1.5	2.1	4.2	5.9

Source: Douglass North, *The Economic Growth of the United States, 1790–1860* (1961; New York: W.W. Norton, 1966), 258.

Analyzing the Source

REFLECTING ON THE SOURCE

1. Using your notes on page 181, what types of methods and sources were used in compiling the data presented in these tables? Depending upon the types of sources they are using, do you find some of the tables more convincing than others? Why or why not?

2. What factors other than type of labor (slave or free) might have accounted for the differences in Helper's totals for Northern and Southern agricultural output in Sources 1, 2, and 3? Why or why not would a per acre figure, such as that provided in Source 3, be a more accurate measure of the efficiency of free versus slave labor than state-by-state totals, such as those given in Source 2?

3. Compare Helper's per capita wealth figures in Source 6 with the per capita income figures provided by Fogel and Engerman in Sources 7 and 8. If Helper wanted his figures to prove the superiority of free over slave labor, why was it to his advantage to measure the per capita wealth of urban populations rather than the entire Northern and Southern populations? Likewise, why do you suppose Fogel and Engerman emphasized regional and national comparisons in their per capita income figures?

MAKING CONNECTIONS

4. What does the data on patents in Sources 4 and 5 tell you about how Southerners and Northerners chose to invest the capital they put into increasing agricultural production? What sort of incentive did a Northern farmer have for investing in new technology that a Southern farmer did not?

5. What does the data on urbanization and manufacturing in Sources 9, 10, and 11 tell you about the comparative positions of the Northern and Southern economies in these categories? Why would measures of urban population growth and manufacturing output be important in discussions of the efficiency of slave versus free labor?

6. Having reviewed the information provided in these tables, how would you formulate a definition for economic efficiency that could be applied to both slave and free labor? How would your definition incorporate measures of both inputs (for example, land, labor, technology) and outputs?

Beyond the Source

The divergent paths toward economic development taken by the North and South during the first half of the nineteenth century had important ramifications for each region. On the eve of the Civil War, the South led the world in cotton production, but it lagged behind the North in population, manufacturing, and wealth. During the war, the North's superior industrial capacity sustained the war effort, while the South's economy withered under a Union naval blockade that closed access to international markets. Cotton planters' profits evaporated during the war, and emancipation destroyed the property value they claimed in their slaves. An economic system that had prospered in the South since the 1790s utterly collapsed by 1865. Recovery came slowly. In the war's aftermath, cotton prices fell and the South's economy stagnated. Yet Southern farmers, white and black alike, continued to cultivate cotton at the expense of other crops. While the rest of the nation experienced unparalleled growth in urbanization, industrialization, and agricultural output, the South remained locked in a cycle of low productivity and profits.

Economic historians debate the reasons for this stagnation as vociferously as they do the efficiency of antebellum slavery. Some attribute it to the destruction the Civil War visited upon the South's economic infrastructure, including its plantations, urban centers, and railroad lines. Others emphasize the loss in property and capital that the planter class faced as a result of emancipation. Still others emphasize external factors, such as the decline in the world demand for cotton, which had little to do with the political or social consequences of the Civil War.

Invariably, studies of the South's postwar economy address the problem of labor and race relations. Planters were stripped of their most valuable asset when the Emancipation Proclamation and Thirteenth Amendment ended slavery. The former slaves were set free with no assets of their own in the form of land, livestock, tools, or cash. Both of these groups needed each other to survive, but their relationship was strained by years of racial antagonism. Planters tried to replicate the old system of slavery as closely as possible by signing the freedmen to labor contracts that tied them to the land for a year or more at a time. The freedmen preferred to work their own land on their own terms, but if that was not an option, they accepted tenancy on white-owned land, so long as they could work free from the white supervision that had been the hallmark of antebellum plantations. Gradually, there evolved in the South a system of sharecropping, in which black farmers lived and worked on land owned by their former masters, paying rent by surrendering a percentage of their crop at the end of the year.

This system gave the freedmen and women the autonomy they desired, but it also had its drawbacks. Landlords demanded that they cultivate a cash crop, typically cotton, to use as payment for their rent. This led to an intensification of cotton cultivation at a time when its value was declining, drawing precious capital and labor away from the production of livestock and subsistence crops that would have improved the farmers' material welfare. Also, because landlords and local merchants controlled the farmers' access to provisions and supplies, sharecroppers went into debt that bound them to the land from one generation to the next. Cotton's stranglehold on Southern farmers would not be broken until the twentieth century, when a combination of crop failures caused by boll weevil infestations and black migration to Northern cities finally ended the sharecropping system.

Finding and Supplementing the Source

The seventh U.S. census, which provided the basis of Helper's data in *The Impending Crisis*, was originally published in Washington, D.C., in 1853. A modern edition is United States Census Office, *The Seventh Census of the United States, 1850: Embracing a Statistical View of Each of the States and Territories* (New York: N. Ross, 1990). The Web site of the U.S. Census Bureau (**census.gov**) is a good place to start Internet searches for census information, but bear in mind that its online data focuses on the most recent U.S. census in 2000. For a Web site that provides access to data from every U.S. census since 1790, see the University of Virginia Geospatial and Statistical Data Center's United States Historical Census Data Browser (**fisher.lib.virginia.edu/census/**). For a useful introduction to the methods of econometrics, see Pat Hudson, *History by the Numbers: An Introduction to Quantitative Approaches* (London: Arnold Publishers, 2000).

The most famous work to apply econometrics to the study of American slavery is Robert William Fogel and Stanley L. Engerman, *Time on the Cross: The Economics of American Negro Slavery,* 2 volumes (Boston: Little, Brown and Company, 1974). Volume 1 presents the book's argument in language aimed at the general reader; Volume 2, *Evidence and Methods,* contains source materials and appendixes useful to anyone interested in the authors' methodology. Fogel and Engerman have since qualified and elaborated on their interpretation of slavery in *Without Consent or Contract: The Rise and Fall of American Slavery* (New York: W. W. Norton, 1989).

Fogel and Engerman's argument that antebellum slavery was economically efficient and provided a higher standard of living for slaves than contemporary wage laborers in the North ignited a firestorm of criticism. Two important works that take aim at Fogel and Engerman's methods and conclusions are Paul A. David, Herbert G. Gutman, Richard Sutch, Peter Temin, and Gavin Wright, *Reckoning with Slavery: A Critical Study in the Quantitative History of American Negro Slavery* (New York: Oxford University Press, 1976), and Herbert G. Gutman, *Slavery and the Numbers Game: A Critique of "Time on the Cross"* (Urbana: University of Illinois Press, 1975). Both of these books make for compelling reading in how historians argue over the meaning of statistical evidence.

The scholarly debate over slavery's efficiency has continued in several important works based on econometrics. Gavin Wright's *The Political Economy of the Cotton South: Households, Markets, and Wealth in the Nineteenth Century* (New York: W. W. Norton, 1978) makes the case for the inefficiency of slave labor. Wright's *Old South, New South: Revolutions in the Southern Economy since the Civil War* (New York: Basic Books, 1986) and Roger L. Ransom and Richard Sutch's *One Kind of Freedom: The Economic Consequences of Emancipation* (Cambridge: Cambridge University Press, 1977) apply econometrics to the study of the Southern economy after the Civil War. Mark M. Smith, *Debating Slavery: Economy and Society in the Antebellum American South* (Cambridge: Cambridge

University Press, 1998) provides an excellent, brief overview of the debate over the economics of slavery.

Other significant works that address the economics of slavery in the antebellum South but without relying on econometrics for their methodology include Kenneth M. Stampp's *The Peculiar Institution: Slavery in the Ante-Bellum South* (New York: Alfred A. Knopf, 1956), Eugene D. Genovese's *The Political Economy of Slavery* (New York: Pantheon, 1965) and *Roll, Jordan, Roll: The World the Slaves Made* (New York: Pantheon, 1974), and James Oakes's *The Ruling Race: A History of American Slaveholders* (New York: Alfred A. Knopf, 1982).

CHAPTER 10

The West in Jacksonian Arts

George Catlin's Paintings of American Indians

During the Jacksonian era, it was hard to enjoy American arts and literature without bumping into Indians making their final exits. James Fenimore Cooper's novel *The Last of the Mohicans* (1826) popularized the figure of the stoic, lone Indian observing the passing of his people. Theatergoers flocked to see John Augustus Stone's *Metamora; or, the Last of the Wampanoags* (1829), a play that retold the story of Metacom, or King Philip, the doomed leader of a seventeenth-century Indian war in New England. People who preferred seeing real Indians to fictional ones attended lectures given by western Indians touring eastern cities. The most famous of these was Black Hawk, a chief of the Sac and Fox nation in Illinois, who came to the nation's capital in 1833 as a prisoner of war but gained celebrity status after speaking engagements in Baltimore, Philadelphia, and New York. The "vanishing Indian" became a permanent fixture in the cultural landscape of Jacksonian America; as soon as one exited, another appeared to deliver a heartfelt elegy to his people and lament his "last of" status.

An art exhibition that opened in New York City in 1837 did for the vanishing Indian in American painting what *The Last of the Mohicans* and *Metamora; or, the Last of the Wampanoags* had done for him on page and stage. George Catlin's Indian Gallery featured almost five hundred paintings of Indians, mostly portraits, but also scenes of hunting, religious ceremonies, and village life. His exhibition also included tools, weapons, clothing, and other artifacts associated with the paintings' subjects. Catlin had painted every single one of the works featured in the exhibition, and he proudly proclaimed their unrivaled authenticity, claiming that he had visited fifty Indian nations from the western reaches of the Missouri River to the southwestern plains of Texas.

Born in Wilkes-Barre, Pennsylvania, in 1796, Catlin spent his formative years in the East, practicing law in Connecticut and then moving to Philadelphia in 1821 to make his living as an artist. He specialized as a painter of miniatures, palm-sized portraits of loved ones in an age before photography, but he longed to devote his talents to a greater purpose. He found his inspiration in 1829 when a delegation of western Indians visited Philadelphia. The exotic appearance and noble carriage of these strangers, so unlike any people Catlin had ever seen before, convinced him to abandon his work and move to St. Louis, where he would seek out and paint Indians still untouched by white society. As Catlin described it in his book *Letters and Notes on the Manners, Customs, and Condition of the North American Indians* (1841), he used his paints and brushes to record "the living manners, customs, and character of an interesting race of people, who are rapidly passing away from the face of the earth, lending a hand to a dying nation who have no historians or biographers of their own to portray with fidelity their native looks and history."

For Catlin, there were two types of Indians: those who retained their "original" character and those who had fallen into their "secondary" character. The difference between the two was exposure to what whites called civilization. In Catlin's view, those Indians who still lived removed from civilization were uncorrupted and worthy of preservation on canvas. Those who traded and lived among whites, even on the frontier, were diminished physically and morally by the evils of "whisky, the small-pox, and the bayonet." Catlin had no doubt that the western expansion of the United States would mean the ultimate extinction of all Indian peoples; those still in their original state were doomed to assume their secondary character before too long. Thus, he undertook his work with great urgency, enlisting the aid of federal Indian superintendent William Clark (of Lewis and Clark fame) to find and paint as many as possible of those Indians still living in their original condition. As Catlin described it, "the traveler who would see these people in their native simplicity and beauty, must needs be hastily on his way to the prairies and Rocky Mountains, or he will see them only as they are now seen on the frontiers, as a basket of *dead game*, harassed, chased, bleeding, and dead."

Between 1832 and 1836, Catlin made five trips into Indian country from his base in St. Louis. The first and longest of these was a steamboat journey of almost two thousand miles up the Missouri River, to its confluence with the Yellowstone River in modern North Dakota. During this trip, Catlin painted 170 canvases and encountered Indians barely known to Americans outside of a small coterie of fur traders, military personnel, and government agents. In the next five years, Catlin also traveled southwest into the Arkansas Territory and north into the upper Mississippi Valley and western Great Lakes, but none of those trips matched in scale or productivity his first journey up the Missouri. When he returned east with his Indian Gallery in 1837, Catlin had already acquired a reputation (much of it due to his own tireless self-promotion) as an inland Columbus, the first and final witness to the Indians of the Great Plains in their natural state.

Catlin's approach to his Indian subjects reflected the political climate in which he lived and worked. Catlin headed for St. Louis in 1830, the same year in which Congress, at the urging of President Andrew Jackson, passed the Indian Removal Act. By this legislation, Congress authorized the forced eviction of Indians east of the Mississippi to reservations in the West. The act was aimed primarily at several Indian nations in the Southeast that were resisting efforts by state governments there to appropriate their land and extend legal jurisdiction over them. The Cherokees, Creeks, Choctaws, Chickasaws, and Seminoles—known collectively as "the Five Civilized Tribes" because of their adoption of European-style government, farming, and property law after the American Revolution—had no interest in surrendering their lands or sovereignty to Georgia, Alabama, Mississippi, and Tennessee. Jackson, who had risen to fame fighting Indians in the 1810s, had no interest in protecting their territorial or political autonomy.

Supporters of Indian removal justified this policy with language very similar to that used by Catlin to explain why he went west in 1830. They claimed that Indians and whites could not peacefully coexist; invariably, contact and trade with whites led to the cultural and physical degeneration of the Indians. Removal across the Mississippi, where Indians could live free from the corruption of white society, was their only hope for forestalling their extinction. Of course, the experience of the Cherokees and other Indian nations that had managed to adapt and even in some cases flourish as whites invaded their homelands proved otherwise, but in the 1830s, Jackson and his supporters did not want to recognize such an alternative to removal. In 1831, the Supreme Court ruled that dispossessing the Cherokees against their wishes was unconstitutional. However, the Supreme Court had no power to enforce its decision; that job rested with the executive branch of the federal government. As president, Jackson chose to ignore the Supreme Court's ruling, thus enabling the states to proceed with Indian removal unhindered.

A painter brings more to the canvas than just paints and brushes. In Catlin's case, the distinction he drew between Indians in their original and secondary character was a product of political and cultural attitudes surrounding Indian removal in the 1830s. The "vanishing Indian" he took as his subject was a literary and political invention of his time. Nevertheless, Catlin did go west, meet hundreds of Indians, and create a rich visual documentation of their lives.

Using Paintings as a Source

Scholars interested in Catlin's work have always been mindful of his commercial motives. Catlin was an entrepreneur as well as an artist. He took seriously his self-appointed charge as historian to the Indians, but he also tried constantly to cultivate a paying audience for his Indian Gallery. During his journeys west in the 1830s, he wrote dispatches to eastern newspapers describing his travels and adventures. As early as 1833, he exhibited selections of his paintings in Pittsburgh, Louisville, and Cincinnati. And although he told his audiences that his work was self-financed, he sought the patronage of Indian agents, military officers, and congressmen whom he thought might convince the federal government to purchase his collection for a hefty sum.

Catlin's commercial motives and relentless self-promotion colored the reception of his work from the start. Many of his contemporaries involved in the fur trade found his written accounts of the Indians of the upper Missouri to be exaggerated or misleading, and they ridiculed his claims to being the first white man to visit the sacred pipestone quarries of the Sioux in western Minnesota. One of the pioneering scholars of American anthropology, Henry Rowe Schoolcraft, took issue with Catlin's depiction of the Mandans' O-kee-pa ceremony, calling it sensationalistic and without basis in fact. To counter such attacks, Catlin published statements by other western travelers corroborating his work, and he never missed the opportunity to have a touring group of Indians visit his gallery and testify to its accuracy.

Art historians have also criticized Catlin's work on aesthetic grounds. Catlin placed an obvious priority on quantity over quality in his art and worked at a breakneck pace. The hurried nature of much of his work is evident in the broad strokes he used, especially in his landscapes. As for his portraits, it is important to remember that before painting Indians, Catlin had earned his living as a miniaturist. He preferred to paint sitting figures and was most adept at faces and busts. Many of his full-length portraits are oddly proportioned, featuring improperly sized bodies or limbs. There is no doubt that Catlin was an artist of tremendous output; whether he was one of tremendous skill is debatable.

His defenders emphasize his significance as an innovator in American painting. Previous artists had painted Indian subjects, but always in the comfort of their studios. Catlin was the first to bring his paints and canvases to the Indians in their camps and villages, giving his work an unprecedented realism. His assembly-line style and output also reflected the dynamic quality of Jacksonian society. Catlin was constantly on the move, adapting his work to his surroundings, finding new subjects and trying new ways of painting them. While he may not have been the most technically proficient painter in nineteenth-century America, his work reflected the kinetic, innovative spirit of the Jacksonian era.

It is harder to determine what Catlin's paintings can tell us about the Indians themselves. Indians are ubiquitous in his work, even his landscapes, yet they are silent. Catlin occasionally recorded the reactions his subjects had to his paintings in his letters and journals but with the same air of self-congratulation evident throughout his published writings. Generally, Indians enjoyed the novelty of having their portraits painted by an artist who visited their villages, but some Sioux medicine men warned that Catlin used his craft to capture Indian souls. At the very least, the fact that Catlin conducted his work without threats or injuries to his person or property indicates that his Indian hosts offered no united or sustained resistance to his work.

After taking account of all the biases Catlin brought to his work—his commercial motives, the political climate of Indian removal, his prejudices against

Indians who lived among whites and his idealized vision of those who did not—the reliability of his paintings as a historical source remains in question. Catlin's work ignored the world inhabited by the Five Civilized Tribes and other eastern Indians who had lived for generations among whites, but what can it tell us about those he encountered west of the Mississippi?

Advantages and Disadvantages of Working with Paintings

Few readers are willing to suffer voluntarily through James Fenimore Cooper's novels today, but historians still find them a useful source for understanding the origins of the "vanishing Indian" motif in America literature. So too can Catlin's art help explain the prejudices and assumptions that shaped Indian policy in the Jacksonian era. While it is tempting to evaluate Catlin's paintings by our modern standards of what constitutes good art, it is more fruitful for the historian to ask why an artist wishing to produce commercially viable and historically significant work in the 1830s would have pursued Native Americans as subjects. To understand why Catlin's work appealed to the audiences who paid to see it is to gain insight into American attitudes about the West and Indians at that time.

Another advantage to using Catlin's work is what it can tell us about the life and culture of its subjects. Catlin preferred portraits, but he also painted scenes of Indian religious ceremonies, games, and hunting. These works provide some of the earliest and most complete visual records of Indian life on the Great Plains. In the case of the Mandans, a Missouri Valley tribe practically wiped out by a smallpox epidemic in 1837, Catlin's work is indispensable for documenting Indians that very few other whites ever encountered.

Despite these obvious strengths in Catlin's work, it is important to remember that many contemporaries questioned Catlin's reliability as an eyewitness to Indian cultures. He ranged far and wide during the years he spent in the West, but he did not settle in any one place long enough to learn native languages or knit himself into the fabric of native communities. Unlike fur traders who often married into Indian families, Catlin developed no kinship ties or other bonds of lasting intimacy among his subjects. He had to rely on traders and government agents as his interpreters, and he lost much of their support when he published reports in newspapers critical of the fur trade, which in Catlin's opinion corrupted Indian morals and society. As noted earlier, his detractors also accused him of engaging in sensationalism whenever it served his commercial purposes. It is useful, therefore, to look for evidence within Catlin's work that contradicts his claim that his Indian subjects lived in a natural state untainted by white contact.

Consider for example the image on page 202, the frontispiece (an illustration that appears at the start of a book) to Catlin's *Letters and Notes on the Manners, Customs, and Condition of the North American Indians*. This self-portrait, titled *The Author Painting a Chief, at the Base of the Rocky Mountains*, depicts Catlin in the process of painting Máh-To-Tóh-Pa, or Four Bears, a chief of the Mandans (see Source 2, p. 206).

What does this frontispiece tell Catlin's readers about his work?

Catlin has posed his subject in front of Siouan buffalo-hide tipis, rather than the wood and earth lodges of the Mandans

Note the rifle of non-Indian origin

What do the Indians' expressions tell you about the way Catlin promoted himself?

Careful examination of this image illustrates some of the advantages and disadvantages associated with using Catlin's work as a historical source. On the one hand, it provides a visual introduction to how Catlin went about his work and how he self-consciously fashioned his identity as an artist (note his confident stance, his awestruck audience). The image, however, also confuses elements of Mandan and Sioux culture in a way that suggests Catlin was more concerned with dramatic effect than factual consistency in this painting. Catlin claimed that his Indian subjects still lived in a natural state untainted by contact with whites, but items of non-Indian origin were often included in his paintings. Besides the rifle, what other evidence in this painting contradicts his claim?

Catlin premised his work on a dichotomy that held very little meaning to his Indian subjects. As an artist, he wanted to freeze time, to capture Indians in their "original" character before they slipped into their degraded "secondary" character. His work shows little interest in documenting the long-term process of cultural adaptation that all Indians experienced in the wake of white contact and that was well underway when he arrived on the Great Plains in the 1830s. Indeed, it may be argued that the Indians Catlin painted never really existed. French, Spanish, and American traders had long preceded him on the Missouri, and the Indians he painted in their supposed natural state showed much evidence of that contact, particularly in their material culture. Historians using Catlin's paintings must bear in mind that many of his subjects were already quite familiar with the world he came from and anxious to expand their trade and diplomacy with it. As living, breathing human beings, they contradicted the very ideas and sentiments Catlin wished to convey in his work.

Working with the Source

It will be helpful as you examine Catlin's paintings to reflect on two related questions: what information does the painting convey about its subject, and what evidence does it present of contact and exchange between Indians and whites? The table on page 204 will help you record your reactions.

	What information does this painting convey about its subject?	What evidence does this painting present of contact and exchange between Indians and whites?
1. Shón-Ka-Ki-He-Ga		
2. Máh-To-Tóh-Pa		
3. La-Dóo-Ke-A		
4. Pshán-Shaw		
5. Jú-Ah-Kís-Gaw		
6. Wi-Jún-Jon		
7. Fort Pierre		
8. Buffalo Hunt		
9. Buffalo Chase		
10. Bird's-Eye View		
11. Sioux Encamped		
12. The Cutting Scene		

The Source: Paintings from George Catlin's Indian Gallery, 1832–1839

Catlin provided a title for each one of his paintings and a brief description of its subject in his exhibition catalog. Each portrait was titled in a similar manner: Catlin rendered the subject's name phonetically, followed by a version in English. In keeping with modern cataloguing practices, the caption for each of the paintings included here also includes the subject's tribal affiliation as Catlin identified it, followed in some cases by the preferred modern usage (in parentheses), and the year in which Catlin painted it.

Shón-Ka-Ki-He-Ga, Horse Chief, Grand Pawnee Head Chief, Pawnee, 1832

Catlin's experience as a miniaturist is evident in this portrait, which features only the subject's torso and head. The round object hanging from beads around Shón-Ka-Ki-He-Ga's neck is a peace medal, distributed by the United States government to allied Indian chiefs.

Source: Smithsonian American Art Museum: 1985.66.99.

Máh-To-Tóh-Pa, Four Bears, Second Chief, in Full Dress, Mandan (Numakiki), 1832

Máh-To-Tóh-Pa's appearance in this portrait has come to define what novels, films, and other popular media regard as the authentic attire of an Indian chief: a full-length feathered headdress complemented by buffalo horns, beaded leggings and moccasins, and a shirt featuring pictographs of native design. Catlin purchased the outfit from Four Bears and featured it in his Indian Gallery.

Source: Smithsonian American Art Museum: 1985.66.128.

3 *La-Dóo-Ke-A, Buffalo Bull, A Grand Pawnee Warrior,* Pawnee, 1832

This unfinished portrait (only the torso and head of the subject are complete) tells the viewer about the process of Catlin's work from the field to the exhibit hall. He concentrated on the subject's head and face during a sitting and often left other details to be completed in his studio in St. Louis.

Source: Smithsonian American Art Museum: 1985.66.100.

Pshán-Shaw, Sweet-Scented Grass, Twelve-Year-Old Daughter of Bloody Hand, Arikara (Sahnish), 1832

Catlin's Indian Gallery included far fewer portraits of Indian women than men, an imbalance due in part to his working methods. The traders, agents, and military officers he traveled with transacted most of their business with Indian males. The girl in this portrait was the daughter of Bloody Hand, a chief who also posed for Catlin. Most of Catlin's female subjects were relatives of distinguished males he also painted.

Source: Smithsonian American Art Museum: 1985.66.125.

5 | *Jú-Ah-Kís-Gaw, Woman with Her Child in a Cradle*, Ojibwa (Chippewa), 1835

This portrait of an Indian woman and her child also depicts a cradleboard, an object of native manufacture used to hold and carry infants.

Source: Smithsonian American Art Museum: 1985.66.186.

Wi-Jún-Jon, Pigeon's Egg Head (The Light) Going to and Returning from Washington, Assiniboine (Nakoda), 1837–1839

This "before and after" portrait was one of Catlin's most overtly political and frequently reproduced works. Catlin first encountered Wi-Jún-Jon (and painted a portrait of him) in 1831, when the warrior was en route to Washington, D.C., to meet President Jackson. Eighteen months later, Catlin met him again, this time returning from Washington "in the dress and with the airs of a civilized beau." According to Catlin, Wi-Jún-Jon soon fell into disgrace, the stories of his eastern travels earning him the reputation of an "unexampled liar." He was eventually murdered by his own people.

Source: Smithsonian American Art Museum: 1985.66.474.

Fort Pierre, Mouth of the Teton River, 1200 Miles above St. Louis, 1832

Named for fur trader Pierre Chouteau, this fort was on the Missouri River in Sioux country. The American Fur Company maintained a trading post there. French traders had been active on the upper Missouri since the eighteenth century.

Source: Smithsonian American Art Museum: 1985.66.384.

Buffalo Hunt under the Wolf-Skin Mask, 1832–1833

Catlin painted several scenes of buffalo and buffalo hunting on the Great Plains. Indians used a variety of methods to hunt buffalo, including driving them into water, snow banks, or over bluffs. In this scene, Indian hunters approach a buffalo herd disguised as animals.

Source: Smithsonian American Art Museum: 1985.66.414.

Buffalo Chase, A Surround by the Hidatsa,
Hidatsa (Minitari), 1832–1833

Note the difference in the hunting techniques used here and in Source 8 on page 212. Several Indian nations on the Great Plains, most notably the Comanche and the Sioux, adopted horses for transportation after Spanish colonists from Mexico brought this animal north of the Rio Grande in the seventeenth century.

Source: Smithsonian American Art Museum: 1985.66.409.

Bird's-Eye View of the Mandan Village, 1800 Miles above St. Louis, Mandan (Numakiki), 1837–1839

Plains Indian cultures included mobile hunter-gather societies such as the Sioux and more sedentary farming societies such as the Mandans, depicted here with their distinctive dome-shaped lodges.

Source: Smithsonian American Art Museum: 1985.66.502.

Sioux Encamped on the Upper Missouri, Dressing Buffalo Meat and Robes, Western Sioux (Dakota), 1832

This scene conveys information about the gender division of labor within Plains Indian communities. The female figures in the lower left foreground and right background are dressing buffalo hides, while males return from the hunt with horses loaded with more hides. Buffalo meat is drying on racks arranged around the tipis.

Source: Smithsonian American Art Museum: 1985.66.377.

12 *The Cutting Scene, Mandan O-Kee-Pa Ceremony,*
Mandan (Numakiki), 1832

Catlin's paintings of the Mandan O-kee-pa ceremony, an annual initiation and fertility rite, were some of the most controversial in his Indian Gallery. According to Catlin, young men inside a medicine lodge were suspended from cords anchored in their chests and shoulders until they lost consciousness. Catlin's critics claimed that he fabricated many of the gruesome details in his visual and textual descriptions of O-kee-pa, a charge he adamantly denied. The decimation of the Mandans by smallpox in 1837 made corroboration of Catlin's claims difficult, and the debate over the accuracy of his descriptions of this ceremony continued for the rest of his life.

Source: Denver Art Museum, The William Sr. and Dorothy Harmsen Collection.

Analyzing the Source

REFLECTING ON THE SOURCE

1. Catlin claimed that he painted Indians in their natural state, untouched by white contact. Judging from these paintings, what values did Catlin associate with the Indians' "original" character, and how did he think contact with whites altered that character?

2. In the table on page 204, you listed evidence from the paintings of contact and exchange between Plains Indians and whites that predated Catlin's western journeys. How do these paintings depict the impact that such contact had on the Indians' material culture or subsistence patterns?

3. Paintings often say as much about the artist who creates them as the subjects they depict. What do these paintings tell you about Catlin and his world? Which of these paintings endorse or contradict the notion of the "vanishing Indian" that was so popular in nineteenth-century American literature? What commentary do they offer on the politics of Indian removal?

MAKING CONNECTIONS

4. Most of Catlin's paintings were portraits, but he did a fair number of landscapes and village scenes as well. Judging from the works you have examined here, what kinds of topics or themes was he trying to address when he painted a landscape or village scene? Do such works have a different impact on the viewer than his portraits?

5. In Chapter 1, you learned how historians use archaeological evidence to reconstruct the European colonization of eastern North America from the Indians' perspective. How might Catlin's paintings be used in conjunction with archaeological evidence to document the collision of natives and newcomers on the Great Plains? What sort of information can these paintings convey that archaeological sources cannot?

6. Historians confront potentially unreliable sources all the time, yet seldom choose to discard them altogether. Knowing what you do about the methods and motives behind Catlin's work, how would you make use of this source to study American Indians in the Jacksonian era? What do you think are the chief liabilities of this source, and how might you compensate for those weaknesses through the use of other sources? What do you see as the chief benefit of using Catlin's paintings as a historical source?

Beyond the Source

When Catlin's efforts to sell his Indian Gallery to the federal government failed, he took it to Europe. In 1839 he sailed for England with more than five hundred of his paintings, along with his collection of Indian artifacts, a full-size Crow Indian lodge, and two grizzly bears (both very much alive and not at all pleased with their travel arrangements; one took off the nose of a sailor who got too close). As this inventory might suggest, the European version of the Indian Gallery was one part art exhibit and one part circus. To attract audiences, Catlin dressed himself and a few assistants in Indian costume and reenacted scenes depicted in his paintings. In 1843, a group of Ojibwas already in England joined Catlin's entourage and proved so popular that he hired small parties of Indians to accompany the Indian Gallery to Paris and Brussels.

Despite drawing large audiences, Catlin could not pay his bills, and he ended up in debtors prison in 1852. Bankruptcy forced him to sell off his original collection of paintings. To avoid his creditors, he traveled extensively, including trips to South America to paint Indians there. By 1870, he had completed a second set of six hundred paintings, known as the "Cartoon Collection" because much of it was based on sketches he had made of his original paintings before selling them off. In 1870, he returned to the United States to have his work exhibited at the Smithsonian Institution. Once again, he pinned his hopes for solvency on convincing the government to purchase his collection, but those plans were unrealized when he died in 1872.

While Catlin was touring Europe and dodging creditors, great changes were afoot for the Indian peoples he had painted in the 1830s. Catlin may have imagined them as frozen in amber, unspoiled by contact with the outside world, but as his own paintings suggested, they had been in touch with Europeans for quite some time. The pace of change wrought by such contact increased markedly during the 1830s and 1840s, as steamboats, white migration to the West, and the resettlement of Indians evicted from their eastern homelands transformed the landscape of the Great Plains. Smallpox epidemics in the 1830s took a devastating toll on many of the Missouri Valley's sedentary tribes, such as the Mandans, tipping the balance of power there in favor of the horse-powered Sioux. Those Indian nations most adept at using horses to hunt buffalo experienced an increase in power and population between 1830 and 1850 that defied any notion of a "vanishing Indian." However, within a generation they faced the problem of the vanishing buffalo, which was hunted to near extinction by whites and Indians alike after the Civil War. Had Catlin returned to the Great Plains in 1870, he would have encountered a world far different from the one he had left thirty-three years earlier.

Catlin's career may not have gone as planned, but his work had a lasting impact on American cultural attitudes about Indians. In going west to learn about Indians firsthand, he continued an intellectual inquiry initiated by Thomas Jefferson with the Lewis and Clark expedition. By the time of Catlin's death, a new generation of artists were continuing his work, only now with cameras instead of paints and canvas. Anthropologists followed in their wake in the twentieth century, using new technologies in sound recording and filmmaking to document Indian life.

Catlin's career represented another strain of the American cultural fascination with Indians as well, one that equated the "vanishing Indian" with an opportunity to make a buck. The profits that eluded Catlin in the 1830s and 1840s flowed into the hands of promoters like Buffalo Bill Cody between 1880 and 1920, when Wild West shows toured eastern cities and European countries, recreating buffalo hunts, stagecoach raids, and even Custer's Last Stand. By the 1920s, the "vanishing Indian" had made it to the silver screen, giving rise to one of the most popular genres of twentieth-century American film, the Western. *Last of the Mohicans* and *Dances with Wolves*, two films released in the 1990s and now staples of cable television, testify to the enduring appeal of the themes Catlin explored in his art in the 1830s. In the long history of the European-Indian encounter, Catlin stands somewhere between Thomas Jefferson and P. T. Barnum, a figure who made the Indian an object of both scholarly inquiry and commercial exploitation.

Finding and Supplementing the Source

Catlin never succeeded in his efforts to sell his Indian Gallery to the United States government, but the private collector who purchased the first incarnation of the Indian Gallery in 1852 ultimately donated it to the Smithsonian Institution in Washington, D.C. A major exhibit of Catlin's work at the Renwick Gallery of the Smithsonian American Art Museum in 2002–2003 inspired this chapter. The catalog of that exhibit provides an excellent overview of Catlin's life and work, as well as full-color reproductions of his most famous paintings. See George Gurney and Therese Thau Heyman, editors, *George Catlin and His Indian Gallery* (Washington, D.C.: Smithsonian American Art Museum, 2002). The exhibit may be viewed online at **americanart.si.edu/collections/exhibits/catlin/index.html**. Another useful study of Catlin's art is William H. Truettner, *The Natural Man Observed: A Study of Catlin's Indian Gallery* (Washington, D.C.: Smithsonian Institution Press, 1979).

Catlin published many works in his lifetime aimed at drawing attention to his Indian Gallery. The most important of these is the two-volume *Letters and Notes on the Manners, Customs, and Condition of the North American Indians* (1841; repr., Minneapolis: Ross and Haines, 1965). It details his western trips in the 1830s and features engravings of his paintings.

Two books useful for exploring the cultural and political climate that produced the "vanishing Indian" theme in American arts are Anthony F. C. Wallace, *Jefferson and the Indians: The Tragic Fate of the First Americans* (Cambridge: Harvard University Press, 1999), and Brian W. Dippie, *The Vanishing American: White Attitudes and U.S. Indian Policy* (1982; repr., Lawrence: University of Kansas Press, 1991). Jill Lepore's *The Name of War: King Philip's War and the Origins of American Identity* (New York: Random House, 1998) contains an excellent chapter on the cultural significance of the play *Metamora; or, the Last of the Wampanoags*, and the autobiography of Sac and Fox chief Black Hawk, first published in 1833, provides an important literary complement to Catlin's paintings. For a modern edition, see Donald Jackson, editor, *Black Hawk: An Autobiography* (Urbana: University of Illinois Press, 1955).

For a good overview of the changing circumstances of Plains Indian life during Catlin's lifetime, see Richard White, "The Winning of the West: The Expansion of the Western Sioux in the Eighteenth and Nineteenth Centuries," *Journal of American History* 65 (1978): 319–43. The legacy of Catlin's work in American art and popular culture can be explored in Joy S. Kasson, *Buffalo Bill's Wild West: Celebrity, Memory, and Popular History* (New York: Hill and Wang, 2000); L. G. Moses, *Wild West Shows and the Images of American Indians, 1883–1933* (Albuquerque: University of New Mexico Press, 1996); and Alfred L. Bush and Lee Clark Mitchell, *The Photograph and the American Indian* (Princeton, N.J.: Princeton University Press, 1994).

CHAPTER 11

Conversions and Camp Meetings in the Second Great Awakening

Autobiographies by African American Women

Zilpha Elaw was born to free African American parents in Philadelphia sometime around 1790. Her mother died when she was twelve and her father a year and a half later. Zilpha spent her teen years living and working in the household of a Quaker couple. Her guardians treated her kindly, but at age fourteen she was overwhelmed by a sense of her own sinfulness, and as she described it, "my spirits became greatly depressed, and I wept excessively." Elaw found no comfort until she began attending the meetings of a new religious denomination known as Methodists. After experiencing a vision of Jesus Christ while engaged in her chores, Elaw embraced the Methodist faith wholeheartedly. At a prayer meeting led by a traveling minister, she rose from her seat and announced her readiness to accept Christ as her savior. That moment of spiritual rebirth marked the start of a new life for Elaw, one transformed by the "tide of divine comforts" that her conversion experience had unleashed in her soul.

Elaw married two years later and moved with her husband to New Jersey. She soon regretted marrying someone who, "though a very respectable young man . . . was not a Christian." She knew that scripture demanded that she submit to her husband's authority, but she resisted when he tried to convince her to renounce her church membership and join him in "the merriments of the world," such as music and dancing. She went so far as to accompany him to a ballroom once, but the discomfort she experienced there caused her to "weep before God." After witnessing the "ill success of this wretched experiment," her husband never asked her to join him at a dance again.

In 1823, Elaw's husband died, and she found herself freed from the bonds of wifely duty to pursue her faith with a new vigor. Acting on a divine calling she had received while attending a Methodist revival several years earlier, she placed her children in the care of a relative and moved back to Philadelphia, preaching to audiences of black and white listeners without the support or approval of any religious authority other than her conscience. Her ministry took her to Maryland and Virginia, where she preached before slaves and slaveholders, and then back into the northern states of Pennsylvania, New Jersey, and New England. In 1840, she crossed the Atlantic to preach in England, where she published *Memoirs of the Life, Religious Experience, Ministerial Travels and Labours of Mrs. Zilpha Elaw, an American Female of Colour, Together with Some Account of the Great Religious Revivals in America (Written by Herself)*. This self-published book provides practically all we know about Elaw's life and work; while it mentions her intentions to return to the United States, no record exists of her life after the autobiography's publication in 1846.

Elaw's spiritual journey was mirrored by many other Americans who participated in the Second Great Awakening, a wave of religious revivalism that swept through the United States between 1800 and 1840. Like the first Great Awakening of the mid-eighteenth century, this movement was spread by itinerant ministers who traveled from one pulpit to the next, preaching a message of personal salvation that appealed to audiences across a wide cross section of American society: male and female, black and white, rich and poor. Revivalist preachers were not sticklers for doctrine or theology, nor did they did insist that their audiences subscribe to a particular denominational creed. Rather, they spoke of divine inspiration and personal redemption in Christ: each individual needed to recognize and repent his or her own sins and ask for God's saving grace. Those who received it would be "born again" into the fellowship of Christian believers, regardless of their social, racial, or religious background. This emphasis on personal faith, conversion, and redemption has come to define what is commonly called the evangelical tradition in American religion.

The first Great Awakening had primarily affected churches already well-established in British North America: the Congregationalists of New England, Presbyterians of the Middle Colonies, and Anglicans of the South. The Second Great Awakening, on the other hand, powered the expansion of two Protestant denominations relatively new to North America in the 1790s: Methodists and Baptists. Baptists had their roots in the religious ferment of the Protestant Reformation. They were distinguished from other Protestant denominations chiefly by their practice of adult baptism, after a believer had experienced a transformational conversion experience. Methodism, which originated in eighteenth-century England, likewise taught that God directly intervened in the believer's life, and it encouraged its adherents to seek that divine guidance through the everyday practice of personal piety and devotions.

Baptists and Methodists were also innovative in how they spread their evangelical message. Unlike other Protestant denominations of the time, they did not require their clergy to hold college degrees, and they encouraged lay preaching. In 1800 and 1801, Methodist preachers on the Kentucky frontier pioneered another distinctive element of American evangelical Protestantism, the camp meeting. To reach as many potential converts as possible, preachers held meetings out of doors that lasted for days and even weeks. People from the surrounding countryside traveled to such sites, pitched tents for accommodations, and spent their time living, eating, and praying together in a communal religious celebration that resembled a modern-day outdoor rock festival, only without the $5 bottled water. Baptist and Methodist preachers also sought audiences among social groups long ignored or excluded by more established churches. On the frontier, where other churches were often unable to keep pace with western migration, revivalist ministers known as circuit riders traveled constantly between isolated communities, creating and attending to new congregations. In rapidly growing cities, revivalists sought converts among immigrants and urban workers who had lost touch with traditional religious institutions. And in the South, revivalists found receptive audiences among slaves and poor whites whose spiritual needs had long been denied or neglected by the planter class. Historians estimate that somewhere between 10 and 20 percent of the nation's population participated in the Second Great Awakening, but its greatest impact was felt by those social groups that had been previously unchurched in American society. By 1850, Baptists and Methodists were the two largest Protestant denominations in the United States.

Elaw's personal experience within this tide of revivalism illuminates another important aspect of the Second Great Awakening: the ways in which African Americans and women used it to open avenues for themselves into American public life. When Elaw converted, she joined a congregation that was part of the African Methodist Episcopal (AME) Church, the first religious denomination founded in the United States by African Americans. The AME Church had its roots in the Methodist outreach that gained white and black converts in the 1790s, but black Methodists formed their own institutional structure when white Methodists began insisting on racial segregation within their churches. The number and size of AME churches grew as more African Americans were drawn to Christianity during the Second Great Awakening, and those churches became the spiritual and social center of many free black communities.

The evangelical message of the Second Great Awakening also appealed to many women, white and black, who felt a calling to preach the gospel. Christian churches had prohibited women from being ordained or preaching in public since the days of Saint Paul. Citing biblical injunctions against women speaking in church, male clergy told women that their place was within the home, where they were to attend to the spiritual needs of others as wives, mothers, and neighbors. Women were excluded from the universities that granted the credentials for a career in the ministry. During the Second Great Awakening, these strictures on female preaching loosened. Methodists and Baptists recognized the importance of male and female "lay exhorters" in reaching potential converts. Audiences at camp meetings did not insist that their preachers carry divinity degrees or licenses; they gave the pulpit to anyone who had the power to move them in word and song. Female preachers such as Zilpha Elaw usually got their start by leading prayer meetings in private homes. As their reputations grew, local ministers invited them to preach from their pulpits and missionary societies funded their tours to other regions. If church authorities refused to grant approval or financial backing, they went on the road anyway, relying on their audiences for support. The success of such female preachers contradicted the notion that women served God first as wives and mothers and openly challenged whites' racist assumptions about the spiritual fitness of African Americans.

The Second Great Awakening primed the United States for many of the social transformations associated with the Jacksonian era. Circuit-riding and camp meetings made religion more egalitarian and democratic, shifting power from established churches and clergy to new denominations that attracted believers from among the poor and unlettered. The revivals also fueled a spirit of perfectionism that inspired a wide range of social reform movements in the Jacksonian era. The evangelical message that sin could be washed away and spiritual purity renewed by being born again encouraged fellow believers to join cause in reforming American society from the inside out, purging it of its sins in preparation for Christ's second coming on earth. Temperance societies, abolitionism, and even the women's rights movement had their origins in the crusading spirit that animated lay preachers and converts like Zilpha Elaw.

Using Autobiographies as a Source

A small but significant number of African American women wrote autobiographies inspired by their experiences in the Second Great Awakening. Collectively, these autobiographies mark the emergence of a genre in African American literature that complements the more famous slave narratives of the nineteenth century. Slave narratives may have been more widely read, but they were overwhelmingly written by or about male slaves. The spiritual autobiography was a distinctly female genre that had its roots in a tradition of female authorship in American religious literature. Whereas a slave narrative usually told a story about the subject's tribulations under slavery and his escape from it, the spiritual autobiography focused on the personal psychology of religious experience, the struggles with sin and temptation, the joys of conversion and God's grace, and the difficulties and triumphs of leading a Christian life. Similar themes of bondage (whether in slavery or sin) and redemption (whether by escape or salvation) shaped both genres, but the spiritual autobiography was by its nature more introspective and offered a more sustained look inside the mind and heart of its author.

Spiritual autobiographies from the Second Great Awakening followed a common pattern. The author paid little attention to her life prior to her conversion, providing only brief biographical information about birth, parentage, and childhood. Conversion, the moment of spiritual rebirth, marked the start of the story, which then continued on through various stages of trial and renewal. These autobiographies placed a great deal of emphasis on the author's calling from God to spread the gospel, and the story's dramatic tension usually came from antagonists who tried to thwart that calling. Any number of characters fell into this category—Satan, church leaders, slaveholders—but they typically were powerful males who criticized female preaching as uneducated, unlicensed, and unwarranted by scriptural authority. Women preachers of the Second Great Awakening defended themselves by recounting the dreams and visions in which their calling had been revealed to them, comparing themselves to Moses, Jonah, and other reluctant prophets who had had no choice but to follow God's will.

Here is a brief excerpt from Zilpha Elaw's autobiography. As you read it, note how she uses scripture to challenge those who would dismiss her preaching as unlearned.

Cites scripture to defend preachers, such as herself, who have no formal education

Author of the New Testament's Book of Revelations, based on an apocalyptic vision

Thinly veiled reference to college-educated clergy and church officials who would question the spiritual worthiness of the revivals

Divine oracle mentioned in the Old Testament

Spiritual fervor

[M]en of high repute for learning and wisdom, have been sent over [from Britain] to ascertain the nature, as well to investigate the means and extent of those great transatlantic revivals [in America]: what report of the good land they returned with, I have not been informed, but generally I have found that the wise and learned have seldom experienced much of the heavenly discipline of God's Holy Spirit; "the world by wisdom knew not God" (1 Cor. 1:21); and though many Christians are at immense pains to acquire the wisdom of this world, God bringeth it to nought, and taketh them in their own craftiness; He hideth His counsel from the "wise and prudent, and revealeth it to babes" (Matt. 11:25). The man who would judge of so high a matter as a revival of the kingdom of heaven upon earth, must be spiritual (he need not be learned) himself; for the spiritual man judgeth all things; yea, even the deep things of God, yet he himself is judged of no man, for no man can fathom the sacred Urim and Thummim, or as St. John says, the holy anointing or unction which abides in his soul.[1]

In this excerpt, Elaw defends herself by citing passages and figures from the Bible that elevate divine inspiration over worldly wisdom. She answers her critics not only by proving her familiarity with scripture but also by comparing herself to oracles and saints that served as the mouthpieces of God. This brief

[1] Zilpha Elaw, *Memoirs of the Life, Religious Experience, Ministerial Travels and Labours of Mrs. Zilpha Elaw, an American Female of Colour, Together with Some Account of the Great Religious Revivals in America (Written by Herself)* (London: Zilpha Elaw, 1846); reprinted in William L. Andrews, editor, *Sisters of the Spirit: Three Black Women's Autobiographies of the Nineteenth Century* (Bloomington: Indiana University Press, 1986), 11.

passage also tells us something about the extent of biblical literacy in nineteenth-century America. The ease and frequency with which Elaw cites scripture is indicative of how pervasive Bible reading was in the Anglo-American world at this time. Even those believers who were not literate themselves heard the Bible read and preached from frequently enough to be able to understand scriptural references that present-day readers might find obscure.

Advantages and Disadvantages of Working with Autobiographies

On the surface, autobiographies would appear to be the most reliable and transparent of historical sources. They are by definition firsthand accounts, and who knows the story of a person's life better than that person herself? It is important to remember, however, that writing an autobiography is an act of self-invention; anyone who takes up the task usually has a specific purpose in mind. The most famous autobiographies in American literature, from the *Autobiography of Benjamin Franklin* to the *Autobiography of Malcolm X*, are still read today not because they offer the most complete retelling of the subject's life but because of what they tell us about how that person created an identity for public consumption. An obituary or encyclopedia entry can provide the details of a person's life—when and where she was born, the names of her spouse and children, where she worked and how she died—but an autobiography tells the reader what that person thought of herself and how she consciously chose to present herself to others.

Spiritual autobiographies also open an important window for historians into the nature of religious experience. The history of religion is not the same as church history. The latter tends to focus on institutions and ideas: how churches get created, how theologies evolve, how believers interact with non-believers. The personal psychology of religious belief is much more difficult to recover from historical sources. American Protestantism has always emphasized literacy and introspection, two characteristics that encouraged believers to keep spiritual journals. Religious revivals like the Second Great Awakening, however, often attracted people who lacked the literacy or time for such journal writing, and the published sermons of evangelical preachers failed to capture the drama and appeal of their oral delivery. Spiritual autobiographies, therefore, offer one of the few means by which historians can recapture the personal dimension of the Second Great Awakening, from the inner turmoil of conversion to the social bustle of camp meetings.

When reading autobiographies, it is also important to remember that they are often written with the aid of an editor or amanuensis, someone who writes down oral testimony. This is especially true in the case of nineteenth-century African American authors, many of whom were illiterate former slaves. In such cases, the narrative's subject dictated her life story to someone who then sponsored its publication for a specific purpose, such as promoting Christianity or attacking slavery. We tend to assume that an autobiography moves directly from its subject to its reader, but in fact, no autobiography is entirely free from editorial intrusion and filtering. In our modern celebrity culture, an embarrassed movie star or sports figure occasionally confesses to having not read his or her own ghostwritten "autobiography"; such gaffes should serve as a reminder that the subject and author of an autobiography are not always the same. Whenever you read such a source, keep that distinction in mind and try to determine whether the words appear to be coming directly from the autobiography's subject or by way of a narrator or editor claiming an "as told to" authority over the material.

Likewise, it is important to ask questions about the intended audience for the autobiography you are reading. Did the person who published this book hope to win souls, free slaves, or make some money? Where was it likely to be sold and read? Spiritual autobiographies were usually published as brief religious tracts and sold along with other devotional and inspirational literature at camp meetings and similar religious gatherings. None of those you will examine in this chapter achieved bestseller status, and their circulation among slaves was severely limited by the antiliteracy laws in Southern slave codes. African American women may have been the subjects of these autobiographies, but the manner in which they were published and read meant that for the most part they followed conventions shaped chiefly by white society.

Working with the Source

In each of the selections included in the following section, the subject describes her conversion and calling to preach. Use the table on page 228 to summarize how each woman experienced these events.

	Conversion experience	Calling to preach	Audience for her ministry	Opposition encountered to her ministry
Zilpha Elaw				
Sojourner Truth				
Elizabeth				

The Source: Three Autobiographies by African American Women

 Memoirs of the Life, Religious Experience, Ministerial Travels and Labours of Mrs. Zilpha Elaw

For information on the life of Zilpha Elaw, see the introduction to this chapter.

About this time,[1] the Methodists made their first appearance in that part of the country, and I was permitted to attend their meetings once a fortnight, on the Sabbath afternoons, from which I derived great satisfaction; but the divine work on my soul was a very gradual one, and my way was prepared as the dawning of the morning. I never experienced that terrific dread of hell by which some Christians appear to have been exercised; but I felt a godly sorrow for sin in having grieved my God by a course of disobedience to His commands. . . . I at length proved the verification of the promise, "They that seek shall find" (Luke 11:9); for, one evening whilst singing one of the songs of Zion, I distinctly saw the Lord Jesus approach me with open arms, and a most divine and heavenly smile upon his countenance. As He advanced towards me, I felt that his very looks spoke, and said, "Thy prayer is accepted, I own thy name." From that day to the present I have never entertained a doubt of the manifestation of his love to my soul. . . .

As I was milking a cow and singing, I turned my head; and saw a tall figure approaching, who came and stood by me. He had long hair, which parted in the front and came down on his shoulders; he wore a long white robe down to the feet; and as he stood with open arms and smiled upon me, he disappeared. I might have tried to imagine, or persuade myself, perhaps, that it had been a vision presented merely to the eye of my mind; but, the beast of the stall gave forth her evidence to the reality of the heavenly appearance; for she turned her head and looked round as I did; and when she saw, she bowed her knees and cowered down upon the ground. I was overwhelmed with astonishment at the sight, but the thing was certain and beyond all doubt. I write as before God and Christ, and declare, as I shall give an account to my Judge at the great day, that

[1] When Elaw was an adolescent.

Source: Memoirs of the Life, Religious Experience, Ministerial Travels and Labours of Mrs. Zilpha Elaw, an American Female of Colour, Together with Some Account of the Great Religious Revivals in America (Written by Herself) (London: Zilpha Elaw, 1846); reprinted in William L. Andrews, editor, *Sisters of the Spirit: Three Black Women's Autobiographies of the Nineteenth Century* (Bloomington: Indiana University Press, 1986), 55–57, 64–67, 90–91.

every thing I have written in this little book, has been written with conscien-
tious veracity and scrupulous adherence to truth. . . .

In the year 1817, I attended an American camp-meeting. Oh, how I should
like our dear English friends to witness some of our delightful camp-meetings,
which are held in the groves of the United States. . . .

In order to form a camp-meeting, when the place and time of meeting has
been extensively published, each family takes its own tent, and all things necessary for lodgings, with seats, provisions and servants; and with wagons and
other vehicles repair to the destined spot, which is generally some wildly rural
and wooded retreat in the back grounds of the interior: hundreds of families,
and thousands of persons, are seen pressing to the place from all quarters; the
meeting usually continues for a week or more: a large circular enclosure of
brushwood is formed; immediately inside of which the tents are pitched, and
the space in the centre is appropriated to the worship of God, the minister's
stand being on one side, and generally on a somewhat rising ground. It is a
scaffold constructed of boards, and surrounded with a fence of rails.

In the space before the platform, seats are placed sufficient to seat four or
five thousand persons; and at night the woods are illuminated; there are generally four large mounds of earth constructed, and on them large piles of pine
knots are collected and ignited, which make a wonderful blaze and burn a long
time; there are also candles and lamps hung about in the trees, together with a
light in every tent, and the minister's stand is brilliantly lighted up; so that the
illumination attendant upon a camp-meeting, is a magnificently solemn scene.
The worship commences in the morning before sunrise; the watchmen proceed
round the enclosure, blowing with trumpets to awaken every inhabitant of this
City of the Lord; they then proceed again round the camp, to summon the in-
mates of every tent to their family devotions; after which they partake of breakfast, and are again summoned by sound of trumpet to public prayer meeting at
the altar which is placed in front of the preaching stand. Many precious souls
are on these occasions introduced into the liberty of the children of God; at the
close of the prayer meeting the grove is teeming with life and activity; the
numberless private conferences, the salutations of old friends again meeting in
the flesh, the earnest inquires of sinners, the pressing exhortations of anxious
saints, the concourse of pedestrians, the arrival of horses and carriages of all descriptions render the scene portentously interesting and intensely surprising.
At ten o'clock, the trumpets sound again to summon the people to public worship; the seats are all speedily filled and as perfect a silence reigns throughout
the place as in a Church or Chapel; presently the high praises of God sound
melodiously from this consecrated spot, and nothing seems wanting but local
elevation to render the place a heaven indeed. It is like God's ancient and holy
hill of Zion on her brightest festival days, when the priests conducted the pro-
cessions of people to the glorious temple of Jehovah. . . .

I, for one, have great reason to thank God for the refreshing seasons of his
mighty grace, which have accompanied these great meetings of his saints in
the wilderness. It was at one of these meetings that God was pleased to separate

my soul unto Himself, to sanctify me as a vessel designed for honour, made meet for the master's use. Whether I was in the body, or whether I was out of the body, on that auspicious day, I cannot say; but this I do know, that at the conclusion of a most powerful sermon delivered by one of the ministers from the platform, and while the congregation were in prayer, I became so overpowered with the presence of God, that I sank down upon the ground, and laid there for a considerable time; and while I was thus prostrate on the earth, my spirit seemed to ascend up into the clear circle of the sun's disc; and, surrounded and engulphed in the glorious effulgence of his rays, I distinctly heard a voice speak unto me, which said, "Now thou art sanctified; and I will show thee what thou must do." I saw no personal appearance while in this stupendous elevation, but I discerned bodies of resplendent light; nor did I appear to be in this world at all, but immensely far above those spreading trees, beneath whose shady and verdant bowers I was then reclined. When I recovered from the trance or ecstasy into which I had fallen, the first thing I observed was, that hundreds of persons were standing around me weeping; and I clearly saw by the light of the Holy Ghost, that my heart and soul were rendered completely spotless—as clean as a sheet of white paper, and I felt as pure as if I had never sinned in all my life; a solemn stillness rested upon my soul:

> "the speechless awe that dares not move,
> And all the silent heaven of love."

Truly I durst not move, because God was so powerfully near to me; for the space of several hours I appeared not to be on earth, but far above all earthy things. I had not at this time offered up public prayer on the camp ground; but when the prayer meeting afterwards commenced, the Lord opened my mouth in public prayer; and while I was thus engaged, it seemed as if I heard my God rustling in the tops of the mulberry-trees. Oh, how precious was this day to my soul! I was after this very frequently requested to present my petitions to the throne of grace in the public meetings at the camp. . . .

I returned home in April, 1828,[2] and remained there a few days. During my stay home, I was one day exercised with devout contemplations of God, and suddenly the Spirit came upon me, and a voice addressed me, saying, "Be of good cheer, and be faithful; I will yet bring thee to England and thou shalt see London, that great city, and declare my name there." I looked round to ascertain from whence and from whom the voice proceeded, but no person was near me; my surprise was so great that my very blood seemed to stagnate and chill in my veins: it was evidently the Spirit of the Lord whose I am, and whom I serve, who had spoken to me; and my soul responded to His word, saying, "The will of the Lord be done in and by me on earth, as it is by His servants in Heaven." My mind was at this time very much perplexed as to what was the will of God concerning me: I was in doubt as to what I ought to do; but, after

---

[2] Elaw had been on a preaching tour.

a few days, I took my journey again to Philadelphia, with the intention of visiting the southern slave-holding states of America; here I saw my dear daughter, and remained with my friends during some few weeks; but the confusion of my mind still continued, and whenever I opened a Bible, where ever I visited, as well as at my apartments, the book of the prophet Jonah was perpetually presented before me. I mentioned to my friends the uncertainty of my mind as to what the Lord required me to do, the propriety of a voyage to England, and my repeatedly opening in the Bible at the book of Jonah; and they assured me that if it was God's will that I should then visit England, He would make it appear, and smooth the way for me in His own good time.

I therefore rested upon this assurance; and while I yet abode in Philadelphia, I dreamed one night, that I saw two ships cleared out of the docks there, bound for England, and I was not on board either of them. I then concluded that the time for my journey to England had not yet come; and being now satisfied on this matter, I started off for the southern territories of the United States, where slavery is established and enforced by law. When I arrived in the slave states, Satan much worried and distressed my soul with the fear of being arrested and sold for a slave, which their laws would have warranted, on account of my complexion and features. On one occasion, in particular, I had been preaching to a coloured congregation, and had exhorted them impressively to [ac]quit themselves as men approved of God, and to maintain and witness a good profession of their faith before the world, &c. I had no sooner sat down, than Satan suggested to me with such force, that the slave-holders would speedily capture me, as filled me with fear and terror. I was then in a small town in one of the slave states; and the news of a coloured female preaching to the slaves had already been spread widely throughout the neighborhood; the novelty of the thing had produced an immense excitement and the people were collecting from every quarter, to gaze at the unexampled prodigy of a coloured female preacher. I was sitting in a very conspicuous situation near the door, and I observed, with very painful emotions, the crowd outside, pointing with their fingers at me, and saying "that's her," "that's her"; for Satan strongly set before me the prospect of an immediate arrest and consignment by sale to some slave owner. Being very much alarmed, I removed from my seat to a retired part of the room, where, becoming more collected, I inquired within myself, "from whence cometh all this fear?" My faith then rallied and my confidence in the Lord returned, and I said, "get thee behind me Satan, for my Jesus hath made me free." My fears instantly forsook me, and I vacated my retired corner, and came forth before all the people again; and the presence and power of the Lord became greatly manifested in the assembly during the remainder of the service. At the earnest request of the friends, I consented to preach there again on the following Lord's-day morning, which I accordingly did.

2   *Narrative of Sojourner Truth, a Bondswoman of Olden Time*

Sojourner Truth was born a slave in New York in the 1790s. She was known as Isabella until she took the name Sojourner Truth at the outset of her preaching career in 1843. She gained her freedom in 1827 under a gradual emancipation law passed in New York and moved from the Hudson Valley to New York City, where she worked as a domestic servant and associated with several radical religious groups, including the Millerites, who believed that Christ's Second Coming was imminent. After embracing her calling to preach, she traveled throughout the Northeast and took a leading role in both the abolitionist and women's rights movements. In 1856 she moved to Michigan but remained active as a touring preacher and speaker during the Civil War and Reconstruction period, meeting President Lincoln in the White House in 1864. She died in Battle Creek, Michigan, in 1883.

Truth was illiterate. She dictated the *Narrative of Sojourner Truth* to an amanuensis (note that the story is told in the third person) and published it in 1850. The excerpts below are from a subsequent edition published in 1878. Her immersion in the Second Great Awakening and abolitionist movement make her narrative an interesting amalgam of spiritual auto-biography and slave narrative.

[Truth] says that God revealed himself to her, with all the suddenness of a flash of lightning, showing her, "in the twinkling of an eye, that he was *all over*"— that he pervaded the universe—"and that there was no place where God was not." She became instantly conscious of her great sin in forgetting her almighty Friend and "ever-present help in time of trouble." All her unfulfilled promises arose before her, like a vexed sea whose waves run mountains high; and her soul, which seemed but one mass of lies, shrunk back aghast from the "awful look" of Him whom she had formerly talked to, as if he had been a being like herself; and she would now fain had hid herself in the bowels of the earth, to have escaped his dread presence. But she plainly saw there was no place, not even in hell, where he was not: and where could she flee? Another such "a look," as she expressed it, and she felt that she must be extinguished forever, even as one, with the breath of his mouth, "blows out a lamp," so that no spark remains.

A dire dread of annihilation now seized her, and she waited to see if, by "another look," she was to be stricken from existence, swallowed up, even as the fire licketh up the oil with which it comes in contact.

When at last the second look came not, and her attention was once more called to outward things, she . . . exclaim[ed] aloud, "Oh, God, I did not know you were so big," walked into the house, and made an effort to resume her work. But the workings of the inward man were too absorbing to admit of

Source: Narrative of Sojourner Truth, a Bondswoman of Olden Time (1850; repr., Battle Creek, Mich.: Sojourner Truth, 1878), 65–67, 99–101, 115–18.

much attention to her avocations. She desired to talk to God, but her vileness utterly forbade it, and she was not able to prefer a petition. "What!" said she, "shall I lie again to God? I have told him nothing but lies; and shall I speak again, and tell another lie to God?" She could not; and now she began to wish for someone to speak to God for her. Then a space seemed opening between her and God, and she felt that if someone, who was worthy in the sight of heaven, would but plead *for* her in their own name, and not let God know it come from *her,* who was so unworthy, God might grant it. At length a friend appeared to stand between herself and an insulted Deity; and she felt as sensibly refreshed as when, on a hot day, an umbrella had been interposed between her scorching head and a burning sun. But who was this friend? Became the next inquiry. . . .

"Who *are* you?" She exclaimed, as the vision brightened into a form distinct, beaming with the beauty of holiness, and radiant with love. She then said, audibly addressing the mysterious visitant—"I *know* you, and I *don't* know you." Meaning, "You seem perfectly familiar; I feel that you not only love me, but that you always *have* loved me—yet I know you not—I cannot call you by name." When she said, "I know you," the subject of the vision remained distinct and quiet. When she said, "I don't know you," it moved restlessly about, like agitated waters. So while she repeated, without intermission, "I know you, I know you," that the vision might remain—"Who are you?" was the cry of her heart, and her whole soul was in one deep prayer that this heavenly personage might be revealed to her, and remain with her. At length, after bending both soul and body with the intensity of this desire, till breath and strength seemed failing, and she could maintain her position no longer, an answer came to her, saying distinctly, "It is Jesus." "Yes," she responded, "it is *Jesus.*"

Previous to these exercises of the mind, she heard Jesus mentioned in reading or speaking, but had received from what she heard no impression that he was any other than an eminent man, like a Washington or a Lafayette. Now he appeared to her delighted mental vision as so mild, so good, and so every way lovely, and he loved her so much! And, how strange that he had always loved her, and she had never known it! And how great a blessing he conferred, in that he should stand between her and God! And God was no longer a terror and dread to her. . . .

Her next decision was, that she must leave the city;[1] it was no place for her; yea, she felt called in spirit to leave it, and to travel east and lecture. She had never been further east than the city, neither had she any friends there of whom she had particular reason to expect anything; yet to her it was plain that her mission lay in the east, and that she would find friends there. She determined on leaving; but these determinations and convictions she kept close locked in her own breast, knowing that if her children and friends were aware of it, they would make such an ado about it as would render it very unpleasant,

---

[1] New York City.

if not distressing to all parties. Having made what preparations for leaving she deemed necessary, which was, to put up a few articles of clothing in a pillow-case, all else being deemed an unnecessary incumbrance, about an hour before she left, she informed Mrs. Whiting, the woman of the house where she was stopping, that her name was no longer Isabella, but SOJOURNER; and that she was going east. And to her inquiry, "What are you going east for?" her answer was, "The Spirit calls me there, and I must go."

She left the city on the morning of the 1st of June, 1843, crossing over to Brooklyn, L. I.;[2] and taking the rising sun for her only compass and guide, she "remembered Lot's wife."[3] And hoping to avoid her fate, she resolved not to look back till she felt sure the wicked city from which she was fleeing was left too far behind to be visible in the distance; and when she first ventured to look back, she could just discern the blue cloud of smoke that hung over it, and she thanked the Lord that she was thus far removed from what seemed to *her* a second Sodom.

. . . Her mission was not merely to travel east, but to "lecture," as she designated it; "testifying of the hope that was in her"—exhorting the people to embrace Jesus, and refrain from sin, the nature and origin of which she explained to them in accordance with her own most curious and original views. Through her life, and all its chequered changes, she has ever clung fast to her first permanent impressions on religious subjects. . . .

When Sojourner had been at Northampton[4] a few months, she attended another camp-meeting, at which she performed a very important part.

A party of wild young men, with no motive but that of entertaining themselves by annoying and injuring the feelings of others, had assembled at the meeting, hooting and yelling, and in various ways interrupting the services, and causing much disturbance. Those who had the charge of the meeting, having tried their persuasive powers in vain, grew impatient and tried threatening.

The young men, considering themselves insulted, collected their friends, to the number of a hundred or more, dispersed themselves through the grounds, making the most frightful noises, and threatening to fire the tents. It was said the authorities of the meeting sat in grave consultation, decided to have the ring-leaders arrested, and sent for the constable, to the great displeasure of some of the company, who were opposed to such an appeal to force and arms, be that as it may, Sojourner, seeing great consternation depicted in every countenance, caught the contagion, and, ere she was aware, found herself quaking with fear.

Under the impulse of this sudden emotion, she fled to the most retired corner of a tent, and secreted herself behind a trunk, saying to herself, "I am

---

[2] Long Island, in New York.

[3] Lot's wife was an Old Testament figure who turned to stone when she looked back as she fled the destruction of Sodom and Gomorrah.

[4] The Northampton Association was a utopian community in present-day Florence, Massachusetts.

the only colored person here, and on me, probably, their wicked mischief will fall first, and perhaps fatally." But feeling how great was her insecurity even there, as the very tent began to shake from its foundations, she began to soliloquize as follows:

Shall I run away and hide from the Devil? Me, a servant of the living God? Have I not faith enough to go out and quell that mob, when I know it is written—"One shall chase a thousand, and two put ten thousand to flight"? I know there are not a thousand here; and I know I am a servant of the living God. I'll go to the rescue, and the Lord shall go with and protect me.

"Oh," said she, "I felt as if I had *three hearts*! And that they were so large, my body could hardly hold them!"

She now came forth from her hiding place, and invited several to go with her and see what they could do to still the raging of the moral elements. They declined, and considered her wild to think of it.

The meeting was in the open fields—the full moon shed its saddened light over all—and the woman who was that evening to address them was trembling on the preacher's stand. The noise and confusion were now terrific. Sojourner left the tent alone and unaided, and walking some thirty rods to the top of a small rise of ground, commenced to sing, in her most fervid manner, with all the strength of her most powerful voice, the hymn on the resurrection of Christ—

> It was early in the morning—it was early in the morning,
>   Just at the break of day—
> When he rose—when he rose—when he rose,
>   And went to heaven on a cloud. . . .

As she commenced to sing, the young men made a rush towards her, and she was immediately encircled by a dense body of the rioters, many of them armed with sticks or clubs as their weapons of defence, if not of attack. As the circle narrowed around her, she ceased singing, and after a short pause, inquired, in a gentle but firm tone, "Why do you come about me with clubs and sticks? I am not doing harm to anyone." "We aren't going to hurt you old woman; we came to hear you sing," cried many voices simultaneously. "Sing to us, old woman," cries one. "Talk to us, old woman," says another. "Pray, old woman," says a third. "Tell us your experience," says a fourth. "You stand and smoke so near me, I cannot sing or talk," she answered.

"Stand back," said several authoritative voices, with not the most gentle or courteous accompaniments, raising their rude weapons in the air. The crowd suddenly gave back, the circle became larger, as many voices again called for singing, talking, or praying, backed by assurance that no one should be allowed to hurt her—the speakers declaring with an oath that they would "*knock down*" any person who would offer her the least indignity.

She looked about her, and with her usual discrimination, said inwardly—"Here must be young men in all this assemblage, bearing within them hearts susceptible of good impressions. I will speak to them." She did speak; they silently heard, and civilly asked her many questions. It seemed to her to be given her at the time to answer them with truth and wisdom beyond herself. Her speech had operated on the roused passions of the mob like oil on agitated waters; they were, as a whole, entirely subdued, and only clamored when she ceased to speak or sing. Those who stood in the background, after the circle was enlarged, cried out, "Sing aloud, old woman, we can't hear." Those who held the sceptre of power among them requested that she should make a pulpit of a neighboring wagon. She said, "If I do, they'll overthrow it." "No, they shan't—he who dares hurt you, we'll knock him down instantly, d——n[5] him," cried the chiefs. "No we won't, no we won't, nobody shall hurt you," answered the many voices of the mob. They kindly assisted her to mount the wagon, from which she spoke and sung to them about an hour.

[5] Damn.

 ## Elizabeth, a Colored Minister of the Gospel, Born in Slavery

The subject of this autobiography is known only by the name Elizabeth, and what details we know of her personal life come from the narrative. She was born a slave in Maryland in 1766 and gained her freedom at age thirty. When she was forty-two, she began a preaching career that did not end until she was in her eighties. Late in life she dictated her life story to some Quaker friends. It was published posthumously in 1889.

In the eleventh year of my age, my master sent me to another farm several miles from my parents, brothers and sisters, which was a great trouble to me. At last I grew so lonely and sad I thought I should die, if I did not see my mother. I asked the overseer if I might go, but being positively denied, I concluded to go without his knowledge. When I reached home my mother was away. I set off and walked twenty miles before I found her. I staid with her for several days, and we returned together. Next day I was sent back to my new place, which renewed my sorrow. At parting, my mother told me that I had "nobody in the wide world to look to but God." These words fell upon my heart with ponderous weight, and seemed to add to my grief. I went back repeating as I went, "none but God in the wide world." On reaching the farm, I found the overseer was displeased at me for going without his liberty. He tied me with a rope, and gave me some stripes of which I carried the marks for weeks.

Source: Elizabeth, a Colored Minister of the Gospel, Born in Slavery (Philadelphia, 1889), reprinted in Bert James Loewenberg and Ruth Bogin, editors, Black Women in Nineteenth-Century American Life: Their Words, Their Thoughts, Their Feelings (University Park: Pennsylvania State University Press, 1976), 128–34.

After this time, finding as my mother said, I had none in the world to look to but God, I betook myself to prayer, and in every lonely place I found an altar. I mourned sore like a dove and chattered forth my sorrow, moaning in the corners of the field, and under the fences.

I continued in this state for about six months, feeling as though my head were waters, and I could do nothing but weep. I lost my appetite, and not being able to take enough food to sustain nature, I became so weak I had but little strength to work; still I was required to do all my duty. One evening, after the duties of the day were ended, I thought I could not live over the night, so threw myself on a bench, expecting to die, and without being prepared to meet my Maker; and my spirit cried within me, must I die in this state, and be banished from Thy presence forever? I own I am a sinner in Thy sight, and not fit to live where thou are. Still it was my fervent desire that the Lord would pardon me. Just at this season, I saw with my spiritual eye, an awful gulf of misery. As I thought I was about to plunge into it, I heard a voice saying "rise up and pray," which strengthened me. I fell on my knees and prayed the best I could the Lord's prayer. Knowing no more to say, I halted, but continued on my knees. My spirit was then taught to pray, "Lord have mercy on me, Christ save me."

Immediately there appeared a director, clothed in white raiment. I thought he took me by the hand and said, "come with me." He led me down a long journey to a fiery gulf, and left me standing upon the brink of this awful pit. I began to scream for mercy, thinking I was about to sink to endless ruin. Although I prayed and wrestled with all my might, it seemed in vain. Still I felt all the while that I was sustained by some invisible power. At this solemn moment, I thought I saw a hand from which hung, as it were, a silver hair, and a voice told me that all the hope I had of being saved was no more than a hair; still, pray and it will be sufficient. I then renewed my struggle, crying for mercy and salvation, until I found that every cry raised me higher and higher, and my head was quite above the fiery pillars. Then I thought I was permitted to look straight forward and saw the Saviour standing with his hand stretched out to receive me. An indescribably glorious light was in Him, and He said, "peace, peace, come unto me." At this moment I felt that my sins were forgiven me, and the time of my deliverance was at hand. I sprang forward and fell at his feet, giving Him all the thanks and highest praises, crying, Thou hast redeemed me. Thou hast redeemed me to thyself. I felt filled with light and love. At this moment I thought my former guide took me again by the hand and led me upward, till I came to the celestial world and to heaven's door, which I saw was open, and while I stood there, a power surrounded me which drew me in, and I saw millions of glorified spirits in white robes.

After I had this view, I thought I heard a voice saying, "Art thou willing to be saved?" I said, "Yes Lord." Again I was asked, "Art thou willing to be saved in my way?" I stood speechless until he asked me again, "Art thou willing to be saved in my way?" Then I heard a whispering voice say, "If thou art not saved in the Lord's way, thou canst not be saved at all"; at which I exclaimed, "Yes Lord, in thy own way." Immediately a light fell upon my head, and I was filled with light and I was shown the world lying in wickedness, and was told I must go there, and call the people to repentance, for the day of the Lord was at hand;

and this message was as a heavy yoke upon me, so that I wept bitterly at the thought of what I should have to pass through. While I wept, I heard a voice say, "weep not, some will laugh at thee, some will scoff at thee, and the dogs will bark at thee, but while thou doest my will, I will be with thee to the ends of the earth."

I was at this time not yet thirteen years old. The next day, when I had come to myself, I felt like a new creature in Christ, and all my desire was to see the Saviour. . . .

I did not speak much till I had reached my forty-second year, when it was revealed to me that the message which had been given to me I had not yet delivered, and the time had come. As I could read but little, I questioned with myself how it would be possible for me to deliver the message, when I did not understand the scriptures. I went from one religious professor to another, enquiring of them what ailed me; but of all these I could find none who could throw any light upon such impressions. They all told me there was nothing in Scripture that would sanction such exercises. It was hard for men to travel, and what would women do? These things greatly discouraged me, and shut up my way, and caused me to resist the spirit. After going to all that were accounted pious, and receiving no help, I returned to the Lord, feeling that I was nothing, and knew nothing and wrestled and prayed to the Lord that He would fully reveal his will, and make the way plain.

Whilst I thus struggled, there seemed a light from heaven to fall upon me which banished all my desponding fears, and I was enabled to form a new resolution to go on to prison and to death, if it might be my portion; and the Lord showed me that it was his will I should be resigned to die any death that might be my lot, in carrying his message, and be entirely crucified to the world, and sacrifice all to his glory that was then in my possession, which his witnesses, the holy Apostles, had done before me. It was then which I could rejoice day and night, and I walked and talked with God, and my soul was illuminated with heavenly light, and I knew nothing but Jesus Christ, and Him crucified.

One day, after these things, while I was at my work, the Spirit directed me to go to a poor widow, and ask her if I might have a meeting at her house, which was situated in one of the lowest and worst streets in Baltimore. With great joy she gave notice, and at the time appointed I appeared there among a few colored sisters. When they had all prayed, they called upon me to close the meeting, and I felt an impression that I must say a few words; and while I was speaking, the house seemed filled with light; and when I was about to close the meeting, and was kneeling, a man came in and stood till I arose. It proved to be a watchman.[1] The sisters became so frightened, they all went away except the one who lived in the house, and an old woman; they both appeared to be much frightened, fearing they should receive some personal injury, or be put out of the house. A feeling of weakness came over me for a short time, but I soon grew warm and courageous in the Spirit. The man then said to me, "I was sent here to break up your meeting. Complaint has been made to me that the

---

[1] Police officer.

people round here cannot sleep for the racket." I replied, "a good racket is better than a bad racket. How do they rest when the ungodly are dancing and fiddling till midnight? Why are not they molested by the watchmen? And why should we be for praising God, our Maker? Are we worthy of greater punishment for praying to Him? And are we to be prohibited from doing so, that sinners may remain slumbering in their sins?" Speaking several words more, he turned pale and trembled, and begged my pardon, acknowledging that it was not his wish to interrupt us, and that he would never disturb a religious assembly again. He then took leave of me in a comely manner and wished us success.

Our meeting gave great offence, and we were forbid holding any more assemblies. Even the elders of our meeting joined with the wicked people, and said such meetings must be stopped, and that woman quieted. But I was not afraid of any of them and continued to go, and burnt with a zeal not my own. . . .

We went on for several years, and the Lord was with us with great power it proved, to the conversion of many souls, and we continued to grow stronger. . . .

I also held meetings in Virginia. The people there would not believe that a colored woman could preach. And moreover, as she had no learning, they strove to imprison me because I spoke against slavery: and being brought up,[2] they asked by what authority I spake? and if I had been ordained? I answered, not by the commission of men's hands: if the Lord had ordained me, I needed nothing better.

As I travelled along through the land, I was led at different times to converse with white men who were by profession ministers of the gospel. Many of them, up and down, confessed they did not believe in revelation, which gave me to see that men were sent forth as ministers without Christ's authority. In a conversation with one of these, he said, "You think you have these things by revelation, but there has been no such thing as revelation since Christ's ascension." I asked him where the apostle John got his revelation while he was in the Isle of Patmos.[3] With this, he rose up and left me, and I said in my spirit, get thee behind me Satan.

I visited many remote places, where there were no meeting-houses, and held many glorious meetings, for the Lord poured out his Spirit in sweet effusions. I also travelled to Canada, and visited several settlements of colored people, and felt an open door amongst them.

Analyzing the Source

REFLECTING ON THE SOURCE

1. Compare and contrast the conversion experiences depicted in each narrative. What events or emotions seemed to trigger their visions of God? What do their stories tell you about the practice and beliefs of African American Christianity in the early nineteenth century?

[2] Before a judge.

[3] A reference to Saint John, author of the New Testament Book of Revelations.

2. Compare and contrast how each author depicted her calling to preach. How did they initially react to that calling, and what prompted them to answer it? What opposition did they face to their ministries? What do these narratives tell you about their relationship with their audiences at camp meetings and prayer groups?

3. Elaw and Truth published their narratives during the prime of their lives; Elizabeth's is a memoir composed in old age. Elaw wrote her narrative; Truth and Elizabeth dictated theirs to others. How should these differences affect your use of these autobiographies as historical sources on the Second Great Awakening?

MAKING CONNECTIONS

4. How does the depiction of womanhood in these narratives compare to that found in Chapter 8, "Family Values: Advice Literature for Parents and Children in the Early Republic"? Where did white and black notions of femininity converge in early nineteenth-century America, and how did they differ? How did female African American preachers challenge the gender roles and assumptions of middle-class society?

5. What was the most significant factor in shaping the identity of the subjects of these autobiographies: their gender, race, social origin, or religion? Where do you see in these sources expressions of solidarity with other African Americans, other women, or fellow evangelical Christians?

6. What connection, if any, do these narratives suggest between the Second Great Awakening and the abolitionist and women's rights movements of the Jacksonian era? Why do you suppose African American women and evangelical Christians were attracted to these political causes?

Beyond the Source

African American women played a significant role in the Second Great Awakening, but their churches never opened positions of leadership to them. During the 1790s, Methodists and Baptists actively sought African American converts and allowed women substantially more influence in their church governance than did other Protestant denominations, but as these faiths moved from the fringes of American society into the middle class, they retreated from their initial racial tolerance and gender equality. During the Jacksonian era, male clergy and church officials were more likely to brand outspoken women as "disorderly" and threaten them with excommunication. Even the AME Church, which was strongly committed to racial equality, remained steadfastly male in its clergy and governance. Delegates at the AME Church's 1852 General Conference voted overwhelmingly against a resolution to license female preachers.

Nevertheless, evangelical religion provided white and black women with a means of challenging their exclusion from public life. Female benevolent societies dedicated to promoting Christian morals, missions, and charitable work were a fixture of Jacksonian society. Claiming a moral authority rooted in their experience as mothers and wives, women used these organizations to gain a voice in public affairs and to criticize the imbalance of power between men and women. Female temperance societies attacked drunkenness by demonizing the male drunkard, who wasted his family's money, beat his wife, and abandoned his children. The abolitionist movement attracted women from evangelical backgrounds who found slavery morally reprehensible because it denied the integrity of the slave's soul and subjected the slave family to sexual abuse, cruelty, and separation. Abolitionists imitated many of the techniques of evangelical camp meetings to spread their message, including outdoor rallies, spoken testimonials from runaway slaves and former slaveholders, and traveling lecturers who spread the antislavery message in the style of circuit-riding ministers.

African American women preachers varied in their approach to discussing slavery. Some, like Elizabeth, avoided the topic and focused instead on spiritual matters. Doing so enabled them to bring their ministry to slaves in the South without being assaulted or jailed as abolitionists in disguise. Elizabeth continued her travels until the 1850s, when the infirmities of old age forced her to retire among Quaker friends in Philadelphia. We do not know what became of Zilpha Elaw after she published her autobiography in 1846. Sojourner Truth, on the other hand, found fame during the 1840s as an abolitionist and women's rights activist. She joined forces with abolitionists William Lloyd Garrison, Frederick Douglass, and Harriet Beecher Stowe, and in 1851 she gave a famous speech at a women's rights convention in Akron, Ohio, in which she defended the rights of African American women with the famous phrase, "ar'n't I a woman?" After the Civil War, Truth advocated voting rights for blacks and women. Her remarkable public career, from the 1840s through the 1870s, illustrated the lasting impact that the Second Great Awakening had on American society and the transformations it wrought in the spiritual and political lives of women who embraced its evangelical message.

Finding and Supplementing the Source

Many of the works of early female African American writers have been reprinted in modern editions in the series *The Schomburg Library of Nineteenth-Century Black Women Writers*, general editor Henry Louis Gates Jr., published by Oxford University Press. One volume in the series that is particularly relevant to the genre of spiritual autobiography is Susan E. Houchins, editor, *Spiritual Narratives* (New York: Oxford University Press, 1988). Three spiritual autobiographies, including Zilpha Elaw's, are reprinted in full in William L. Andrews, editor, *Sisters of the Spirit: Three Black Women's Autobiographies of the Nineteenth Century* (Bloomington: Indiana University Press, 1986). *Black Women in Nineteenth-Century American Life: Their Words, Their Thoughts, Their Feelings*, edited by Bert James Loewenberg and Ruth Bogin (University Park: Pennsylvania State University Press, 1976), contains edited selections from twenty-four African

American women writers, both famous and obscure. It is a valuable collection for comparing the female voice in spiritual autobiographies with that found in slave narratives and political tracts.

For an excellent introduction to the Second Great Awakening and its impact on nineteenth-century American culture, see Nathan O. Hatch, *The Democratization of American Christianity* (New Haven: Yale University Press, 1989). Paul E. Johnson and Sean Wilentz's *The Kingdom of Matthias: A Story of Sex and Salvation in Nineteenth-Century America* (New York: Oxford University Press, 1995) tells an interesting story about the Second Great Awakening in New York that features Sojourner Truth. For the role women have played in shaping evangelical Protestantism, see Marilyn J. Westerkamp, *Women and Religion in Early America, 1600–1850: The Puritan and Evangelical Traditions* (New York: Routledge, 1999), and Susan Juster, *Disorderly Women: Sexual Politics and Evangelicalism in Revolutionary New England* (Ithaca, N.Y.: Cornell University Press, 1994).

For a comparative history of the origins and spread of the AME Church, see James T. Campbell, *Songs of Zion: The African Methodist Episcopal Church in the United States and South Africa* (New York: Oxford University Press, 1995), and for a study of gender in the AME Church, see Jualynne E. Dodson, *Engendering Church: Women, Power, and the AME Church* (Lanham, Md.: Rowman and Littlefield Publishers, 2002). Gary B. Nash's *Forging Freedom: The Formation of Philadelphia's Black Community* (Cambridge: Harvard University Press, 1988) provides important background on the social origins of African American Methodism. For African American women in the nineteenth century, see Deborah Gray White, *Ar'n't I a Woman? Female Slaves in the Plantation South* (New York: W. W. Norton, 1985). Nell Irvin Painter examines the career of Sojourner Truth in *Sojourner Truth: A Life, a Symbol* (New York: W. W. Norton, 1996).

CHAPTER 12

On and Off the Record

Diplomatic Correspondence on the Eve of the Mexican-American War

President James K. Polk did not like to work on Sundays. A strict observer of his religious principles, he preferred to follow the biblical command to rest on the Sabbath. He had even banned dancing in the White House. Nevertheless, on Sunday, May 10, 1846, he broke from his usual custom and spent the day at his desk. The news he had received the night before was very good, good enough, one might imagine, for Polk to allow himself to dance a private little jig. A courier had arrived late on Saturday to inform the president that U.S. troops under the command of General Zachary Taylor had been attacked by a Mexican military patrol just north of the Rio Grande two weeks earlier. Polk had decided earlier in the day on Saturday to ask Congress for a declaration of war against Mexico, but the news from the Rio Grande was exactly the kind of provocation he needed to clinch his case. And so, on Sunday he revised the message he intended to send to Congress the following day, incorporating the news about General Taylor and stating in no uncertain terms that "Mexico has . . . invaded our territory and shed American blood upon American soil. . . . War exists, and notwithstanding all our efforts to avoid it, exists by the act of Mexico."

Three days later Congress gave Polk the declaration of war he wanted. When the Mexican-American War ended two years later, Mexico ceded one half of its territory to the United States, comprising all or parts of the modern states of California, Arizona, New Mexico, Texas, Nevada, Utah, Colorado, and Wyoming (see Map 12.1). The war with Mexico was the crowning achievement of Polk's administration. During his four years in office (1845–1849), the United States experienced its most significant territorial expansion since the Louisiana Purchase.

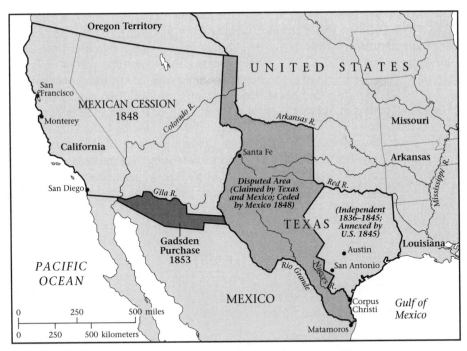

Map 12.1 Territory Contested between the United States and Mexico, 1845–1853
The annexation of Texas by the United States in 1845 created the disputed area of possession between Mexico and the United States shown here. The historic border between Mexico and Texas had been the Nueces River, but Texans, backed by President James K. Polk, argued that the border was the Rio Grande. The Mexican-American War (1846–1848) resolved this dispute in the Americans' favor and led to the Mexican cession of California and New Mexico. The Gadsden Purchase in 1853 completed the modern U.S.-Mexican border. Source: Adapted from Bradford Perkins, *The Cambridge History of American Foreign Relations*, Vol. 1, *The Creation of a Republican Empire, 1776–1865* (Cambridge: Cambridge University Press, 1993), 184.

The rapid unfolding of events in late April and early May 1846 may make it seem as though the Mexican-American War started accidentally. Two military forces, both far removed from their nation's capitals, engaged each other on a remote, contested border. Certainly, the words Polk chose so carefully for his war message conveyed a sense of unanticipated emergency, of hostilities already commenced by a treacherous enemy against unsuspecting Americans. However, the events that preceded Polk's war message were the culmination of an ongoing diplomatic crisis. On Friday, May 9, an envoy Polk had sent to Mexico returned to Washington, D.C., and reported on the Mexican government's refusal to receive him. Before the news arrived of the skirmish on the Rio Grande, Polk intended to make this diplomatic rebuff the centerpiece of his war message to Congress.

The diplomatic showdown between the United States and Mexico had been brewing since the United States annexed Texas a year earlier. A former province of Mexico, Texas had fought a successful war of independence in 1835–1836. Following that conflict, Texas had been a thorn in the side of U.S.-Mexican relations. In 1846, Mexico still regarded Texas as a rebellious province within its borders. While it may have grudgingly accepted the reality of Texan independence, it was loathe to accept the idea of Texas joining the United States, which would endanger Mexico's control over its other northern provinces of New Mexico and California. Anglo-Americans in Texas, many of them slaveholders from the southern United States who had migrated there in the 1820s, supported annexation, although a minority of them liked the idea of remaining independent. In the United States, the annexation of Texas was a political hot potato. Southerners generally supported it because it would open new territory for their slave-based plantation economy. Northerners opposed it for exactly the same reason, fearing that the addition of such a large slave state would upset the balance of power between free and slave states within the union. In Europe, Great Britain and France watched the crisis brewing over annexation closely. Both countries were creditors of Mexico and interested in the disposition of its northern territories.

The likelihood of annexation increased when Polk was elected president in November 1844. A southern Democrat, slaveholder, and ardent expansionist, he made no secret of his desire to see Texas, California, and Oregon incorporated into the union and his willingness to go to war to achieve it. The spirit and rationale behind Polk's aggressive expansionism was summed up in the phrase "manifest destiny," coined by a newspaper editor in 1845 to describe what he believed was God's divine plan for the United States to extend its dominion across the North American continent. Polk skillfully balanced different constituencies to put his plans in motion. To appease Northerners, he pursued the U.S. claim against Britain for the Oregon country, so that the admission of Texas to the union could be balanced with an additional free state. To cement Texans' support for annexation, he endorsed their claim that their border with Mexico extended as far south as the Rio Grande and as far west as Santa Fe, the capital city of New Mexico. Polk knew the Mexican government would find this border unacceptable. Mexico had long maintained that its historic border with Texas was the Nueces River, one hundred miles north of the Rio Grande and far removed from Santa Fe (see Map 12.1 on page 245). The president also kept a close eye on Britain and France, for fear that they would try to use their own diplomacy with Mexico to acquire new colonies in North America.

When Congress voted to annex Texas, Mexico broke off diplomatic relations with the United States and sent troops north to the Rio Grande. Polk ordered a U.S. naval squadron into the Gulf of Mexico to menace the Mexican seaport of Vera Cruz, and he sent troops to occupy the disputed territory between the Nueces River and the Rio Grande. These maneuvers by the Mexican and U.S. governments set the stage for the hostilities that prompted Polk to revise his war message on May 10.

Mexico was not anxious for war, but it did not wish to lose its northern provinces either. Since achieving its independence from Spain in 1821, Mexico had suffered from a succession of weak, poorly financed governments. The chief source of political power in the nation was the army, but it was also the chief source of political instability, as military coups undid one attempt at constitutional government after another. To complicate matters, Mexico's provinces north of the Rio Grande were rich in resources but poor in people. The largest populations in California, New Mexico, and Texas were Native Americans who were not particularly interested in submitting to Mexico or any other foreign power. Spanish missionaries and colonists had established various settlements in the northern provinces before 1800, but these communities were isolated from each other and Mexico City. In brief, Mexico's hold on its territory north of the Rio Grande was tenuous but too valuable to give up.

All of the military posturing between Mexico and the United States was accompanied by quieter efforts to mend the rift between the two nations. Polk, despite his hawkish public demeanor, knew that war with Mexico would not be easy. It would require military organization and spending on a scale unprecedented for the federal government, which had not managed its last major war with a foreign power, the War of 1812 with Britain, very well. Aware of the financial straits of the Mexican government, Polk thought he might be able to purchase a settlement to the dispute over Texas and perhaps even acquire New Mexico and California in the deal. He encouraged his secretary of state, James Buchanan, to pursue this option through both official and unofficial diplomatic channels.

The U.S. declaration of war against Mexico in May 1846 would indicate that Buchanan failed. The two nations did not renew normal diplomatic relations until peace was restored two years later. Describing Buchanan's efforts as a failure, however, raises some important questions about the purposes and methods behind Polk's foreign policy. Was Polk ever genuinely interested in making the sort of compromises that would have been necessary to avoid war? Did he and Buchanan set out to find a solution to this crisis or did they purposely exacerbate it so they would have justification for going to war? Historians interested in answering these questions look for answers in the documentary record of official and unofficial communications between Buchanan, his foreign agents, and the Mexican government.

Using Diplomatic Correspondence as a Source

During the nineteenth century, the United States conducted its foreign relations according to conventions inherited from Europe and standardized at the Congress of Vienna in 1815. Generally speaking, there were three types of personnel who dealt directly with foreign governments. First, ambassadors carried out official communication between governments. Until the 1890s, the United States avoided using the title "ambassador" because it smacked of Old World aristocracy. Instead, the federal government granted its highest-ranking diplomats the title of "envoy extraordinary and minister plenipotentiary," a mouthful that was usually shortened to "minister." A minister led the embassy or "legation" established in the capital city of a foreign country and typically had several assistants ranked in descending order below him as counselors, secretaries, and agents. Consuls were a second category of foreign service personnel, appointed to protect and assist a nation's citizens traveling, doing business, or living abroad. Consuls kept offices in foreign seaports and commercial centers as well as capitals. Unlike an embassy or legation, a consular office did not conduct official diplomacy, but it did serve as eyes and ears for its government in a foreign nation. Commissioners made up the third category of diplomatic personnel, and they were usually appointed for specific tasks, such as negotiating treaties or initiating relations with another country.

While the minister to a foreign country carried out much of his duties in person, all his official business was documented in written correspondence. Such business followed an elaborate etiquette observed by the minister and his host government. When an envoy or minister arrived in a foreign country, he presented his credentials, the papers authorizing their appointment, to the foreign secretary (the equivalent of the secretary of state in the United States). If the foreign secretary approved the credentials, he "recognized" the minister, allowing him to conduct business with the government and granting him immunity from its laws. Issues of rank, precedent, and precise language weighed heavily on such occasions. Depending upon a diplomat's official title and the wording of his credentials, he may or may not gain access to senior officials of government. If the foreign secretary refused to recognize him, he received no more favor or protection than any other foreign citizen in that country.

Governments also conducted diplomacy through unofficial channels. Confidential agents were hired by their home governments to serve as informants. They received specific instructions with their appointment but were expected to keep such information secret and to assume the character of a private citizen when abroad. They did not carry formal credentials and therefore did not enjoy diplomatic immunity or any other privileges associated with diplomatic rank. Oftentimes, they were businessmen who lived abroad, knew the native language well, and had cultivated relationships with people of influence and power. In an age before international communication by telephone or television, their correspondence with government officials back home gave forthright assessments and advice that contrasted sharply with the highly stylized, restrained language of official diplomatic correspondence. The term "confidential agent" may call to mind images of espionage and skullduggery, but their work was usually more mundane, consisting chiefly of reading the local newspapers and meeting privately with influential officials. Nevertheless, confidential agents provided the primary means of what we call today "intelligence gathering" about foreign governments.

The difference between the official and unofficial diplomacy conducted over the Texas annexation crisis is best grasped through the metaphor of a play or ballet. Official diplomacy between the United States and Mexico was conducted by high-ranking foreign service personnel trained in the specialized language and manners of their profession. Their performance, however, was shaped by the maneuvers of lower-ranking officials and confidential agents, who could express themselves more bluntly because they worked behind the scenes. To reconstruct fully the Texas annexation crisis, the historian must pull back the curtain and scrutinize the unofficial channels of diplomacy as well as the official ones. Only then will the entire process become clear.

Consider the style and tone of the two letters below (from William R. Manning, editor, *Diplomatic Correspondence of the United States: Inter-American Affairs, 1831–1860*, 8:699–700, 760). The first, an example of official diplomatic correspondence, is from the Mexican minister in Washington, D.C., to John C. Calhoun, the secretary of state for President John Tyler, Polk's predecessor in office; in this letter the Mexican minister formally breaks diplomatic relations with the United States after the congressional vote to annex Texas. The second, an example of unofficial diplomatic correspondence, is from a confidential agent working for the United States in Mexico City, writing to Secretary of State James Buchanan, who succeeded Calhoun when Polk was inaugurated in March 1845, about his impression of the Mexicans.

JUAN N. ALMONTE, MEXICAN MINISTER TO THE UNITED STATES, TO JOHN C. CALHOUN, SECRETARY OF STATE OF THE UNITED STATES, WASHINGTON, D.C., MARCH 6, 1845

WASHINGTON, D.C.

The Undersigned, Envoy Extraordinary and Minister Plenipotentiary of the Mexican Republic, has the honour to address the Honourable John C. Calhoun Secretary of State of the United States of America, with the object of making known to him the profound regret, with which he has seen, that the General Congress of the Union has passed a law, giving its consent, and admitting into the American Confederacy, the Mexican Province of Texas.

Note the precise, legalistic tone of this letter

The Undersigned . . . sees consummated on the part of the American Government, an act of aggression, the most unjust which can be found recorded in the annals of modern history, namely—that of despoiling a friendly nation like Mexico, of a considerable portion of her territory. . . .

Stops short of calling the annexation an act of war but makes clear that he sees it as justification for one

The Undersigned will say in conclusion to the Honourable Secretary of State of the United States, in order that he may be pleased to communicate it to the President of these States; that in consequence of this law against which he has just protested, his mission near this Government has ceased from this day. Wherefore the Undersigned prays the Honourable Secretary of State, to be pleased to deliver to him his

He observes the official channel of communication from the secretary of state to the president

Polite request signals the end of formal diplomatic relations

passports, as he has made arrangements to leave this city without delay for New York.

WILLIAM S. PARROTT, CONFIDENTIAL AGENT OF THE UNITED STATES TO MEXICO, TO JAMES BUCHANAN, SECRETARY OF STATE OF THE UNITED STATES, OCTOBER 11, 1845

Private and Confidential   Mexico

Parrott intends to speak frankly, in words not meant for public exposure

MY DEAR SIR: Although I am but a neophyte in diplomacy, I am an American, and believe that in every emergency, in which I have been placed, by chance or otherwise, I have not been found wanting—

Beginner. Why would he point out his lack of experience as a diplomat?

In the discharge of the important trust confided to me in Mexico, I have followed my instructions to the letter, not my personal desire to see this people well flogged by Uncle Sam's boys, ere we enter upon negotiation—

Note colloquial, even folksy, tone

Before

I have suffered more, perhaps, than any other American citizen, at their [the Mexicans'] hands. I know them better, perhaps, than any other American citizen and I am fully persuaded, they never can love or respect us, as we should be loved and respected by them, until after we shall have given them a positive proof of our superiority.

Bases his conclusion on his first-hand experience with the Mexicans

Both of these letters refer to a potential military response to the crisis, but they are strikingly different in their language and tone. Almonte maintains an air of formality and politeness even as he breaks diplomatic relations. His carefully chosen words make clear that Mexico sees annexation as an act of aggression. Parrott, on the other hand, offers no pretence of formality. After proudly admitting his lack of diplomatic expertise, he bluntly advises the secretary of state that only war will bring this dispute to a successful resolution.

Advantages and Disadvantages of Working with Diplomatic Correspondence

There are several advantages to working with diplomatic correspondence when studying foreign relations. First, unlike newspaper stories and political speeches intended for public audiences, official diplomatic correspondence was intended for a much smaller audience of officials who controlled the reins of power in foreign affairs. While its specialized language can be difficult to comprehend at first (not unlike the legal documents you encountered in Chapter 6), it does lay out very precisely the issues that divided Mexico and the United States on the eve of war.

A second advantage derives from reading together two types of diplomatic correspondence: that between nations and that between officials and agents of a single nation. The former has the highly stylized, legalistic language one would expect; the latter is much more plainspoken and reveals the ambitions behind the artifice of the first. Instructions from the secretary of state to ministers and agents in the field lay out the objectives of foreign policy in a bareknuckled way not found in carefully crafted political speeches or official correspondence with other governments. Likewise, the reports that confidential agents and consuls sent back from the field often have an "off-the-record" honesty to them that that can be invaluable for revealing the prejudices and assumptions behind foreign policy.

A disadvantage to bear in mind when working with diplomatic correspondence before the twentieth century is the time involved in transmitting it. Communication between the secretary of state and his agents in foreign nations had to be carried by hand in the 1840s, and if a letter was delayed, the information it contained might arrive after important policy decisions had been made. The telegraph was a new technology in 1846 and did not reach beyond cities on the east coast of the United States. Steamships and specialized courier riders sped the mail, but important communications could still be lost or delayed en route. Most correspondence from U.S. agents in Mexico City to Washington, D.C., first traveled overland to Vera Cruz and then by ship to Havana, Cuba, where it was transferred to another ship headed for New Orleans. After arriving in New Orleans, it took a minimum of three more days to reach Washington, D.C. Agents in the field tried to compensate for the unreliability of long distance communication by writing many letters, so that if one were lost, another containing similar information might arrive safely. Nevertheless, the delay involved in international correspondence should make you think twice about what role these letters played in decision making at home.

You should also bear in mind the domestic politics that can influence foreign policy. Then as now, high-ranking diplomatic officials were political appointees typically being rewarded for their support of the president and his party. They did not necessarily occupy their posts because of their familiarity or sympathy with the foreign nation to which they were posted; they might in fact be downright ignorant about it. Likewise, career foreign service personnel seldom commanded the political influence necessary to sway policy decisions made by the president and secretary of state.

Diplomatic correspondence will not reveal the full process of decision making in foreign policy. In the case of the Texas annexation crisis, it cannot tell you what sorts of political pressures Polk faced at home: What was the tide of public opinion about war with Mexico? Did some members of Congress want to extract political favors from Polk before agreeing to vote for a declaration of war? How much influence did Buchanan have within Polk's administration? Historians turn to other sources to answer those questions. In studying the origins of the Mexican-American War, they have usually read diplomatic correspondence in conjunction with Polk's diary, his messages to Congress, and the vast literature produced in the popular press about the annexation of Texas.

Working with the Source

In the next section, you will read selections from diplomatic correspondence involving U.S.-Mexican relations between March 1845 and March 1846. Much of it deals with Secretary of State James Buchanan's efforts to handle the annexation crisis by gathering information about Mexico's preparedness for war, its willingness to cede California and New Mexico, and the potential for intervention by Great Britain or France.

The letters fall into two general categories: correspondence exchanged between officials of the U.S. and Mexican governments, and correspondence exchanged between Buchanan and his agents in Mexico. As you read them, use this table to organize and record your reactions. The table asks you to describe the tone of the letters, meaning the subtle (and sometimes not so subtle) role that word choice and style played in conveying the author's objectives and designs.

LETTERS BETWEEN U.S. AND MEXICAN OFFICIALS			
Source	Author's Title	Subjects Discussed in Letter	Tone of Letter
1. Buchanan to Almonte			
7. Peña to Black			
11. Castillo y Lanzas to Slidell			

LETTERS BETWEEN BUCHANAN AND U.S. AGENTS IN MEXICO			
Source	Author's Title	Subjects Discussed in Letter	Tone of Letter
2. Buchanan to Parrott			
6. Buchanan to Black			
8. Buchanan to Slidell			
10. Buchanan to Slidell			
12. Buchanan to Slidell			
3. Parrott to Buchanan			
5. Parrott to Buchanan			
4. Black to Buchanan			
9. Slidell to Buchanan			
13. Slidell to Buchanan			

The Source: Diplomatic Correspondence Concerning the Annexation of Texas, March 10, 1845–March 18, 1846

 ## U.S. Secretary of State James Buchanan to Juan N. Almonte, Mexican Minister to the United States, March 10, 1845

When Polk was inaugurated in March 1845, his secretary of state, James Buchanan, inherited the crisis in U.S.-Mexican relations caused by the annexation of Texas.

WASHINGTON, D.C.

The Undersigned, Secretary of State of the United States, has received the note of General Almonte, the Envoy Extraordinary and Minister Plenipotentiary of the Mexican Republic of the 6th instant,[1] addressed to his predecessor, the Honorable John C. Calhoun, protesting, in the name of his Government, against the resolution of the late Congress for annexing Texas to the United States; and he has submitted the same to the President.

In answer, the Undersigned is instructed to say, that the admission of Texas as one of the States of this Union having received the sanction both of the legislative and Executive Departments of the government, is now irrevocably decided, so far as the United States are concerned. Nothing but the refusal of Texas to ratify the terms and conditions on which her admission depends, can defeat this object. It is therefore, too late at present to reopen a discussion which has already been exhausted, and again to prove that Texas has long since achieved her independence of Mexico, and now stands before the world, both *de jure*[2] and *de facto*,[3] as a sovereign and independent State amid the family of nations. Sustaining this character and having manifested a strong desire to become one of the members of our Confederacy, neither Mexico nor any other nation will have just cause of complaint against the United States for admitting her into this Union.

The President nevertheless sincerely regrets that the government of Mexico should have taken offence at these proceedings; and he earnestly trusts that it

[1] This month.

[2] By law.

[3] By fact.

Source: William R. Manning, editor, *Diplomatic Correspondence of the United States: Inter-American Affairs, 1831–1860* (Washington, D.C.: Carnegie Endowment for International Peace, 1937), 8:163.

may hereafter be disposed to view them in a more favorable and friendly light. Whilst entering upon the duties of the Presidential office, he cheerfully declares in advance, that his most strenuous efforts shall be devoted to the amicable adjustment of every cause of complaint between the two Governments, and to the cultivation of the kindest and most friendly relations between the sister Republics.

The Undersigned has the honor to transmit to General Almonte his passport according to his request, and to assure him of his distinguished consideration and regard.

2 *Secretary of State James Buchanan to William S. Parrott, Confidential Agent of the United States to Mexico,* March 28, 1845

Shortly after the break in formal diplomatic relations between the United States and Mexico, President Polk appointed William S. Parrott a confidential agent in Mexico City. Parrott was a merchant who, like many foreign businessmen, also held an outstanding claim of debt against the Mexican government.

WASHINGTON, D.C.

Sir: All diplomatic intercourse having been suspended between the governments of the United States and Mexico, it is the desire of the President to restore such an intercourse if this can be effected consistently with the national honor. To accomplish this purpose he has deemed it expedient to send a confidential agent to Mexico, and reposing confidence in your abilities and patriotism, has selected you as a proper person to execute this important trust. Your success may mainly depend upon your perfect command of temper in all situations and under all circumstances, and upon your prudence in refraining from the least intimation that you are a Government agent, unless this should become indispensable to the success of your mission. . . . From your long residence in Mexico and your thorough acquaintance with the Mexican people and their language, the President considers you peculiarly qualified for the trust and indulges in favorable anticipation of your success.

You will proceed without delay by the most expeditious route to the City of Mexico, and will there ascertain the temper and tone of the present Mexican Government towards the United States. . . . The great object of your mission and that which you will constantly keep in view in all your proceedings, is to reach the President and other high officers of the Mexican government and

Source: Manning, *Diplomatic Correspondence of the United States,* 8:164–65.

especially the Minister of Foreign Affairs; and by every honorable effort to convince them that it is the true interest of their country, as it certainly is, to restore friendly relations between the two Republics. Should you clearly ascertain that they are willing to renew our diplomatic intercourse, then and not till then you are at liberty to communicate to them your official character and to state that the United States will send a Minister to Mexico as soon as they receive authentic information that he will be kindly received. . . .

Whilst, therefore, you ought not to conceal that the reünion of Texas with the United States is already decreed and can never under any circumstances be abandoned, you are at liberty to state your confident belief that in regard to all unsettled questions, we are prepared to meet Mexico in a most liberal and friendly spirit. . . .

William S. Parrott, Confidential Agent of the United States to Mexico, to Secretary of State James Buchanan, April 29, 1845

MEXICO

. . . If it be true that climate forms the character of a nation, that the character of a nation forms its Government, and that the Government forms its manners, morals and institutions, judging from what Mexico has been; it is not probable she will find more repose, hereafter or for years to come, than she has hitherto enjoyed—Prone to revolution and change, as she is; distracted by opposing factions nearly equally balanced, it is hardly reasonable to suppose that, the present Government can be of long duration . . . The people know not what they want, nor is there, a man in the country, of sufficient moral courage and prestige to establish any stable form of Government, out of the chaos that now exists—Each prominent individual in the country, has his party, and each party is plotting against all others to obtain power, however ephemeral, with a view to personal emolument, at the expense of the nation and happiness of its people. . . .

My instructions are deposited in safety, I keep no copies of my communications to the Department, so as not, under the most unfavorable turn things might take, to be taken by surprise.

Source: Manning, *Diplomatic Correspondence of the United States,* 8:712–13.

John Black, United States Consul at Mexico City, to Secretary of State James Buchanan, June 21, 1845

John Black was the American consul in Mexico City. He became the highest-ranking U.S. diplomatic official in Mexico when the U.S. minister there, Wilson Shannon, returned home after the break in formal diplomatic relations in March 1845.

MEXICO

. . . It is not known what course Mexico will take, in respect to the question of Annexation of Texas to the United States, but no doubt she will make some noise, and as far as threats, and words, and paper war will go, we shall no doubt have enough of it, but I do not think the present Government has any serious idea of carrying on any other kind of war, against us,—though forced by the opposition to put itself in a belligerent attitude, to show its patriotism.—Neither do I think, that the opposition who appear to be so eager for war, and are urging on the Government to that extremity, would, if they themselves were in power, or should hereafter get into power, ever seriously think of entering into a war, (in earnest,) with the United States.

It is true our defenceless citizens in different parts of the Country, on account of existing difficulties, will be likely to suffer in their persons and property from unjust and arbitrary acts of the Mexican Authorities, and it is from this kind of depredations we have the most to fear.

Source: Manning, *Diplomatic Correspondence of the United States,* 8:728–29.

 ## William S. Parrott, Confidential Agent of the United States to Mexico, to Secretary of State James Buchanan, August 26, 1845

MEXICO

. . . A declaration of war with the United States is not now spoken of; nor was it ever seriously contemplated—The Government at one time, intended to concentrate a force on the frontier of Texas, sufficient to have annoyed its inhabitants, perhaps to have imprisoned one of its Courts of Justice; but even this is not now contemplated—The face of things have changed, and no additional

Source: Manning, *Diplomatic Correspondence of the United States,* 8:746–47.

force will be sent to the Frontier, unless the Government, intimated as it is, should be compelled to do so by an insincere opposition—There is a desire, even publickly manifested, to receive a commissioner from the United States, and every vessel that arrives . . . is said to have one on board—

I have good reasons to believe that, an Envoy from the United States would not only, be well received; but that his arrival would be hailed with joy—An Envoy possessing suitable qualifications for this Court, might with comparative ease, settle, *over a breakfast,* the most important national question, while such as we have lately had here would make matters worse—An Envoy to this Court, should speak the language of the country, should be accessible and affable in his deportment, to insure the success of his mission. . . .

6   *Secretary of State James Buchanan to John Black, United States Consul at Mexico City,* September 17, 1845

WASHINGTON, D.C.

. . . He [President Polk] is anxious to preserve peace, although prepared for war.

Actuated by these sentiments, the President has directed me to instruct you in the absence of any Diplomatic Agent in Mexico, to ascertain from the Mexican Government whether they would receive an Envoy from the United States entrusted with full power to adjust all the questions in dispute between the two Governments. Should the answer be in the affirmative such an Envoy will be immediately despatched to Mexico.

If the President were disposed to stand upon a mere question of etiquette, he would wait until the Mexican Government, which had suspended the Diplomatic relations Between the Two Countries, should ask that they may be restored. But his desire is so strong to terminate the present unfortunate state of our relations, with that Republic, that he has consented to waive all ceremony and take the initiative.

Concerning the most politic and judicious mode of communicating with the Mexican Government, you will consult Dr. Parrott, a Citizen of the United States now in Mexico. He is a discreet man, well acquainted with public affairs and possesses my confidence. . . .

I need scarcely warn you to preserve the most inviolable secrecy in regard to your proceedings, making no communication to any person with the exception of Dr. Parrott, not indispensable to the accomplishment of the object. There will be a vessel of War at Vera Cruz ready to receive your Despatch for this Department, and to convey it to the United States with the least possible delay . . .

Source: Manning, *Diplomatic Correspondence of the United States,* 8:167–68.

7 *Manuel de la Peña, Minister of Foreign Affairs of Mexico, to John Black, United States Consul at Mexico City,*
October 15, 1845

On October 10, 1845, John Black met privately with Mexico's foreign minister (the equivalent of the U.S. secretary of state), Manuel de la Peña, to propose that the United States send a commissioner to Mexico to negotiate a settlement to the annexation crisis. Peña responded positively to the idea but insisted that the United States withdraw its naval squadron from the waters off of Vera Cruz first.

Confidential   MEXICO

. . . As my Government believes this invitation to be made in good faith, and with the real desire that it may lead to a favourable conclusion, it also hopes that the Commissioner will be a person endowed with the qualities proper for the attainment of this end; that his dignity prudence and moderation, and the discreatness and reasonableness of his proposals, will contribute to calm as much as possible, the just irritation of the Mexicans; and in fine, that the conduct of the Commissioner, on all points, may be such as to persuade them, that they may obtain satisfaction for their injuries, through the means of reason and peace, and without being obliged to resort to those of arms and force.

What my Government requires above all things is, that the mission of the Commissioner of the United States, and his reception by us, should appear to be always absolutely frank and free, from every sign of menace or coercion; and thus Mr. Consul while making known to your Government, the disposition on the part of that of Mexico, to receive the Commissioner, you should impress upon it, as indispensable, the previous recall of the whole naval force, now lying in sight of our port of Vera Cruz. Its presence would degrade Mexico, while she is receiving the Commissioner, and would justly subject the United States to the imputation of contradicting by acts, the vehement desire of conciliation peace and friendship, which is professed and asserted by words. . . .

Source: Manning, *Diplomatic Correspondence of the United States,* 8:763.

8   *Secretary of State James Buchanan to John Slidell, Appointed United States Minister to Mexico,* November 10, 1845

After learning of Peña's positive response to Black, Polk appointed John Slidell, a prominent Democrat, Louisiana slaveholder, and ardent expansionist, to serve as his commissioner to Mexico. Buchanan made clear in his instructions to Slidell the president's priorities for negotiating with Mexico.

WASHINGTON, D.C.

. . . In the present crisis of the relations between the two countries, the office for which you have been selected is one of vast importance. To counteract the influence of foreign Powers, exerted against the United States in Mexico & to restore those ancient relations of peace and good will which formerly existed between the Governments and the citizens of the sister Republics, will be principal objects of your mission. The wretched condition of the internal affairs of Mexico, and the misunderstanding which exists between her Government and the Ministers of France and England, seem to render the present a propitious moment for the accomplishment of these objectives. From your perfect knowledge of the language of the country, your well known firmness and ability, and your taste and talent for society, the President hopes that you will accomplish much in your intercourse with the Mexican authorities and people. . . .

In your negotiations with Mexico, the independence of Texas must be considered a settled fact, and is not to be called in question. . . .

It may, however, be contended on the part of Mexico, that the Nueces and not the Rio del Norte,[1] is the true western boundary of Texas. I need not furnish you arguments to controvert this position. You have been perfectly familiar with the subject from the beginning, and know that the jurisdiction of Texas has been extended beyond that river and that representatives from the country between it and the Del Norte have participated in the deliberations both of her Congress and her Convention. Besides, this portion of the territory was embraced within the limits of ancient Louisiana.

The case is different in regard to New Mexico. Santa Fe, its capital, was settled by the Spaniards more than two centuries ago; and that province has been ever since in their possession and that of the Republic of Mexico. The Texans never have conquered or taken possession of it, nor have its people ever been represented in any of the Legislative Assemblies or Conventions.

The long and narrow valley of New Mexico or Santa Fe is situated on both banks of the upper Del Norte, and is bounded on both sides by mountains. It is

---

[1] The Rio Grande.

Source: Manning, *Diplomatic Correspondence of the United States,* 8:172–81.

many hundred miles remote from other settled portions of Mexico, and from its distance, it is both difficult and expensive to defend the inhabitants against the tribes of fierce and warlike savages that roam over the surrounding country. For this cause it has suffered severely from their incursions. Mexico must expend far more in defending so distant a possession than she can possibly derive benefit from continuing to hold it.

Besides, it is greatly to be decided that our boundary with Mexico should now be established in such a manner as to preclude all future difficulties and disputes between the two Republics. A great portion of New Mexico being on this side of the Rio Grande and included within the limits already claimed by Texas, it may hereafter, should it remain a Mexican province, become a subject of dispute and a source of bad feeling between those who, I trust, are destined in future to be always friends.

On the other hand, if in adjusting the boundary, the province of New Mexico should be included within the limits of the United States, this would obviate the danger of future collisions. Mexico would part with a remote and disturbed province, the possession of which can never be advantageous to her; and she would be relieved from the trouble and expense of defending its inhabitants against the Indians. Besides, she would thus purchase security against their attacks for her other provinces West of the Del Norte; as it would at once become the duty of the United States to restrain the savage tribes within their limits and prevent them from making hostile incursions into Mexico. From these considerations and others which will readily suggest themselves to your mind, it would seem to be equally the interest of both Powers, that New Mexico should belong to the United States.

But the President desires to deal liberally by Mexico. You are therefore authorized to offer to assume the payment of all the just claims of our citizens against Mexico, and, in addition, to pay five millions of dollars, in case the countries from the mouth of the Rio Grande, up the principal stream to the point where it touches the line of New Mexico, thence West of the river, along the exterior line of that province and so as to include the whole within the United States until it again intersects the river, thence up the principle stream of the same to its source and thence due north until it intersects the forty second degree of north latitude.

A boundary still preferable to this, would be an extension of the line from the north west corner of New Mexico, along the range of mountains, until it would intersect the forty second parallel. . . .

There is another subject of vast importance to the United States, which will demand your particular attention. From information possessed by this Department, it is to be seriously apprehended that both Great Britain and France have designs upon California. . . . whilst this Government does not intend to interfere between Mexico and California, it would vigorously interpose to prevent the latter from becoming either a British or a French Colony. You will endeavor to ascertain whether any such design exists, you will exert all your energies to prevent an act which, if consummated, would be so fraught with danger to the best interests of the United States. . . .

The possession of the Bay and harbour of San Francisco, is all important to the United States. The advantages to us of its acquisition are so striking that it would be a waste of time to enumerate them here. If all these should be turned against our country, by the cession of California to Great Britain our principal commercial rival, the consequences would be most disastrous.

The Government of California is now but nominally dependent on Mexico and it is more than doubtful whether her authority will ever be re-instated. Under these circumstances, it is the desire of the President that you shall use your best efforts to obtain a cession of that Province from Mexico to the United States. Could you accomplish this object, you would render immense service to your country and establish an enviable reputation for yourself. Money would be no object when compared with the value of the acquisition. Still the attempt must be made with great prudence and caution, and in such a manner as not to alarm the jealousy of the Mexican Government. Should you, after sounding the Mexican authorities on the subject, discover a prospect of success, the President would not hesitate to give, in addition to the assumption of the just claims of our citizens on Mexico, twenty five millions of dollars for the cession. Should you deem it expedient, you are authorized to offer this sum for a boundary, running due West from the southern extremity of New Mexico to the Pacific ocean, or from any other point on its western boundary, which would embrace Monterey within our limits. . . .

9 John Slidell, Appointed United States Minister to Mexico, to Secretary of State James Buchanan, December 17, 1845

MEXICO

. . . The most absurd reasons have been advanced against my recognition,[1] so absurd indeed that they would appear scarcely credible to any one, not upon the spot, unacquainted with the character of the people and ignorant of the manner in which affairs are here conducted—The objections stated were that my credentials did not appear to have been given with the sanction of Congress, that my appointment had not been confirmed by the Senate, that this Government had agreed only to receive a commissioner and that consequently the appointment of an Envoy Extraordinary and Minister Plenipotentiary was not in accordance with the letter of the 15th October from the Minister of Foreign Affairs to Mr. Black,[2] That this letter only contemplated negotiation upon

---

[1] Slidell is referring to the Mexican government's refusal to accept his credentials.

[2] See Source 7 on page 259.

Source: Manning, *Diplomatic Correspondence of the United States,* 8:777–81.

the subject of Texas, and finally to cap the climax of absurdity, that my powers were not sufficient. I hope before the closing of this despatch, to obtain information of the precise grounds upon which the Council finally decided to recommend that I should not be received . . .

Your instructions direct me to bear & forbear much for the purpose of promoting the great objects of my mission, and caution me against raising any points of honor, with a people so feeble and degraded. As for myself, personally, I should feel very indifferent to any questions of mere etiquette, but in my representative capacity I ought not silently to suffer any mark of disrespect. Although not yet recognized by this Government, as the person with whom it is willing to enter upon official relations, so far as my own is concerned, I am its representative here and all other considerations apart, the interests of my mission with a people attaching peculiar importance to forms, require that I should not allow any violation of accustomed courtesies to pass unnoticed. My present intention is to address a note to the Minister of Foreign Relations couched in the most respectful terms, attributing the omission to address me by my proper title to inadvertence, and suggesting the expectation that it will not be repeated. This however, I shall not do without proper reflection, and consultation of precedents if any such can be found. There is less reason for immediate reply, as I am satisfied that nothing is to be gained by pressing upon the Government at this moment; their existence hangs by a thread, and they retain power not by their own force, but solely by the inability of their opponents to agree among themselves . . .

10 *Secretary of State James Buchanan to John Slidell, Appointed United States Minister to Mexico,* January 20, 1846

WASHINGTON, D.C.

. . . Should the Mexican Government, by finally refusing to receive you, consummate the act of folly and bad faith of which they have afforded such strong indications, nothing will then remain for this Government but to take the redress of the wrongs of its citizens into its own hands.

In the event of such a refusal, the course which you have determined to pursue is the proper one. You ought, in your own language, so to conduct yourself as to throw the whole odium of the failure of the negotiation upon the Mexican Government; point out, in the most temperate manner, the inevitable consequences of so unheard of a violation of all the usages which govern the intercourse between civilized nations; and declare your intention to remain in

Source: Manning, *Diplomatic Correspondence of the United States,* 8:185–86.

Mexico until you can receive instructions adapted to the exigencies of the case. This sojourn will afford you an honorable opportunity to watch the course of events and avail yourself of any favorable circumstances which, in the mean time, may occur. . . .

In the mean time the President, in anticipation of the final refusal of the Mexican Government to receive you, has ordered the army of Texas to advance and take position on the left bank of the Rio Grande, and has directed that a strong fleet shall be immediately assembled in the Gulph of Mexico. He will thus be prepared to act with vigor and promptitude the moment that Congress shall give him the authority. . . .

 11   *Joaquín M. de Castillo y Lanzas, Minister of Foreign Affairs of Mexico, to John Slidell, Appointed United States Minister to Mexico,* March 12, 1846

> Joaquín M. de Castillo y Lanzas succeeded Manuel de la Peña as Mexico's foreign minister in December 1845.

Mexico

The Undersigned, Minister of Foreign Relations and Government of the Republic . . . make[s] known to Mr. Slidell . . . that the Mexican Government cannot receive him as Envoy Extraordinary & Minister Plenipotentiary to reside near it.

And here might the undersigned terminate his note, if reasons of great weight did not convince him of the necessity of making some reflections in this place; not through fear of the consequences which may result from this decisive resolve, but through the respect which he owes to reason and to justice.

It is true that this warlike display, with which the American Union presents herself, — by sea, with her squadrons on both coasts; by land, with her invading forces advancing by the northern frontiers — at the same time, that by her Minister Plenipotentiary propositions are made for conciliation, and accommodation, would be a sufficiently powerful reason for not listening to them, so long as all threatening should not be withdrawn, even to the slightest appearance of hostility. But even this is waived by the Government of the Republic, in order that it may in all frankness & loyalty enter into the discussion, relying solely upon reason and facts. A simple reference to the truth, plainly stated, suffices to show the justice by which Mexico is upheld in the question now under discussion.

Source: Manning, *Diplomatic Correspondence of the United States,* 8:818–22.

The vehement desire of the Government of the United States, to extend its already immense territory at the expense of that of Mexico, has been manifest for many years; and it is beyond all doubt, that in regard to Texas at least, this has been their firm and constant determination: for it has been so declared categorically & officially by an authorized representative of the Union, whose assertion, strange & injurious as was its frankness, has nevertheless not been belied by the United States. . . .

Thus, this incorporation of a territory which had constituted an integral part of that of Mexico during the long period of the Spanish dominion, and after her emancipation for so long a term without any interruption whatever, and which moreover had been recognized & sanctioned by the Treaty limits between the Mexican Republic and the United States of America; this annexation was effected by the reprobated means of violence and fraud. . . .

Civilized nations have beheld with amazement, at this enlightened and refined epoch, a powerful & well consolidated State, availing itself of the internal dissensions of a neighbouring nation, putting its vigilance to sleep by protestations of friendship, setting in action all manner of springs and artifices, alternately plying intrigue & violence, and seizing a moment to despoil her of a precious part of her territory, regardless of the incontrovertible rights of the most unquestionable ownership and the most uninterrupted possession.

Here, then, is the true position of the Mexican Republic: despoiled, outraged, contemned, it is now attempted to subject her to a humiliating degradation. The sentiment of her own dignity will not allow her to consent to such ignominy. . . .

It follows, that if war should finally become inevitable, and if in consequence of this war the peace of the civilized world should be disturbed, the responsibility will not fall upon Mexico. It will all rest upon the United States, to them will the whole of it belong. Not upon Mexico, who, with a generosity unequalled, admitted the American citizens who wished to colonize in Texas; but upon the United States, who, bent upon possessing themselves, early or late, of that territory, encouraged emigration thither, with that view; in order that, in due time, its inhabitants, converting themselves from colonists into its masters, should claim the country as their own, for the purpose of transferring it to the United States. Not upon Mexico, who having in due season protested against so enormous a transgression, wished to remove all cause for controversy & hostility; but upon the United States, who, to the scandal of the world, and in manifest violation of treaties, gave protection and aid to those guilty of a rebellion so iniquitous. Not upon Mexico, who, in the midst even of injuries so great & so repeated, has shewn herself disposed to admit propositions for reconciliation; but upon the United States, who pretending sincerely to desire a friendly and honourable accommodation, has belied by their acts the sincerity of their words. Finally, not upon Mexico, who, putting out of view her own dearest interests, through her deference for peace, has entertained as long as was wished the propositions which with this view might be made to her: but upon the United States, who, by frivolous pretexts, evade the conclusion of such an arrangement; proposing peace, at the very moment when they are causing their squadrons & their troops to advance upon the ports & the frontiers of Mexico; exacting an humiliation, impossible to be submitted to, in order to find a pretext, if no reason can be found, which may occasion the breaking out of hostilities.

Secretary of State James Buchanan to John Slidell, Appointed United States Minister to Mexico, March 12, 1846

In December 1845, General Mariano Paredes led a military coup in Mexico City and installed himself as the head of the new government. This sudden change in the political climate of Mexico raised the possibility of renewing negotiations over Texas, especially since the Paredes government needed money to solidify its position at home.

WASHINGTON, D.C.

The President [Polk] believes . . . you ought to return to the City of Mexico, if this be practicable consistently with the national honor. . . . It appears from your despatch No. 7, that the Government of Paredes is now tottering for want of money. It would be easy for you to make known to him in some discreet manner that the United States were both able and willing to relieve his administration from pecuniary embarrassment, if he would do us justice and settle the question of boundary between the two Republics. A treaty for this purpose, under your instructions, if ratified by Mexico and transmitted to the United States, could be returned in a brief space with the ratification of the President and Senate. In the meantime, Paredes could command immediately funds on such an assurance. . . .

We have received information from different quarters, in corroboration of your statement, that there may be a design on the part of several European Powers to establish a monarchy in Mexico. It is supposed that the clergy would generally favor such a project and that a considerable party already exists among the people which would give it their countenance and support. It is believed by many that this party will continue to increase in consequence of the successive revolutions which may afflict that country, until at length a majority of the people will be willing to throw themselves into the arms of a monarch for security and protection. Indeed, rumor has already indicated the King, in the person of the Spanish Prince Henry, the son of Francisco de Paula, and the rejected suitor of Queen Isabella.

Source: Manning, *Diplomatic Correspondence of the United States,* 8:189–92.

These may be, and probably are, idle speculations, but they come to us in such a shape that they ought not to be wholly disregarded. It will be your duty to exercise your utmost vigilance in detecting this plot and its ramifications, if any such exists. Should Great Britain and France attempt to place a Spanish or any other European Prince upon the throne of Mexico, this would be resisted by all the power of the United States. In opposition to such an attempt, party distinctions in this country would vanish and the people would be nearly unanimous. It is unnecessary to state to one so well informed upon the subject as yourself, the reasons why the United States could never suffer foreign Powers to erect a throne for a European Prince on the ruins of a neighboring Republic, without our most determined resistance. . . .

13 *John Slidell, Appointed United States Minister to Mexico, to Secretary of State James Buchanan,* March 18, 1846

Slidell failed in his efforts to negotiate with the Paredes government. He wrote this letter while en route out of Mexico and reached the White House on May 8. The next day, Polk drafted his war message to Congress.

Private   JALAPA[1]

MY DEAR SIR: I have nothing to add to the accompanying dispatches, except to say that while at Vera Cruz, I will make arrangements to convey by express to the Pacific Squadron, any orders which may be sent there. There can be no difficulty in doing this if a steamer convey the first intelligence of war to Vera Cruz, it can be kept secret until the express is well on its way to Mexico. I do not know that I can give any useful information at Washington, but should you think my presence there desirable, I will cheerfully make the journey.

I expect to receive my passports on Thursday next, (24 instant) & in that case I ought to reach New Orleans, about the 5 April. . . . it is no easy matter to preserve one's *sang froid*[2] with these people. Depend upon it, we can never get along well with them, until we have given them a good drubbing.

[1] A Mexican city between Mexico City and Vera Cruz.
[2] Grace under pressure.
Source: Manning, *Diplomatic Correspondence of the United States,* 8:832.

Analyzing the Source

REFLECTING ON THE SOURCE

1. Briefly describe the nature of the "intelligence" that Parrott, Black, and Slidell provided for Buchanan. On what basis did they make their judgments about the Mexican government and people? How did Buchanan use the information they provided him?

2. How did the subject matter of letters exchanged between the United States and Mexico differ from that in letters exchanged between Buchanan and his agents in Mexico? What topics or issues were addressed in one that were not addressed in the other?

3. How do the letters written by Mexican officials present Mexico's position on the annexation of Texas? How does their version of events differ from that provided by Buchanan's agents in Mexico?

MAKING CONNECTIONS

4. Was there a significant difference in the tone of letters exchanged between Mexican and American officials and those exchanged between Buchanan and his agents in Mexico? If so, how would you describe this difference, and what do you think accounts for it? How does Buchanan's correspondence with his agents reflect the organization and operations of the U.S. foreign service in the 1840s?

5. How did Parrott, Black, and Slidell describe Mexicans? What evidence do you see in their letters of racism or ethnocentrism that may have influenced their advice to Buchanan? Did such prejudices change in any significant ways over time?

6. Judging from the diplomatic correspondence you have read here, what do you think was the ultimate objective of the Polk administration's foreign policy in regard to Mexico? Did Polk want to avoid a war or generate one? Should Buchanan's diplomatic efforts to advance Polk's aims be defined as a failure or success?

Beyond the Source

The Mexican-American War proved to be as politically controversial for the Polk administration as was the annexation of Texas. Northern Whigs openly condemned "Mr. Polk's War" as an unjust territorial grab undertaken at the behest of Southern slaveholders. As the war progressed and American troops occupied Mexico City, some American expansionists supported an "All Mexico" movement to incorporate the conquered nation into the United States. Others balked at such a plan, calling the United States a white man's republic that could not possibly assimilate such a large and racially distinct population. Polk did not support the All Mexico movement, but he did want more from the conquered enemy than a Texas border at the Rio Grande. Through the Treaty of Guadalupe Hidalgo, which ended the war in February 1848, the United States acquired California and New Mexico, about one-third of Mexico's national territory, for a payment of $15 million and an agreement to assume any debts owed by Mexico to U.S. citizens.

Victory over Mexico brought its own problems. Despite the successful prosecution of the war, Polk chose not to run for reelection in 1848, and he died shortly after leaving office. He was succeeded by Zachary Taylor, a hero from the Mexican-American War nominated by the Whigs, even though he had no previous connection to the party. Sectional tensions between free and slave states intensified in the wake of Mexico's defeat, as the federal government anticipated the admission of new states carved from its conquests. Everyone knew that Oregon, over which the Polk administration had reached a negotiated settlement with Britain, would enter the union as a free state. New Mexico and much of the rest of the nation's new Southwest were too arid to support a plantation economy, but California beckoned to northerners and southerners alike. At the outset of the Mexican-American War, some antislavery congressmen introduced a piece of legislation called the Wilmot Proviso, which stipulated that any territory acquired from the war would be "free soil," or closed to slavery. Southern congressmen believed such a measure violated the property rights of slaveholders. They blocked its passage, but the legislative battle over the Wilmot Proviso led to the creation of the Free Soil Party, which further polarized the sectional debate. As the nation moved into the 1850s, it still had no workable method for resolving the issue of slavery's expansion.

Meanwhile, eleven thousand Mexicans in Texas, New Mexico, and California now found themselves living within the borders of the United States. Polk had wanted Mexico's territory, not its people. The presence of even this small number of Mexicans within the newly acquired territory presented a challenge to American race relations, which had for so long been defined by opposing categories of black and white. The fact that many Mexicans were the product of intermarriage between Spanish colonizers and Native Americans aroused the racial prejudices of Anglo-Americans, who legally barred interracial marriage in many states. Social and legal custom in the American West treated Mexican-Americans as second-class citizens because in the eyes of the white ruling class, they were a "mongrel" race.

History has a way of turning the tables. According to the 2000 U.S. Census, Hispanics are now the largest minority group in the nation, and two-thirds of them are of Mexican heritage. Demographers project that within a few decades, Hispanics will make up the majority of the populations of Texas and California, two of the largest and most politically influential states in the union. While Polk and his contemporaries may have balked at extending citizenship to Mexicans living there in 1848, the reality more than 150 years later is that the American Southwest is defined culturally and politically by historical ties to Mexico that no foreign policy or war could erase.

Finding and Supplementing the Source

The records of nineteenth-century U.S. foreign relations are scattered through a number of institutions, including the U.S. Congress, the National Archives, and the Library of Congress. If you are interested in working in these materials but do not live near Washington, D.C., it is best to consult a number of documents collections published in the early twentieth century. The diplomatic correspondence you read in this chapter was selected from William R. Manning, editor, *Diplomatic Correspondence of the United States: Inter-American Affairs, 1831–1860,* 12 volumes (Washington, D.C.: Carnegie Endowment for International Peace, 1932–1939). Another important collection for presidential papers related to diplomatic affairs is James D. Richardson, compiler, *A Compilation of the Messages and Papers of the Presidents, 1789–1902,* second edition, 10 volumes (Washington, D.C.: Bureau of National Literature and Art, 1910). Polk's diary is available in Milo Milton Quaife, editor, *The Diary of James K. Polk during His Presidency, 1845–1849,* 4 volumes (Chicago: A. C. McClurg, 1910).

The most thorough study of the Texas annexation crisis in U.S.-Mexican relations is David M. Pletcher, *The Diplomacy of Annexation: Texas, Oregon, and the Mexican War* (Columbia: University of Missouri Press, 1973). Also see Frederick Merk with Lois Bannister Merk, *The Monroe Doctrine and American Expansionism, 1843–1849* (New York: Alfred A. Knopf, 1967), and Samuel Flagg Bemis, *The Latin-American Policy of the United States: An Historical Interpretation* (New York: W. W. Norton, 1943). Charles Sellers explores the origins and operation of Polk's foreign policy in *James K. Polk, Continentalist, 1843–1846* (Princeton, N.J.: Princeton University Press, 1966). A study that measures the cultural impact of the Mexican-American War on the United States is Robert W. Johannsen, *To the Halls of the Montezumas: The Mexican War in the American Imagination* (New York: Oxford University Press, 1985). Two useful studies of manifest destiny and American racial attitudes are Reginald Horsman, *Race and Manifest Destiny: The Origins of American Racial Anglo-Saxonism* (Cambridge: Harvard University Press, 1981), and Thomas R. Hietala, *Manifest Design: Anxious Aggrandizement in Late Jacksonian America* (Ithaca, N.Y.: Cornell University Press, 1985).

CHAPTER 13

The Illustrated Civil War

Photographers on the Battlefield

On September 17, 1862, Union and Confederate armies collided in the small western Maryland town of Sharpsburg. The ensuing Battle of Antietam, named after a nearby creek where much of the action took place, was the bloodiest day of the Civil War. Seventy-five thousand Union troops, led by General George B. McClellan, suffered more than twelve thousand casualties. The Confederate Army of fifty-two thousand men, led by General Robert E. Lee, suffered almost fourteen thousand casualties. Put another way, the combined armies of the Union and Confederacy experienced an astounding 20 percent casualty rate: one in five soldiers was either killed, wounded, or missing in action by the end of the day.

The Battle of Antietam was nominally a victory for McClellan because Lee's troops withdrew from the field first. In Washington, D.C., President Abraham Lincoln had been hoping for news of a decisive Union victory to prime public opinion for the Emancipation Proclamation and to improve Republican fortunes in the upcoming congressional election. Instead, Lincoln grew incensed when McClellan failed to pursue Lee's badly damaged army as it retreated into Virginia. His patience worn thin by McClellan's constant foot-dragging, Lincoln traveled to the Antietam battlefield to discuss the matter in person. In a letter to his wife about that meeting, Lincoln noted, "General McClellan and myself are to be photographed . . . if we can be still long enough. I feel General McClellan should have no problem." A few weeks later, Lincoln relieved McClellan of his command.

Lincoln and McClellan did indeed pose for a battlefield portrait (see Source 3 on p. 282), but their photographer took some other pictures as well. About one month after the battle, its horrible cost was brought home to the American public when Mathew Brady opened an exhibit at his New York City gallery of photographs taken at Sharpsburg. Brady and other photographers had been taking pictures related to the war since it had commenced in early 1861, but those were mostly portraits of soldiers. What was different about Brady's Antietam exhibit was the inclusion of images of corpses, horribly twisted, mangled, and bloated from the summer sun, strewn across the fields of Sharpsburg. In a review published on October 20, 1862, the *New York Times* praised Brady for his realism:

> Mr. Brady has done something to bring home to us the terrible reality and earnestness of war. If he has not brought bodies and laid them in our door-yards and along the streets, he has done something very like it. At the door of his gallery hangs a little placard, "The Dead of Antietam." Crowds of people are constantly . . . bending over photographic views of that fearful battle-field, taken immediately after the action. . . . there is a terrible fascination about it that draws one near these pictures, and makes him lo[a]th to leave them. You will see hushed, reverend groups standing around these weird copies of carnage, bending down to look in the pale faces of the dead, chained by the strange spell that dwells in dead men's eyes.

Ironically, Brady had not taken any of the photographs that he exhibited in his gallery that October. Although his name had become synonymous with photography in America during the 1850s, his poor eyesight meant that he rarely operated the cameras that made him famous. Instead, Brady hired and trained others to do much of the work associated with the photographs published under his name. The Antietam images were taken by Alexander Gardner, who managed a gallery owned by Brady in Washington, D.C. A few months before the Battle of Antietam, Gardner joined General McClellan's staff as its official photographer. This appointment enabled him to travel with the army and to photograph battlefields immediately before and after action took place. It was this sort of inside access that gave his Antietam photographs the stunning immediacy and realism that entranced the crowds in Brady's gallery.

Gardner's Antietam photographs were a tremendous commercial success, but Gardner was not pleased that Brady published them without giving him credit. The two men parted ways a few months later and became commercial rivals for the rest of the war, with Gardner working out of his own gallery in Washington, D.C. (see Figure 13.1). Brady, who had made his name in the 1850s as the photographer of the nation's leading citizens, continued to publish photographs of famous figures and landmarks associated with the war. In the meantime, Gardner led a new wave of photographers who focused their work on images of wartime destruction: battlefield dead, blasted buildings, and landscapes transformed by the hard hand of war.

Photographers such as Brady and Gardner produced a rich visual record of the Civil War. Previous wars had been photographed: military portraits and landscapes date to the Mexican-American War (1846–1848) and the British-Russian Crimean War (1854–1856). Both of those conflicts, however, occurred

Figure 13.1 Photographer Unknown, "Gardner's Gallery" This undated photograph shows what the exterior of an urban photographer's gallery looked like. Note the billboards advertising the different types of photographs and photographic services available, as well as the prominent advertisement for "Views of the War."
Source: Library of Congress, Prints and Photographs Division, LC-BH837-207.

when the technology of photography was in its infancy, and their battlefields were far removed from the cities where photographers worked. The Civil War was different in two significant ways. First, the war's eastern theater of operations was close to urban centers such as Washington, D.C., that already had a commercial photography industry. Second, the consumer market for photographs in the United States had expanded exponentially during the 1850s because of technological improvements that made photographs affordable to just about everyone. Photographs had been a novelty of the well-to-do in the 1840s; by 1860 they were knit into the fabric of American culture, thanks in part to the relentless innovation and promotion of entrepreneurs such as Mathew Brady and Alexander Gardner.

Photography had a profound impact on how Americans experienced the Civil War. As the review of Brady's Antietam exhibit indicates, photography brought the violence and destruction of the battlefield to the doorsteps of the American public and elicited a strong emotional response, even from people far removed from the fighting. Photographers such as Brady and Gardner cultivated their reputations as the war's most accurate and impartial observers, describing their work as a visual record unvarnished by sentimentality or political bias. They also turned the war into a commodity available for purchase. Their claims to rendering the war in objective, unfiltered truthfulness must be weighed against their efforts to market the war for public consumption in a way that suited their own commercial and artistic purposes.

Using Civil War Photographs as a Source

In 1860, there were more than three thousand photographers working in the United States. During the Civil War, they took tens of thousands of pictures of military subjects: individual and group portraits of soldiers, scenes of camp life and field hospitals, battlefield and city landscapes, railroad depots, fortifications, and shipyards. In order to use these images as a source, you must first familiarize yourself with the history, technology, and terminology of nineteenth-century photography.

The age of photography began with the invention of the daguerreotype in the late 1830s. Named for one of its inventors, Jacques Mandé Daguerre, the daguerreotype was a fixed image produced on a silver-coated copper plate. Shortly after Daguerre introduced his invention in Europe, Samuel F. B. Morse brought the technology to America, where he taught the craft to several students, including Mathew Brady. Daguerreotypists opened studios in American cities during the 1840s, drawing as their customers members of the urban middle and upper classes, who sat for their portraits individually, with their children, or as married couples. A successful daguerreotypist ran a kind of factory, keeping a public gallery/reception area where he displayed samples of his work to attract customers, a studio where he posed his subjects, and backrooms where craftsmen prepared and developed his plates and fit them into handsomely ornamented frames for display at home. As one of many daguerreotypists in New York competing for business, Brady built his reputation by photographing famous politicians, authors, and actors, styling himself the "national historian," and publishing *The Gallery of Illustrious Americans*, an illustrated book based on his daguerreotypes, in 1850.

The next great leap in photography's development came in the mid-1850s with the invention of the wet-plate process. Unlike the daguerreotype, which was a one-time, nonreproducible image, the wet-plate process used glass plates immersed in a solution of photosensitive chemicals to produce negative images from which "positive" paper copies could be made, much like negatives from camera film work today. The wet-plate process expanded the market for photography, making possible mass-produced copies and enlargements suitable for exhibit or sale. Two important product innovations based on this improved technology occurred in the years just before the Civil War. The stereograph was a double image produced by fitting two lenses on a single camera. When viewed through a stereoscope, a handheld device that could be purchased from a photographer's studio, it produced a three-dimensional effect. Stereoscopes helped turn the viewing of photographs into a leisure activity that could occur in every home. The carte-de-visite was a small print made by fitting four lenses onto one camera, which produced four identical images on a single plate. Prints from such a negative, when cut into quarters, were used as calling cards. Brady led the way in marketing them as collector's cards (sometimes called album cards), selling cartes-de-visite of famous figures in numbered series much like baseball cards are sold and collected today.

Paper reproduction in such formats made photographs available to even working-class folk. A portrait-sized print might cost $1.50, a stereoscope 50 cents, and a carte-de-visite only 25 cents. When Union and Confederate armies mobilized in 1861, soldiers in uniform rushed to have their portraits taken as souvenirs of their service or as keepsakes for loved ones at home. The vast majority of the tens of thousands of Civil War photographs fall into this category. Once photographers realized the demand that the war was creating for their services, they expanded their work to include other subjects that they thought might turn a profit.

Advantages and Disadvantages of Working with Civil War Photographs

The most obvious advantage to using such photographs as a historical source was one immediately realized by the government and military. Photography made possible the recording and communication of visual information with much greater speed and detail. Armies had long relied on sketch artists to record useful information about the scene of battle. During the Civil War, generals added photographers to their staffs so that they could make images of fortifications, bridges, railroads, and natural landmarks, not to mention portraits of themselves as they sallied forth into history. Military photographers also aided in the reproduction of maps. Ever since, historians have used these images to reconstruct the military history of the war, from engagements on rural battlefields like Antietam to scorched-earth attacks on cities such as Richmond and Charleston.

Cultural and social historians find many advantages to working with these photographs as well. How people create visual images of war tells us much about the values and emotions they associate with it. Paintings, drawings, and photographs of battlefields are as much attempts to create meaning out of the violence and death of warfare as are letters home, diary entries, or memoirs. Before the invention of photography, the visual record of American warfare was usually created by painters who worked long after the battle raged. John Trumbull was the most famous battle scene painter of the American Revolution, and the federal government commissioned his work for the new nation's Capitol in the early nineteenth century. Compare his *Death of General*

George Washington leading the Continental Army forward

Compare Mercer's facial expression with that of the dead soldier in the foreground of O'Sullivan's image

Mercer dies in close proximity to the enemy, witnessing the tide of battle around him

Mercer at the Battle of Princeton, New Jersey, 3 January 1777 (above) with the most famous photograph from the Gettysburg battlefield, Timothy O'Sullivan's "A Harvest of Death, Gettysburg, Pennsylvania" (on p. 277). Both depict battlefield carnage, but convey very different messages to their viewers.

Trumbull's painting, which he started ten years after the Battle of Princeton took place, makes Mercer's death heroic: he dies with sword in one hand, his other hand grasping the bayonet that will deliver his fatal wound. He literally stares death in the face, gazing directly into the eyes of his adversary. The worth of his sacrifice is evident by the action occurring behind him. While Mercer dies, General George Washington leads the Continental Army forward to victory.

Now consider O'Sullivan's 1863 photograph "A Harvest of Death," which he took two days after the fighting at Gettysburg had ceased. Corpses litter the battlefield to the horizon. Their horrible disfiguration is most evident on the figure in the foreground, whose mouth gapes open and whose face, stomach, and hands have bloated in the process of decomposing. Off in the distance, a

The photo's title, "A Harvest of Death," calls to mind the fields on which the battle took place and invokes popular images of the Grim Reaper

Compare the shadowy figure on horseback to Washington's figure in Trumbull's painting

No evidence here that these dead soldiers ever saw the faces of their enemy

figure shrouded in mist appears on horseback, but this is not the confident commanding officer of Trumbull's painting. Rather, it is a ghostly presence surveying the battlefield, a Grim Reaper–like figure come to collect his harvest. Unlike Trumbull's painting, this photograph shows no evidence that these soldiers died in hand-to-hand combat or ever stared into their enemies' eyes. They are as anonymous as they are lifeless. This image, one of the most widely reproduced battlefield photographs of the war, challenges the notions of military sacrifice and valor celebrated in Trumbull's painting. It testifies to the crisis that the massive casualties of the Civil War caused in the traditional values nineteenth-century Americans associated with military service.

Studying these photographs also reveals much about how civilians experienced the war. Photographers such as Brady and Gardner sold prints of their work almost as quickly as they made them, constructing a history of the war for public consumption while the conflict was still underway. Stereographs brought the war into the home for viewing the same way television does today, and cartes-de-visite made celebrities out of political and military leaders of the war. By studying the arrangement of photographs in private collections or in the catalogues that advertised them for sale, historians can recover the civilian effort to interpret the war, to make sense of the brutality and destruction the war unleashed.

One disadvantage of working with Civil War photographs is that there was no "blanket coverage" of the war by photographers. Their work favored the North and East at the expense of the South and West. The photography industry in the Confederacy all but collapsed after 1861 as the economic privations of the war increased. Also, the further removed the scene of battle was from eastern urban centers, the less likely it was to be photographed. Antietam and Gettysburg were the most thoroughly photographed battlefields of the war. Not coincidentally, both were within ninety miles of Washington, D.C., where Brady and Gardner had galleries. By contrast, little to no photographic evidence exists of many campaigns west of the Appalachian Mountains.

Another disadvantage to bear in mind when looking at Civil War photographs is the technological limits on photographing battles as they occurred. Cameras had to be mounted on tripods and required exposure time measured in minutes rather than a fraction of a second. Photographers had to bring all of their equipment into the field within darkrooms on wheels, because the glass plates had to be prepared, exposed, and developed in one continuous process, before their chemical coating dried and rendered them useless. As one historian of nineteenth-century photography has noted, these technical limitations meant that we have many "before" and "after" images of Civil War battlefields but no "during," because the photographers and their equipment were not mobile enough to capture the actual battles.

The chief disadvantage to working with Civil War photographs is that the photographers manipulated their subjects, dead as well as living, for commercial purposes. Brady, Gardner, and their peers were businessmen, and they took pictures that they thought would sell. If they could increase sales by posing their subjects in a particular manner, they did not hesitate to do so. Then and now, people invoked the phrase "the camera never lies" to emphasize the impartiality and truthfulness of photography. Knowing something about how Civil War photographs were made, however, should dissuade you from taking that adage too literally when dealing with this source. Of course, when soldiers, officers, and civic leaders posed for their portraits, they assumed postures and carried props meant to broadcast their bravery, leadership, or virtue. But because of the long exposure time required for early photographs, even less formal scenes of camp life or field hospitals had to be carefully arranged by their photographers. One might assume that photographs of corpses on the battlefield were the least posed of the photographer's subjects, but Gardner and his associates moved bodies, added props, and altered backgrounds to achieve the effect they desired. Whenever you use a Civil War photograph as a source, it is best to ask yourself, what did the photographer want to convey in this image? If you assume that every photograph was posed in the sense that the photographer went through a long and complicated process to produce it, then you will be better equipped to answer that question and less likely to assume that the camera presented an unfiltered representation of its subject.

Working with the Source

The table below will help you record your impressions of photographs you will examine in the next section.

Source	What is the subject matter of this photograph?	What information, ideas, or emotions did the photographer want to convey in this image?
1. Lieut. Washington and Capt. Custer		
2. Gen. Robert B. Potter and Staff		
3. Lincoln at Antietam		
4. Gettysburg		
5. Ruins of Charleston		
6. Brig. Gen. McLaughlin		
7. Culpeper "Contrabands"		
8. African American Soldiers		
9. Antietam, Bodies for Burial		
10. A Contrast		
11. He Sleeps His Last Sleep		
12. Body of Soldier in Wheat Field		
13. Field Where General Reynolds Fell		
14. Fort Mahone		
15. Cold Harbor, Virginia		

The Source: Photographs of Civil War Battlefields and Military Life, 1861–1866

BATTLEFIELD MILITARY PORTRAITS

Many soldiers posed in uniform for formal portraits before they left home. Photographers also brought their cameras to military camps near battlefields, to capture armies at work.

 ## James F. Gibson, "Lieut. Washington, a Confederate Prisoner, and Capt. Custer, U.S.A.," 1862

This photograph, published in one of Alexander Gardner's catalogs, has an interesting history. Confederate lieutenant James Barroll Washington was taken prisoner during McClellan's Peninsula Campaign in Virginia. Captain George Armstrong Custer, a Union officer who would achieve fame at Gettysburg a year later (and a different kind of notoriety at Little Big Horn in 1876) was an old friend of Washington's. Upon finding the two chatting amiably, James Gibson decided to photograph them. Washington called out for a young African American boy to join them. An illustration based on this image subsequently appeared in *Harper's Weekly* under the title "Both Sides, the Cause."

Source: Library of Congress, Prints and Photographs Division.

Mathew Brady, "Gen. Robert B. Potter and Staff of Seven, Recognized Capt. Gilbert H. McKibben, Capt. Wright, A.A.G. Also Mr. Brady, Photographer," c. 1863

Brady owed his reputation in the 1850s to photographing famous people, so it is not surprising that during the war, he devoted much of his work on the battlefield to taking pictures of officers and their staffs. A relentless self-promoter, he also had a penchant for inserting himself into his own work. General Potter is the bareheaded figure at the center of this image. Brady, in civilian clothes, leans against a tree to the right.

Source: National Archives and Records Administration.

Alexander Gardner, "President Lincoln on Battle-Field of Antietam," 1862

Gardner took this photograph when President Lincoln traveled to Antietam in October 1862 to confer with General McClellan. McClellan is to the left of Lincoln, standing in profile and facing the President. McClellan's staff forms an arc around the two figures.

Source: Amon Carter Museum, Fort Worth, Texas.

BATTLEFIELD LANDSCAPES AND CITYSCAPES

Photographers often took pictures of battlefield landscapes and cityscapes, juxtaposing civilian and military life or depicting the destructive effects of the war.

Timothy O'Sullivan, "Pennsylvania, Gettysburg 07/1863," 1863

O'Sullivan worked with Gardner in photographing the Gettysburg battlefield. This image, taken from a hill south of the town's center, shows the small remnant of a military camp after most of the Union and Confederate forces had withdrawn. During the Civil War, many small towns saw their farms and fields occupied by armies that dwarfed the local population.

Source: National Archives and Records Administration.

George P. Barnard, "Ruins of Charleston, S.C.," 1866

Photographer George P. Barnard documented the devastating impact of war on the South. This image shows one of the South's greatest cities in ruins, with solitary human figures scattered about, contemplating the destruction.

Source: Beinecke Rare Book and Manuscript Library, Yale University.

AFRICAN AMERICANS IN MILITARY LIFE

African Americans, free and enslaved, worked on and near Civil War battlefields as soldiers and laborers. Slaves who ran away from their masters and sought refuge with the Union Army were known as "contrabands." Before the Emancipation Proclamation, they occupied a limbo between freedom and slavery. Union officers did not have the legal authority to free them, but neither did they wish to return them to their former homes, where their labor might benefit the Confederate war effort. Many contrabands ended up in battlefield and camp photographs.

Mathew Brady, "Portrait of Brig. Gen. Napoleon B. McLaughlin, Officer of the Federal Army, and Staff, Vicinity of Washington, D.C.," 1861

This photograph from early in the war is typical of Brady's portraits of Union officers and their staffs (see Source 2 in this chapter). Sometimes these portraits included African Americans, posed in subservient positions to indicate their status as servants.

Source: Library of Congress, Prints and Photographs Division.

7 *Timothy O'Sullivan, "Culpeper, Va. 'Contrabands,'"* 1863

African Americans worked for Union and Confederate armies in a number of capacities. These two men are pictured outside of a cook's tent at a Union camp.

Source: Library of Congress, Prints and Photographs Division.

Photographer Unknown, "African American Soldiers with Their Teachers and Officers," date unknown

Many African Americans, including contrabands, enlisted in the Union Army and were photographed in uniform. These recruits posed with their white commanding officers and female teachers. Instead of bearing arms, the recruits hold books.

Source: Library of Congress, Prints and Photographs Division.

BATTLEFIELD DEAD

Battlefield dead made up only a tiny fraction of Civil War photographs, but they became some of the most enduring visual images of the war. To take them, a photographer had to arrive on the battlefield before corpses were buried, usually within two days of the fighting. Gardner's and O'Sullivan's photographs from Antietam and Gettysburg are the most famous of this category, but equally powerful ones were taken after other battles in the war's eastern theater, including Cold Harbor and Petersburg, both in Virginia.

 ### *Alexander Gardner, "Antietam, Md. Bodies of Dead Gathered for Burial,"* 1862

This image, one of the Antietam series exhibited in Mathew Brady's New York gallery, presents a line of corpses arranged as if in formation. No single soldier is identified; they appear as an anonymous mass. The line running across the photograph is from a crack in the original glass plate.

Source: Library of Congress, Prints and Photographs Division.

Alexander Gardner, "A Contrast. Federal Buried; Confederate Unburied, Where They Fell on the Battle Field of Antietam," 1862

This is a stereograph of one of Gardner's Antietam photographs. It juxtaposes the marked grave of Union officer John A. Clark with the unburied corpse of an anonymous Confederate.

Source: Collection of the New-York Historical Society.

Entered according to Act of Congress, in the year 1863, by Alex. Gardner, in the Clerk's Office of the District Court of the District of Columbia.

Alexander Gardner, "He Sleeps His Last Sleep," 1862

As he did with the image shown in Source 10, Gardner sold stereographs and album cards of this Antietam photograph via his catalogue. Unlike most of his other photographs of the dead from the Battle of Antietam, this one shows a single casualty far removed from any other fallen soldiers. Gardner's catalogue caption for this image read: "A Confederate Soldier, who after being wounded, had evidently dragged himself to a little ravine on the hill-side, where he died."

Source: Collection of the New-York Historical Society.

Entered according to Act of Congress, in the year 1864, by Alex. Gardner, in the Clerk's Office of the District Court of the District of Columbia.

12   *James F. Gibson, "Battlefield of Gettysburg—Body of a Soldier in 'the Wheat Field,' Evidently Killed by the Explosion of a Shell,"* 1863

Photographers manipulated their subjects, even dead ones, to achieve the desired effect. Gibson accompanied Gardner to Gettysburg to take photographs after the battle. In his catalogue, Gardner described this anonymous soldier as a sharpshooter, but a sharpshooter would not have affixed a bayonet to his weapon. Also, by the time photographers reached battlefield corpses, their weapons had usually been collected by the victorious army or by scavengers. The weapon shown here is a "prop gun" placed there by Gibson or Gardner; it shows up in several of their Gettysburg photographs. The photographer has also placed an unexploded shell near the corpse's right knee to suggest the source of the horrible wound in the abdomen. It is more likely that a pig fed on the body shortly after death. The dismembered hand and canteen in the right foreground are also likely props.

Source: Library of Congress, Prints and Photographs Division.

Timothy O'Sullivan, "Field Where General Reynolds Fell, Gettysburg," 1863

This image from the Gettysburg battlefield stands in sharp contrast to the caption Gardner chose for it. Reynolds was the highest-ranking Union officer killed at Gettysburg and became in death one of the battle's heroes. This image offers no trace of Reynolds (in fact, he was killed in a wooded area), only anonymous, bloodied, and bloated corpses.

Source: Amon Carter Museum, Fort Worth, Texas.

T. C. Roche, "... View of the Covered Ways inside the Rebel Fort Mahone, Called by the Soldiers 'Fort Damnation' ... Taken the Morning after the Storming of Petersburgh, Va. 1865," 1865

T. C. Roche, a former cameraman for Mathew Brady, documented the Union Army's assault on Petersburg, a vital railroad junction in Virginia, in April 1865. This stereographic image of a solitary Confederate soldier lying dead in one of the trenches built to defend the city anticipates the photographs that would document trench warfare in World War I. The spiked device in the foreground is a cheval-de-frise, a type of movable fortification designed to slow an enemy advance.

Source: Collection of the New-York Historical Society.

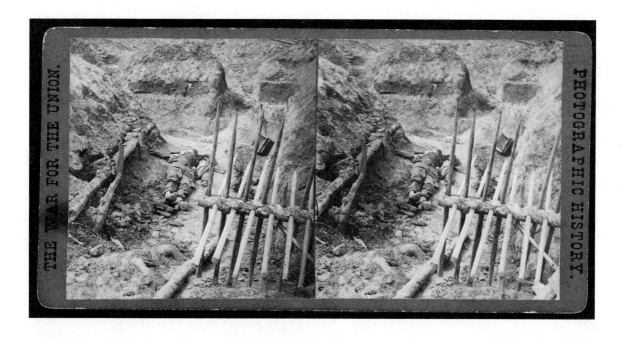

John Reekie, "Cold Harbor, Va. African Americans Collecting Bones of Soldiers Killed in Battle," 1865

John Reekie was a cameraman for Alexander Gardner and worked with him documenting the final weeks of the war in Virginia in 1865. In this photograph, a burial party made up of African American males is collecting and interring the skeletal remains of soldiers who had died on the Cold Harbor battlefield almost a year earlier. The figures working in the background suggest that Reekie has captured them "in action," but bear in mind that the exposure time required for such a photograph would have meant that they were posed. The glass plate used to make this image has been damaged, as evidenced by the crack across the photograph and the missing shard on the right-hand side.

Source: Library of Congress, Prints and Photographs Division.

Analyzing the Source

REFLECTING ON THE SOURCE

1. Overall, would you describe these photographs as critical of the war or supportive of it? Does your answer to this question vary if you ask it of individual groups of photographs (for example, "Battlefield Military Portraits," or "African Americans in Military Life") rather than the entire lot?

2. How is death presented and interpreted in these photographs? How do the images challenge the notions of military glory and valor embodied in earlier military art such as Trumbull's *Death of General Mercer* (p. 276)? Compare the notes you took on Sources 9, 10, 13, and 15 with those you took on Sources 11, 12, and 14. What messages do you think photographers were trying to convey when they "posed" the dead either as individuals or in groups?

3. Civil War photographers marketed their work to a civilian audience. What needs do you think these images fulfilled for the civilian population during and after the war? How might the visual record of the war differed if the South had been able to sustain a photography industry as productive as the North's during the war?

MAKING CONNECTIONS

4. How do these photographs present African Americans and the role they played in the Civil War? Did the depiction of African Americans in these images change over time? How does that depiction compare to what you have learned about African Americans and slavery in earlier chapters?

5. Compare these photographs with the Catlin paintings you studied in Chapter 10. In what ways did these photographers approach their subjects in a manner similar to Catlin's? How do their artistic and commercial motives compare? How did the new technology of photography alter the purpose and method by which artists and journalists attempted to record history?

6. Compare these images to the visual records you have seen of warfare in the twentieth and twenty-first centuries (for example, photographs, films, documentaries, newscasts). In what ways did the Civil War establish precedents for the ways in which our modern society uses visual images to transmit and document information from the battlefield for the civilian population?

Beyond the Source

Some Civil War photographers collected the best of their work into albums for sale to the public. Gardner's two-volume *Gardner's Photographic Sketch Book of the Civil War* (first edition, 1865) offered a selection of one hundred of his most popular photographs, arranged to provide a chronological narrative of the war, but its $150 price tag put it far beyond the reach of most American consumers. Such collections had a limited reach because of their expense. For most people, their visual record of the Civil War remained a portrait of a soldier in uniform or a few stereographs or cartes-de-visite purchased from a catalogue or at a photographer's gallery.

After the war, Gardner took his camera west to photograph the Union Pacific Railroad expedition of 1867, landscapes, and American Indians. He also pioneered the use of "mug shots," taking photographs of criminals for the police department of Washington, D.C. He died in 1882, leaving behind a reputation as one of the most innovative photographers of the nineteenth century. Mathew Brady spent much of his career after the Civil War trying to sell off his collection of negatives so that he could lift himself out of debt. Always more of an impresario than an actual working photographer, he continued to live in a high style long after he could afford to do so, seeking out the celebrities who had made his early work famous. In 1872, Congress approved purchasing Brady's collection for $25,000. Despite this deal, he declared bankruptcy a few years later and spent much of the rest of his life shuttling between New York and Washington, D.C., trying to recover his solvency. He died in 1896, regarded as the Civil War's greatest photographer, even though he took very few of the pictures published under his name.

The work of Civil War photographers like Brady and Gardner marked the birth of photojournalism. For the first time, photographers used their craft to convey news of the world around them to a waiting public. The Civil War forever wedded the camera to the civilian experience of American warfare. During the war, the popular press had to rely on images reproduced from engravings, although many of those were based on photographs. By World War I, printing technology allowed for photographic reproductions in newspapers and magazines. During World War II, newsreel footage of Pacific and European battlefields brought the war home to Americans, but these images were heavily edited by the government to limit the public's exposure to the sort of carnage depicted in Civil War battlefield photographs. The Vietnam War was America's first televised war, and much of the public's discontent with that conflict can be traced to the images broadcast into American living rooms every night by photojournalists working half a world away. During the U.S.-Iraq War in 2003, the phrase "embedded journalist" entered the American lexicon, as reporters traveling with military personnel used digital technology to transmit war coverage to American televisions in real time. They are the modern descendants of Alexander Gardner and other Civil War photographers who attached themselves to military units so they could gain access to battlefields. In many respects, however, Gardner and his contemporaries enjoyed greater freedom in deciding what to report and how to publish it than military journalists do today. The camera may never lie, but the constant improvement in photographic technology since the 1860s does not necessarily mean that images produced by it today are any more truthful or complete than those produced during the Civil War.

Finding and Supplementing the Source

The two most significant collections of Civil War photographs may be found at the Library of Congress and the National Archives in Washington, D.C. Both of these institutions have Web sites that will introduce you to their collections and help you navigate them. The Library of Congress's *Selected Civil War Photographs* Web site is part of its American Memory project and is available at **memory.loc.gov/ammem/cwphtml/cwphome.html.** For the National Archives, see *Pictures of the Civil War* under its Research Room Web site, available at **archives.gov/research_room/research_topics/civil_war/civil_war_photos.html.**

There are also many print resources available for researching and identifying Civil War photographs. A good place to start in this regard is the six-volume series published by the National Historical Society, *The Image of War* (Garden City, N.Y.: Doubleday, 1981–1984). Alexander Gardner's *Gardner's Photographic Sketch Book of the Civil War,* first published in 1865, is available in a modern edition published by Dover Publications of New York in 1959.

There are thousands of books that include reproductions of Civil War photographs, but few have the background information that will enable you to study them in a scholarly manner. A noteworthy study of Alexander Gardner's work is D. Mark Katz, *Witness to an Era: The Life and Photographs of Alexander Gardner* (Nashville, Tenn.: Rutledge Hill Press, 1991). Mary Panzer provides the same for Mathew Brady in *Mathew Brady and the Image of History* (Washington, D.C.: Smithsonian Institution Press, 1997). William Frassanito's studies of photographs associated with particular Civil War campaigns are based on superior historical detective work—see *Gettysburg: A Journey in Time* (New York: Charles Scribner's Sons, 1975); *Antietam: The Photographic Legacy of America's Bloodiest Day* (1978; repr., New York: Simon and Schuster, 1995); and *Grant and Lee: The Virginia Campaigns, 1864–65* (New York: Charles Scribner's Sons, 1983). For an excellent introduction to the cultural significance of photography in nineteenth-century America, see Alan Trachtenberg, *Reading American Photographs* (New York: Hill and Wang, 1989).

CHAPTER 14

Political Terrorism during Reconstruction

Congressional Hearings and Reports on the Ku Klux Klan

Elias Thomson was an old man in 1871. Born a slave in Spartanburg County, South Carolina, he had lived his entire life on the plantation of Dr. and Mrs. Vernon. When he gained his freedom in 1865, he continued to live there, farming land he rented from his former masters. Thomson's daily life after the war must have gone on much the same as it did before, but freedom did bring some opportunities he was anxious to seize, even at his advanced age. In particular, the ratification of the Fifteenth Amendment in March 1870 guaranteed him the right to vote. Thomson exercised that right in the fall of 1870, casting his ballot in the state and congressional elections for the Republican ticket.

Late one night the following May, a group of men disguised in hoods appeared on his doorstep. They dragged him from his home and told him to start praying, for "your time is short." When Thomson refused, they pointed pistols at his head and asked him, "Who did you vote for?" Thomson responded that he had voted for Claudius Turner, a neighbor whom he held in high esteem. The disguised men told him he had made the wrong choice and whipped him. They told Thomson to remain silent about what had happened and left him with a final warning: "We will have this country right before we get through."

Elias Thomson was one of many Southern men and women to suffer at the hands of the Ku Klux Klan between 1867 and 1871. In fact, his home in Spartanburg, South Carolina, was at the center of one of the most violent and prolonged outbreaks of Klan violence during Reconstruction. The Klan had first appeared there in 1868, using intimidation, arson, whippings, sexual assault, and murder to keep potential Republican voters away from the polls in that year's election. Despite such efforts, the state government remained in the hands of the Republicans, and the Klan temporarily receded as a public threat. Klan violence rose again, however, with the next election in 1870 and became more intense as white and black Republicans tried to mobilize the vote. In addition to intimidation and physical assaults on potential black voters, Klansmen burned black churches, schools, and homes and murdered black men who had enrolled in the state militia. In several counties of the Carolina up-country, where white and black populations were roughly equal or whites held a slight majority, the Klan conducted these crimes without fear of prosecution. Local sheriffs failed to make arrests, and if they did, white juries refused to render guilty verdicts. In some up-country counties, such as Spartanburg, state Republican officials estimated that practically all of the white adult male population belonged to the Klan or sympathized with it.

The Ku Klux Klan was of very recent origins in 1871 but had spread quickly throughout the former Confederate states. It was founded in 1867 by a group of Confederate veterans in Pulaski, Tennessee, who initially intended for it to be nothing more than a social club, similar in purpose and organization to the Freemasons and other secret fraternal orders popular with American males in the nineteenth century. Like the Freemasons, early Klan members created their own ritual, costume, and hierarchy from a mishmash of precedents in ancient mythology: the name "Ku Klux" was derived from the Greek word *kuklos*, meaning circle, and one of the titles in the organization was "Grand Cyclops." As the Klan spread, however, it acquired a different purpose. In Tennessee and the Carolinas in 1868, local "dens" of the Klan began acting as vigilantes, calling themselves "regulators" or "night riders" who enforced law and order according to local custom rather than the dictates of the postwar state governments created by Congress and the Republican Party. Never a centralized organization to begin with, local Klansmen operated autonomously and rarely cooperated with each other beyond the county level. Regardless of that fragmentation, the primary targets of their terrorism remained the same: any blacks who challenged white supremacy by daring to vote, teach, or acquire land, and "carpetbaggers," white Northerners who came to the South after the war to seek their fortunes or to assume office in the Reconstruction state governments.

The violence and intimidation the Klan visited upon freedmen and women and white Republicans seriously challenged the federal government's plans for the postwar South. After passing the Civil Rights Act of 1866, congressional Republicans had pegged their hopes for Reconstruction on enfranchising the former slaves as full and equal U.S. citizens. In this manner, the freedmen would become a core constituency for the Republican Party in the South and prevent the defeated Confederates from reassuming control of government and society there. The ratification of the Fourteenth Amendment in 1868 made this plan part of the Constitution by granting the freedmen and women U.S. citizenship and guaranteeing them equal protection under the law. When some Southern states failed to extend their franchise to the freedmen, Republicans in Congress responded with the Fifteenth Amendment, which prohibited states from denying the right to vote to any citizen because of "race, color, or previous condition of servitude."

Republicans had great success in passing their legislative agenda for Reconstruction in Washington, D.C., but the enforcement of those laws in the South remained very much in question. The twenty thousand federal troops stationed in the South in 1867 were not nearly enough to pacify regions such as the Carolina up-country, where the Klan was at its greatest strength. Furthermore, military officers were reluctant to assume control over matters of law enforcement without specific requests from civilian authorities to do so, lest they alienate the defeated Southern white population even further. As news of the Klan's expansion and pervasive influence in the South made its way to the nation's capital, Republican leaders agreed that further legislation to counteract it was necessary.

In a special message to Congress in December 1870, President Ulysses S. Grant noted that the Klan and similar organizations were using violence to prevent citizens from voting in the Southern states. Acting on a request he had received from the governor of North Carolina for assistance, he asked Congress to investigate the matter. Congress formed a committee to review affairs in North Carolina, and then in April 1871, it created another, much larger committee to expand the investigation into other states. This group, titled the Joint Select Committee to Inquire into the Condition of Affairs in the Late Insurrectionary States, was composed of seven senators and fourteen representatives, thirteen of whom were Republicans and eight of whom were Democrats.

At approximately the same time that it formed the Joint Select Committee to investigate the Klan, Congress also passed the Ku Klux Klan Act. This law gave the president the power to use federal troops and courts to protect the lives, property, and rights of U.S. citizens in the South. For the first time, crimes committed by private persons against other citizens became eligible for prosecution under federal rather than state law. Provisions included in the Ku Klux Klan Act effectively gave the president the ability to declare martial law in any state or region he deemed under Klan influence. The most controversial of these provisions concerned suspension of the writ of habeas corpus, a cornerstone of American civil liberties. The writ of habeas corpus protects citizens from unlawful imprisonment by requiring that any person placed under arrest be charged with a specific crime and placed on trial. By allowing the president to suspend it, Congress made it possible for suspected Klansmen to be jailed indefinitely. Many congressmen, even some Republicans, questioned the constitutionality of this provision and of the Ku Klux Klan Act in general, but the majority who supported the law believed the Klan could not be defeated without such a powerful weapon.

Congressmen formulated and debated this legislation in Washington while freedmen and women in the South confronted the Klan face to face. Casting a ballot or even expressing an interest in voting could put a former slave's life in jeopardy. Those who joined militias, held office, or tried to improve their economic circumstances faced similar reprisals, while the promise of assistance from Washington must have seemed far off indeed. In 1871, a showdown was brewing between the Ku Klux Klan and the federal government that placed people like Elias Thomson squarely in the middle of the battle to determine Reconstruction's fate in the postwar South.

Using Congressional Hearings and Reports as a Source

The Joint Select Committee undertook one of the most far-reaching congressional investigations ever conducted up to that time. During the summer and fall of 1871, it heard testimony from witnesses in Washington, D.C., and sent subcommittees to interview witnesses throughout the South. Most of its work was concentrated on North Carolina and South Carolina, where the activities and impact of the Klan were reported to be most severe, but committee members also visited Alabama, Florida, Georgia, Mississippi, and Tennessee, compiling a record of testimony that numbered in the thousands of pages. In February 1872, the Joint Select Committee submitted this testimony and its reports to Congress. The majority report, signed by every Republican on the committee, endorsed the Ku Klux Klan Act of 1871 and recommended continuing the president's powers to combat the Klan through the use of federal troops, courts, and suspension of the writ of habeas corpus. The minority report, signed by every Democrat on the committee, did not deny the existence of Klan-related violence but blamed it on misguided federal Reconstruction policy, which had left the Southern states in the hands of carpetbaggers and former slaves.

Advantages and Disadvantages of Working with Congressional Hearings and Reports

Since its publication in 1872, historians have found the thirteen volumes of the Joint Select Committee's report a remarkably detailed and comprehensive source for studying Reconstruction in the South. One of its chief advantages as a source is its sheer size. The committee conducted its work thoroughly, and the hundreds of witnesses who testified before it represented a broad spectrum of Southern society: white and black, rich and poor, male and female, Republican and Democrat. One historian has called their testimony "the richest single source" for understanding Southern society during the Reconstruction era. In the case of freedmen and women, testimony before the committee provides invaluable first-person narratives of what the transition from bondage to freedom was like.

Another advantage of working with this source has to do with the methods by which the Joint Select Committee collected its evidence. Its procedures resembled legal hearings: oaths were administered to witnesses, and witnesses were subjected to cross-examination, all in meetings open to the public. No witnesses appeared anonymously or gave secret testimony. While those procedures may have prevented many from testifying for fear of reprisals, they nevertheless lent an air of authenticity to the witnesses' descriptions of the Klan that was not necessarily accorded to rumors or sensationalistic stories reported in the press. The Klan conducted its terrorism under cover of night and in disguise. By its very nature, it did not submit willingly to public scrutiny. For the most part, however, the witnesses who appeared before the committee in Southern towns and counties were eyewitnesses to the Klan's activities, making their testimony the most complete and reliable account of this secret organization's operations during Reconstruction.

The disadvantages associated with using the Joint Select Committee's report stem mostly from its inherent political biases. The Republicans who dominated the Joint Select Committee by a two-to-one margin were most interested in finding evidence that the Klan was a conspiratorial organization bent on depriving black and white Republicans of their civil and political liberties. Such evidence could be used to justify imposing martial law in those regions affected by the Klan. Democrats accused the Republicans of using the committee to drum up stories of Klan brutality and lawlessness that could be publicized to Republican advantage in the upcoming election of 1872. While the Democrats on the committee could not deny the violence of the Klan, they used their questioning of witnesses to cast doubt on its political motives, depicting Klansmen instead as isolated, ill-advised characters pushed to extremes by desperation and offended honor. It is important to remember that Congress had already passed the Ku Klux Klan Act when the Joint Select Committee conducted its work. Given that the committee's majority was made up of the same Republicans who had passed that piece of legislation, how likely was it that the committee's findings would challenge its enforcement? By passing the Ku Klux Klan Act *before* its investigation of the Klan, Congress clearly anticipated the outcome of the Joint Select Committee's work.

As you read the testimony, you will quickly realize that neither the Republicans nor the Democrats on the Joint Select Committee resembled neutral fact finders. Each side brought an agenda to the proceedings that influenced the nature of the testimony before the committee. Consider, for example, these excerpts from the testimony of D. H. Chamberlain, the Republican attorney general of South Carolina, given before the committee in Washington, D.C., on June 10, 1871. A good historian quickly learns to read between the lines of such evidence, looking carefully at the questions as well as the answers to determine what biases and ulterior motives shaped the construction of this source.

D. H. Chamberlain, sworn and examined.

By the Chairman:

> *Question:* How long have you been a resident of the State?
>
> *Answer:* I have been a resident there since December, 1865.
>
> *Question:* Please go on and state to the committee the knowledge you have acquired, from your official position, as to the efficiency with which the laws are executed throughout the State of South Carolina, and the protection afforded to life and property in the State. Make your statement in general terms.
>
> *Answer:* The enforcement of the law has, from time to time, been very much interrupted and disturbed from special causes; lately by what are popularly known as Ku-Klux operations. . . .

By Mr. Van Trump:

> *Question:* You say you went to South Carolina in 1865?
>
> *Answer:* Yes, sir.
>
> *Question:* How long after the termination of the war; what part of the year?
>
> *Answer:* I went in December, 1865.
>
> *Question:* From where did you go?
>
> *Answer:* From Massachusetts. I had been in the Union army during the war. I settled at Charleston in December, 1865, and remained there, and my residence is there now, although I have to be at the capital of the State most of the time.

Margin notes:

An oath to tell the truth similar to that given in a court of law

Republican senator John Scott of Pennsylvania chaired the committee and typically initiated the questioning

Returns to the subject of Chamberlain's background, seeking to discredit him as a carpetbagger

Invites Chamberlain to speak freely about law enforcement

Philadelph Van Trump, a Democratic representative from Ohio, typically led the cross-examination

One other disadvantage to bear in mind about the Joint Select Committee's report is that while the committee's hearings had the appearance of legal proceedings, they did not work with the same standards of evidence as a court of law. In particular, the Republican majority of the committee was willing to accept hearsay, what someone had heard but not personally witnessed, as evidence. Democrats on the committee objected mightily to this, likening it to accepting rumors and gossip as facts. They equated the two-dollars-a-day allowance the committee paid to witnesses with bribery and accused the local Republican officials of coaching witnesses as well. In the thousands of pages of testimony in the Joint Select Committee's report, some witnesses do appear more reliable than others. As a historian, you face a twofold task in dealing with this source. First, you have to keep track of the information it provides you about the persons and events involved in the Klan's activities. Second, you must judge whether the evidence you are reading is reliable, by establishing your own measures for assessing its truthfulness: Is the testimony hearsay or an eyewitness account? Does the witness contradict himself or herself under cross-examination? What evidence is there, if any, of outside pressure or influence on the witness's testimony?

Working with the Source

As you read the sources in the next section, use the tables on page 305 to organize your notes on what they tell you about the Klan's operations in South Carolina and the federal government's response to them. For Sources 1 through 5, summarize what the witnesses said about the Klan's actions and the purposes behind them in the first column of the first table. In the second column, note the type of evidence each witness presented: was it a firsthand account? hearsay? personal opinion? For Sources 6 and 7, summarize how each report described the Klan in the first column, and in the second column, note each report's assessment of the federal response to it.

	Description of the Klan's Actions and Purposes	Type of Evidence Provided
1. Samuel T. Poinier		
2. D. H. Chamberlain		
3. Elias Thomson		
4. Lucy McMillan		
5. Mervin Givens		

	Description of the Klan	Assessment of Federal Response to the Klan
6. Majority Report		
7. Minority Report		

The Source: Testimony and Reports from the Joint Select Committee to Inquire into the Condition of Affairs in the Late Insurrectionary States

All of the testimony that follows is taken from the Joint Select Committee's investigation of the Ku Klux Klan in South Carolina. Sources 1 and 2 come from testimony heard in Washington, D.C., while Sources 3, 4, and 5 are from testimony heard in Spartanburg, South Carolina. Sources 6 and 7 are excerpts from the committee's majority and minority reports, which were completed after the investigation was over.

Testimony of Samuel T. Poinier, Washington, D.C., June 7, 1871

Poinier was a Republican newspaper editor and a federal tax collector in South Carolina at the time of his testimony.

Samuel T. Poinier sworn and examined.

By the Chairman:[1]

Question: Please state in what part of South Carolina you reside.
Answer: In Spartanburg County, the most northern county in the State.
Question: How long have you resided there?
Answer: Since February, 1866; a little over five years.
Question: From what part of the United States did you go to South Carolina?
Answer: I went there from Louisville, Kentucky. . . . I went there in 1866 with no intention whatever of remaining. I went entirely for social reasons, to marry, and I was persuaded to stay there. My wife was a native of Charleston, and I found her up in Spartanburg after the war, where a large number of Charleston people went during the bombardment of the city. . . .
Question: Were you in the Union Army?
Answer: Yes, sir: I went out from Kentucky.
Question: Proceed with your statement.

[1] Republican senator John Scott from Pennsylvania.
Source: United States Congress, *Report of the Joint Select Committee to Inquire into the Condition of Affairs in the Late Insurrectionary States,* vol. 2, *South Carolina, Part I* (Washington, D.C.: Government Printing Office, 1872), 25–28, 33–34.

Answer: Just before our last campaign,[2] it was May a year ago, I . . . identi-fied myself publicly with the republican party. I made my paper a republican paper. I did everything I could in the last State election for the reelection of Governor Scott[3] and our other State officers. From that time I have been in very deep water. . . . I was ordered away last fall, immediately after our last election, in November. It was soon after the first appearance of this Ku-Klux organiza-tion, or whatever it is. Soon after these outrages occurred in our county I re-ceived a note ordering me away from there, stating that I must leave the county; that all the soldiers of the United States Army could not enable me to live in Spartanburg. . . . two days prior to our election, a party of disguised men went, at night, and took out two white men and three negroes, one of them a colored woman, and whipped them most brutally. Two of them were managers of the box[4] at that election; and the men told them that if they dared to hold an election at that box they would return and kill them. That was the first ap-pearance of any trouble in the State. . . .

Question: Were those people of whom you spoke in disguise?

Answer: They were all in disguise. One of the colored men who were whipped swore positively as to the identity of some of them, and the parties were arrested, but nothing could ever be done with them; they proved an *alibi*, and some of them have since gone to Texas. . . .

Question: Go on and state any similar occurrences in that county since that time . . .

Answer: Since that time outrages of that nature have occurred every week. Parties of disguised men have ridden through the county almost nightly. They go to a colored man's house, take him out and whip him. They tell him that he must not give any information that he has been whipped. They tell him, more-over, that he must make a public renunciation of his republican principles or they will return and kill him. . . .

Question: Do the facts that have transpired and the manner in which they have occurred satisfy you of the existence of the organization in that portion of South Carolina?

Answer: Yes, sir; I have no doubt of it in the world. I have received anony-mous communications signed by the order of "K.K.K.," directing me to leave the county, stating that I could not live there; that I was a carpet-bagger. But personally I have never met with any trouble.

By Mr. Van Trump:[5]

Question: You have a connection with the partisan press there?

Answer: Yes, sir. I am editing a republican paper.

Question: Do you advocate the cause of the negro in your paper?

---

[2] The election of 1870.

[3] Robert K. Scott was the Republican governor of South Carolina.

[4] Ballot box.

[5] Democratic representative Philadelph Van Trump from Ohio.

Answer: Not the negro especially. I advocate the general principles of republicanism.

Question: You support the whole republican doctrine in your paper?

Answer: So far as general principles go, I do. I do not approve or uphold the State government in many of its acts; but, so far as the general principles of republicanism are concerned, I uphold it very strongly. I advocate the right of the colored people to vote and to exercise their civil and political privileges. . . .

Question: These men who assert that their object is to put down the negro and get possession of the Government are prominent men, are they not?

Answer: Yes, sir.

Question: Can you name a single man?

Answer: Well, I cannot name anybody specially who has made such a remark, but I hear it in the hotels.

Question: Have you yourself heard them make the remark?

Answer: I have heard the remark made; it is a common thing.

Question: Is it not rather an uncommon remark?

Answer: It is not, there.

Question: You cannot recollect the name of a single person who has made that declaration?

Answer: No sir, I cannot recall any now.

2　*Testimony of D. H. Chamberlain,*
Washington, D.C., June 10, 1871

Chamberlain was a Republican and the attorney general of South Carolina.

D. H. Chamberlain, sworn and examined.

By the Chairman:

Question: How long have you been a resident of the State?

Answer: I have been a resident there since December, 1865.

Question: Please go on and state to the committee the knowledge you have acquired, from your official position, as to the efficiency with which the laws are executed throughout the State of South Carolina, and the protection afforded to life and property in the State. Make your statement in general terms.

Answer: The enforcement of the law has, from time to time, been very much interrupted and disturbed from special causes; lately by what are popularly known as Ku-Klux operations. There have been a great many outrages committed, and a great many homicides, and a great many whippings. I speak

Source: Report of the Joint Select Committee, vol. 2, South Carolina, Part I, 48–51.

now, of course, of what I have heard; I have never seen any outrages committed myself; I am simply stating what I believe to be fact. . . .

Question: In what part of the State are these offenses committed which you attribute to the influence of this organization?

Answer: Notably in Spartanburg, Newberry, Union, and York Counties; those are the principal counties that have been the scenes of these disturbances. But they have extended into Laurens, Chester, and Lancaster Counties.[1] . . .

Question: Have there been any convictions for these offenses in the State, so far as your information goes; offenses committed by these organized bands?

Answer: No sir, no convictions, and no arrests, except in the case of this wounded Ku-Klux.[2] . . .

By Mr. Van Trump:

Question: You say you went to South Carolina in 1865?
Answer: Yes, sir.
Question: How long after the termination of the war; what part of the year?
Answer: I went in December, 1865.
Question: From where did you go?
Answer: From Massachusetts. I had been in the Union army during the war. I settled at Charleston in December, 1865, and remained there, and my residence is there now, although I have to be at the capital of the State most of the time.

By Mr. Stevenson:[3]

Question: When did it first come to your knowledge that this organization existed in the State of South Carolina?

Answer: It would be difficult to say. My conviction that there is such an organization has grown up very gradually. . . . I cannot fix the date exactly.

Question: Had you any knowledge of the fact that there were acts of violence and disorders in that State about the time of the election in 1868?

Answer: Yes, sir.

Question: Had you any information of the sending of arms at that time into that State?

Answer: O, I remember that a great many arms were purchased by private individuals, if you refer to that. I know that at the time, during the canvass,[4] there was considerable excitement when it was understood that the democrats,

---

[1] All seven of these counties were in the piedmont or up-country region of South Carolina, where the black and white populations were roughly equal.

[2] Chamberlain is referring to a Klansman wounded during a raid on the Newberry County Courthouse. He was jailed and then released on bail and subsequently either died while in the care of a friend or was spirited away by friends to avoid prosecution.

[3] Republican representative Job Stevenson from Ohio.

[4] Campaigning for votes.

as we call them, were arming themselves with Winchester and Henry rifles, or something of the kind.

Question: Repeating rifles?

Answer: Yes, sir. . . .

By Mr. Blair:[5]

Question: Did you have any actual knowledge of the fact that the democrats were then arming?

Answer: No, sir.

Question: Then you make this statement as a rumor merely?

Answer: Well, yes, sir; I should use, perhaps, a little stronger term than rumor. I had heard it so often that it came to be a belief with me, but it was hearsay. . . .

Question: Was it a common report that those arms all went into the hands of democrats?

Answer: As I heard it, it was understood that those arms were imported into the State upon order of individuals. I do not know but a republican might have had his order filled, but the belief was that they were generally ordered by democrats.

By Mr. Stevenson:

Question: You have no knowledge of any general arming among the republicans at that time?

Answer: No, sir.

Question: You were a republican, then, were you not?

Answer: Yes, sir.

By Mr. Blair:

Question: Did not the republicans have arms?

Answer: O, yes.

By Mr. Van Trump:

Question: Did not the negroes have arms?

Answer: Yes, sir; it is very common for people to have their shot-guns, to have some kind of arms. I suppose that in this instance people thought that there was an unusually large number brought in at a particular time, and that they were not for sporting purposes. They were repeating rifles.

Question: Have you been a politician for any part of your life?

Answer: No, sir; I do not think I have ever been a politician.

Question: Have you never heard a thousand rumors during an election that had no foundation in fact?

Answer: Yes, sir; many of them.

Question: Got up for excitement merely?

Answer: Yes, sir.

[5] Democratic senator Frank Blair from Michigan.

Testimony of Elias Thomson,
Spartanburg, South Carolina, July 7, 1871

Elias Thomson (colored) sworn and examined.

By the Chairman:

> *Question:* Where do you live?
> *Answer:* Up on Tiger River, on Mrs. Vernon's plantation.[1]
> *Question:* What do you follow?
> *Answer:* Farming.
> *Question:* Do you live on rented land?
> *Answer:* Yes, sir.
> *Question:* How much have you rented?
> *Answer:* I think about fifty acres.
> *Question:* How long have you been living there?
> *Answer:* Ever since the surrender; I never left home.
> *Question:* Have you ever been disturbed any up there?
> *Answer:* Yes, sir.
> *Question:* How?

Answer: There came a parcel of gentlemen to my house one night—or men. They went up to the door and ran against it. My wife was sick. I was lying on a pallet, with my feet to the door. They ran against it and hallooed to me, "Open the door, quick, quick, quick." I threw the door open immediately, right wide open. Two little children were lying with me. I said, "Come in gentlemen." One of them says, "Do we look like gentlemen?" I says, "You look like men of some description; walk in." One says, "Come out here; are you ready to die?" I told him I was not prepared to die. "Well," said he, "Your time is short; commence praying." I told him I was not a praying man much, and hardly ever prayed; only a very few times; never did pray much. He says, "You ought to pray; your time is short, and now commence to pray." I told him I was not a praying man. One of them held a pistol to my head and said, "Get down and pray." I was on the steps, with one foot on the ground. They led me off to a pine tree. There was three or four of them behind me, it appeared, and one on each side, and one in front. The gentleman who questioned me was the only one I could see. All the time I could not see the others. Every time I could get a look around, they would touch me on the side of the head with a pistol, so I had to keep my head square in front. The next question was, "Who did you vote for?" I told him I voted for Mr. Turner—Claudius Turner, a gentleman in the neighborhood. They said, "What did you vote for him for?" I said, "I thought a good deal of him; he was my neighbor." I told them I disremembered who was on the ticket besides, but they had several, and I voted the ticket. "What did you do that for?" they said. Says I, "because I thought it was right."

---

[1] The Vernons were Thomson's former masters.

Source: Report of the Joint Select Committee, vol. 2, South Carolina, Part I, 410–15.

They said, "You thought it was right? It was right wrong." I said, "I never do anything hardly if I think it is wrong; if it was wrong, I did not know it. That was my opinion at the time and I thought every man ought to vote according to his notions." He said, "If you had taken the advice of your friends you would have been better off." I told him I had. Says I, "You may be a friend to me, but I can't tell who you are." Says he, "Can't you recognize anybody here?" I told him I could not. "In the condition you are in now, I can't tell who you are." One of them had a very large set of teeth; I suppose they were three-quarters of an inch long; they came right straight down. He came up to me and sort of nodded. He had on speckled horns and calico stuff, and had a face on. He said, "Have you got a chisel here I could get?" I told him I hadn't, but I reckoned I could knock one out, and I sort of laughed. He said, "What in hell are you laughing at? It is no laughing time." I told him it sort of tickled me, and I thought I would laugh. I did not say anything then for a good while. "Old man," says one, "have you got a rope here, or a plow-line, or something of the sort?" I told him, "Yes; I had one hanging on the crib." He said, "Let us have it." One of them says, "String him up to this pine tree, and we will get all out of him. Get up, one of you, and let us pull him up, and he will tell the truth." I says, "I can't tell you anything more than I have told. There is nothing that I can tell you but what I have told you and you have asked me." One man questioned me all this time. One would come up and say, "Let's hang him a while, and he will tell us the truth"; and another then came up and said, "Old man, we are just from hell; some of us have been dead ever since the revolutionary war." . . . I was not scared, and said, "You have been through a right smart experience." "Yes," he says, "we have been through a considerable experience." One of them says, "we have just come from hell." I said, "If I had been there, I would not want to go back." . . . Then they hit me thirteen of the hardest cuts I ever got. I never had such cuts. They hit me right around my waist and by my hip, and cut a piece about as wide as my two fingers in one place. I did not say a word while they were whipping, only sort of grunted a little. As quick as they got through they said, "Go to your bed. We will have this country right before we get through; go to your bed," and they started away. . . .

   Question: Who is Claudius Turner?

   Answer: He is a gentleman that run for the legislature here. He was on the ticket with Mr. Scott.

   Question: The republican ticket?

   Answer: Yes, sir; the radical[2] ticket. . . .

By Mr. Van Trump:

   Question: Explain to me, if you can, if the object of this Ku-Klux organization is to intimidate the colored people, why they were so particular as to make you promise, under penalty of death, that you would never disclose the fact that you had been visited; do you understand why that is?

_____

[2] Radical Republicans were known for their support of black suffrage and the disenfranchisement of former Confederate military and civilian officers.

Answer: I can explain this fact this far: You know when they said to me to not say anything about this matter, I asked them what I must say, and when I asked, "What must I say? I will have to say something," they said, "What are you going to say?" I said, "What must I say?" He said, "Are you going to tell it?" I told them, "I have to say something, of course, and what must I say; what can I say?" Then they said, looking straight at me—

Question: Why is it that so often in giving your testimony you have to get up and make gesticulations like an orator? Have you been an orator?

Answer: No, sir, but I was showing the way they did me, and what they said to me. They said, "You just let me hear of this thing again, and we will not leave a piece of you when we come back."

Question: To whom have you talked lately about this case, or consulted here in town?

Answer: I have not consulted much about it.

Question: How long have you been waiting to be examined?

Answer: Since Tuesday about 10 o'clock.

Question: Have any white republicans been to see you?

Answer: No, sir; nobody at all.

Question: Did you see them?

Answer: I don't know who the republicans are here. I may have seen some.

Question: Do you pretend to say that since Tuesday you have not talked with any white about your case?

Answer: With none about the Ku-Klux matter.

Testimony of Lucy McMillan,
Spartanburg, South Carolina, July 10, 1871

Lucy McMillan (colored) sworn and examined.

By the Chairman:

Question: Where do you live?

Answer: Up in the country. I live on McMillan's place, right at the foot of the road.

Question: How far is it?

Answer: Twelve miles.

Question: Are you married?

Answer: I am not married. I am single now. I was married. My husband was taken away from me and carried off twelve years ago.

Question: He was carried off before the war?

Answer: Yes, sir; the year before the war; twelve years ago this November coming.

Source: Report of the Joint Select Committee, vol. 3, South Carolina, Part 2, 604–7.

Question: How old are you now?

Answer: I am called forty-six. I am forty-five or six.

Question: Did the Ku-Klux come where you live at any time?

Answer: They came there once before they burned my house down. The way it happened was this: John Hunter's wife came to my house on Saturday morning, and told they were going to whip me. I was afraid of them; there was so much talk of Ku-Klux drowning people, and whipping people, and killing them. My house was only a little piece from the river, so I laid out at night in the woods. The Sunday evening after Isham McCrary[1] was whipped I went up, and a white man, John McMillan, came along and says to me, "Lucy, you had better stay at home, for they will whip you anyhow." I said if they have to, they might whip me in the woods, for I am afraid to stay there. Monday night they came in and burned my house down; I dodged out alongside of the road not far off and saw them. I was sitting right not far off, and as they came along the river I knew some of them. I knew John McMillan, and Kennedy McMillan, and Billy Bush, and John Hunter. They were all together. I was not far off, and I saw them. They went right on to my house. When they passed me I run further up on the hill to get out of the way of them. They went there and knocked down and beat my house a right smart while. And then they all got still, and directly I saw the fire rise.

Question: How many of these men were there?

Answer: A good many; I couldn't tell how many, but these I knew. The others I didn't. . . .

Question: What was the reason given for burning your house?

Answer: There was speaking down there last year and I came to it. They all kept at me to go. I went home and they quizzed me to hear what was said, and I told them as far as my senses allowed me.

Question: Where was this speaking?

Answer: Here in this town. I went on and told them, and then they all said I was making laws; or going to have the land, and the Ku-Klux were going to beat me for bragging that I would have land. John Hunter told them on me, I suppose, that I said I was going to have land. . . .

Question: Was that the only reason you know for your house being burned?

Answer: That is all the reason. All the Ku-Klux said all that they had against me was that I was bragging and boasting that I wanted the land. . . .

By Mr. Van Trump:

Question: Do you mean to say that they said they burned the house for that reason?

Answer: No sir; they burned the house because they could not catch me. I don't know any other reason. . . .

Question: Who was John Hunter?

Answer: He is a colored man. I worked for him all last summer. I worked with him hoeing his cotton and corn.

---

[1]Another freedman who testified before the committee in Spartanburg.

Question: What was he doing with these Ku-Klux?

Answer: I don't know. He was with them. . . .

Question: How did you come to be named Lucy McMillan?

Answer: I was a slave of Robert McMillan. I always belonged to him.

Question: You helped raise Kennedy and John?[2]

Answer: Not John, but Kennedy I did. When he was a little boy I was with him.

Question: Did he always like you?

Answer: Yes, sir. They always pretended to like us.

Question: That is while you were a slave?

Answer: Yes, sir, while I was a slave, but never afterward. They didn't care for us then.

[2] Sons of Robert McMillan.

5   *Testimony of Mervin Givens,*
Spartanburg, South Carolina, July 12, 1871

Mervin Givens (colored) sworn and examined.

By Mr. Stevenson:

Question: Your name in old times was Mery Moss?

Answer: Yes, sir; but since freedom I don't go by my master's name. My name now is Givens.

Question: What is your age?

Answer: About forty I expect. . . .

Question: Have you ever been visited by the Ku-Klux?

Answer: Yes, sir.

Question: When?

Answer: About the last of April.

Question: Tell what they said and did.

Answer: I was asleep when they came to my house, and did not know anything about them until they broke in on me.

Question: What time of night was it?

Answer: About twelve o'clock at night. They broke in on me and frightened me right smart, being asleep. They ordered me to get up and make a light. As quick as I could gather my senses I bounced up and made a light, but not quick enough. They jumped at me and struck me with a pistol, and made a knot[1] that you can see there now. By the time I made the light I catched the voice of them, and as soon as I could see by the light, I looked around and saw by the

[1] Bump.

Source: Report of the Joint Select Committee, vol. 2, South Carolina, Part 2, 698–700.

size of the men and voice so that I could judge right off who it was. By that time they jerked the case off the pillow and jerked it over my head and ordered me out of doors. That was all I saw in the house. After they carried me out of doors I saw nothing more. They pulled the pillow-slip over my head and told me if I took off they would shoot me. They carried me out and whipped me powerful.

Question: With what?

Answer: With sticks and hickories. They whipped me powerful.

Question: How many lashes?

Answer: I can't tell. I have no knowledge at all about it. May be a hundred or two. Two men whipped me and both at once.

Question: Did they say anything to you?

Answer: They cursed me and told me I had voted the radical ticket, and they intended to beat me so I would not vote it again.

Question: Did you know any of them?

Answer: Yes, sir; I think I know them.

Question: What were there names?

Answer: One was named John Thomson and the other was John Zimmerman. Those are the two men I think it was.

Question: How many were there in all?

Answer: I didn't see but two. After they took me out, I was blindfolded; but I could judge from the horse tracks that there were more than two horses there. Some were horses and some were mules. It was a wet, rainy night; they whipped me stark naked. I had a brown undershirt on and they tore it clean off. . . .

By Mr. Van Trump:

Question: There were, then, two men who came to your house?

Answer: Yes, sir; that was all I could see.

Question: Were they disguised?

Answer: Yes, sir.

Question: How?

Answer: They had on some sort of gray-looking clothes, and much the same sort of thing over their face. One of them had a sort of high hat with tassel and sort of horns.

Question: How far did John Thomson live from there?

Answer: I think it is two or three miles.

Question: Were you acquainted with him?

Answer: Yes, sir.

Question: Where?

Answer: At my house. My wife did a good deal of washing for them both. I was very well-acquainted with their size and their voices. They were boys I was raised with. . . .

Question: Did you tell anybody else it was John Thomson?

Answer: I have never named it.

Question: Why?

Answer: I was afraid to.

Question: Are you afraid now?

Answer: I am not afraid to own the truth as nigh[2] as I can.

Question: Is there any difference in owning to the truth on the 12th of July and on the 1st of April?

Answer: The black people have injured themselves very much by talking, and I was afraid.

Question: Are you not afraid now?

Answer: No, sir; because I hope there will be a stop put to it. . . .

Question: Do you think we three gentlemen can stop it?

Answer: No, sir; but I think you can get some help.

Question: Has anybody been telling you that?

Answer: No, sir; nobody told me that. . . .

Question: Why did you not commence a prosecution against Thomson and Zimmerman?

Answer: I am like the rest, I reckon; I am too cowardly.

Question: Why do you not do it now; you are not cowardly now?

Answer: I shouldn't have done it now.

Question: I am talking about bringing suit for that abuse on that night. Why do you not have them arrested?

Answer: It ought to be done.

Question: Why do you not do it?

Answer: For fear they would shoot me. If I were to bring them up here and could not prove the thing exactly on them, and they were to get out of it, I would not expect to live much longer.

[2] Near.

Majority Report of the Joint Select Committee to Inquire into the Condition of Affairs in the Late Insurrectionary States, February 19, 1872, Submitted by Luke P. Poland

Poland was a Republican representative from Vermont.

The proceedings and debates in Congress show that, whatever other causes were assigned for disorders in the late insurrectionary States, the execution of the laws and the security of life and property were alleged to be most seriously

Source: Report of the Joint Select Committee, vol. 1, *Reports of the Committee,* 2–3, 98–99.

threatened by the existence and acts of organized bands of armed and disguised men, known as Ku-Klux. . . .

The evidence is equally decisive that redress cannot be obtained against those who commit crimes in disguise and at night. The reasons assigned are that identification is difficult, almost impossible; that when this is attempted, the combinations and oaths of the order come in and release the culprit by perjury either upon the witness-stand or in the jury-box; and that the terror inspired by their acts, as well as the public sentiment in their favor in many localities, paralyzes the arm of civil power. . . .

The race so recently emancipated, against which banishment or serfdom is thus decreed, but which has been clothed by the Government with the rights and responsibilities of citizenship, ought not to be, and we feel assured will not be left hereafter without protection against the hostilities and sufferings it has endured in the past, as long as the legal and constitutional powers of the Government are adequate to afford it. Communities suffering such evils and influenced by such extreme feelings may be slow to learn that relief can come only from a ready obedience to and support of constituted authority, looking to the modes provided by law for redress of all grievances. That Southern communities do not seem to yield this ready obedience at once should not deter the friends of good government in both sections from hoping and working for that end. . . .

The law of 1871[1] has been effective in suppressing for the present, to a great extent, the operations of masked and disguised men in North and South Carolina. . . . The apparent cessation of operations should not lead to a conclusion that community would be safe if protective measures were withdrawn. These should be continued until there remains no further doubt of the actual suppression and disarming of this wide-spread and dangerous conspiracy.

The results of suspending the writ of *habeas corpus* in South Carolina show that where the membership, mysteries, and power of the organization have been kept concealed this is the most and perhaps only effective remedy for its suppression; and in review of its cessation and resumption of hostilities at different times, of its extent and power, and that in several of the States where it exists the courts have not yet held terms at which the cases can be tried, we recommend that the power conferred on the President by the fourth section of that act[2] be extended until the end of the next session of Congress.

For the Senate:	For the House of Representatives:
JOHN SCOTT, Chairman	LUKE P. POLAND, Chairman
Z. CHANDLER[3]	HORACE MAYNARD[4]

[1] The Ku Klux Klan Act.

[2] To suspend the writ of habeas corpus.

[3] Republican senator from Michigan.

[4] Republican representative from Tennessee.

BENJ. F. RICE[5]   GLENNI W. SCOFIELD[6]

JOHN POOL[7]   JOHN F. FARNSWORTH[8]

DANIEL D. PRATT[9]   JOHN COBURN[10]

                                     JOB E. STEVENSON

                                     BENJ. F. BUTLER[11]

                                     WILLIAM E. LANSING[12]

[5] Republican senator from Arkansas.

[6] Republican representative from Pennsylvania.

[7] Republican senator from North Carolina.

[8] Republican representative from Illinois.

[9] Republican senator from Indiana.

[10] Republican representative from Indiana.

[11] Republican representative from Massachusetts.

[12] Republican representative from New York.

 7

Minority Report of the Joint Select Committee to Inquire into the Condition of Affairs in the Late Insurrectionary States, February 19, 1872, Submitted by James B. Beck

Beck was a Democratic representative from Kentucky.

The atrocious measures by which millions of white people have been put at the mercy of the semi-barbarous negroes of the South, and the vilest of the white people, both from the North and South, who have been constituted the leaders of this black horde, are now sought to be justified and defended by defaming the people upon whom this unspeakable outrage had been committed. . . .

There is no doubt about the fact that great outrages were committed by bands of disguised men during those years of lawlessness and oppression. The natural tendency of all such organizations is to violence and crime. . . . It is so everywhere; like causes produce like results. Sporadic cases of outrages occur in every community. . . . But, as a rule, the worst governments produce the most disorders. South Carolina is confessedly in the worst condition of any of the States. Why? Because her government is the worst, or what makes it still worse,

Source: Report of the Joint Select Committee, vol. 1, *Reports of the Committee,* 289, 463–64, 514–16, 588.

her people see no hope in the future. . . . There never was a Ku-Klux in Virginia, nobody pretends there ever was. Why? Because Virginia escaped carpet-bag rule. . . .

The Constitution was trampled under foot in the passage of what is known as the Ku-Klux law; a power was delegated to the President which could be exercised by the legislative authority alone; whole communities of innocent people were put under the ban of executive vengeance by the suspension of the writ of *habeas corpus* at the mere whim and caprice of the President; and all for what? For the apprehension and conviction of a few poor, deluded, ignorant, and unhappy wretches, goaded to desperation by the insolence of the negroes, and who could, had the radical authorities of South Carolina done their duty, just as easily have been prosecuted in the State courts, and much more promptly and cheaply, than by all this imposing machinery of Federal power, through military and judicial departments. . . .

. . . The antagonism, therefore, which exists between these two classes of the population of South Carolina does not spring from any political cause, in the ordinary party sense of the term; but it grows out of that instinctive and irrepressible repugnance to compulsory affiliation with another race, planted by the God of nature in the breast of the white man, perhaps more strongly manifested in the uneducated portion of the people, and aggravated and intensified by the fact that the Negro has been placed as a *ruler* over him. . . .

We feel it would be a dereliction of duty on our part if, after what we have witnessed in South Carolina, we did not admonish the American people that the present condition of things in the South cannot last. It was an oft-quoted political apothegm, long prior to the war, that no government could exist "half slave and half free." The paraphrase of that proposition is equally true, that no government can long exist "half black and half white." If the republican party, or its all-powerful leaders in the North, cannot see this, if they are so absorbed in the idea of this newly discovered political divinity in the negro, that they cannot comprehend its social repugnance or its political dangers; or, knowing it, have the wanton, wicked, and criminal purpose of disregarding its consequences, whether in the present or in the future, and the great mass of American white citizens should still be so mad as to sustain them in their heedless career of forcing negro supremacy over white men, why then "farewell, a long farewell," to constitutional liberty on this continent, and the glorious form of government bequeathed to us by our fathers. . . .

The foregoing is a hurried, but, as we believe, a truthful statement of the political, moral, and financial condition of the State of South Carolina, under the joint rule of the Negro and the "reconstructive" policy of Congress.

FRANK BLAIR

T. F. BAYARD[1]

S. S. COX[2]

---

[1] Democratic senator from Delaware.

[2] Democratic representative from New York.

JAMES B. BECK

P. VAN TRUMP

A. M. WADDELL[3]

J. C. ROBINSON[4]

J. M. HANKS[5]

[3] Democratic representative from North Carolina.
[4] Democratic representative from Illinois.
[5] Democratic representative from Arkansas.

Analyzing the Source

REFLECTING ON THE SOURCE

1. Using your notes from the first table on page 305, describe the actions and purposes witnesses attributed to the Ku Klux Klan in South Carolina. How did the descriptions of the Klan differ between witnesses examined in Washington, D.C. (Sources 1 and 2) and those examined in South Carolina (Sources 3, 4, and 5)? How would you explain those differences?

2. Briefly compare the nature of evidence presented in the testimony: How did it differ between black and white witnesses? In what ways did the Klan's attacks on blacks differ from those on white Republicans? What do you think accounts for such differences?

3. What patterns did you find in the cross-examination of witnesses? How did Van Trump and other Democrats on the committee seek to discredit or shape the testimony they heard, and do you think they succeeded in any instances? Which witnesses do you think were most successful in answering their cross-examinations? Did any of the witnesses contradict themselves?

MAKING CONNECTIONS

4. Consider whether the majority and minority reports (Sources 6 and 7) could have been written before the committee heard any witnesses. Using your notes from the second table on page 305, do you think any of the congressmen sitting on the committee had their minds changed about the Ku Klux Klan or the federal government's response to it by the testimony they heard? What specific examples or passages from the reports would you use to support your answer?

5. What does this source tell you about the limits of federal power during Reconstruction? According to the testimony and reports, what accounted for the breakdown of law and order in South Carolina, and how was it most likely to be restored? How did Republicans and Democrats differ in this regard?

6. Judging from the testimony of witnesses you have read here, how might you use this source to study the social and economic conditions of the freedmen

and women of the South during Reconstruction? What evidence does the testimony of Thomson, McMillan, and Givens (Sources 3, 4, and 5) provide of the ways in which African American men and women valued and acted on their freedom after 1865? Judging from this evidence, what limits did whites try to impose on that freedom?

Beyond the Source

As noted in the Joint Select Committee's majority report, the Ku Klux Klan Act of 1871 did succeed in suppressing the Klan's activities in those regions where it was enforced. In October 1871, while the Joint Select Committee was still at work, President Grant suspended the writ of habeas corpus in nine South Carolina counties, including Spartanburg, and sent in federal troops to arrest approximately 1,500 suspected Klansmen. Even more Klansmen fled the region to avoid prosecution. In a series of trials managed by U.S. Attorney General Amos Akerman in late 1871 and in 1872, about ninety Klansmen were sentenced to prison terms ranging from three months to ten years. Most of those given long sentences were released within a year or two, under amnesty offered by President Grant. Overall, very few Klansmen were ever brought to meaningful justice for their crimes, but by the election of 1872, reports of Klan terrorism had declined considerably and the organization's ability to intimidate black voters appeared to have been broken.

During the 1920s, the Ku Klux Klan was revived by whites who felt threatened by Catholic and Jewish immigrants as well as by African Americans. At its peak, this version of the Klan included three million members and spilled beyond the South into western and northern states. After ebbing in the 1940s, the Klan surged again during the civil rights movement of the 1950s and 1960s. This incarnation was much smaller than its predecessor in the 1920s but more violent in its resistance to racial equality. Today a number of white supremacist organizations continue to call themselves the Ku Klux Klan, but they are poorly organized and constantly at odds with each other and with similar hate groups on the far right of American politics.

In the larger story of Reconstruction, it would seem that the Ku Klux Klan Act and the congressional investigation of the Klan were shining examples of how the federal government and the freedmen and women of the South acted in partnership to advance the cause of racial justice and equality in the United States. Unfortunately, these successes were short-lived. During his second term, Grant reduced considerably the number of federal troops posted in the South, and the Republicans split between a liberal faction still committed to racial equality and a more conservative faction willing to jettison Reconstruction policies and black voters in return for political compromises with Democrats on other issues.

The third branch of the federal government did not help African Americans in their pursuit of equality either. In two cases from the 1870s, the

Supreme Court interpreted the Fourteenth Amendment in such a way that it severely restricted the federal government's ability to intervene on behalf of private citizens when their civil and political rights were violated. In the *Slaughterhouse Cases* (1873), the Court ruled that the Fourteenth Amendment protected only those rights that were derived directly from the federal government, most of which dealt with matters of interstate or foreign travel or business; the civil rights of most concern to blacks in the South still fell under the jurisdiction of state courts and law enforcement. In *U.S. v. Cruikshank* (1876), the Court ruled that the Fourteenth Amendment empowered the federal government only to prosecute violations of civil rights by the states, not by individual persons (violations in that category still fell under state jurisdiction). The combined effect of these two decisions was to place responsibility for protecting the rights of the South's African American population under the authority of the state governments, while making any federal intervention on their behalf similar to that pursued under the Ku Klux Klan Act unconstitutional.

After the last of the former Confederate states had fallen back into Democratic hands in 1877, Southern whites found new ways to confine blacks to second-class citizenship that were far more subtle than the Klan's political terrorism. Insulated from federal intervention by the Supreme Court's decisions and congressional indifference, Southern states passed laws that disenfranchised blacks by imposing poll taxes and literacy tests. They also erected a system of social segregation known as Jim Crow laws that limited black access to education and economic opportunity. When blacks challenged this system, mobs and night riders responded with the same methods used by the Klan, most notably lynching and arson, to prevent any sustained resistance to white rule. Not until the civil rights movement of the 1950s would the federal government again embrace the cause of racial justice in the South with the same vigor it had shown during its battle against the Klan in 1871.

Finding and Supplementing the Source

Like all federal government reports, the Joint Select Committee's report was published by the Government Printing Office in Washington, D.C. In every state, libraries designated as federal repositories receive copies of such publications, and your college or university library may in fact be one. The full citation for the report is *Report of the Joint Select Committee to Inquire into the Condition of Affairs in the Late Insurrectionary States*, 13 volumes (Washington, D.C.: Government Printing Office, 1872). It can also be found under the title *Senate Reports*, 42d Congress, 2d sess., no. 41 (serial 1484–96) or *House Reports*, 42d Congress, 2d sess., no. 22 (serial 1529–41). Some libraries may also catalogue it under the title printed on the spine of each volume, *The Ku Klux Conspiracy*. Volume 1 contains the majority and minority reports, and the subsequent volumes contain the verbatim testimony of witnesses before the committee.

For a more accessible selection of the testimony heard by the Joint Select Committee, see Albion W. Tourgée, *The Invisible Empire* (1880; repr., Baton Rouge: Louisiana State University Press, 1989). Tourgée was a disillusioned carpetbagger when he published his autobiographical novel about Reconstruction, *A Fool's Errand*, in 1879. A year later, he published *The Invisible Empire* as an exposé of the Ku Klux Klan. For the definitive modern study of the Ku Klux Klan during Reconstruction, see Allen W. Trelease, *White Terror: The Ku Klux Klan Conspiracy and Southern Reconstruction* (New York: Harper and Row, Publishers, 1971). The Klan's place in the wider current of political violence in the Reconstruction-era South is explained in George C. Rable, *But There Was No Peace: The Role of Violence in the Politics of Reconstruction* (Athens: University of Georgia Press, 1984). The best comprehensive history of Reconstruction, Eric Foner's *Reconstruction: America's Unfinished Revolution, 1863–1877* (New York: Harper and Row, Publishers, 1988), also provides a good summary of the Klan's origins and role in Reconstruction. For a study of the constitutional significance of the Ku Klux Klan Act and similar Reconstruction-era legislation, see Harold M. Hyman, *A More Perfect Union: The Impact of the Civil War and Reconstruction on the Constitution* (New York: Alfred A. Knopf, 1973). The film *Birth of a Nation* (1915), directed by D. W. Griffith and based on Thomas Dixon's popular novel *The Clansman* (1905), is a stunning example of how the Klan was mythologized during the Jim Crow era as an organization that defended white Southerners against the depredations of Northern carpetbaggers and black Republicans during Reconstruction.

Documenting the Source

Whenever you use another researcher's work as a source in your own writing, whether you quote the researcher's words directly or rely on the researcher's evidence and theories to support your arguments, you must include documentation for that source. This is equally true when using a map, photograph, table, or graph created by someone else. The reasons for this are twofold. First, to avoid any possibility of plagiarism, you must always include proper documentation for *all* source materials. Second, a proper citation gives important information to your reader about where to find a particular source, be it on a Web site, in a book at the library, or in an archive in your local community.

When documenting sources, historians use a standard form based on the recommendations published in *The Chicago Manual of Style*. All of the following documentation models are based on the guidelines published in the fifteenth edition of *The Chicago Manual of Style* (Chicago: The University of Chicago Press, 2003). These examples are based on the sources that appear in both volumes of *Going to the Source*. The diversity of the examples will give you some sense of the variety of source types that you may encounter in your research. For each source type, you will see a citation style that can be used for either a footnote, which appears at the bottom of the page of text, or an endnote, which appears at the end of a chapter or at the end of the whole text. This will be followed by an example of how this source type would be cited in a bibliography. Two examples are provided because footnote/endnote citation style is slightly different from bibliography citation style.

The examples provided here will help you address many of the documentation issues associated with source types that you come across in your research. However, this guide is not a comprehensive list, and as you dig further into the past, you may uncover source types that are not covered in this brief guide. For additional information about documenting sources in the *Chicago* style, please see **bedfordstmartins.com/resdoc**.

Documentation Basics

The question to keep in mind when you are wondering what to include in a citation is this: what does my reader need to know in order to *find* this source? When citing sources internally, you should use the footnote or endnote style. Footnotes and endnotes are used to document specific instances of borrowed text, ideas, or information. The first time you cite a source, you need to include the full publication information for that source—the author's full name, source title (and subtitle, if there is one), and facts of publication (city, publisher, and date)—along with the specific page number that you are referencing.

1. David Paul Nord, *Communities of Journalism: A History of American Newspapers and Their Readers* (Urbana: University of Illinois Press, 2001), 78.

If you refer to that source later in your paper, you need to include only the author's last name, an abbreviated version of the title, and the page or pages cited.

4. Nord, *Communities of Journalism,* 110–12.

A bibliography is used in addition to footnotes or endnotes to list all of the works you consulted in completing your paper, even those not directly cited in your footnotes. The sources included in your bibliography should be listed alphabetically, so the citation style for a bibliographic entry begins with the author's last name first.

Nord, David Paul. *Communities of Journalism*: *A History of American Newspapers and Their Readers*. Urbana: University of Illinois Press, 2001.

BOOKS

■ *Standard format for a book*

The standard form for citing a book is the same whether there is an editor or an author, the only difference being the inclusion of "ed." to indicate that an editor compiled the work.

FOOTNOTE/ENDNOTE:

1. Tim Johnson, ed., *Spirit Capture: Photographs from the National Museum of the American Indian* (Washington, DC: Smithsonian Institution Press, 1998), 102.

BIBLIOGRAPHY ENTRY:

Johnson, Tim, ed. *Spirit Capture: Photographs from the National Museum of the American Indian*. Washington, DC: Smithsonian Institution Press, 1998.

■ Book with two or more authors or editors

When citing a source from a book with two or three authors or editors, you need to include the names of all of the authors (or editors) in the order that they appear on the title page. If a work has more than three authors, you need to include all of the names in your bibliography. However, in your footnotes or endnotes, you need only include the name of the lead author followed by "and others" or "et al.," with no intervening comma.

FOOTNOTE/ENDNOTE:

2. Graham Russell Hodges and Alan Edward Brown, eds., *"Pretends to Be Free": Runaway Slave Advertisements from Colonial and Revolutionary New York and New Jersey* (New York: Garland, 1994), 58.

BIBLIOGRAPHY ENTRY:

Hodges, Graham Russell, and Alan Edward Brown, eds. *"Pretends to Be Free": Runaway Slave Advertisements from Colonial and Revolutionary New York and New Jersey*. New York: Garland, 1994.

■ Edited book with an author

Sometimes a book will have an author and an editor. In that case, you need to include both the author's and editor's names.

FOOTNOTE/ENDNOTE:

3. Hilda Satt Polacheck, *I Came a Stranger: The Story of a Hull-House Girl*, ed. Dena J. Polacheck Epstein (Urbana: University of Illinois Press, 1991), 36.

BIBLIOGRAPHY ENTRY:

Polacheck, Hilda Satt. *I Came a Stranger: The Story of a Hull-House Girl*. Edited by Dena J. Polacheck Epstein. Urbana: University of Illinois Press, 1991.

■ *Multivolume book*

If you are referring to a specific volume in a multivolume work, you need to specify which volume you used. This information should come before the page reference toward the end of the citation.

FOOTNOTE/ENDNOTE:

4. Bernard Bailyn, ed., *The Debate on the Constitution: Federalist and Anti-Federalist Speeches, Articles, and Letters during the Struggle over Ratification* (New York: Library of America, 1993), 2:759–61.

BIBLIOGRAPHY ENTRY:

Bailyn, Bernard, ed. *The Debate on the Constitution: Federalist and Anti-Federalist Speeches, Articles, and Letters during the Struggle over Ratification.* 2 vols. New York: Library of America, 1993.

Sometimes individual volumes in a multivolume work have separate volume titles. When citing a particular volume, you should include the volume title first followed by the name of the complete work.

FOOTNOTE/ENDNOTE:

5. Robert M. Yerkes, *Psychological Examining in the United States Army*, vol. 15, *Memoirs of the National Academy of Sciences* (Washington, DC: Government Printing Office, 1921), 145.

BIBLIOGRAPHY ENTRY:

Yerkes, Robert M. *Psychological Examining in the United States Army.* Vol. 15 of *Memoirs of the National Academy of Sciences.* Washington, DC: Government Printing Office, 1921.

■ *Book with an anonymous author*

Many books printed in the nineteenth century were published anonymously. If the author was omitted on the title page, but you know from your research who the author is, insert the name in square brackets; if you do not know who the actual author is, begin the citation with the work's title. Avoid using "Anonymous" or "Anon." in citations. As originally published, the author of *The Mother's Book* was listed as "Mrs. Child," so this citation includes that information along with the full name in brackets.

FOOTNOTE/ENDNOTE:

6. Mrs. [Lydia Maria] Child, *The Mother's Book* (Boston: Carter, Hendee, and Babcock, 1831), 23.

BIBLIOGRAPHY ENTRY:

Child, [Lydia Maria]. *The Mother's Book*. Boston: Carter, Hendee, and Babcock, 1831.

■ *Book-length work within a book*

Sometimes, the source that you are using may be a book-length work that has been reprinted within a longer work. In that case, you need to include both titles along with the editor of the longer work.

FOOTNOTE/ENDNOTE:

7. Zilpha Elaw, *Memoirs of the Life, Religious Experience, Ministerial Travels and Labours of Mrs. Zilpha Elaw, an American Female of Colour, Together with Some Account of the Great Religious Revivals in America (Written by Herself)*, in *Sisters of the Spirit: Three Black Women's Autobiographies of the Nineteenth Century*, ed. William L. Andrews (Bloomington: Indiana University Press, 1986), 55–91.

BIBLIOGRAPHY ENTRY:

Elaw, Zilpha. *Memoirs of the Life, Religious Experience, Ministerial Travels and Labours of Mrs. Zilpha Elaw, an American Female of Colour, Together with Some Account of the Great Religious Revivals in America (Written by Herself)*. In *Sisters of the Spirit: Three Black Women's Autobiographies of the Nineteenth Century*, edited by William L. Andrews. Bloomington: Indiana University Press, 1986.

■ *Chapter from a book*

If you want to cite a particular chapter from a book, you should include the title of the chapter in quotation marks before the title of the book.

FOOTNOTE/ENDNOTE:

8. Vicki L. Ruiz, "The Flapper and the Chaperone," in *From Out of the Shadows: Mexican Women in Twentieth-Century America* (New York: Oxford University Press, 1998), 12–26.

BIBLIOGRAPHY ENTRY:

Ruiz, Vicki L. "The Flapper and the Chaperone." In *From Out of the Shadows: Mexican Women in Twentieth-Century America*. New York: Oxford University Press, 1998.

PERIODICALS

Journals are scholarly publications that are usually published a few times a year. Popular magazines are written for the general public and are most often published on a monthly or weekly basis. Most newspapers are published daily, though some small local papers are published weekly. The following examples demonstrate the style for citing each type of periodical. If you consult an on-line periodical, the style for citing this source would be the same with the addition of the URL at the end of your citation.

■ *Journal articles*

When citing an article from a journal, you need to include the volume number, issue number (when given), and date of publication.

FOOTNOTE/ENDNOTE:

9. Elizabeth A. Fenn, "Biological Warfare in Eighteenth-Century North America: Beyond Jeffery Amherst," *Journal of American History* 86, no. 4 (2000): 1552–80.

BIBLIOGRAPHY ENTRY:

Fenn, Elizabeth A. "Biological Warfare in Eighteenth-Century North America: Beyond Jeffery Amherst." *Journal of American History* 86, no. 4 (2000): 1552–80.

■ *Popular magazines*

When citing material from a popular magazine, you need include only the magazine title followed by the date of publication and the page number(s) for the material. If you are citing from a regular feature of the magazine, you should include the title of the feature in the citation. If there is an author of the magazine article or the magazine's regular feature, the author's name would appear first in your citation, followed by the name of the feature.

FOOTNOTE/ENDNOTE:

10. Can This Marriage Be Saved?, *Ladies' Home Journal*, September 1961, 42.

BIBLIOGRAPHY ENTRY:

Ladies' Home Journal. Can This Marriage Be Saved? September 1961.

■ *Newspaper articles*

When citing newspaper articles, you must include the day, month, and year of publication, and the author if the article had a byline. *Chicago* style allows for page numbers to be omitted because newspapers often publish several editions each day and these editions are generally paginated differently.

FOOTNOTE/ENDNOTE:

11. John Dickinson, "The Liberty Song," *Boston Gazette*, July 18, 1768.

BIBLIOGRAPHY ENTRY:

Dickinson, John. "The Liberty Song." *Boston Gazette*, July 18, 1768.

INTERNET SOURCES

■ *Internet archives*

Because many older sources like newspapers and letters are rare and fragile, researchers often turn to Internet archives such as that of the Library of Congress through which digital copies of these documents are made available. Access to documents on the Internet also allows us to examine materials without having to travel to the archives in which they are housed. To cite a document found on an Internet Web site, you need to provide as much of the following information as possible: the author, the name of the document with original date of publication, the name of the site, the sponsor or owner of the site, and the URL. Sometimes a Web archive will include a document number; when available, you should include this cataloguing number as well.

FOOTNOTE/ENDNOTE:

12. Civil Rights Act of 1964, Document PL 88-352, *International Information Programs*, U.S. State Department, http://usinfo.state.gov/usa/infousa/laws/majorlaw/civilr19.htm.

BIBLIOGRAPHY ENTRY:

Civil Rights Act of 1964. Document PL 88-352. *International Information Programs*, U.S. State Department. http://usinfo.state.gov/usa/infousa/laws/majorlaw/civilr19.htm.

■ *An entire Web site*

To cite an entire Web site, you need include only the author of the site (if known), the name of the site, the sponsor or owner of the site, and the URL.

FOOTNOTE/ENDNOTE:

13. University Libraries of the University of Minnesota, *Sources for Ship Passenger Lists and Emigration Research*, University of Minnesota, http://wilson.lib.umn.edu/reference/shp-gene.html.

BIBLIOGRAPHY ENTRY:

University Libraries of the University of Minnesota. *Sources for Ship Passenger Lists and Emigration Research*. University of Minnesota. http://wilson.lib.umn.edu/reference/shp-gene.html.

OTHER SOURCES

■ *Published letters and other forms of correspondence*

When citing letters, memoranda, telegrams, and the like, you need to include the name of the sender and the recipient along with the date of the correspondence. Memoranda, telegrams, and other forms of communication should be noted as such in your citation after the recipient's name and before the date, but letters do not need to be specifically noted as such. The source cited in the following examples comes from *Foreign Relations of the United States* (FRUS), a valuable resource for historians published by the U.S. State Department. In citing any single document from FRUS, you need to provide the document's specific source, which is provided at the bottom of the document's first page in FRUS, along with the specific volume publication information. Note that these citations specify that the correspondence was a telegram.

FOOTNOTE/ENDNOTE:

14. Henry Byroade to U.S. State Department, telegram, August 4, 1956, from Department of State Central Files, 974.7301/8-456 in *Foreign Relations of the United States*, volume 16 (1955–1957), *Suez Canal Crisis, July 26–December 31, 1956* (Washington, DC, 1990).

BIBLIOGRAPHY ENTRY:

Byroade, Henry. Henry Byroade to U.S. State Department, telegram, August 4, 1956. From Department of State Central Files, 974.7301/8-456, in *Foreign Relations of the United States*, Volume 16 (1955–1957), *Suez Canal Crisis, July 26–December 31, 1956*. Washington, DC, 1990.

■ *Unpublished letters and other forms of correspondence*

Unpublished letters and those that have not been archived should include some indication of this fact, such as "in the author's possession" or "private collection." If the letter was found in an archive, the location of the depository would be included as well. (For information on how to cite material found in an archive, see the section "Photos and other material found in an archive or depository" on p. 334.)

FOOTNOTE/ENDNOTE:

15. Jeff Rogers to William and Adele Rogers, November 10, 1968, in the author's possession.

BIBLIOGRAPHY ENTRY:

Rogers, Jeff. Jeff Rogers to William and Adele Rogers, November 10, 1968. In the author's possession.

■ Court records

When citing legal cases in historical writing, the name of the plaintiff appears first, followed by the name of the defendant, and both names are italicized. The first time you cite the case, you should also include the court and year in which the case was decided. Supreme Court decisions are published by the government in a series called *United States Reports*. When citing Supreme Court decisions, you need to include the name of the case in italics followed by the number of the volume that contains the particular case, the abbreviation "U.S." for *United States Reports*, page numbers, and the date of the decision.

FOOTNOTE/ENDNOTE:

> 16. *Korematsu v. United States,* 323 U.S. 242, 242–48 (1944).

BIBLIOGRAPHY ENTRY:

Korematsu v. United States. 323 U.S., 242, 242–48. 1944.

■ Tables, graphs, and charts

Whenever incorporating statistical data into your work, it is important to document your evidence. If you borrow a table, graph, or chart from another source, you must cite it just as you would quoted material in your text. Include a citation in appropriate footnote format to the source of the borrowed information directly below it. If you change the table, graph, or chart in any way (for example, eliminating unnecessary information or adding another element such as a percent calculation to it), use the phrase "adapted from" in your citation, which signals to the reader that you have altered the original. If a number is used to identify the data in the original source, that information should be included as well at the end of the citation.

FOOTNOTE/ENDNOTE:

> 17. Adapted from Hinton R. Helper, *The Impending Crisis of the South: How to Meet It* (New York: Burdick Brothers, 1857), 71, table XVIII.

Because you wouldn't cite any one particular table in your bibliography, you would follow the style for citing the book, periodical, or Web site where the data you consulted first appeared.

■ Paintings

When citing paintings that appear in a catalogue, archive, or database, it is important to include the catalogue or accession number of the piece of art if available. This documentation will allow other researchers to locate the original source more easily. Generally, specific works of art are not included in your bibliography. However, if a particular painting is important to your research, you may list it in your bibliography by the painter's name first.

FOOTNOTE/ENDNOTE:

18. George Catlin, *Shón-Ka-Ki-He-Ga, Horse Chief, Grand Pawnee Head Chief* (1832, Smithsonian American Art Museum: 1985.66.99).

BIBLIOGRAPHY ENTRY:

Catlin, George. *Shón-Ka-Ki-He-Ga, Horse Chief, Grand Pawnee Head Chief.* 1832. Smithsonian American Art Museum: 1985.66.99.

■ *Photos and other material found in an archive or depository*

Any material found in an archive or depository, be it a photograph, letter, or a map, needs to be cited just as published material would be. The name of the author (or photographer, in the case of photographs) should appear first, followed by the title of the image or document being cited in quotation marks, the date, and the name of the archive or depository. If a source from a collection is important enough to your work, you can mention that source specifically in your bibliography. However, if you make use of more than one photograph or other type of source from a particular collection, you need only cite them generally in your bibliography.

FOOTNOTE/ENDNOTE:

19. George P. Barnard, "Ruins of Charleston, S.C.," 1866, Beinecke Rare Book and Manuscript Library, Yale University.

BIBLIOGRAPHY ENTRY:

Photographs. Beinecke Rare Book and Manuscript Library, Yale University.

■ *Government publications*

The government publishes thousands of pages of documents every year. The format for citing these documents varies slightly from source to source depending on the format of the publication and the source being cited. For example, any testimony given before a congressional committee is usually published in a book. Here the exact name of the committee is given in the title of the work in which the testimony appears. When citing government publications in your bibliography, you would substitute the agency that published the work for the author unless, of course, a particular author has been specified.

FOOTNOTE/ENDNOTE:

20. United States Congress, *Report of the Joint Select Committee to Inquire into the Condition of Affairs in the Late Insurrectionary States,* vol. 2, *South Carolina, Part I* (Washington, DC: Government Printing Office, 1872), 25–28, 33–34.

BIBLIOGRAPHY ENTRY:

United States Congress. *Report of the Joint Select Committee to Inquire into the Condition of Affairs in the Late Insurrectionary States.* Vol. 2, *South Carolina, Part I.* Washington, DC: Government Printing Office, 1872.

Acknowledgments (continued)

Page 13 (Source 4): Courtesy of the State Museum of Pennsylvania, Pennsylvania Historical and Museum Commission.

Page 14 (Source 5): Courtesy of the State Museum of Pennsylvania, Pennsylvania Historical and Museum Commission.

Page 15 (Source 6): Courtesy of the State Museum of Pennsylvania, Pennsylvania Historical and Museum Commission.

Page 16 (Source 7): Courtesy of the State Museum of Pennsylvania, Pennsylvania Historical and Museum Commission.

Page 17 (Source 8): Courtesy of the State Museum of Pennsylvania, Pennsylvania Historical and Museum Commission.

Page 18 (Source 9): Courtesy of the State Museum of Pennsylvania, Pennsylvania Historical and Museum Commission.

Page 19 (Source 10): Courtesy of the State Museum of Pennsylvania, Pennsylvania Historical and Museum Commission.

Page 20 (Source 11): Courtesy of the State Museum of Pennsylvania, Pennsylvania Historical and Museum Commission.

Page 21 (Source 12): Courtesy of the State Museum of Pennsylvania, Pennsylvania Historical and Museum Commission.

Page 22 (Source 13): Courtesy of the State Museum of Pennsylvania, Pennsylvania Historical and Museum Commission.

CHAPTER 4

Page 72: Elizabeth A. Fenn, "Biological Warfare in Eighteenth-Century North America: Beyond Jeffery Amherst," *Journal of American History* 86, no. 4 (March 2000): 1552–80.

CHAPTER 5

Page 91 (Figure 5.1): The Connecticut Historical Society, Hartford, Connecticut.

CHAPTER 8

Page 157 (Figure 8.1): Courtesy of Special Collections, Musselman Library, Gettysburg College, Gettysburg, Pennsylvania.

CHAPTER 9

Page 187 (Source 5): "Patents Granted per Year for Mechanical Devices for Grain and Corn Harvesting, Threshing, and Cutting and for Cotton Harvesting, Picking, and Cutting," adapted from Gavin Wright, *The Political Economy of the Cotton South: Households, Markets, and Wealth in the Nineteenth Century.* Copyright © 1978 by Gavin Wright. Used by permission of W. W. Norton & Company, Inc.

Pages 189–90 (Sources 7 and 8): "Per Capita Income by Region for 1840 and 1860 in 1860 Prices" and "The Relative Level of the Per Capita Income of the South in 1860," adapted from Robert William Fogel and Stanley L. Engerman, *Time on the Cross: The Economics of American Negro Slavery,* 2 vols. Copyright © 1974 by Robert William Fogel and Stanley L. Engerman. By permission of Little, Brown and Company.

Page 192 (Sources 10 and 11): "Regional Patterns of Manufacturing" and "Regional Patterns of Urbanization by Percent of Population," adapted from Gavin Wright, *The Political Economy of the Cotton South: Households, Markets, and Wealth in the Nineteenth Century.* Copyright © 1978 by Gavin Wright. Used by permission of W. W. Norton & Company, Inc.

CHAPTER 10

Page 205 (Source 1): George Catlin, *Shón-Ka-Ki-He-Ga, Horse Chief, Grand Pawnee Head Chief.* Smithsonian American Art Museum. Gift of Mrs. Joseph Harrison Jr.

Page 206 (Source 2): George Catlin, *Máh-To-Tóh-Pa, Four Bears, Second Chief, in Full Dress.* Smithsonian American Art Museum. Gift of Mrs. Joseph Harrison Jr.

Page 207 (Source 3): George Catlin, *La-Dóo-Ke-A, Buffalo Bull, A Grand Pawnee Warrior.* Smithsonian American Art Museum. Gift of Mrs. Joseph Harrison Jr.

Page 208 (Source 4): George Catlin, *Pshán-Shaw, Sweet-Scented Grass, Twelve-Year-Old Daughter of Bloody Hand.* Smithsonian American Art Museum. Gift of Mrs. Joseph Harrison Jr.

Page 209 (Source 5): George Catlin, *Jú-Ah-Kís-Gaw, Woman with Her Child in a Cradle.* Smithsonian American Art Museum. Gift of Mrs. Joseph Harrison Jr.

Page 210 (Source 6): George Catlin, *Wi-Jún-Jon, Pigeon's Egg Head (The Light) Going to and Returning from Washington.* Smithsonian American Art Museum. Gift of Mrs. Joseph Harrison Jr.

Page 211 (Source 7): George Catlin, *Fort Pierre, Mouth of the Teton River, 1200 Miles above St. Louis.* Smithsonian American Art Museum. Gift of Mrs. Joseph Harrison Jr.

Page 212 (Source 8): George Catlin, *Buffalo Hunt under the Wolf-Skin Mask.* Smithsonian American Art Museum. Gift of Mrs. Joseph Harrison Jr.

Page 213 (Source 9): George Catlin, *Buffalo Chase, A Surround by the Hidatsa.* Smithsonian American Art Museum. Gift of Mrs. Joseph Harrison Jr.

Page 214 (Source 10): George Catlin, *Bird's-Eye View of the Mandan Village, 1800 Miles above St. Louis.* Smithsonian American Art Museum. Gift of Mrs. Joseph Harrison Jr.

Page 215 (Source 11): George Catlin, *Sioux Encamped on the Upper Missouri, Dressing Buffalo Meat and Robes.* Smithsonian American Art Museum. Gift of Mrs. Joseph Harrison Jr.

Page 216 (Source 12): George Catlin, *The Cutting Scene, Mandan O-Kee-Pa Ceremony,* 1832, Denver Art Museum Collection, The William Sr. and Dorothy Harmsen Collection, 2001.456. Photo provided by the Denver Art Museum.

CHAPTER 13

Page 273 (Figure 13.1): Photographer unknown, "Gardner's Gallery." Library of Congress, Prints & Photographs Division, LC-BH837-207.

Page 276 (Figure 13.2): John Trumbull, *Death of General Mercer at the Battle of Princeton, New Jersey, 3 January 1777.* Yale University Art Gallery, Trumbull Collection.

Page 277 (Figure 13.3): Timothy O'Sullivan, "A Harvest of Death, Gettysburg, Pennsylvania," 1863, Albumen silver print, P1984.30.36. Amon Carter Museum, Fort Worth, Texas.

Page 280 (Source 1): James F. Gibson, "Lieut. Washington, a Confederate prisoner, and Capt. Custer, U.S.A.," 1862. Library of Congress, Prints & Photographs Division, LC-B8171-0428 DLC.

Page 281 (Source 2): Mathew Brady, "Gen. Robert B. Potter and staff of seven, recognized Capt. Gilbert H. McKibben, Capt. Wright, A.A.G. Also Mr. Brady, photographer," c. 1863. National Archives and Records Administration, 111-B-4.

Page 282 (Source 3): Alexander Gardner, "President Lincoln on Battle-Field of Antietam," 1862. Albumen silver print, P1984.30.23, Amon Carter Museum, Fort Worth, Texas.

Page 283 (Source 4): Timothy O'Sullivan, "Pennsylvania, Gettysburg 07/1863." National Archives and Records Administration, 165-SB-35.

Page 284 (Source 5): George P. Barnard, "Ruins of Charleston, S.C.," 1866. The Beinecke Rare Book and Manuscript Library.

Page 285 (Source 6): Mathew Brady, "Portrait of Brig. Gen. Napoleon B. McLaughlin, officer of the Federal Army, and staff, vicinity of Washington, D.C.," 1861. Library of Congress, Prints & Photographs Division, LC-B8171-7180 DLC.

Page 286 (Source 7): Timothy O'Sullivan, "Culpeper, Va. 'Contrabands,' " 1863. Library of Congress, Prints & Photographs Division, LC-B8171-0221 DLC.

Page 287 (Source 8): Photographer unknown, "African American soldiers and their teachers and officers," date unknown. Library of Congress, Prints & Photographs Division, LC-B8184-10061.

Page 288 (Source 9): Alexander Gardner, "Antietam, Md. Bodies of dead gathered for burial," 1862. Library of Congress, Prints & Photographs Division, LC-B8171-0557 DLC.

Page 289 (Source 10): Alexander Gardner, "A Contrast. Federal buried; Confederate unburied, where they fell on the battle field of Antietam," 1863. Collection of the New-York Historical Society, PR-065-788-1.

Page 290 (Source 11): Alexander Gardner, "He Sleeps his Last Sleep," 1862. Collection of the New-York Historical Society, PR-065-774-2.

Page 290 (Source 12): James F. Gibson, "Battlefield of Gettysburg—Body of a soldier in 'the wheat field,' evidently killed by the explosion of a shell," 1863. Library of Congress, Prints & Photographs Division, LC-8184-7258.

Page 292 (Source 13): Timothy O'Sullivan, "Field Where General Reynolds Fell, Gettysburg," 1863, Albumen silver print, P1984.30.97, Amon Carter Museum, Fort Worth, Texas.

Page 293 (Source 14): T. C. Roche, ". . . View of the covered ways inside the rebel Fort Mahone, called by soldiers 'Fort Damnation' . . . taken the morning after the storming of Petersburgh, Va. 1865." E. & H. T. Anthony, Collection of the New-York Historical Society, PR-065-811-18.

Page 294 (Source 15): John Reekie, "Cold Harbor, Va., African Americans collecting bones of soldiers killed in battle," 1865. Library of Congress, Prints & Photographs Division, LC-B8171-7962 DLC.

Index

Letters in parentheses following page numbers refer to:
(i) illustrations
(f) figures, including charts and graphs
(m) maps